A NEARLY PERFECT SEASON

A NEARLY PERFECT SEASON

The Inside Story of the
1984 San Francisco 49ers

Chris Willis

ROWMAN & LITTLEFIELD
Lanham • Boulder • New York • London

Published by Rowman & Littlefield
A wholly owned subsidiary of The Rowman & Littlefield Publishing Group,
Inc.
4501 Forbes Boulevard, Suite 200, Lanham, Maryland 20706
www.rowman.com

16 Carlisle Street, London W1D 3BT, United Kingdom

British Library Cataloguing in Publication Information Available

Library of Congress Cataloging-in-Publication Data

Willis, Chris, 1970–
A nearly perfect season : the inside story of the 1984 San Francisco 49ers / Chris Willis.
    p. cm.
Includes bibliographical references and index.
ISBN 978-1-4422-3641-7 (hardcover : alk. paper) — ISBN 978-1-4422-3642-4 (ebook)
1. San Francisco 49ers (Football team)—History. I. Title.
GV956.S3W55 2014
796.332'74097946109048—dc23
2014007268

Printed in the United States of America

This book is dedicated to the four players and three coaches from the 1984 San Francisco 49ers team no longer with us:

John Ayers, Gary "Big Hands" Johnson, Carl Monroe, and Freddie Solomon; Norb Hecker, Bobb McKittrick, and head coach Bill Walsh

CONTENTS

1984 SAN FRANCISCO 49ERS

Cast of Characters

PLAYERS

#68, John Ayers, guard
#76, Dwaine Board, defensive end
#57, Dan Bunz, linebacker
#95, Michael Carter, defensive tackle
6, Matt Cavanaugh, quarterback
#87, Dwight Clark, wide receiver
#29, Mario Clark, cornerback
#89, Earl Cooper, tight end
#33, Roger Craig, running back
#51, Randy Cross, guard
#74, Fred Dean, defensive end
#50, Riki Ellison, linebacker
#55, Jim Fahnhorst, linebacker
#71, Keith Fahnhorst, offensive tackle
#54, Ron Ferrari, linebacker
#81, Russ Francis, tight end
#86, John Frank, tight end
#49, Jeff Fuller, safety
#24, Derrick Harmon, running back
#22, Dwight Hicks, safety
#28, Tom Holmoe, safety

#97, Gary Johnson, defensive tackle
#94, Louie Kelcher, defensive tackle
#66, Allan Kennedy, offensive tackle
#42, Ronnie Lott, cornerback
#53, Milt McColl, linebacker
#62, Guy McIntyre, guard
#43, Dana McLemore, cornerback/kick returner
#32, Carl Monroe, running back
#16, Joe Montana, quarterback
#52, Blanchard Montgomery, linebacker
#83, Renaldo Nehemiah, wide receiver
#77, Bubba Paris, offensive tackle
#65, Lawrence Pillers, defensive end
#56, Fred Quillan, center
#64, Jack Reynolds, linebacker
#30, Bill Ring, running back
4, Max Runager, punter
#61, Jesse Sapolu, guard
#90, Todd Shell, linebacker
#67, Billy Shields, offensive tackle
#88, Freddie Solomon, wide receiver
#72, Jeff Stover, defensive end
#79, Jim Stuckey, defensive end
#78, Manu Tuiasosopo, defensive tackle
#58, Keena Turner, linebacker
#26, Wendell Tyler, running back
#99, Michael Walter, linebacker
#14, Ray Wersching, kicker
#27, Carlton Williamson, safety
#85, Mike Wilson, wide receiver
#21, Eric Wright, cornerback

COACHES

Bill Walsh, president/head coach
George Seifert, defensive coordinator
Jerry Attaway, physical development coordinator

Paul Hackett, quarterbacks/wide receivers
Tommy Hart, assistant defensive line
Norb Hecker, linebackers
Sherman Lewis, running backs
Bobb McKittrick, offensive line
Bill McPherson, defensive line
Ray Rhodes, defensive backs
Fred vonAppen, special teams

ADMINISTRATIVE STAFF

Eddie DeBartolo Jr., owner
John McVay, vice president and general manager
Ken Flower, vice president marketing and community affairs
Keith Simon, business manager
Tony Razzano, director of college scouting
Allan Webb, director of pro personnel
Jerry Walker, director of public relations
Neal Dahlen, director of research and development
Ken Dargel, tickets
R. C. Owens, executive assistant

SUPPORT STAFF

Bronco Hinek, equipment manager
Chico Norton, equipment manager emeritus
Roy Gilbert, films director
Robert Yanagi, staff assistant
Michael Olmstead, entertainment director
Teri Hatcher, cheerleader
Nicole Gisele, secretary
Donnan Sinn, researcher
Michael Zagaris, team photographer
Lindsy McLean, trainer
John Miller, assistant trainer
Don Klein, 49ers radio (play-by-play)

Don Heinrich, 49ers radio (color)
Ted Robinson, 49ers radio (pregame/postgame)

PREFACE

In the fall of 1984 I turned fourteen years old. I was a skinny eighth grader living in Columbus, Ohio, thinking about playing high school football in a year. Playing in the NFL was just a pipe dream, but I enjoyed watching the games every Sunday of that 1984 season, especially the games played by a team that was more than 2,000 miles away from the Buckeye State. The San Francisco 49ers were led by my favorite player, Joe Montana, and I read anything I could find on the 1984 team. Whether it was *Pro Football Weekly*, *Football Digest*, or *Sports Illustrated*, I wanted to learn more about the 49ers. I also watched every game I could. Since the Browns or Bengals usually played at 1:00 p.m. on most Sundays, I was able to watch many of the 49ers games at 4:00 p.m., mainly on CBS, or on ABC's *Monday Night Football*. It was a joy to watch Montana's passing wizardry and the hard-hitting 49ers defense churn out victory after victory.

That fall I enjoyed watching the NFL and the 49ers so much that, right before the conference championship games to decide who went on to play in Super Bowl XIX, I created a six-page magazine called *Touchdown!* On the last page I pasted four photos of the remaining teams, including one of Joe Montana running the ball against the New York Giants in the divisional round. While researching this book, I came across my initial foray into publishing. Looking at this juvenile attempt at sports writing thirty years later, it's hard to believe that I've written a book about the 1984 49ers.

Looking back at it now, it must have been in my blood all along to tell the story of the 1984 49ers and what a journey it was. Researching and writing about a great group of men who came within one play of a perfect season has been the most enjoyable time of my writing career. When I started this project I didn't know what kind of response I would get from the coaches and players of the 1984 49ers. I was surprised. Over an eight-month period (between December 2012 and August 2013), I interviewed either in person or by phone nearly fifty players, coaches, and front-office personnel from the team.

Before I interviewed anyone, I had a chance to read all the game recaps in the San Francisco newspapers, and, more importantly, I watched every 49ers network game on DVD. It was amazing to review every play from that phenomenal season. I felt like I had a front-row seat at Candlestick Park. It was a joy to watch Bill Walsh's West Coast offense with Joe Montana under center and George Seifert's multidimensional defense that allowed a league-low 227 points. Watching every game and talking to the coaches and players from that team was a football lesson I won't soon forget.

This great group of men gave me their time and energy, telling me stories and recollections of a team that would be the first in NFL history to go 15–1 in the regular season. Running back Roger Craig told me with a smile that he enjoyed training camp so much he called it "heaven." Linebacker Jim Fahnhorst revealed the joy of playing that season with his older brother Keith, calling it "a chance of a lifetime." Linebacker Ron Ferrari told me on the phone that the 1984 49ers not only cared for each other, but "absolutely loved each other. Of course that was modeled by our owner [Eddie DeBartolo] . . . and Bill Walsh loved us. He tried to stay away and act like a coach, but we knew he cared." They reflected on their time in a city that cherished their efforts on the field and on how they came together as a team for one common goal—to win the Super Bowl. Which they did in spectacular fashion over the more publicized Miami Dolphins at nearby Stanford Stadium in Palo Alto.

It was a team made up of great ownership and front-office personalities, a Hall of Fame head coach and his ten assistants, and a roster of fifty-two men who all knew their specific roles and played nearly perfect football for an entire season. Every man in the organization and on the team contributed to make the 1984 San Francisco 49ers one of the greatest teams to ever play in NFL history. This is their story.

ACKNOWLEDGMENTS

After spending nearly two years researching and writing about the 1984 San Francisco 49ers, I feel I don't have enough words to thank all of the people who helped me complete this book. First and foremost I want to thank Keena Turner, 49ers vice president of football affairs, who was also a starting linebacker with the 1984 49ers. He was the first person I talked to about this project, and if it hadn't been for his support and help, this book would never have been written. I thank him for sitting down with me for an interview as well as for providing the contacts I needed to get this project off the ground. Keena, you went far beyond the call of duty. Also, big thanks to Angela Banister, 49ers executive administrative assistant, for all her help with my visit to the 49ers facility.

I am also indebted to Craig Walsh, son of the late 49ers Hall of Fame coach Bill Walsh. He spent nearly two hours with me talking about his father and allowed me to go through some of his game plans and meeting tapes. Learning more about Bill Walsh from Craig was a football lesson I won't soon forget.

I couldn't have finished this project without the help of Jerry Walker of the 49ers Hall of Fame, who was the 49ers director of public relations in 1984. I had a great time interviewing him in Palo Alto, and his tour of the old 49ers facility at 711 Nevada Street in Redwood City was a memorable afternoon. I still can't believe the 49ers headquarters was there in that two-story "treasure." Thanks again for showing me through the old place.

Once again I want to thank Stephen Ryan, senior editor at Rowman & Littlefield, for believing in preserving the history of professional football. This is our fifth book together and I can't think of another editor I would rather work with. I also want to thank Rowman & Littlefield and its professional staff in putting this book together, especially Christen Karniski, associate editor, and Kellie Hagan, production editor, for answering all my questions. They are a joy to work with.

As for all the players, coaches, and front-office personnel of the 1984 49ers who gave me their time and energy while I conducted my interviews, I am forever grateful. Not only are they a great group of football players and coaches, but they are simply a great group of people. Whether you talked to me for a half hour or two hours, every person I interviewed gave me unbelievable insight into one of the NFL's greatest teams. It's been thirty years since that championship season, but the people I interviewed gave me a front-row seat to that special year. I thank every one of them from the bottom of my heart. In person I was able to interview Roger Craig, Allan Kennedy, Milt McColl, Guy McIntyre, Dana McLemore, Bill McPherson, John McVay, Bill Ring, Keena Turner, Jerry Walker, Craig Walsh, and Michael Zagaris; by phone, Jerry Attaway, Dwaine Board, Dan Bunz, Michael Carter, Mario Clark, Earl Cooper, Neal Dahlen, Fred Dean, Riki Ellison, Jim Fahnhorst, Keith Fahnhorst, Ron Ferrari, Ken Flower, Nicole Gisele, Paul Hackett, Derrick Harmon, Tom Holmoe, Louie Kelcher, Blanchard Montgomery, Renaldo Nehemiah, Lawrence Pillers, Ray Rhodes, Max Runager, George Seifert, Billy Shields, Jeff Stover, Jim Stuckey, Manu Tuiasosopo, Wendell Tyler, Fred vonAppen, Michael Walter, Ray Wersching, Carlton Williamson, and Mike Wilson.

An extra thank-you goes to the San Francisco 49ers organization and the York family. I especially want to thank Bob Lange, 49ers director of public relations and his staff, Mike Chasanoff, Dan Beckler, and Kyle Koger, for all their help over the past two years with this project. They are the best at what they do.

Several other interviews were done that I want to acknowledge. Thanks to Don Klein and Ted Robinson for talking to me about their involvement in the 49ers radio broadcasts during the 1984 season. I am grateful to Michael Olmstead, 1984 49ers entertainment director who runs e2k Entertainment, for telling me about the events held at Candlestick Park during that year. And a big thank-you goes to Willie Brown, former mayor of San Francisco, who discussed his passion for the 49ers and his involvement with the Fred Dean holdout. Kudos to Nicole Gisele, who was secretary for Bill Walsh, for taking the time to talk about her former boss. Ladd McKittrick, thanks for your time talking about your father. Again, thank you all!

Also, thanks goes to Kelly Norris (operations manager for e2k), Jason Greenberg (producer/communication director for e2k), Alyssa Romano (manager of personalities and properties at Octagon), Lindy Pickin-paugh (Bernstein Global Wealth Management), Song Schreiber (Willie Brown Jr. Inc.), and Gillian Chavez (executive assistant to Brigham Young University athletic director Tom Holmoe) for helping me set up interviews.

While visiting San Francisco I stayed with two families that made me feel at home: Carla and Caleb Houser and John Richards and his wife, Angela. Thanks for allowing me to stay with you. Each visit was wonder-ful, including attending four football games in four days with John. I will always remember your generosity and my last game at Candlestick Park with you. I'm thankful to call you my friend.

More thanks goes to all the San Francisco–area sportswriters who covered the 49ers in 1984: Frank Blackman, Frank Cooney, John Crumpacker, and Art Spander from the *San Francisco Examiner*; Low-ell Cohn, Glenn Dickey, Tom Fitzgerald, and Ira Miller from the *San Francisco Chronicle*; and Mark Purdy from the *San Jose Mercury News*.

I also want to thank my friends with the Professional Football Re-searchers Association (PFRA). First, I want to thank the late Bob Car-roll, who passed away in August 2009, for his help and guidance during the fifteen years I knew him. Bob published my very first article in PFRA's *Coffin Corner* back in 1994, and I will always be grateful for his generosity. You are still missed. Thanks to Tod Maher for making cop-ies of all the 1984 49ers game recaps from microfilm. I've been in your shoes, so it means a lot to me that you agreed to sit there making copy after copy after copy. Thanks Roy Sye, Andy Piascik, Ken Crippen, and PFRA president Mark Ford. Lastly, thanks to Coach T. J. Troup. I truly enjoy our phone calls. Thanks for listening the past two years about the 1984 49ers. I'm also glad you were able to enjoy the 49ers win against the Dolphins at Candlestick in 2012. It was a great time.

I also want to thank fellow authors Sal Paolantonio (ESPN), Dan Daly, Allen Barra, Jim Dent, and Ray Didinger for their advice over the past couple of years—keep up the good work. Thanks, S. L. T., for all your support and help on this project. It means a lot to me. I would also like to thank my colleagues at NFL Films: Dave Plaut, Pete Frank, Neil Zender, Pat Kelleher, Kevin McLoughlin, Jeremy Swarbrick, and especially Diane Kimball. You always go beyond the call of duty, so thanks, Di! Special thanks to the late Steve Sabol, president of NFL Films, who gave me my start here. I loved working for you, and I miss you every day.

Kudos go to all the librarians, organizations, and websites that helped me during my journey. Thanks to the San Jose (California) Public Library, Stanford University Library (Media-Microtext Center, Green Library), eBay, timeanddate.com, newspaperarchive.com, and Lexis-Nexis. A big thank you to Tony Rohatch of Mancave Memorabilia of San Carlos, California, for allowing me to conduct the Roger Craig interview at his store.

I want to thank current NFL commissioner Roger Goodell and his staff. I also want to thank Rita Benson LeBlanc of the New Orleans Saints for her advice and support. I've known her for more than a decade now and through all my book projects she always has my best interests at heart.

Thanks to my brothers, Rhu and Adrian, for their support. And to my best friend, Jennifer Heinz, for her continued support and friendship. Although she couldn't care less about football, she is always there for me, and I couldn't have asked for a better friend during the past fifteen years. Thanks also to her husband, Craig, my buddy Sean Heinz—a future quarterback—and little Ellie. To my mother, Tina, thanks for all your love and inspiration in helping me finish this book. I know I couldn't have done it without you. And thanks to my father, Roy Willis, who passed away in 2008. You gave me my passion for reading and writing—while being a book dealer for nearly three decades. I miss you so much and I hope you're proud of what I've accomplished here. Finally, thank you, Stephanie Titus, for all your support, generosity, and love with helping me finish this book.

INTRODUCTION

The Speech—1983 NFC Championship Game,
San Francisco 49ers at Washington Redskins,
January 8, 1984

The capacity crowd at RFK Stadium in Washington, D.C., was jumping up and down so hard that the stands were literally bouncing and making the whole stadium shake. The Washington Redskins, the NFL's defending champs, were leading the San Francisco 49ers 21–0 in the 1983 NFC Championship Game. On a cool and cloudy January day in the nation's capital, the game entered the fourth quarter with the Redskins just fifteen minutes away from a return trip to the Super Bowl.

After a third quarter that saw the 49ers defense give up a pair of touchdowns, the coda began when head coach Bill Walsh, who just two years earlier had led the Cinderella 49ers to a Super Bowl victory, chatted strategy with his star quarterback Joe Montana. The teacher and student were about to mount a furious comeback that would put more than 55,000 screaming fans on the edges of their seats.

On the first drive of the final quarter Montana completed five of eight passes and a five-yard touchdown to wide receiver Mike Wilson. The 49ers defense, which had been on its heels, was now bending but not breaking. The unit forced a Redskins field goal attempt, which was missed badly by Mark Moseley. Incredibly it was his fourth missed kick of the game. Walsh wasted no time in attacking the Redskins defense. He went for it all and Montana would deliver. Behind perfect protection Montana took a seven-step drop and lofted a beautiful, deep pass down the middle of the field. Wideout Freddie Solomon streaked past Redskins speedy cornerback Darrell Green to haul in a seventy-six-yard touchdown. With less than ten minutes left in the game, the 49ers trailed by just one touchdown, 21–14.

The comeback was on. The whole stadium and the television audience watching on CBS could feel the momentum shift to the 49ers side. The first play from scrimmage after the Solomon touchdown confirmed it, as 49ers defensive end Dwaine Board, who had thirteen sacks during the regular season, dropped Joe Theismann for a huge loss. Two plays later the Skins punted the ball back to the red-hot 49ers offense. Taking over at their own forty-seven-yard line, Walsh and Montana went back to work.

Montana sixteen-yard pass to tight end Eason Ramson.
Wendell Tyler three-yard run.
Montana twenty-two-yard pass to wide receiver Mike Wilson.
Montana twelve-yard touchdown pass to Mike Wilson. Extra point good.

In a blur the drive was over. Four plays, fifty-three yards. Touchdown. The capacity crowd was now dead silent. The loud cheers heard just a few minutes earlier were now coming from the 49ers bench. The clock showed 7:08 remaining in the fourth quarter. In little more than half a quarter, the 49ers erased a twenty-one point Redskins lead. The 49ers were in the midst of the greatest comeback in NFL postseason history. No team had come back this far in the playoffs, and the 49ers were doing it on the road against the NFL's defending champions, who were 14–2 in 1983 and had scored the most points ever—541—in a single season.

With less than seven minutes remaining, the Redskins offense went back to its bread-and-butter pounding of the ball with its All-Pro running back John Riggins. During the 1983 regular season, Riggins would rush for more than 1,300 yards and a then–NFL record twenty-four touchdowns. His three carries for twenty-five yards gave the Redskins some much-needed breathing room. Riggins was stopped for no gain. The game was then put into the hands of the officials. On second down Theismann threw a deep pass down the sidelines for Art Monk, but 49ers cornerback Eric Wright was right by his hip giving him no space.

The ball sailed over both of their heads out-of-bounds. Incomplete. But the official on the sidelines threw a flag. Pass interference on Wright. With two and a half minutes remaining, instead of facing third-and-ten, the Redskins were given twenty-seven yards in field possession on the penalty.[1]

Television replays showed Wright with his hand barely touching Monk's hip as the ball sailed a few yards out-of-bounds. "The ball was completely not catchable. There was a flag. They ended up changing the rule that the ball had to be catchable in order for there to be interference," recalled Dwight Hicks, defensive back, in a 2005 interview.[2]

Two plays later, on third-and-fifteen from the 49ers thirteen-yard line, Theismann threw another incomplete pass, and the Redskins had to settle for a field goal. Oh, wait, another flag. This time cornerback Ronnie Lott was called for defensive holding as the pass was incomplete on the other side of the field. Once again replays showed Lott barely touching a receiver—this time away from the play. The Redskins would get a new set of downs near the two-minute warning.

The 49ers defense stiffened, but the hourglass was running out. Walsh had to use his last two timeouts. So instead of a Redskins field goal attempt with perhaps 1:40 left on the clock, Moseley, after four missed field goals, booted a twenty-five yarder to give the Redskins a 24–21 lead with just forty seconds remaining. Four plays later Montana threw a desperation interception on the last play of the game. The comeback was over. As the Redskins headed to the Super Bowl, the dejected 49ers headed to the locker room.

Below RFK Stadium in the visitor's locker room, the atmosphere was not a pretty scene for a team that was ready to return to the Super Bowl. Emotions boiled over for many of the 49ers. "It was the first time I saw a whole bunch of grown men crying, sad, and depressed. I mean, they gave their hearts and souls to get back to the top. It was very emotional," said linebacker Dan Bunz.[3] "God, it was a tough, hard-fought game. It brings back so many memories. One, it's the only game I cried at. . . . Just giving it our all, and to lose that game when we had all the momentum going forward in the fourth quarter, but we did. It set the resolve and the tone for us moving forward," said defensive end Jim Stuckey.[4]

At this moment something magical happened. A special team came together. "I mean, we were really, really upset about that game, because we thought that we should've won," recalled running back Roger Craig. "It motivated us the next year to come back to being better."[5]

The players, coaches, and front-office staff, both physically and emotionally drained from the loss, gathered in an intimate circle. After a few words from head coach Bill Walsh, one of the 49ers defensive leaders stood up to speak. Pro Bowl free safety Dwight Hicks spoke from the heart, delivering a passionate speech that would carry the 49ers resolve into the next season.

> We let this one slip away, fellas. Get a grasp on yourself and the situation. Let yourself realize this rotten feeling of defeat. We don't want to feel this again, especially in a big game such as this. Sure, we could blame the officiating; there are a lot of things we can blame on why we lost this game. But the bottom line—we didn't play well enough to win. We should be packing for Tampa and Super Bowl XVIII right now, but instead our season is over. Let's capture this moment and each and every one of us pledge right now not to feel this rotten feeling again. Don't forget it. Remember this feeling because we don't want to ever feel like this again. We will play Washington next year, we will beat them, and we will begin building toward a trip to Super Bowl XIX! We can do it! We will do it!"[6]

"I was defensive captain of that team [1983]. I was just compelled to get up and say something because, first, I just looked around and some guys were crying, we were very defeated and felt cheated," recalled Hicks in a 2005 interview.[7]

"When we went into the locker room Dwight Hicks got up and talked to the team. He made a point that we don't want to feel like this again, and we're going to get to work right now. When we come back for the next season, we're gonna be ready to take this thing all the way. All the players and coaches in there listened to the speeches. The team took off," said Ray Rhodes, defensive backs coach.[8]

Hicks's speech touched everybody in the room, not just players and coaches. "Everybody was upset. I mean everybody was crying, and when Dwight got up and spoke, he gave me goose bumps when he was speaking," said Jerry Walker, director of public relations. "From that moment on, that whole season [1984] was when we decided we were going to win the Super Bowl."[9]

The flight to San Francisco carried a disappointed but determined squad back to the West Coast. "I maintained from the time that it happened on that plane ride back from Washington that it set the foundation for our championship team in 1984. This was a team that was bound and determined that this was not going to be their legacy to lose this game this way. I was just overwhelmed with the maturity and the sense of purpose . . . on that plane ride. And you know we had some great leaders. I mean, obviously Ronnie Lott on defense and Dwight Clark and, of course, Joe Montana. The off-season was a strong one," said Paul Hackett, quarterbacks/wide receivers coach.[10]

"[That game] just ignited us. I think it was unsaid—the type of competition and camaraderie and cohesiveness that we had with the leadership of Eddie DeBartolo and Bill Walsh and the rest of the coaches—that we just expected to come back the next year. Be ready and just be fueled by the fire to play and get to the Super Bowl," said tight end Earl Cooper.[11]

As the sun set over the nation's capital, a luxury DC-10 flew back to San Francisco, setting the stage for a nearly perfect season by a nearly perfect team.

Part I

The Team

I

EDDIE D.

Being an owner is a support function. If an owner doesn't have the brains to hire good people and then stay out of the action himself, then he has no business in sports.
—Eddie DeBartolo Jr., 49ers owner[1]

As the 49ers slowly walked into the locker room at RFK Stadium with their heads down and tears in their eyes, one man stood tall, all five feet eight of him. Eddie DeBartolo Jr., the thirty-seven-year-old owner of the 49ers, remained surprisingly calm. "Going into the locker room, Eddie and the people he was with seemed to be upbeat," said George Seifert, 49ers defensive coordinator. "Normally when we lost a game all hell would break loose, particularly a game as meaningful as the championship game. So I was impressed by the fact that there was ownership and they were in a positive mood."[2]

DeBartolo Jr. had gained a reputation for wearing his emotions on his sleeve and never apologizing for it. His personality was all about hugs and kisses. He was colorful and vibrant, showing off his Italian heritage every moment he could, which seemed to be the opposite of his father. Eddie Sr. was more reserved and got away with nods and smiles. They shared one common trait, however—the drive to be successful. They lived to work. As a result, the DeBartolo Corporation became one of the most successful companies in the country.

Edward DeBartolo Sr. was born Anthony Paonessa in Youngstown, Ohio, the son of Italian immigrants, and began working early in construction, writing bids for various construction projects at the age of thirteen for his stepfather's company. While in high school, he assumed the surname of his stepfather, Michael DeBartolo, as a tribute to him.[3]

While studying civil engineering at the University of Notre Dame, Eddie Sr. also worked at night as a concrete foreman on projects around South Bend. He returned to his hometown and after five years of working for his stepfather, he started his own company in 1937, building single-family residences. After army service in Korea during World War II, he founded the Edward J. DeBartolo Corporation.

It has been said that the future belongs to those who can anticipate it—something Eddie Sr. did very well. He accumulated his fortune by being among the first to build regional shopping malls just before the wave of suburban development. The first, a 48,000-square-foot plaza that opened in 1948, was seen as a radical design—mostly due to its size—and was followed three years later by the seventeenth mall, Boardman Plaza in Youngstown, the company's first "major" shopping center.[4]

During the ensuing ten years DeBartolo and his company continued to build shopping centers across the Midwest, and by 1965 he was dubbed the "Plaza King" with more than 100 projects to his credit. The company's success continued in the 1970s with the flagship project, Cleveland's Randall Park Mall, which opened in 1976 with five anchor stores and more than 200 retail shops sprawling over 2.2 million square feet of land.

By 1984 there were more than fifty DeBartolo malls from Pennsylvania to California. The company's huge success in real estate allowed the family to branch out into other areas, including professional sports. DeBartolo invested in racetracks, including Thistledown in Cleveland and the luxurious Louisiana Downs near Shreveport, and he was owner of the NHL's Pittsburgh Penguins and its home, the Civic Arena.

Eddie Jr. grew up knowing that he wanted to be in the family business. At the age of twelve Eddie worked for his father's company doing every odd job in the book, including gardening and shoveling snow at the mall locations, continuing into high school and college as a laborer on DeBartolo construction crews. "We have a family motto, 'work harder than you play' and I have, right from the time I was a youngster," once claimed Eddie Jr.[5]

After graduating from the University of Notre Dame in 1968, Eddie Jr. went to work for the DeBartolo Corporation. He quickly received a crash course in how to run a successful business, taking an executive training program where he moved from department to department learning the many facets of the company. In 1971 he was named vice president, and five years later he was appointed executive vice president and assumed leadership of the mammoth in-house DeBartolo staff of some 300 engineers, architects, designers, financiers, leasing agents, lawyers, and operations teams, along with advertising, public relations, and marketing personnel. In 1979 he was promoted to president and chief administrative officer. While becoming a success at the DeBartolo Corporation, he spent quality time learning how to treat people.

"When my father started the company he always treated people first class no matter where they were, no matter who they were," commented Eddie DeBartolo Jr. in a 2012 interview. "They could've been a maintenance man; they could've been somebody working in the kitchen or . . . his senior vice president. [He] always treated people like they were part of his family. If anybody had a problem, they could come to him or anybody else in the family, and they did. It really was a family and that's what I wanted to do. I wanted to carry that on into San Francisco and into the football operation."[6]

The two men were inseparable while overseeing a multimillion dollar enterprise. "When he got out of the army, my father had about $5,000 and he invested in two duplexes," Eddie Jr. said once to a sportswriter. "His first shopping center was a three-store strip center in Youngstown. My father and I spent a tremendous amount of time together. He's really become more like my brother. We have coffee every morning at six.

"We develop from concept to completion. Then we manage and operate. We never sell anything. One hundred percent owned by us. We design everything ourselves. We look at everything as a total entity. We're concerned not with what we've done, but what we are going to do next. Our philosophy is to keep moving, keep building."[7]

Eddie Sr. was often described as a soft-spoken, unassuming man, a characterization that seems far removed from his public persona as a shrewd businessman and tough negotiator. He had a legendary work ethic that started early in the day and it rubbed off on his son. His fourteen-hour workdays began at 5:30 a.m., when he arrived at the office. He worked seven days a week and was never seen by employees—or 49ers players and staff—without a suit and tie. Eddie Jr. always joined his father in the predawn hours at the company's work sites for coffee from a Styrofoam cup and discussed business.

As the company blossomed Eddie married his childhood sweetheart Cynthia (known as Candy) Papalia and went on to have three daughters, Lisa Marie (1969), Tiffanie Lynn (1970), and Nicole Anne (1975). In 1977 the DeBartolos were about to get into the pro football business. After the family's first foray into sports with the Penguins, Eddie De-Bartolo Jr., barely thirty years old, helped negotiate the purchase of the NFL's San Francisco 49ers. "It took an awful lot of negotiation," recalled Eddie Jr. "After many days of talks, always very aboveboard and very pleasant—and, of course, we were flying back and forth from Youngstown—we finalized the deal. . . . I just remember sitting in the company jet on the way back to Youngstown and thinking, 'That's it, then; we're going to do it.' And all of sudden we were in the football business."[8]

As soon as the deal was signed detractors in San Francisco emerged to criticize the young, handsome, Italian outsider from northwest Ohio. On the surface, as some writers penned, the purchase of the 49ers was a gift from his father. But as the West Coast was about to find out, it would be hard to imagine Eddie Sr. spending seventeen million dollars on a mere diversion for his son. This was a successful and motivated family that wanted to prove that it could win and excel in the arena of professional sports. The 49ers purchase was also a chance for Eddie Jr. to step out of his father's shadow.

A winning atmosphere wasn't part of Eddie Jr.'s inheritance when he acquired the San Francisco 49ers. It's safe to say that the previous owners—the Morabito sisters and Franklin Mieuli (owner of the NBA's Golden State Warriors)—didn't anticipate the impact the Notre Dame alumnus would have on the NFL when they sold him the 49ers. Being only thirty years old when he took over the 49ers in the spring of 1977, much was said about Eddie Jr.'s ability (or lack thereof) to run an NFL team.

His first move was to fire head coach Monte Clark, who was very popular with fans and media, at the family's introductory press conference at the Fairmont Hotel in downtown San Francisco. "Does everyone fully realize that we made an investment of seventeen million?" DeBartolo told the local media. "This is a business, not a play toy. We're not going to placate personalities. We have to run the team our way."

The young owner's remarks weren't viewed kindly by the press. The next two years didn't get any easier for young Eddie D.[9]

During that time the organization was in chaos. The 49ers were losers on and off the field. Eddie Jr. tried to reorganize the franchise by hiring general manager Joe Thomas, a family friend, who had earned a reputation for building winning teams based on sound personal decisions while working with the Minnesota Vikings, Miami Dolphins, and Baltimore Colts.

However, it didn't take Eddie Jr. long to see that Thomas's way of doing things wasn't going to work. The 49ers reverted to their losing ways with a 5–9 record in 1977. Coach Ken Meyer was fired and Thomas brought in Pete McCulley, a loyal Thomas supporter from the Colts. He never finished the 1978 season. Fired after the ninth game (1–8), McCulley was replaced by Fred O'Connor (1–6). The 1978 season ended with a 2–14 record. On top of the poor coaching hires, Thomas made an ill-advised trade before the season to acquire an aging O. J. Simpson from the Buffalo Bills. Thomas gave up second- and third-round picks in 1978, first-round (which turned out to be the number-one pick overall) and fourth-round picks in 1979, and a second-round pick in 1980. The future didn't look bright in the City by the Bay.

Eddie Jr. knew the two years under Thomas was a mistake. But the young owner quickly learned from his initial failure. "You take a licking, but you have to keep ticking," reflected DeBartolo in 1981. "Joe Thomas had become an island unto himself. You can't become an island when you're in the entertainment business. You can never be bigger than what you're trying to do. He couldn't take the gas. It wasn't easy for any of us. If I was going to be in Youngstown, Ohio, and still be the owner of a San Francisco team, then I had to have somebody very visible who would be able to take the heat."

DeBartolo continues, "As the last, Joe [Thomas] was communicating with no one. He wasn't talking to the media; he wasn't talking to me. What concerned me as much as our record is the fact that our image and status in the community had suffered. Our family has always been in the people business, and that means doing things in a first-class manner, being fair and cooperating as much as possible with the public and the media."[10]

Thomas's reign with the 49ers was littered with terrible mistakes. He began his tenure by taking down the pictures of former 49ers greats at the 49ers facility and ordering them burned. He wanted no signs of past glory (luckily, a public relations assistant had most of the pictures stored in the basement). Thomas told 49ers legends Hugh McElhenny and Y. A. Tittle that their days of special privileges were over. He abolished the kids' section at Candlestick Park, fired cheerleaders, and even canceled the team's Christmas card. Young DeBartolo saw his franchise become the laughingstock of the NFL, both on and off the field. Something needed to be done. "Being an owner is a support function. If an owner doesn't have the brains to hire good people and then stay out of the action himself, then he has no business being in sports," commented DeBartolo.[11]

Eddie D.'s vision of a first-class sports organization was nowhere to be found. Fans took out their frustrations on the young owner. "The fan reaction was not complimentary to him. We'd go to games and the fans would be throwing beer at him. There were some nasty confrontations. He was a young guy learning what this is all about," said Ken Flower, former 49ers administrative assistant under DeBartolo.[12] "We didn't have good teams," recalled Eddie DeBartolo in *The Team of the Decade*. "God, I was booed. I got hit with things at the stadium; I was spit on. It was a very tough few years. And there were times when I thought, 'This is crazy; who needs this? Is this really worth it?' But you stop and say, 'Well, let's try and get things together. Let's try and regroup, get the troops together, put the wagons in a circle, and we'll see what we can do.' And you know that's about the time I met Bill Walsh."[13]

The next decision was Eddie Jr.'s alone. He wouldn't listen to any of the people around the league who were advocating that he hire a head coach and a general manager. He only wanted one man and that man was in his own backyard. All he had to do was convince Bill Walsh of Stanford University to join him in the National Football League.

2

THE GENIUS

Genius? Genius? Beethoven was a genius. Einstein was a genius. I just taught a bunch of grown men how to play a game.
—Bill Walsh, 49ers head coach[1]

On November 27, 1978, the heart and soul of the city of San Francisco changed forever. Just hours before the San Francisco 49ers were to host the Pittsburgh Steelers on Monday Night Football at Candlestick Park, a horrific event would shock the City by the Bay. With a revolver in his pocket, a depressed former city supervisor, Dan White, snuck into city hall through a basement window and assassinated San Francisco mayor George Moscone and city supervisor Harvey Milk, the first openly gay person elected to public office in California.

Just a week before the assassination of Moscone and Milk, the city was shaken by the Jonestown tragedy in Guyana, where more than nine hundred people from the religious cult the Peoples Temple died from cyanide poisoning. The Peoples Temple headquarters had been in San Francisco since the mid-1970s. The city was just processing the Jonestown tragedy when it was rocked by the Moscone and Milk assassinations at 11:00 a.m. on November 27.

That day unbelievable grief and sorrow filled the city. The only person who seemed to be immune to the loss of two very popular city officials was Joe Thomas. As news of the assassinations reached the NFL office, officials debated whether the game between the 49ers and Steelers should be played. Looking out for his own safety, Thomas wanted to cancel the game, because he thought he would be next. "I knew then that I had to make a change," reflected Eddie DeBartolo Jr. after witnessing Thomas's reaction to the city's pain that day. NFL commissioner Pete Rozelle, a graduate of the University of San Francisco, said the game should be played to help the city heal. That night Eddie D. decided that he needed new leadership to run his franchise. He also saw a Steelers team—with a record of 11–1 at that time who would go on to win the Super Bowl that year—dismantle his weak 49ers. Behind three touchdown passes from Terry Bradshaw and a defense that forced five interceptions, the Steelers cruised to a 24–7 victory in front of a somber Candlestick crowd.[2]

The 49ers finished a 2–14 season under the failed leadership of Joe Thomas. Something needed to be done. The team and city needed a savior. Little did they know he was already in the Bay area.

Bill Walsh (born November 30, 1931) grew up in an industrious family in Los Angeles, where his father worked for the Chrysler Corporation and ran a private automotive business. The family moved to Oregon following Bill's sophomore year in high school but quickly returned to California, settling in Hayward, near San Francisco's East Bay. He stayed at Hayward High School long enough to win a running back job on the varsity football team. His skills, however, were insufficient to attract a scholarship from a big-name college.

Following high school Walsh enrolled at San Mateo Junior College, playing quarterback for two years. He then transferred to San Jose State where he majored in education and played end for coach Bob Bronzan. In 1956 after a stint in the army at Fort Ord, he became a graduate assistant in physical education at his alma mater. He rejoined his former coach, Bronzan, who recognized his pupil's aptitude for coaching and was willing to do anything to help the young coach. He was the first to recognize Walsh's genius for drawing up complicated plays. In turn Walsh absorbed everything Bronzan presented to him.

"He had a great football mind. He was a theorist and an excellent teacher who set a standard as to the detail of everything he coached and the organizational system he set up," said Bill Walsh of his mentor. "He coached football like it was a science, a skilled sport instead of just head bashing."[3] In later years Walsh would credit Bronzan for his decision to go into the coaching profession.

Bronzan could see that Walsh was burning to succeed as a football coach and was bursting with ideas. When Walsh completed his master's studies at San Jose (his thesis was titled "Defensing the Pro-Set Formation"), his mentor wrote an impressive recommendation for Walsh's placement file, saying, "I predict Bill Walsh will become the outstanding football coach in the United States."[4] Walsh's first head coaching job was at Washington Union High School in Fremont, California, in 1957. (His yearly $4,650 salary included teaching physical education.) He turned the school's previous three-year record of 1–26 into a conference championship team with a 9–1 record in his second season. His success led him to an appointment as defensive coordinator on Marv Levy's University of California staff in 1960 before moving on to Stanford in 1963 as administrative assistant and secondary coach for John Ralston.

Learning from Levy and Ralston gave Walsh an even bigger thirst for the intrinsic technical aspect of the sport. Although Walsh was coaching on the defensive side of the ball, his mind wasn't far from developing the short passing game that would be called the "West Coast offense." His professional football apprenticeship began in 1966 with a season as offensive backfield coach for the AFL's Oakland Raiders under head coach Al Davis, giving him another mentor who would show him how to use the passing game as a weapon.

But after the one season with the Raiders Walsh's career reached a crossroads. After a decade in the profession Walsh was now married to Geri with two boys, Steve and Craig. His family needed stability. So in 1967 he taught a class at San Jose City College while waiting to see if he would be admitted to Stanford's Graduate School of Business. But football wasn't totally out of his system. That fall he was head coach of the San Jose Apaches of the minor league Continental Football League. "My father would be driving down the road, using his index finger, and crafting plays as he was driving. I watched this as I was growing up," said Craig Walsh, son of Bill Walsh.[5] Then in early 1968 Walsh got an unexpected phone call.

That fall the American Football League gave Paul Brown an expansion team that he quickly named the Cincinnati Bengals. One of his first phone calls was to Bill Walsh to see if he wanted a job as wide receivers coach. Walsh agreed to get back into coaching full time. His second year with the Bengals, he added quarterback coaching to his responsibilities and eventually offensive coordinator. "The eight years with Paul Brown at Cincinnati were the most valuable I could have," Walsh commented in 1984. "The atmosphere for teaching and coaching was ideal. I had a lot of autonomy. By the second year I began to take the responsibility to call 50 to 60 percent of the plays."[6]

The legendary Brown stressed theory, organization, and teaching— all things that Walsh believed were at the heart of coaching football. He knew the time spent with Brown would lead him to a head coaching position. While in Cincinnati, Walsh gained the reputation as an offensive genius. Building Brown's offense around the short passing game, Walsh taught his quarterbacks how to attack a defense not by just throwing deep passes, but by using the whole field. The West Coast offense was developed in Cincinnati.

WEST COAST OFFENSE

The West Coast offense reversed traditional football thinking that the run sets up the pass. Walsh instead used short, horizontal passes to spread out the defense, relying on his receivers to gain yards after the catch. The system was based on short timing routes and three- to five-step drops to get rid of the ball quickly. Defenses would subsequently focus on those short routes, opening up opportunities to run the ball.[7]

But the West Coast offense was a philosophy as much as a scheme. It preached precision and preparation. Walsh was meticulous with his play calling, eventually scripting fifteen to twenty-five plays of the game ahead of time. This allowed him to gauge the defense's tendencies as the game unfolded so that he could exploit them later. That ability—to recognize the holes and weaknesses in a defense and react accordingly—is just as important as the plays themselves in the West Coast offense. Bill Walsh was superior at making such assessments, and for this reason his genius went beyond the X's and O's.

His system also relied on running backs who could catch the ball out of the backfield. On any given play, a running back could be asked to fulfill the role of a receiver in order to create mismatches for the defense. Walsh attacked every inch of the football field, and with Cincinnati's early teams, he had to do it to be successful.

Being an expansion team, the Bengals had to find creative ways of moving the ball to get first downs. During his time in Cincinnati, Walsh helped quarterbacks Greg Cook, Virgil Carter, and especially Ken Anderson to become successful signal callers, giving Walsh a platform in the coaching industry. "There's no special secret to what I have learned or what I know about the passing game," he stated. "I simply spent a lot of time and put in a lot of hard work mastering techniques of the passing game, techniques that I believe in. As an assistant coach, I decided eventually that the way to succeed was to establish a reputation in one area, and I did that with the pass offense."[8]

The perfect match lasted eight years while Walsh waited for Brown to retire and leave the Bengals to him, his protégé. Brown retired after the 1975 season, but to everyone's surprise he chose Bill Johnson, the Bengals longtime offensive line coach, as his successor. There was a sense that Walsh cast too large a shadow for Brown's taste, that Walsh was not willing to stay in the background, that he pushed for attention. At forty-four years old, after putting in twenty years of coaching, Walsh wanted to be a head coach.

Feeling hurt, Walsh left the Bengals after his contract expired to become offensive coordinator with the San Diego Chargers under Tommy Prothro. There he helped future Hall of Famer Dan Fouts to his best year as a pro, completing nearly 58 percent of his passes for a career high 2,535 yards. His year in San Diego led him to be hired as head coach at Stanford University. At Stanford his two signal callers, Guy Benjamin (1977) and Steve Dils (1978), led the NCAA in passing and were named All Americans despite being unknown commodities prior to playing for Walsh. His two Stanford teams were 17–7 overall and captured bowl wins at the conclusion of both seasons: the Sun and Bluebonnet bowls.

It was before the 1978 Bluebonnet Bowl that Walsh and Eddie DeBartolo met for the first time. After the assassinations of Moscone and Milk and the Monday night debacle against the Steelers, DeBartolo looked into hiring a new man to lead his organization. He wanted Bill Walsh. Through Ron Barr, the Stanford play-by-play man, a meeting was arranged for the two men on the second Saturday in December.

In a room at the Fairmont Hotel in San Francisco Eddie DeBartolo and Bill Walsh met to discuss the 49ers situation. It didn't take long for each man to realize that it was going to be a perfect match. "I just knew it. And I think he knew it too," recalled Eddie DeBartolo years later. "I think I knew after five or six minutes that it would be a good relationship."[9]

After talking about football, philosophy, family, and values, DeBartolo tentatively agreed to hire Walsh as his next head coach. The meeting lasted less than an hour. Because Walsh still had to coach Stanford against Georgia in the Bluebonnet Bowl, nothing was finalized or signed. On New Year's Eve DeBartolo held a party in Youngstown to watch the game and brag about his new hire. Unfortunately Stanford fell behind 22–0 and cleared out the party early. Young Eddie sat watching in disbelief, wondering, "Did I make another mistake?"

Then in the second half Walsh and his team mounted a furious comeback against the Bulldogs, winning 25–22, making DeBartolo breathe a little easier. On January 9, 1979, Eddie DeBartolo hired Bill Walsh as the franchise's eleventh head coach, paying him $160,000 a year (compared to $48,000 at Stanford). Walsh was ready to get to work. Little did he know that he didn't have much waiting for him.

BILL WALSH'S STANDARD OF PERFORMANCE

After two decades in coaching and learning from great mentors such as Bob Bronzan, Marv Levy, John Ralston, Al Davis, and, most importantly, Paul Brown, Walsh was ready to put his philosophy into practice. He called it "a standard of performance." It was his playbook for success, teamwork, hard work, and leadership. It was more than just X's and O's.

Walsh's philosophy, which he would teach to the whole 49ers organization, had as much to do with values, principles, and ideals as it did with blocking, tackling, and passing. It had more to do with the mental than the physical. "It began with the fundamental assertion, regardless of your specific job, it is vital to our team that you do that job at the highest possible level in all its various aspects, both mental and physical," wrote Walsh in his playbook.[10] He wanted perfection from his staff and players.

This standard of performance included everybody from coaches and players to marketing, office personnel, groundskeepers, and even the receptionists who answered the phones. There was a page in the playbook for every employee. Everybody was accountable and everybody in the 49ers organization was important regardless of job title. Walsh created an environment in which everybody in the 49ers organization adhered to his standard of performance, and over time it became second nature to anyone who came into the organization to work at a first-class level both on and off the field. "Dad wanted everyone to work as a team and as a family," said Craig Walsh.[11] It was the same philosophy that DeBartolo had.

After a short time on the job Walsh meet with DeBartolo. Walsh explained that he was having a hard time finding a general manager. When DeBartolo hired Walsh, he gave his coach the power to make all football decisions including personnel. At that time most GMs answered to the owner, not the head coach, and they had the authority to hire and fire the head coach. GMs selected the players, and the coach trained them. Walsh eventually suggested that he be named general manager and director of football operations. He'd find someone to run the administrative details, but the entire organization would be under a single operational authority.

DeBartolo loved everything about Walsh: his enthusiasm, intelligence, and, more importantly, his organizational detail. Walsh had a plan for everything in the organization from running the offense, to hiring a secretary, to maintaining the practice field. Walsh was the anti–Joe Thomas. DeBartolo would give Walsh the keys to the 49ers kingdom. As Walsh finished explaining his plan, Eddie got excited about the idea. "Great," he said. "Let's do it."[12]

Walsh had written four specific guidelines for hiring front-office personnel, which he would follow.

1. I needed to feel comfortable with them, because I knew there would be difficult times, stressful times, when people can misunderstand each other. At such times, any little idiosyncrasy is magnified. Differences can become monumental if people are unable to have an open exchange on an ongoing basis. In critical management positions, you prefer to work with somebody you've known well or known for a long time, so you can gauge how he'll react to the pressures of an intense, highly competitive atmosphere.

2. I wanted functional intelligence, because I knew that one person who is not very bright but very aggressive in pushing ideas can destroy an organization. He can steamroll others, so you waste time undoing the damage he's done.

3. We needed knowledge and experience in the business dynamics of the National Football League. It takes many years to understand the NFL's operational procedures.
4. I wanted people who would be enthusiastic and inquisitive and who would thrive on work.[13]

His first major hire was John Ralston, his former employer with Stanford, who would stay for two seasons as vice president for administration. He supported Walsh as he began setting up his organizational structure. The second hire was John McVay, who had four decades of experience coaching and playing. An Ohio native from famed Massillon High School, McVay played collegiately at Miami of Ohio for Woody Hayes and Ara Parseghian. A three-year starter at center, he won All Midwest and team MVP honors during his final season. His coaching career began with a ten-year tenure (1953–1962) at Canton Central Catholic High School in Ohio before joining Duffy Daugherty's staff at Michigan State. Following three years there, McVay took over as head coach at the University of Dayton and led the Flyers to their first winning season in ten years when they finished 8–2 in 1966.

After leaving Dayton McVay joined the New York Giants in late 1975 as an assistant coach in charge of research and development but was elevated to head coach by owner Wellington Mara to replace the fired Bill Arnsparger. Two and a half years later McVay himself was fired after compiling a 14–25 record. Walsh knew that McVay didn't want to coach anymore, so he hired him as his director of player personnel. From the very beginning McVay could see that the DeBartolos wanted to have a model franchise. "I remember being in Youngstown. Bill and I were there and we had a meeting essentially with Eddie and with Eddie's dad, Senior. I remember Senior saying to us directly so that we understood it. He says, 'I want everything to be first class.' We said, 'Yes, sir.' He said, 'Did you understand? I want everything first class.' And Eddie said, 'Yes, that's the way we want to operate.' And that's the way we operated. Everything was first class," said John McVay, vice president and general manager.[14]

Coming into a new environment in San Francisco, McVay was given more jobs than any other employee under Walsh. "I used to jokingly refer to my job as 'I'm in charge of everything that nobody else wants to do.' I was the liaison guy with the equipment guys, the trainers, with the scouts, with the pro personnel stuff. I had plenty to do," said McVay. "But I came in as director of player personnel because I was convinced and hell-bent on making sure that we had as much good personnel as we could possibly get for the coaches, and that was my main function."[15]

Walsh and McVay complemented each other well in setting up a first-class organization. McVay had a keen eye for talent and knew the NFL's ins and outs of obtaining players via trades, waiver wire, and injuries lists. He was also in charge of the scouting staff and prepared the 49ers college draft strategy. McVay worked behind the scenes, letting Walsh stay in front of the public and media. Walsh usually came up with an idea, but it was McVay who would accomplish it. It was a perfect match.[16]

From the time he took over, Walsh was looking for players who could make a big difference on the field. The 1979 roster didn't have many. He inherited an offensive line that become the nucleus of a future Pro Bowl front, featuring guards John Ayers and Randy Cross, center Fred Quillan, and tackle Keith Fahnhorst. He had a kicker, Ray Wersching, a speedy but inconsistent wide receiver, Freddie Solomon, and two young linebackers in Willie Harper and Dan Bunz. Walsh had precious little beyond that. Yet he turned the team into a Super Bowl champion within three years.

With McVay as director of player personnel and newly hired Tony Razzano as head of scouting, the 49ers would be built through the draft. "Our basic improvement will come through the draft. We have a football team that's void of players," proclaimed Bill Walsh.[17] And indeed they did. In 1979 Walsh selected his franchise quarterback.

From the beginning Walsh had a knack for spotting talent and then developing it to the fullest. His touch was never more apparent than in his selection of Notre Dame quarterback Joe Montana in the third round (the eighty-second choice overall) of the 1979 draft. Although he had Steve DeBerg on his roster, Montana would be the signal caller Walsh would groom. Walsh transformed DeBerg from the NFL's twenty-eighth ranked passer in 1978 to the thirteenth leading passer in 1979—a year in which DeBerg attempted and completed more passes than any quarterback in NFL history. He handed the job to Joe Montana at midseason in 1980, and Montana responded by completing 64 percent of his passes, a club record. Also that year Montana engineered the greatest comeback in NFL history by leading the 49ers from a 35–7 halftime deficit against the New Orleans Saints to a 38–35 overtime win. But the real magic was yet to come.

Walsh also drafted wide receiver Dwight Clark in the tenth round of the '79 draft, who quickly became Montana's favorite target. He knew the draft was the basis for building, but only the basis. That same year he signed two key free agents, defensive end Dwaine Board, who was cut from the Pittsburgh Steelers, and safety Dwight Hicks, who was cut by the Detroit Lions and Philadelphia Eagles. In 1980 he drafted running back Earl Cooper (first round), defensive end Jim Stuckey (first round), linebackers Keena Turner (second round) and Bobby Leopold (eighth round), and signed former Jets defensive end Lawrence Pillers as a free agent. But it was the 1981 draft and season that ignited San Francisco's winning ways and elevated Bill Walsh to "genius" status.

After going 2–14 in 1979 and 6–10 in 1980, the 49ers were showing signs of turning the corner from laughingstock to a competitive football franchise. "We were trying to build the team in segments as we went along," said McVay, director of player personnel in 1980. "We went through those stages where we were just trying to build different sections of the team."[18] But one part of the team was still dragging the defense down—the secondary. In 1980 the 49ers finished twenty-seventh in pass defense—only the Cleveland Browns were worse—by allowing 3,958 passing yards and twenty-nine touchdowns. Quarterbacks completed 66 percent of their passes against a secondary that had players rotating on a weekly basis. Only free safety Dwight Hicks showed promise.

In the '81 draft Walsh knew he needed some defensive backs. He drafted three-quarters of a championship secondary. He selected cornerback Ronnie Lott of USC in the first round, cornerback Eric Wright of Missouri in the second round, and safety Carlton Williamson of Pittsburgh in the third round. The trio joined Hicks to make a formidable secondary that would change the attitude and culture of the 49ers defense. Before the season Walsh and his staff picked up free agent linebacker Jack "Hacksaw" Reynolds from the divisional rival Los Angeles Rams and in midseason traded for pass-rushing specialist Fred Dean from the San Diego Chargers.

The 1981 season was magical for the 49ers. Joe Montana came of age, the newly built secondary was spectacular, and Bill Walsh showed his genius. After a 13–3 regular season, the 49ers defeated the New York Giants in the divisional round to set up the game that would start a dynasty.

The 1981 NFC Championship Game between the 49ers and the Dallas Cowboys ended with "the Catch," a six-yard touchdown from Joe Montana to Dwight Clark, which gave back to the city of San Francisco its heart and soul. Just three years after the doom and gloom of Jonestown and the Moscone and Milk assassinations, the 49ers and their silver-haired head coach lifted the city to new heights. Two weeks later on January 24, 1982, in Detroit, Michigan, the mission was complete when the 49ers defeated the Cincinnati Bengals, Walsh's former team, 26–21 to win Super Bowl XVI.

In just three years Walsh implemented his standard of performance throughout the 49ers organization and, with the backing and support of owner Eddie DeBartolo, began building what would become the 1984 team. He continued to hire and promote key personnel within the 49ers organization. During the magical 1981 season, Walsh hired Jerry Walker and Neal Dahlen.

Walker was hired as assistant director of public relations under George Heddleston. Two years later he replaced Heddleston as director. "Bill, when he talked in staff meetings, [would say] everybody on the staff directory deserves respect. If I ever hear of anybody not getting respect, I'm going to come see you. The secretary, the equipment guy—everybody deserves respect, and they are part of this team and that's when people talk about 49er family, everybody contributed," said Walker.[19]

Neal Dahlen was a local high school coach who knew 49ers defensive line coach Bill McPherson from when Coach Mac recruited one of Dahlen's players for UCLA. One summer Dahlen asked McPherson if he could help out with the 49ers during training camp. So in 1981 Dahlen worked training camp and helped the 49ers to their first Super Bowl win. Walsh and John McVay saw how hard Dahlen worked. "At first I didn't have much contact with Walsh. Then [through] the year I'd go work at the high school, and then work the afternoons at the 49ers. Tony Razzano and John McVay eventually asked me if I could work full time and I did," said Dahlen.[20]

Walsh confided in Dahlen and expanded his responsibilities. "Bill got to know me a little bit more, I guess, and he asked me to be with him at every practice. So I was with him at every practice and he bounced things off me every once in a while," said Dahlen. "If there was something administrative that we needed to do while he was stuck on the field, he'd ask me to go do it. I'd go in and make a phone call or do something that needed to be done while practice went on. Of course, I saw a lot of football on the practice field all those years I was there."[21]

"I was impressed by Bill, his intellect and creativity. Really, he was the chief football officer as the head coach there," continued Dahlen. "He kind of ran everything . . . and he organized it similar to Paul Brown's organization. As long as I knew him, he was an extremely impressive guy."[22] Walsh was impressed with Dahlen and his knowledge of the game. He leaned on him and in 1984 gave him the title of director of research and development. Throughout the season he helped George Seifert and the defensive coaches break down film of their opponents.

In 1982 Walsh was not enjoying the rewards of winning a Super Bowl. He was thinking about stepping away from coaching. That season the 49ers started the season with two close losses to the Raiders and Broncos, then the NFL suffered through a seven-week player's strike, disrupting the season for Walsh. The 49ers would never recover from the strike, finishing the season with a dismal 3–6 record. In the season finale, with an outside shot at the NFL's expanded playoffs, the 49ers lost to the Rams 21–20, when their game-winning field goal attempt was blocked. A distraught Walsh, who took every loss harder than anyone else, thought about stepping aside as 49ers head coach and remaining as general manager.

"A loss was terrible for him. His expectations were high. He started to think 'I'm the guy who has to win these games.' He really wouldn't celebrate a victory unless it was a Super Bowl. He was so hard on himself. I would go over and he would have a glass of wine and just beat himself up," said Craig Walsh.[23]

After several meetings with DeBartolo in Youngstown, Walsh was urged by his boss to remain as head coach. After going back and forth for several weeks, Walsh finally emerged from his disappointment of the strike season to return as the 49ers head man. "I'm more optimistic than I've been before any season since I came here," Walsh said in 1983. "I know that the time for me to get out of coaching and concentrate solely on the other roles of my job is not now. I'm very optimistic about this season." DeBartolo was equally excited about Walsh's new-found energy. "Bill is the difference in the 49ers being recognized as a force to be dealt with in the National Football League," said DeBartolo before the 1983 season. "I want it to stay that way." DeBartolo rewarded Walsh by giving him DeBartolo's former title of president and promoting John McVay to general manager. More changes were on the way in San Francisco.[24]

3

THE COACHING STAFF

It was a wonderful working environment. [Bill Walsh] wouldn't have tolerated anybody getting cranky with anybody else in the meeting.
—Fred vonAppen, 49ers special teams coach[1]

After the disaster of the 1982 strike season, Walsh looked to not only improve his team on the field, but to improve his coaching staff as well. Walsh turned the same sharp eye on his assistant coaches that he used to evaluate his layers. Within his "standard of performance" he wanted knowledgeable, driven, hard-working assistants. Over the years he would record the specific requirements he was looking for when hiring a coach.

PREREQUISITES FOR ASSISTANT COACHING POSITIONS

a. He must have a complete working knowledge of the game, because the players respect that above everything else. Athletes can be coached in almost any style if they're confident that the coach really knows what he's doing. The players must know that the coach is up to date and contemporary in his approach and able to adjust quickly to the tactics of different opponents.
b. Coaches must be able to effectively implement a program for each player that best develops his individual skills. Taking a personal interest in each of his players, regardless of their roles, is

absolutely essential. If you combine that with expertise, a coach
will fully develop the skills and effectiveness of the athletes.

c. You must have people who can communicate well under the
stress of a season, so you need the kind of personality that can
work with others. There's a broad range in that area. Not everybody is ideally suited to working well with just anyone.

d. The ability to express oneself is vital, because a logical, articulate
person is best suited for teaching. If he can both impart what he
knows to the player and deal with others under stress, he's your
man.

e. The coaching ethic of commitment and personal sacrifice is the
basis of the job. There are some who just can't bring themselves
to work a coach's long hours. By and large, those men have elimi-
nated themselves by the time you get to the NFL level. It takes a
person who can enthusiastically accept the values and philosophy
of a head coach.

f. The chemistry of the staff is vital. Everyone has his own distinct
personality, so you must bring together a group of men who will
not only work smoothly with the head coach, but also with other
coaches and with the players.[2]

In sum, "The life of the assistant coach must be a labor of love. These
are men who are totally committed to the game. The sacrifices in time
and effort, the lack of long-term security, the relatively modest com-
pensation, and, in a sense, obscurity can be equated only with a sincere
dedication. It's almost a 'calling.'"[3]

Walsh thought his staff needed new energy and ideas on and off the
field. He wanted to make some changes so the failure of 1982 wouldn't
happen again.

TRANSITION OF THE 1982 STAFF TO THE 1983 STAFF

Gone from the 1982 coaching staff would be defensive coordinator
Chuck Studley, special teams and wide receivers coach Milt Jackson,
running backs coach Billie Matthews, strength and conditioning coach
Al Vermeil, and quarterbacks coach Sam Wyche, who left to become
the head coach at Indiana University. "Coaching changes can be benefi-

cial to an organization, they bring new expertise, they help sort out responsibilities again, they bring revitalization," commented Walsh in 1983.[4]

For his defensive coordinator Walsh looked in-house to replace Studley. He tapped defensive backs coach George Seifert. "I named George because of the absolute importance of the defensive backfield. The secondary play and pass defense and the development of pass coverage was critical. If [there was] any weakness in our defense under Chuck Studley, it was pass coverage. Chuck had concentrated on stopping the run because he was originally a defensive line coach. So it was decided that Bill [McPherson] would concentrate on the job of stopping the run and George would concentrate on pass defense," Walsh once said about hiring forty-three-year-old Seifert as his defensive coordinator.[5] In his 1990 autobiography, *Building a Champion*, Walsh explained why Seifert was the right choice:

"George Seifert had had just two years' experience in the NFL before becoming defensive coordinator, because his previous career was at the college level. He was an excellent technician and taskmaster. He had a gifted mind and was extremely organized.

"George had a unique aptitude for the technical aspects of the game. He was not a light, quick-witted, amusing type of coach, but a very demanding, no-nonsense, business-oriented man who quickly got the respect of his players because of his expertise and concentration and his willingness to work long hours. That wore people out, but it proved to be very successful. There were endless meetings with George and the players, but he put together a style of defense that was fully dimensional with a flexibility that enabled it to deal effectively with new and varied offenses. George's defenses were often a step ahead of everybody."

Walsh continued, "I was also involved with defense approach and philosophy and with player substitution and overall game strategy. During the game, I concentrated on our fourth-quarter strategy. During the week, it was very important that we coordinate defensive and offensive game plans. I would ask George how he wanted to plan the game. Then, I would tell him how many points we anticipated and how many first downs we would register in the process. Example: if George was wary of an opponent's quick-strike ability, our offensive game plan would emphasize ball control. If the opponent was a ball-control team, George would design a higher-risk defense to get the ball back as quickly as possible.[6]

A native of San Francisco, George Seifert grew up in the city's Mission District and graduated from Polytechnic High School, located across the street from Kezar Stadium, the 49ers former home field. He played offensive tackle, end, and linebacker on Poly's football team and enjoyed one of the special perks of attending Poly: students served as ushers at 49ers home games at Kezar. Seifert went on to play guard and linebacker at the University of Utah, where he began his coaching career as a graduate assistant in 1964. After a one-year stint as head coach at Westminster College in Salt Lake, Seifert moved on as an assistant at Iowa (1966), Oregon (1967–1971), and Stanford (1972–1974) and as head coach at Cornell (1975–1976) before Walsh hired him as secondary coach at Stanford in 1977.

When Walsh went to the 49ers, Seifert stayed at Stanford in the fall of 1979, where his secondary finished second in the Pac-10 in pass defense. The following year Walsh convinced Seifert to join him in San Francisco as secondary coach. "Well, I think in many ways I'd grown up. The most formative years of my coaching, I worked for Bill at Stanford and then the years with San Francisco before I became the coordinator. So I understood the expectations and the detailed part of the way we approached the game was important. I saw the success because of that," said Seifert. "I was pretty detailed, at any rate, because of my sense for technique. I was kind of a technique freak. So I was really into that. And then watching Bill, the way he handled things from a specific standpoint in designing plays, and having to defend his plays all the time in practice. . . . You develop a sense and a feel for the offense and how to defend one of the most complex offenses in football. So that carried over into defending our opponents, and it was a great help and a great teaching aid."[7]

To replace Seifert as defensive backs coach, Walsh promoted former 49ers player Ray Rhodes, who had served the previous two seasons as assistant defensive backs coach under Seifert. "Bill was a mentor; he was a guy who I looked at as a father figure. Then getting the opportunity to work under him, I learned so much about football," said Rhodes. "He'd say 'your goal should be wanting to be the best position coach that you can possibly be. You want to be known as the best secondary coach or the best linebacker coach in the league. That's when you arrive as a coach. When your peers around the league respect what they see on tape of how your players are playing. You gotta realize that's what you're judged by.' Everybody knew his role [on the 49ers]. I was really impressed with him . . . how he looked at the game and dissected it. I still don't think Bill gets the credit he deserves for the way he turned the whole organization around."[8]

Like his mentor, Rhodes could see the detailed organization that Seifert would bring to his new role. "George was a tremendous defensive-minded coach. I have great respect for George. . . . He was one of those guys who was very meticulous about everything: detail, detail, detail. He made sure that there were no situations going into a game that we weren't prepared for or hadn't worked on," said Rhodes. "He made sure that he took care of every little detail. George was an intense guy. He was very intense in everything and I learned a lot of football from George Seifert."[9]

Seifert worked hand in hand with defensive line coach Bill McPherson, who had been with the 49ers since 1979 and who had known Walsh from his high school coaching days. "We had known each other when he coached in Fremont [Washington Union High School] in the East Bay and I coached at Bellarmine Prep. We later met at some coaches' clinics," remembered McPherson. "He was always very nice."[10] After twelve seasons as defensive coordinator at Santa Clara, McPherson moved to UCLA, where he coached three seasons (1975–1977) under Dick Vermeil. In 1978 he followed Vermeil to coach linebackers with the Philadelphia Eagles. Walsh hired McPherson, who wanted to return to California, as his linebackers coach in 1979. The following season he took over the defensive line. From the beginning McPherson could see that Walsh had a plan to run his team and would put the entire plan in motion.

"He came into the organization and cleared the building out," said McPherson. "I mean the gardeners, people at the front desk who answer the phone, everyone. In fact, that was one of my first jobs. He said 'Coach Mac, you're in charge of getting somebody to take care of the field, the practice fields.' . . . that was my role."[11]

McPherson became Seifert's right-hand man when it came to stopping the run. "I might have the basic design ideas initially, but as far as the specifics, Bill McPherson was our secret weapon as defensive line coach. [He] formed a foundation for so much [of our] success," said Seifert.[12]

Coach Mac had a wealth of knowledge about defensive line play that he passed on to young players like Dwaine Board and Jim Stuckey. "When I got drafted in 1980 I learned more from Coach Mac in the first two weeks of training camp than I did all four years at Clemson," said defensive end Jim Stuckey. "He was a really good defensive line coach who could teach you individually. He was able to teach technique."[13]

Rounding out the defensive coaches was Norb Hecker. Hired by Walsh as defensive backs coach in 1979, Hecker moved to coaching the linebackers the following season. As a player Hecker was an All-American end at Baldwin-Wallace in northeast Ohio. His professional career began with the Los Angeles Rams, where he played three seasons (1951–1953) and won an NFL championship in 1951. He then played in the CFL in 1954 and returned to the NFL a year later with the Washington Redskins. After his playing days ended Hecker went into coaching and joined Vince Lombardi's staff in Green Bay. He helped coach the Packers to three NFL championships in 1962, 1963, and 1965.

After the third Packers championship, Hecker was hired as the first coach of the expansion Atlanta Falcons. But after two terrible seasons and a 4–23 record, Hecker was fired three games into the 1968 season. The following fall Hecker served as defensive coordinator of the New York Giants before joining the staff at Stanford University three years later. As linebackers coach at Stanford in 1977 under Walsh, Hecker followed Walsh to the 49ers two years later.

Joined by former 49ers star defensive end Tommy Hart as an assistant defensive line coach, Seifert, McPherson, Hecker, and Rhodes made a strong staff on the defensive side of the ball. Whenever he could, Walsh offered suggestions to his defensive coaches. "He liked to go to the defensive staff room and write something on the board. 'You guys check that out' and walk next door to the offensive room. Come back and say, 'what do you guys think of that?' 'Coach, we don't know if it really fits into what we're doing.' He'd kind of give you a funny look and say, 'OK. But next time you better try it,'" said McPherson. "He had a litany of things he wanted to give you before the season started. We called it the litany. One thing was 'listen to what I have to say but you don't have to put it in all the time.' That was really different than anything I had been involved with."[14]

After the disappointment of 1982, Walsh made sure the coaches communicated to the fullest. This was especially true on the offensive side of the ball, where Walsh made the biggest changes. On that side Walsh's secret weapon was already in place: offensive line coach Bobb McKittrick.

McKittrick grew up in Baker, Oregon, where, in the seventh grade, he changed the spelling of his first name from "Bob" to "Bobb" because "I just wanted to be different," revealed McKittrick.[15] Different he was. He was his high school valedictorian and an honor student at Oregon State University, where he played four years at guard for the legendary Tommy Prothro. Following graduation he spent three years in the Marine Corps, where he gained his trademark shaved head and tough exterior. He was known for wearing just a T-shirt and shorts, even on the coldest of days. After leaving the Marines in 1961, McKittrick returned to his alma mater as linebackers and tight ends coach under Prothro, helping the Beavers reach the 1962 Liberty Bowl and the 1965 Rose Bowl. He followed Prothro to UCLA, where he coached the Bruins offensive line in his second consecutive Rose Bowl appearance in 1966.

When Prothro made the jump to the NFL, McKittrick went with him, first to the Los Angeles Rams (1971–1972) and then to the San Diego Chargers (1974–1978). In 1976 he coached the Chargers offensive line alongside then–offensive coordinator Bill Walsh. Although they coached only one season together, Walsh knew that McKittrick was the best offensive line coach in football. When Prothro resigned after the 1978 season, Walsh quickly hired McKittrick as his offensive line coach. "It was Bill's numbering system, his passing plays, but my father had a lot to do with the running game," said McKittrick's son Ladd. "Designing the running plays, the fakes by the quarterback, getting the running back to the hole against what defense—the running game was carried over from the Los Angeles Rams, San Diego Chargers, and now the 49ers."[16] Walsh worked hand in hand with McKittrick on formulating the offensive game plan.

On the practice field McKittrick kept it simple. "Bobb McKittrick was a wonderful person—what a character. He had the most pragmatic approach to coaching. He didn't care about what the stance looked like or what foot you stepped with. Some offensive line coaches are very rigid and militaristic about how things are done. He didn't give a shit about any of that," said Fred vonAppen, special teams coach. "He just [said], 'you gotta block him, now this is how we do it.' Somehow, pragmatically, he would work it out. He had great rapport with his guys."[17]

With McKittrick in place, Walsh would revamp the rest of his offensive staff. Early in 1983 Walsh went looking for a few new assistants. First he hired Sherman Lewis as his running backs coach. A former college All-American back at Michigan State and runner-up for the 1963 Heisman Trophy, Lewis had just finished fourteen seasons as an assistant—the last three as assistant head coach and defensive coordinator—at his alma mater under Duffy Dougherty, Denny Stolz, and Darryl Rogers.

Walsh's second hire was an up-and-coming thirty-five-year-old offensive mind who would replace Sam Wyche as quarterbacks and wide receivers coach. Paul Hackett had played quarterback at UC Davis, where he got his coaching start. Following two seasons there, Hackett moved on to coach quarterbacks at the University of California, where he tutored Steve Bartkowski, the first overall pick in the 1975 draft by the Atlanta Falcons. In 1976 he moved on to USC and enjoyed success with signal callers Vince Evans, Rob Hertel, and Paul McDonald, who set seventeen USC, NCAA, or Pac-10 records. In 1981 Hackett got his first taste of coaching in the NFL with the Cleveland Browns. When Wyche left for Indiana University, Walsh called Hackett.

"I was hired for the quarterbacks, tight ends, and wide receivers at the time. Bill felt it was important to have one person, so that there would be one voice. That was his philosophy in terms of the coaching part; he wanted one guy to be there with him," said Hackett. "When I got there I was anxious to figure out and learn the playbook. He . . . didn't give me a playbook; he took me aside and took me through plays. I really got a hands-on [lesson] with him, just explaining the game and how he coached it. How he coached the quarterbacks and how he coached the wide receivers. It was not at all, 'well, here's the playbook.' It was much more."

Hackett continued, "That's when I first got the inkling of the fact that there would be multiple formations. But the concept and what he was teaching [Joe] Montana was going to be repeated over and over again in a different form. That was really my first introduction. I don't remember him ever plopping a playbook down in front of me because he hand-drew the passing game himself. And I think he probably sat down and did that sometime in the summer or late spring and then put it together as the playbook we took to Rocklin. So it was very personal. It was very—you and me—sort of an extension of him with a perimeter group, explaining to me his philosophy and how to coach and teach his passing game. They usually just hand you a playbook. That was not the case with Bill. He was always a little bit different."[18]

For his third hire, Walsh reached back to his Stanford days for his special teams coach. Fred vonAppen began his coaching career in 1964 at tiny Linfield College in Oregon, where, as a player, he was an all-league selection. He went on to coaching stints at Arkansas, UCLA, Virginia Tech, and Oregon. In 1977 Walsh hired him at Stanford. When Walsh left for the 49ers, vonAppen took a job under Bart Starr as special teams coach with the Green Bay Packers. But after less than two seasons, he returned to college football, first at Arkansas (1981) and back to Stanford (1982).

Walsh really wanted vonAppen to coach his special teams. "At the end of the season I got a call from Bill, and he said he let some people go [and asked if I would be] interested in coming back and being on his staff," said Fred vonAppen. "He said it would be coaching special teams. He offered me the job and I took it."[19]

VonAppen noticed a different atmosphere under Walsh with the 49ers. "Bill had come in and built a structure prior to my arrival, a structure that put them in the first Super Bowl. It was a system of football that was unique to the 49ers. When it was with Stanford, it was unique to Stanford. But a system of how to finish and how to play regardless of opponent . . . was unique to the 49ers," said vonAppen.[20]

That standard of play included giving ample time to the new special teams coach in order for him to achieve perfection. "At that time [I was] the only guy, so I had the entire run of the team except for a few exceptions. He pretty much gave me the run of personnel and he gave me a large block of time to teach. I had half an hour a day to cover six areas of endeavor for special teams," said vonAppen.[21]

Finally, Walsh wanted his team physically and mentally stronger. He wanted a man who could push the team during workouts harder than ever before. To replace Al Vermeil, he hired Jerry Attaway as the 49ers coordinator of physical development. Attaway played college football at

Cal State Sacramento and UC Davis, where his career was cut short by an injury. After graduation, Attaway became an assistant coach at the College of Idaho for three seasons and Utah State for two seasons before being hired as the offensive line coach and coordinator for physical development at USC.

At USC, under the guidance of head coach John Robinson, Attaway helped build a national championship squad. While there he trained future NFL stars such as Marcus Allen, Anthony Munoz, Charles White, Bruce Matthews, Joey Browner, and Chip Banks, as well as future 49ers Ronnie Lott and Riki Ellison. During his five seasons at USC (1978—1982), the Trojans compiled an impressive 48–8–3 record. At first Attaway wasn't sure if he wanted to leave the college game. "I went up there [to San Francisco] with the idea that I didn't want the job, but it would be a great experience to interview with him," said Attaway. "We'd just won a national championship and a couple of Rose Bowls. I was pretty happy. After spending a whole day talking to Walsh, he offered me the job."[22]

Attaway told Walsh that he needed to talk to his boss, John Robinson. "He told me to take the job: 'You've proven that you can coach at this level. This is career advancement. Go try it. If you don't like it, you know you can always come back to college football and coach.' So I did it," said Attaway, who would spend the next twenty-two years with the 49ers.[23]

As the 49ers physical development coordinator, Attaway quickly set up a program to improve the players' nutrition and diet, something Walsh was very interested in bettering on his team. "What people ate didn't match up very well with what they were burning. So one of the things that was a major change was trying to get people to change their eating habits," said Attaway.[24]

In order to track the players' diets, Attaway wanted to use a new state-of-the-art computer program. "When I interviewed with Walsh, he asked me, do I need anything? I said, 'I'd like a piece of software on the computer to help with the nutrition stuff,' He said, 'OK, how much does it cost?' At that time computers were expensive. I want to say the whole thing was about $12,000. So when I was hired, I brought up the computer and software thing, he said, 'Yeah, that's alright.' I said, 'You know it costs $12,000?' He looked at me. He said, 'Jerry, I pay some of these guys damn near a million dollars a year. Do you think I give a fuck about $12,000?'" recalled Attaway.[25]

In 1983 Walsh and the new staff bonded. They worked their butts off to get the team back to the playoffs. Encouraged by Walsh, communication among the staff was not a problem. "He would say if you have an idea that crosses your head . . . bring it up so we can talk about it. It may be so off-the-wall that there's not a chance we're gonna do it, but he said that if we talk about it, then we learn something," said Attaway.[26]

"It was a wonderful working environment. He wouldn't have tolerated anybody getting cranky with anybody else in the meeting," said special teams coach vonAppen. "He'd certainly ask our opinions. He didn't always put them into play, but he'd ask about them. So he was very good about a round table thing, but he was in charge. I don't remember any friction points at all with the staff that year."[27]

The newly hired staff combined with a reenergized Walsh led to a comeback year for the 49ers in 1983. In his first year as president and head coach, Walsh led the 49ers to the playoffs for the second time in three years and just four points shy of returning to the Super Bowl. The tough loss to the Washington Redskins in the 1983 NFC Championship Game would remain with Walsh's staff during the off-season.

The entire eleven-man coaching staff from 1983 would return for the 1984 season and go down as perhaps the best coaching staff in 49ers history. The eleven men combined to coach 137 NFL seasons for the red and gold. Four of those coaches—George Seifert, Ray Rhodes, Bobb McKittrick, and Bill McPherson—were members of all five 49ers Super Bowl wins. That continuity helped the 1984 team gain an edge over the rest of the NFL.

4

BUILDING A CHAMPION

We have a great man in Bill Walsh. It would be a big mistake not to give him the material to work with.
—Eddie DeBartolo Jr., 49ers owner[1]

After the disappointing loss to the Redskins in the 1983 NFC Championship Game, the 49ers got to work rebuilding their roster. Early on the 49ers were dealt a devastating blow when three key defensive players quickly jumped ship for greener pastures by signing with the rival USFL. Linebackers Willie Harper, Bobby Leopold, and defensive tackle Pete Kugler decided to cash in by signing with the spring football league, causing Walsh to reevaluate his needs in the off-season. DeBartolo would give his coach whatever he needed to build a winning team.

"In March [1984] we set some goals for the ball club," explained DeBartolo early in 1984. "Our decision was that we should just be more aggressive. Yes, maybe it had something to do with losing [Pete] Kugler, but not entirely. Look, the USFL has caused salaries to jump about 35 percent. So if our salaries were $10 million, then we should lose about $3.5 million. But you can't sit back and complain about it and become a losing franchise in the process. You have to compete. [That's what we are doing.]"[2]

"Yes, we came back well last season [1983] and maybe that would satisfy some owners. Maybe some would think their team had spent enough because they were strong enough to be in the playoffs. But that would be a mistake. We have a great man in Bill Walsh. It would be a big mistake not to give him the material to work with," continued De-Bartolo.[3]

With ownership behind him Walsh and his staff set out to build a championship team. The core players on the roster were already there. Twenty-four players—including sixteen starters—remained from the 1981 Super Bowl team, and most of them were in the prime of their careers. Looking to get back to the big game, they would be the foundation of the 1984 squad.

49ERS OFFENSE

Quarterbacks

Walsh had his franchise signal caller in Joe Montana. The six-year veteran was entering his fourth full season as the 49ers starting quarterback. In 1983 Montana had thrown for career highs in passing yards (3,910) and touchdowns (26). Most of his teammates knew they were playing with a rare athlete. "I still believe [Montana] was the best quarterback to ever play the game. He had that presence where he wouldn't be a cheerleader, he wouldn't talk a lot, but when he did talk, he was making an important point and everybody listened to him. But he wasn't a cheerleader. Certainly wasn't a cheerleading-type guy, but he knew when to talk and he knew what to say. So we knew he was in charge," said Keith Fahnhorst, offensive tackle. "And he had to answer to Bill, which was a tough position, a tough job, but he always accepted that. Joe was the best, best teammate I ever played with."[4]

"I'd never seen a more competitive person than Joe Montana. He's competitive at everything and a great athlete. You know when Joe gets in that mode that he's going to do his very best. His best was usually always good enough to outdo the other [team]," said Bill Ring, running back. "Joe was an amazing leader just by calming everyone down, just by his presence in saying, 'OK, guys, let's go downfield and put this in' or 'we really need this one. Let's go down and get it.' And he was always very calm. Cool as a cucumber. He never got rattled. I never saw Joe Montana get rattled or even be affected by anything out there. He's always so relaxed, so calm, so in control of everything."[5]

"Well, Joe was Mr. Cool. He was cool under fire. He knew what to do. He studied hard. He knew all his assignments, and he was the leader. He was the type of guy that if you had to have a guy watch your back, I would choose Joe Montana. He's that type of person," said Wendell Tyler, running back.[6]

Montana's backup, Matt Cavanaugh, was obtained in a 1983 trade with the New England Patriots, where he started fifteen games. "Bill always thought that [Cavanaugh] was a very good leader, fiery, threw the ball well. [He] watched him in New England. Bill was always looking to improve. That was the great thing about him. He was always looking to improve the second, third, and fourth guy on the roster, not necessarily the starter," said quarterbacks coach Paul Hackett. "Matt was a powerful, straight, drop-back, fire-the-ball-down-the-field kind of guy, and Bill felt that that would actually be a pretty good complement to Montana. We'd be able to do some things vertically a little more with Matt. . . . He and Montana got along famously, so they were able to learn from each other."[7]

Running Backs

In 1981 Ricky Patton led the 49ers with just 543 yards rushing as Walsh's offense won the Super Bowl as primarily a passing team. The 1984 backfield was stocked with several talented players, and each back knew his specific role. Starting halfback Wendell Tyler was acquired in a trade the day before the 1983 draft from divisional rival Los Angeles Rams, who dumped Tyler to draft Eric Dickerson. "When they traded me I called my wife and she didn't believe me. I was elated because I had seen the 49ers, and they had Joe Montana. They had Dwight Clark. When we played against them, I felt all they needed was a running game. I was just happy to be there. It was like God fulfilled my dream," said Tyler.[8]

Walsh loved Tyler's explosive running style and his ability to catch the football. In his first year with the 49ers in 1983, he rushed for 856 yards and had thirty-four receptions. "I played with Randy Cross at UCLA, so Randy knew what type of athlete I was. Bill Walsh had confidence in me not only to run the ball but to catch it," said Tyler.[9]

"Wendell had an amazing burst. He could accelerate. To this day, I've never seen anyone accelerate faster than Wendell Tyler. He was amazing. When he started to accelerate, he was off to the races. He would hit a hole and boom! He was gone. A lot of guys, they weave and they take their time, but when Wendell saw an opening, he just turned on the after boosters and he was gone. He was an amazing player for us for a long time," said running back Bill Ring.[10]

Tyler turned twenty-nine years old before the 1984 season. He was set for a historic season, and his teammates always knew when he was running the ball well. "Oh yeah, Wendell had a strut like you wouldn't believe. Like, 'Yeah, bring it on.' He'd hang his head a little bit, and he'd swing his arms and walk pigeon-toed, then he always was, like 'Oh, yeah, I'm ready.' You could tell when it was his day to be great," said tight end Earl Cooper.[11]

"You always had to walk. When you were running well, you had the walk. But the walk was a deception walk, confidence walk. What could I say? It was just me. It was something that I was born with. Some of them have it. Some of them don't," said Tyler.[12]

At fullback was Roger Craig, a second-year player out of Nebraska who was selected in the second round of the 1983 draft, forty-ninth overall. Even as a young player Roger Craig brought a veteran work ethic to the 49ers. "Roger, amazing athlete and amazing work ethic. He'd get the ball and he'd run all the way down the field in practice, and I would do the same thing. Get the ball, run it all the way down the field, and come back. Condition himself. He always had that great work ethic. He was always in the weight room. Always studied his plays. Never made mistakes. Just an unbelievable running back for the 49ers," said Ring.[13] Running down the length of the field was something Craig learned from his older brother back in their hometown of Davenport, Iowa. Over the years many players including Jerry Rice would adopt this 49ers technique.

When Craig arrived in San Francisco he learned how to play in the NFL from his new backfield mate. "Yeah, he brought that emphasis [running the length of the field] to the game where maybe I would only run like ten to fifteen [yards]. I'm an older vet, but then I would take Roger in the weight room and show him how to train with the weights so he could take the pounding or we would get on the bike together," recalled Wendell Tyler. "[Our] dynamic was great. We started working together and we started blocking for one another. And that was what the combination was like: me and Roger. Roger was like my son. And that's how we worked it. And Roger accepted that. I knew eventually I would have to give way to Roger but I was able to impart to him what I knew, what I was blessed with."[14]

"Wendell always gave me advice. If I had a question, he'd always answer questions for me. He was like a big brother to me. It was fun. We took care of each other on the football field. He blocked hard for me. I blocked hard for him," said Roger Craig. "Yeah, he had his cool walk. Wendell was cool."[15] In his rookie year Craig made an immediate impact on Bill Walsh's offense with 1,152 total yards and twelve touchdowns.

When both Tyler and Craig joined the 49ers in 1983 they made the backfield a strength, not a weakness. In 1982 the 49ers finished dead last in the NFL in rushing, but in 1983 the dynamic duo helped Walsh's offense finish eighth in the league in rushing yards.

"They did complement each other well. They stayed healthy and they were great blockers there. Can't say more about the guys. They would always come by and say, 'Great block.' Just team players. No big heads. Very, very humble," said Allan Kennedy, offensive tackle. "It was a joy to block for them because you knew they gave it their all. You give them a little crease, and they make you look good and get five, ten yards. If there wasn't any blocking at all, they'd still get yardage and make you look good. Those are what great backs do. They were the best."[16]

Rounding out the backfield was five-feet-eight, 166-pound undrafted free agent Carl Monroe, a second-year player from Utah who missed most of 1983 with a broken foot. He also was counted on to return kicks. Monroe was nicknamed "Prince" because of his uncanny resemblance to the pop singer. Also utilized were Jeff Moore, who was entering his third year with the 49ers as mainly a pass-receiving threat out of the backfield (fifty-six catches and four touchdowns in 1982–1983), and Bill Ring, who was not only the backup fullback to Craig, but the heart and soul of the special teams unit and a 49ers fan favorite. An undrafted running back out of BYU, Ring was cut by the Steelers during training camp in 1980. The following year at a 49ers tryout camp, Walsh noticed the hard-working Ring among the other players. "Bill [Ring] was the lunch pail man. He'd do whatever Bill Walsh wanted him to do. He played special teams, he would go in and make a block if you need it," said Tyler.[17]

Wide Receivers

Heading into the 1984 season the 49ers had one of the strongest receiving corps in the league. The pass-catching group was nearly set heading into the off-season. Starter Dwight Clark, entering his sixth season, was recovering from a knee injury suffered in the 1983 season finale but would be ready to go in 1984. His 297 receptions during the previous four seasons was best among wideouts in the NFL, and his twenty-two touchdowns from Joe Montana made them the most productive passing combination in the NFL.

Opposite Clark was veteran Freddie Solomon, about to begin his tenth season. Acquired by trade in 1978 (in one of Joe Thomas's better moves), Solomon was still able to use his speed to stretch the defense. Beating Redskins cornerback Darrell Green in the championship game illustrated perfectly that he hadn't lost a step. In his six years with the 49ers Solomon had scored thirty-two touchdowns. In 1984 he would find the end zone more than any other 49er. While Clark sat out the 1983 postseason, number-three wide receiver Mike Wilson stepped up and played his best football. Originally drafted by the Dallas Cowboys in the ninth round of the 1981 draft, Wilson was quickly signed by Walsh and the 49ers after he was a late training camp cut. He established himself as a dependable third option, and with Clark out of the 1983 NFC Championship against the Redskins, Wilson scored two touchdowns in the fourth-quarter comeback that fell short.

Wilson learned from the veteran starters before him. "Freddie Solomon was a mentor for me and Dwight [Clark] was a couple of years older than me. He had come in with Joe and they had established a good chemistry and work ethic with each other. So for me to come in after being cut by the Cowboys, we all just worked hard [together]. I think we were technicians. We would dissect you; we would read your coverage; we would adjust on the run. No matter what you threw at us defensively, we always adjusted, so we were going to get open. It was just a matter of having protection. Joe would always get the ball there. So I think the one thing I learned there was just being detailed, real detailed and methodical in dissecting a defense," said Wilson.[18]

The veteran receiving corps was helpful to the younger players, even the running backs. "To be in the West Coast offense, you had to be versatile. You can't just run the ball. You have to learn to catch passes.

You have to learn how to read defenses. So it's a complex system that you have to be tuned in [to]," said Craig. "The older veterans—guys like Freddie Solomon, Dwight Clark, Mike Wilson—all these guys just took the time to help me learn how to run routes and the proper way of catching."[19]

The 49ers fourth receiver was one of Bill Walsh's big experiments. Renaldo Nehemiah was the world's best high hurdler, setting the world record in the 110-meter high hurdles in 1981 with a time of 12.93. Enamored of his blazing speed Walsh signed Nehemiah, who hadn't played organized football since high school, to a football contract in 1982. In two seasons Nehemiah had twenty-five catches for 397 yards (15.9 average) and two touchdowns. "Dwight Clark was professional. I mean, he was intense. Trained at warp speed every day. He had one speed, which was full [speed]. Freddie Solomon, he was sneaky good. He didn't show it, but it just happened. A lot of times it was so deceptive you couldn't tell; it looked like he was not going 100 percent and yet you know the ball is in the air or he had to block someone, he'd find a way to be there and I'd say, 'How did he do that?'" said Nehemiah. "Then, Mike Wilson, he and I were just one year apart, so Mike was still like me, trying to prove himself and trying to get as much playing time and make an impact when he could. We both played behind solid players, so we just tried to make the best of it. But we all had a good time."[20]

"Now the other three [Clark, Solomon, and Wilson] were basically interchangeable, Bill had so much confidence in them, and most importantly, Joe had so much confidence in them that they could really do anything," said Paul Hackett, quarterbacks and wide receivers coach. "All of those guys had an incredible ability to be on the same page almost without saying anything and sometimes without even looking at each other. So the four guys [Clark, Nehemiah, Solomon, and Wilson] really meshed and I think set the standard for allowing Renaldo to improve leaps and bounds in those first couple of years he was with us. I attribute a lot to the way Freddie and Dwight pushed him."[21]

Walsh was always looking for veterans who could contribute, so he signed James Scott, who played seven seasons with the Chicago Bears (177 receptions and twenty touchdowns) to compete for a roster spot.

Tight Ends

Walsh's two tight ends complemented each other very well, too. Earl Cooper, out of Rice University, was Walsh's first-round pick in 1980 as a running back. At six-feet-two, 227 pounds, Cooper ran for more than 700 yards as a rookie, but it was his pass-catching ability that took the NFL by storm. He caught eighty-three passes, an NFL rookie record, and scored a total of nine touchdowns. After Walsh added Tyler and Craig to his backfield, he moved Cooper to tight end to make use of his pass-catching abilities. In early 1981 after playing six seasons with the New England Patriots, three-time Pro Bowl tight end Russ Francis retired from the NFL. Walsh convinced Francis to return to the playing field after sitting out one season. During the 1982 draft, Walsh sent a first- and fourth-round pick to the Patriots for Francis. "Russ is the finest blocking tight end in football," praised Walsh. "He is strong and he has great technique and desire."[22]

"Russ ran good routes. Russ [was] a strong blocker. Sometimes I'm like, 'Man, I wish I had his leverage. I wish I could do some of the things he could do.' But I knew I had to use my footwork and my quickness to be able to get in position to do the things that Russ did. He ran good routes; he could read the coverage. As far as being a character, I think he approached the game the way it should be approached: relaxed, happy-go-lucky, but taking care of business at the same time," said Cooper.[23]

In 1983 Francis and Cooper combined for nearly fifty catches for more than 500 yards and seven touchdowns. Third stringer Eason Ramson, who spent five years with the 49ers, mostly contributed on special teams.

Offensive Line

Montana would be surrounded and protected by a veteran offensive line. Under the tutelage of line coach Bobb McKittrick, no other part of the team had been together as long as the offensive line. At right tackle was the longest-tenured member of the 49ers. In his eleventh season, Keith Fahnhorst was a former second-round pick in 1974 out of the University of Minnesota. Starting eighty-nine consecutive games, he was the glue of the offensive line. "He was pretty much our rock," said offensive tackle Allan Kennedy.[24] In 1984 Fahnhorst would have perhaps his best year as a pro, reaching the Pro Bowl for the first time.

Next to him was right guard Randy Cross, a second-round pick out of UCLA, in his ninth year with the 49ers. Cross was one of the best guards in the NFL, having made the Pro Bowl twice (following the 1981 and 1982 seasons). He had been Fahnhorst's partner on the right side since 1979, when he was moved from center to guard. Communication between the two was uncanny. "It was a good offensive line to play [on]. It's not always communication as far as talking about something or talking during a play. It's a feeling [we] have and if we see a play developing. I would know how Randy [Cross] was gonna react to it before he would, because we'd been playing together for so long," said Keith Fahnhorst. "So let's say it was a game between the defensive end and the defensive tackle. If I saw the end moving in, I knew Randy was going to be there, and I had to get ready for the defensive tackle coming around. It wasn't like, 'Here he comes Randy!' or something like that. That was too late. It was a feeling you had, and I would feel Randy there before [it could be communicated verbally]. That's the way the lines operate. We had a great line."[25]

When Cross moved to guard in 1979, it was to make room for seven-year veteran Fred Quillan, who was a seventh-round pick in 1978 out of Oregon. Anchoring the line at center, Quillan made all the checks and was ragged by teammates for his practice habits. "He had to see the protection and be able to make any adjustments before the snap of the ball. We always gave Fred a lot of trouble—I mean, a lot of crap—because he wasn't the best practice player. He made sure he was ready for the game. So we'd give him crap all week about not working hard. But he was always there on Sunday. Fred was a great communicator; he did a great job," said Keith Fahnhorst.

At left guard was burly John Ayers, in his ninth year with the 49ers, who was an eighth-round pick out of West Texas State in 1976. At six-foot-five and 265 pounds, Ayers was the most underrated guard in the NFL. Over the years he became known for his pass-blocking skills. "John always seemed to have the best pass rusher. His responsibility was going to be the best pass rusher. He was famously good at picking up guys like Lawrence Taylor on the outside, where rushing an outside linebacker like that was kind of a new technique that we hadn't seen a lot before the early 1980s," said Keith Fahnhorst. "Guys like Lawrence

Taylor made a living beating up on offensive running backs who couldn't pass protect well. John was always one of the best at getting out there and being able to pick up outside rushers. He had great feet, probably the best feet. And Bubba [Paris] had some great feet, too, but he was just a youngster. But John had a way of getting out there and being able to control the speed of the rush."[26]

The final building block of the starting offensive line was the "baby" of the group. Six-foot-six, 300-pound tackle William "Bubba" Paris was a second-round pick in 1982 from Michigan. Beginning his third season at left tackle, he was the biggest player on the 49ers squad. He also was the most loquacious. "Bubba [Paris] was newer to the group, so Bubba would pick up some razz from a lot of the guys. That was part of the deal. He had great feet. He was a talented player, too. Bill [Walsh] always liked to have his linemen a little thinner than Bubba wanted to be. So weigh-ins were always an interesting time for Bubba, but he somehow adjusted," said Keith Fahnhorst.[27]

Besides being very talkative, the likable Paris made an instant impression on his teammates because of his size. "Lindsy McLean, our trainer, was from Michigan, too, so he warned us. 'You got Bubba coming in here. I gotta warn you guys, he won't talk and he's a very big person.' I went, 'Oh God'; I was struggling to keep weight at 270. Here's somebody coming in at 300. Just a big, big person there. Great personality and a good person. Just a hell of an athlete, too," said Allan Kennedy.[28]

Backing up the five starters was offensive tackle Kennedy, a free agent signed by the 49ers in 1981 after being released by the Redskins, who had drafted him in the tenth round that year. At six-feet-seven-inches tall and 275 pounds, Kennedy always had a supporter in Bobb McKittrick. "You want to start but Bubba Paris and Keith Fahnhorst were outstanding tackles there, and I knew I had my work cut out for me," said Kennedy. "Coach McKittrick had a lot of faith in me. I worked hard. I was there every day so they [saw that I would] work hard, and I've always done that my entire career because I wasn't blessed with great talent."[29] Kennedy worked hard enough to make the 49ers team in 1981 after getting cut by the Redskins. He helped the team win a Super Bowl ring that season and would provide depth at tackle in 1984.

Jesse Sapolu was an eleventh-round selection in the 1983 draft and started one game that season for Randy Cross. He was counted on as a backup at center and guard. Walt Downing, a six-year vet with the 49ers, helped at guard and center, too. Finally, John MaCaulay, who played for Walsh at Stanford in 1978, was signed as a free agent in 1983 but was never active.

Heading into the 1984 season the 49ers offensive line had started 419 NFL games (397 regular-season and twenty-two playoff games). There was no better unit in the NFL.

"Keith [Fahnhorst] was our rock," said Kennedy. "John Ayers was a pass-blocking fool. No one could get around him. He'd take on Lawrence Taylor. Pull out there and just stop him cold. John was probably our best pass protector and the other three just played great. The four guys in the hole there, you couldn't find a better unit."[30]

49ERS DEFENSE

Defensive Line

Looking at the defensive line early in the off-season, Walsh, John McVay, George Seifert, and defensive line coach Bill McPherson decided more was better. They wanted to rotate as many men as possible to help keep everyone fresh. One of Walsh's key defensive philosophies was to have a fresh pass rush in the fourth quarter. They built the 1984 defensive line with that in mind.

The strength of the 49ers defensive line was the NFL's best defensive end tandem of Dwaine Board and Fred Dean. In 1983 the duo wreaked havoc on NFL quarterbacks, combining for an amazing thirty and a half sacks. Dean's seventeen and a half sacks put him behind only Mark Gastineau of the New York Jets, who led the NFL with nineteen. Dean was the most feared pass rusher in the NFL. Since being acquired in a trade midway through the 1981 season from the San Diego Chargers, he had thirty-two and a half sacks in thirty-six career regular-season games.

"Dwaine [Board] brought an awful lot to the defensive line. You know what I'm saying? He was a particularly strong guy. He and I talked about pass rushing all the time," said Dean. "Dwaine had a particular technique as far as his bull-rushing style, because he could possess it and get around people pretty easy. He played a big part [in what we wanted to do]. Dwaine really made a big difference in our line."[31]

"Dwaine was a student of the game. Mr. Dependable. You could always count on him. Dwaine always amazed me. He knew not only what the defensive line was doing, but he knew what the linebackers were doing, what the defensive backs were doing in every coverage. He was almost like a Joe Montana. Still to this day I've never seen anybody, on any given play, know exactly what the rest of his defensive teammates were doing. I think he was the epitome of our defensive line. You knew what you're going to get from Dwaine Board each and every game. He was a really good pass rusher. He could defend the run and he was a student of the game. I've always admired that. That's probably why he's been coaching all these years," said defensive end Jim Stuckey.[32]

Forty-niners teammates on both sides of the ball could appreciate the talent of the team's best pass rusher. "A great guy. Funny guy. Fred Dean was the most amazing athlete you could ever imagine at his position. He was like Carl Lewis off the starting blocks. His body was just chiseled. No body fat at all and he never lifted a weight, ever. He'd sit in the weight room and smoke Kool cigarettes. He was an amazing guy," said running back Bill Ring.[33]

"His pass-rushing skills were second to none. Never lifted weights and there wasn't an ounce of fat on Fred. He could do things to offensive linemen that nobody else could do. It was the leverage that he brought, the speed, the quickness, the use of his hands. It was amazing to watch. On my best days I could not do the things that Fred Dean did," said Stuckey.[34]

Dean had a unique personality and varied interests that included playing the guitar and piano, singing, writing poetry, cooking, and joking about never lifting weights. When asked how he became so strong Dean would respond, "Every now and then, I get the urge to lift weights . . . and I just go somewhere and lie down until I get over it."[35]

The rest of the 49ers defensive front had size and versatility. Lawrence Pillers, a 1980 free agent pickup from the New York Jets, was about to begin his fifth season with the 49ers and his ninth season overall. He was asked to play both tackle and end. "We were very fortunate to get Pillers. The Jets cut him and he was a really tough run player. He played first down, and he could play end, or he could move inside—very versatile," said McPherson.[36]

His fellow line mates could always tell what kind of mood Pillers was in when he entered the locker room. "Lawrence was a tough guy. He was the toughest. We used to call him the sheriff because he was a tough guy on the defensive line," said Dwaine Board. "We always knew what kind of mood Pillers was in when he came to practice by the hat that he wore! If he wore his Mississippi Highway Patrol hat, you knew he was in a bad mood. [Sometimes] he might be in a good mood, but if he had the Mississippi Highway Patrol Hat on, he wouldn't be dealt with that day."[37]

A former deputy sheriff in Port Gibson, Mississippi, during the off-season, Pillers came to work wearing his patrol hat more often than not. "For some reason, if I had on my [patrol] hat I was going to go hard whether we had shorts on or not. Every time I came out there, I went hard," said Pillers. "Bill Walsh use to tell Coach Mac to get me out of there, [that] I'm gonna to hurt somebody or get hurt, too."[38]

Jeff Stover, who didn't play college football, was found by the 49ers scouting staff when they worked him out in 1982. A former shot-putter at Oregon who twice won Pac-10 crowns, the six-five, 275-pound Stover ran a 4.7 forty at a free agent workout. Quickly recognizing the edge that the raw track athlete gave him on the defensive side, Bill McPherson signed him, much to the chagrin of offensive line coach Bobb McKittrick, who wanted him as a tackle.

"Jeff Stover was an interesting case. Jeff didn't play college football. A fella from one of the junior colleges told me about this guy. He says, 'Mac, you better check him out. Try him out. The guy's strong as a bull. He's fast, too.' So we tried him out. Bobb McKittrick had the flu that day, so Bobb wasn't there to see him. I worked him out and said to coach [Walsh], 'We're signing this guy today.' The guy ran a 4.7, he weighed 270 pounds and was built like a shot-putter. [When] McKittrick saw him, he would cuss at me every other day," said McPherson.[39]

In 1983 Stover set career highs with sixteen tackles and two and a half sacks, impressing his teammates with his pure athletic ability. "Jeff was the epitome of the Olympic athlete. I mean, Jeff was an unbeliev-able physical specimen, just an unbelievable athletic person. Great guy. We were roommates on the road. Very articulate, very goal minded, but the epitome of an athletic specimen. Everything you look for in a defensive lineman," said Stuckey.[40]

Defensive end Jim Stuckey, a 49ers first-round pick in 1980 (with Earl Cooper), was beginning his fifth season with the 49ers. "Stuckey was a real fine football player, and the thing with Stuckey was his attitude toward the game. His attitude in life was always, he was just happy. It's great to be in the NFL, which it is. His thing was, 'Hey, I'm gonna have fun while I'm in the NFL.' Stuckey liked to have fun," said Dwaine Board.[41] At six-feet-four, 253 pounds, Stuckey had started thirty-five games with the 49ers and was counted on to contribute more in 1984. "Very talented, very smart. Did a lot of studying or watching film. He was an outstanding athlete. He took whatever the coaches told him to do and what information they fed him and used it to better his skills and ability," said Pillers.[42]

Defensive end Jim Harty, a second-round choice in 1981, was entering his fourth season on the bubble due to injuries. A foot injury sidelined him in 1983 and he played only five games. But the biggest loss of the defensive line was starting nose tackle Pete Kugler to the USFL. With forty-six tackles, Kugler was second only to Pillers (fifty-two) on the defensive line. Walsh wanted to get a few more bodies on the defensive front and told his defensive line coach to expect more players to rotate in. "[Walsh] said, 'Mac, you're going to have nine guys,' Alright! But that team was a good group. A really good group. They made me look like I knew what I was doing," said McPherson.[43]

Linebackers

The linebacker position suffered two losses in 1983. Gone was thirty-four-year-old Willie Harper, who was slowing down with injuries. Twenty-six-year-old Bobby Leopold was in his prime but needed to be replaced as a starter at outside linebacker. The defensive coaches made a bold move, shifting inside backer Dan Bunz (in his seventh year with 49ers as a first-round pick in 1978) to the outside. The six-feet-four, 225 pounder would play the outside for the first time and on the strong side. "Coaches told me, 'you move outside, we could win. So if you play well, we got a great team, a great defense, we'll be back in the Super Bowl,'" said Bunz. "Inside linebacker is completely different than outside linebacker. Inside you're getting hammered and you gotta make all the calls and adjustments, where outside it's a cat-and-mouse game. It's kind of like playing corner compared to playing free safety or strong safety. You get too aggressive and you lose your guy once in a while, so they told me to watch film." He ended up watching footage of the man he was replacing—Willie Harper. [44]

The other starting outside linebacker was the team's most versatile athlete, Keena Turner, a second-round pick in 1980 out of Purdue playing his fifth year with the 49ers. Entering his prime, Turner was asked not to leave the field—ever. Seifert's situational roster would see continually interchanging parts, but Turner and Dwaine Board would stay on the field all the time. "It just kind of worked out that way that I was a part of most, if not all, of the packages. In 1984 establishing a game for me it was important to be out there on the field and to be part of that group. So, yeah, Dwaine and I worked a lot side by side and were in most of the schemes," said Turner. [45]

All of the 49ers linebackers recognized Turner as a special player. "He was the best athlete, the purest athlete of all of us. He had to be. That was the position he was. He's a great glider, a movement guy. He had a calm demeanor about him. He was really nonconfrontational, much different than Ronnie [Lott], the opposite style in that respect," said linebacker Riki Ellison. [46]

Also on the outside would be Milt McColl, an undrafted free agent in 1981 who had played for Walsh at Stanford. McColl went undrafted primarily because teams knew he would be going to medical school. He helped the linebacking core win Super Bowl XVI. Blanchard Montgomery, a third-round selection in 1983 out of UCLA, was another role player for 49ers linebackers coach Norb Hecker. Montgomery and McColl were also key role players for the 49ers special teams.

On the inside, the linebacker core was led by none other than fifteen-year veteran Jack "Hacksaw" Reynolds. Mr. Professional himself. "Hacksaw was all business. But he understood all the angles in the triangle [guard/center/guard box]. I don't know that there was anybody at that time who really understood and could read it as quickly as he could," said Montgomery. The oldest defensive player in the NFL during the 1984 season—he would turn thirty-seven in November—Reynolds taught many of the 49ers players how to study, watch film, learn to be a pro, and how to be a champion. [47]

"We all benefitted from Hacksaw Reynolds being a part of our group. As a young player, I really learned a lot watching how Jack Reynolds [and Willie Harper], the established veterans in my room, went about their business," said Keena Turner. "And I benefitted from Jack Reynolds and his oddity and his intensity. The thing that got me about Jack was he was an older player. I'd look at him on film and I said, 'That old man's a better football player than I am. How is that? I'm a better athlete than he is.' I really was in that realm of thinking that because you were a great athlete . . . you were [also] a great football player. Well, it didn't, and Hack showed me that, because he wasn't a great athlete anymore, and yet he was a great football player still."[48]

"Hacksaw was a pretty eccentric guy. Everybody got a kick out of his karate chop and frying pan stance. Every time he got into his stance, he would have one hand in a karate chop and the other holding a frying pan, and he would get this look on his face that was so focused," said Milt McColl.[49]

Old and new alike, the 49ers benefited from the work ethic and knowledge of Jack Reynolds whether it was on or off the field, especially one young player who threatened to take his job. "Me and Hacksaw had an interesting relationship because I was obviously a threat to him when I came in as a rookie [in 1983]. I had to be schooled," said Riki Ellison. "First, I didn't have my pencil and paper, and he had a box full of sharpened pencils and paper and he wouldn't share it. He wouldn't share it with me, 'do you come to practice without your helmet on?' So as a young rookie I studied him. I was able to pick up, whether he liked it or not, what he was doing in terms of note taking and the specific areas of being able to start predicting what teams were going to do; what down situations they were going to do; what plays they were gonna do. He was very good at that. I learned more from him in the classroom than on the field. He's one of the greatest linebackers of the game and I was privileged and honored to learn how to play linebacker from him, the mental part of it."

Ellison also remembered Reynolds's unique way of preparing for a game. "At 8:00 in the morning—the game was at 1:00—we were at breakfast. I look up and Hacksaw's in full pads, full gear, eating Wheaties or some shit, and bitching at the coaches about getting out of there because he wanted to be on time. Then he went out, put his helmet on, got in his Corvette, and drove to the stadium."[50]

"We lived in the same apartment complex. I said, 'Come on, we gotta go out to dinner.' He had the same studio apartment, the same setup I had. I walked into his apartment and there's no furniture anywhere except a box mattress. Just a mattress on top of a box spring. That's it. And a sheet pinned to the wall for looking at film from the projector, right next to the bed, with a box of pencils. I'll never forget that," said fullback Bill Ring. [51]

As eccentric as he was, Reynolds had the total respect of his teammates and especially his coaches. "One of the leaders on the 1984 team was Jack 'Hacksaw' Reynolds. Jack was a guy who was very well respected. You're talking about a guy who had the knowledge. . . . Hacksaw brought study habits to the 49ers. He showed everybody how to study the game, the players. He was one of those guys who, every day after practice, [met with] the entire defense after the coaches met with them. He would coach every guy, every guy in that room. He'd keep them there for another hour. But he would go through everything," said Ray Rhodes. [52]

Hacksaw taught a young Riki Ellison how to play. Ellison was a fifth-round pick in the 1983 draft out of USC. He was about to begin his second year with the 49ers. He finished his rookie year third on the team in tackles with seventy-nine, behind only Ronnie Lott (108) and Eric Wright (80). "We called Riki 'Fruit Loops.' He was wild. Riki was another film nut, how he would read things. There was a play that our offense ran with Wendell Tyler running the ball. I don't know how he read it so quick that he was in the backfield. Because he would wipe out Wendell as he was getting the ball. He would fire right through. He had the quickest first three steps that I've ever seen. He was smart, intelligent. He had a bad knee—it was bone on bone, he wore a contraption on his knee his whole career—but he still could move really well. Just a great guy," said linebacker Jim Fahnhorst. [53]

A seventh-round pick in 1982 out of Illinois in his third year with the 49ers, Ron Ferrari gave the linebacking core another versatile athlete playing mainly on passing downs. "Bill [Walsh] made sure that you knew . . . your role. You practiced it," said Ferrari. [54] Ferrari, McColl, and Montgomery were also part of the special teams unit that was the best in the NFL. Every linebacker knew his role and would play a big part in the 49ers defensive success in 1984.

"Each of us had a role to play and we accepted the role. We didn't fight about it . . . like a lot of teams would. It was a contribution across the board. That was very positive for us. I think there's a lot of pride," said Ellison.[55]

"I mean, we all liked each other and you could tell that because we all teased each other. We all focused on the process that year. As Bill likes to say, 'The score takes care of itself.' The prize at the end took care of itself," said Ferrari.[56] "I also think that we had a great attitude and a group of guys who understood their roles, whatever those roles were. We were just really driven toward the perfection of each situation," said Keena Turner, linebacker.[57]

Defensive Backs

Just like the offensive line, the secondary was well stocked and fully loaded with stars. The core of the group was the three draft picks from the 1981 draft. Cornerback Ronnie Lott (fourth season with the 49ers, first-round pick in 1981) was the vocal leader of the defense and one of the best players in the NFL. "Ronnie was the team leader. He was the heart and soul of the 49ers from the time he got there [as] a rookie to the time he left. He didn't need any coaches to handle anything that went on on the field. Ronnie handled it. He was a total team leader," said Dana McLemore, defensive back.[58]

"Ronnie had a great work ethic. He often talked about 'what we gotta do in practice to win the Super Bowl.' If something's not right in practice we'd talk about it. 'Look, we gotta make that play. You gotta be there. In order to win the Super Bowl, this is what's going to happen. We can't make those mistakes. We can't miss the call and blow a coverage because those things can be detrimental.' So we were often working on the fundamentals of our game," said strong safety Carlton Williamson.[59]

On the other side of Lott was cornerback Eric Wright (fourth year with the 49ers, second-round pick in 1981), perhaps the most underrated player in the NFL. In 1983 Wright led the 49ers in interceptions with seven. His position coach, who played defensive back in the NFL for seven years, knew a great corner when he saw one. "Eric was a smooth, fluid athlete. Outstanding cover skills. Pure cover corner. Eric could cover. He was one of the better cover guys I've coached. When he was playing at the top of his game, he was covering like Deion Sanders. Because I coached Deion, too [in 1994]. Eric was the Deion Sanders for the 49ers when he was playing. You're talking about an outstanding cover guy. He was about six-one, a little bit over six feet, and he could cover any of the top receivers who were playing during that time. Eric could cover them all," said Ray Rhodes.[60]

"Eric [Wright] had great height for a cornerback during that era. A lot of cornerbacks were six feet or shorter, but Eric had really deceptive speed because he had long legs. He could really cover ground running, but he didn't look fast. But when he would run with wide receivers, he would be stride-for-stride with a wide receiver on a deep route. He had good hands, great agility, and he would really get down on short, fast, quick receivers because a lot of them weren't as big as they are now. He would find a way to be in the best position to get an interception," said Williamson.[61]

At strong safety was Carlton Williamson, a third-round pick in 1981 in his fourth year with the 49ers. After overcoming a broken leg in 1983 Williamson finished the season with four interceptions and fifty-eight tackles. Like the rest of the secondary, Williamson always wanted to set the tone for the defense with a big hit. "Probably the hardest hitter we had back there. Just a steady ballplayer," said McLemore.[62] "Carlton was a good hitter. Smart. Understood the game. From a coverage standpoint, he did a good job covering, and he was outstanding in the run game because he really came up and put a hit on you," said Rhodes.[63]

Free safety Dwight Hicks joined the 49ers in 1979 as a free agent after being cut in 1978 by the Detroit Lions and Philadelphia Eagles. "Dwight was Mr. Calm. He was our leader. Ronnie was very boisterous and aggressive. He'd get a little short-tempered sometimes in the huddle. It was stress and strain, but Dwight always kept us calm. When there was a big play and the other team was trying to get momentum, Dwight was excellent at keeping us focused, keeping us calm, so we wouldn't come unglued or lose track of what we were trying to accomplish. He made sure that we stuck to our game plan in attacking the team," said Carlton Williamson. "He was like that from day one when he arrived at training camp, because we were there as rookies the week before the veterans came. And when Dwight came in, you could just see the confidence. You could see the intelligence that he had and you welcomed that. As rookies we respected Dwight. He was the last line of defense and sometimes Ronnie and I could be a little more aggressive because we knew Dwight was going to be in position. If the play didn't work out for us, we knew Dwight was back there and would have our back."[64]

Hicks's position coach also noticed his intelligence. "Smart football player. Did a good job anticipating, getting good breaks on the ball from the middle of the field. Understood the game. When I say student of the game, he understood the game. He could anticipate, read quarterbacks well, and he'd get a good jump and get interceptions," said Rhodes.[65]

If Lott was the fire and passion in the 49ers defensive huddle, Hicks was the voice of reason. "When Ronnie got carried away, Hicks was the one who had to calm him down. Yeah, Ronnie was the man for the whole team. But as far as the glue back there that kept everything together, it was Dwight Hicks because, remember, it was Dwight Hicks and the Hot Licks. He had come there before all of us did," said McLemore.[66]

In their three years together, the four starters had combined for more than fifty interceptions. Both Lott and Hicks had been named to the Pro Bowl for three consecutive seasons. In 1984 the foursome would have a season for the ages.

Also in the secondary was safety Tom Holmoe, a fourth-round pick in the 1983 draft; cornerback and kick-return star Dana McLemore, a tenth-round pick in 1982; cornerback Tim Collier, a ten-year veteran of the NFL in his third season with the 49ers; and safety Rick Gervais, a fourth-year player with the 49ers who started five games when Williamson missed the first seven games of 1983 with a broken leg. The backups in the secondary brought confidence to the field whenever they saw action. The unit would not miss a beat. "Tom [Holmoe] knew the defenses really well. We felt that if something should happen to Dwight, Tom would step back there. He knew the calls. He knew all the adjustments that needed to be made, and we had great confidence in all of that," said Carlton Williamson.[67]

"As I look back, we had great leadership. At that point in my career I was a follower. Ronnie was a corner and Dwight was a free safety, so I looked up to those two guys. To this day they are dear friends," said Holmoe. "Those two guys took me under their wing. So I did whatever they did or whatever they said."[68] Holmoe couldn't have had two better role models on the field than the veteran players in the secondary who taught the "49ers way" to the younger players.

Holmoe's coach had the confidence in his ability to play in the NFL. "Holmoe was a sharp kid. He was one of those guys that I took great pride in having an opportunity to work with. Anybody got hurt, he steps right in, and you don't miss a beat. Sometimes when backups go in the game, you worry. Teams start taking advantage, but you couldn't take advantage of Tom. Tom was smart. He understood his role. The thing that was good about the group, those guys all studied. They studied the game and they were really sharp on game day. They understood exactly what needed to be done and they did their job," said Rhodes, defensive backs coach.[69]

As for Dana McLemore, he also brought the extra element of contributing to the return game as one of the NFL's best kick returners. "It was nothing for Dana to make a punt return, to make one or two people miss, and all of a sudden he's running for a touchdown. This was a defensive back, one of our own. So we were just happy to see another way of impacting the game and setting the tone. We took a lot of pride in our secondary with the personnel to really impact the outcome of the game in a positive way," said Carlton Williamson.[70]

"The play was never over with Dana because I've seen him juke one or two guys and I'm like, 'Oh, he's dead.' Then when he does that, of course, I'm kicking myself saying, 'Why am I watching? I should be blocking somebody here.' Man, he could move. The guy could stop on a dime and go lateral as fast as he could go forward and backward. We knew he was good but we saw how special he was," said Ron Ferrari.[71]

Heading into the season George Seifert planned to elevate situational substitutions to an art form. Walsh and general manager John McVay would make sure to get him all the parts he needed.

49ERS SPECIAL TEAMS

KICKER

Going into the 1984 season the 49ers had Ray Wersching as their kicker. The twelve-year veteran had been the 49ers kicker since 1977 after spending the first four years of his career with the San Diego Chargers. "Ray was very businesslike, very hard working, very prideful," said Fred vonAppen, special teams coach. "You look at Ray and you wouldn't think of him as being much of an athlete. He had a funny kind of short-statured, bowlegged body, and yet he took the conditioning seriously. The fact that they would come back every year and [he would] be the top conditioned returnee was remarkable. I mean you would expect some skill position guy to do that but it was an endurance thing and Ray was certainly on top of that."[72]

Wersching always prepared himself well for the upcoming season. He always thought of himself as a member of the team not "just a kicker." "It was an unique experience. I loved it. First day you walked in, they treated you like a teammate, as opposed to a kicker. The mentality was 'you're one of us,'" said Wersching. Wersching always felt like one of the guys. He would also go down with the team's most famous nickname. "I was a hairy guy, had a lot of hair on my back, can't remember who it was, said, 'damn, you have more hair than a mohair sweater.' So that's what stuck, 'Mo-Hair.' I didn't mind it at all; it just confirmed that you're one of the guys," recalled a laughing Wersching.[73]

Like any other kicker, Wersching had his peculiar way of preparing to kick. "It started in San Diego. I wore glasses but I couldn't wear glasses during a game. Things were a little fuzzy, so what I noticed was that the hash marks lined up with the uprights, so that's my reference," said Wersching. "But I didn't know I wasn't looking up, so a reporter said, 'Ray, you know you never look up at the uprights before kicking?' I said, 'No, you're wrong.' So the next time I go out, I notice, 'Damn, you're right, I didn't look up.' It became totally superstitious. I can't look up now, no way in hell. It helped me to focus a little more; it blocked out what the opposing team was doing. The defense tries to distract you, but I was oblivious to that, I had no idea."[74]

In addition to Wersching's superstition about never looking up before kicking, he also observed specific kicking rituals. As he jogged onto the field, he would tap his holder on the shoulder to help line him up. Then pace off his specific yards before lining up to kick. "As for some of the kickers who wanted to be by themselves, I didn't, I wanted to be with the guys—my guys—so I was there," continued Wersching. "I remember one time, we were usually seven and a half yards back from the snap, except for one time I marked off six and a half yards and the damn thing got blocked. From then on I get in the huddle and I tap Joe [Montana] on the shoulders and say, 'Make sure we're at seven and a half yards.' That became superstitious."[75]

In 1984 Wersching would have star quarterback Joe Montana as his holder. "Joe was phenomenal. I didn't care where the snap was—it could've been a wild snap—Joe would get it, and his fluidity—his fluid motion to get the ball back to the proper spot—you were confident that the ball was going to be there. It kind of relaxed you, and your stride to the ball was never interrupted. You never stopped or readjusted or anything like that; the ball was there every time," recalled Wersching. "The confidence he brings into the huddle—the field goal huddle—I can't describe it, other than it relaxed you. It relaxed you and gave you confidence. This is good; this is going to be good. This kicking thing is a mental game. When you have someone like that, it makes it—I don't want to say easier—but it helps. It helps a lot."[76]

Most NFL teams were reluctant to put their starting quarterback as the holder. "He was very professional about doing it," said vonAppen. "I never knew whether he liked doing it or didn't like it. He was fine with doing it."[77] Wersching encouraged Walsh and vonAppen to keep Montana there. "Every year I asked him if he could please hold, then one year, he hurt his back and I had other holders. Other years he said 'can't do it,' so I can't ask him to do it," said Wersching.[78]

As for the long snapper, starting guard Randy Cross handled that role. "Randy would actually lift the ball off the ground and then flip it," said vonAppen. "He would just raise it up for an instant and then throw it. He snapped on punts and field goals. They had a very good relationship, and it was wonderful that it worked as well as it did."[79]

"Randy was the long and short snapper for field goals. He had a knack for it. What he did with not looking up, I would ask him, 'How do you do that?' Every ball was right in the holder's hands. Mine were scattered everywhere when I tried it. Again, that consistency with snapper and holder was perfect," said Wersching.[80]

Punter

Punting was a different story. Walsh was never keen on punters, and going into 1984 he had the incumbent Tom Orosz returning. Orosz averaged only 39.3 yards per punt in 1983, so Walsh brought in veteran

punter Tom Skladany, who had played five seasons with the Detroit
Lions, to compete for the position.

The special teams unit led by coach Fred vonAppen was one of the
best in the NFL. Most of the 49ers key special team contributors returned in 1984. Tom Holmoe, Ron Ferrari, Milt McColl, Dana McLemore, Carl Monroe, Blanchard Montgomery, and Bill Ring were all
back. This unit knew their roles and took pride in being the best in the
NFL. "I didn't play special teams but there's a lot of pride with those
guys. A lot of those guys were on the special teams club. What did they
call themselves, the AWPs? The average white players or something
like that," said a laughing Riki Ellison, linebacker. "So they had a little
group. That was Bill Ring, Ron Ferrari, Milt McColl, probably Wally
[Michael Walter], too. So that was their own group, and they set the
pace and did some outstanding stuff."[81]

"We had some really good special teamers, and they knew their role.
The group was pretty state-of-the-art," said vonAppen. "They were really reliable. True professionals who worked hard every day. It was a good
group to work with."[82]

The 49ers 1984 roster was stacked and deep. Talent was everywhere.
But Walsh, McVay, and the 49ers scouting staff continued to look for
more talent.

5

DRAFT

[Walsh] had a real knack for picking guys. I mean, he would look at some film. There'd be a lot of film or little film. Boom. He might be in the draft room the day of the draft, and he'll say, 'I want to get that [Michael] Carter kid. I want that kid. I saw him a little bit. I want him. I'm going pick him right here.' I mean, he had a knack for talent. He really did.

—Bill McPherson, 49ers defensive line coach[1]

Looking at the roster a month before the NFL draft, Walsh and his staff targeted a few areas they wanted to improve. Most of them were on the defensive line. So Walsh started making some phone calls around the league. On March 16 Walsh sent a draft pick to the Philadelphia Eagles for ten-year veteran linebacker Frank LeMaster. Two weeks later he acquired defensive tackle Louie Kelcher from the San Diego Chargers. Big Louie, who was six feet five and nearly 300 pounds, was a three-time Pro Bowler in his nine years with the Chargers. Seifert wanted him to play nose tackle on run downs. "It was exciting. There really wasn't a selfish bone in anybody as far as trying to determine who got the most playing time, and I knew at that point in my career it was going to be situational. I was happy with that and just having the opportunity to continue my career," said Kelcher. "It was the best decision I made as far as being involved with a team like the 49ers."[2]

Then on April 5 Walsh made a third trade, giving up a fourth-round pick in 1984 and a tenth-round choice in 1985, for another defensive lineman. Six-feet-three, 252-pound Manu Tuiasosopo had played for Bill McPherson at UCLA and was the first-down nose tackle Walsh was looking for. Since being a first-round selection in 1979, Tuiasosopo (whose last name means "happy bird") had started sixty-four games with the Seahawks at three different positions: end, tackle, and nose tackle. He was quickly embraced by the 49ers family despite his long, difficult last name. "It took me four games to figure out how to say his last name," said a laughing Jim Stuckey. "Manu was great. The defensive line was a close-knit group, we were all very close."[3]

Having reached the 1983 AFC Championship Game with the Seahawks, Tuiasosopo initially found it difficult to leave Seattle. That quickly changed. "The two guys who felt like they were taking me under their wing to teach me the 49ers way were Keena Turner and Eric Wright. I remember the first month with the 49ers—those guys reached out and welcomed me with open arms," said defensive tackle Tuiasosopo.[4]

The 49ers veteran players made Manu feel at home. He also felt good about his reunion with his old college coach. "I had a great experience at UCLA playing for Coach Mac. He and Coach [Dick] Vermeil switched me from linebacker to defensive line, and that gave me the opportunity to start," said Tuiasosopo. "Learned a lot from Coach Mac: his style of coaching, relating to the players, and focusing on certain fundamentals. Just a great guy to play for and to learn from."[5]

Walsh then traded two backups, tight end Eason Ramson to the Broncos and guard Walt Downing to the Chargers, to get a few draft picks back. He then turned his full attention to the draft. While working with Paul Brown, Walsh saw how the coaches worked hand and hand with the scouts to evaluate college players. He brought this philosophy to the 49ers.

WALSH'S ASSIGNMENTS TO SCOUTS AND COACHES

"When Bill was with the Cincinnati Bengals, they utilized their coaches to do some of the scouting for the upcoming draft. They became part of their scouting program. So when Bill came to the Niners, he brought some of that philosophy from Paul Brown with him," said John McVay, vice president and general manager. "So Bill would have, for example, the linebackers coach look at the top linebackers—let's say, the top twenty linebackers in the country. We would take that information and blend it with our scouts. We had six scouts that were road scouts and we would blend them together; they worked together at the direction of Eddie and Bill. Sometimes you hear a scout or coach say, 'Coaches coach and scouts scout'; they don't want to blend. But we were able to blend them beautifully and it worked well for us."[6]

Blending his scouts with the coaching staff paid off in a big way during the 1981, 1982, and 1983 drafts. During those three years the 49ers drafted eleven players who would make the 1984 roster, including six starters (Lott, Wright, Williamson, Paris, Craig, and Ellison). "All the coaches went off and scouted. The thing I liked about it [was that] you would look at the draft collectively with everybody. He gave everybody an opportunity to have input. The thing I liked about Bill was the fact that he trusted his coaches. If you liked the guy, he would give you an opportunity to draft that guy. It might not be the round you wanted to draft him in, but he would give you an opportunity to draft that guy," said Ray Rhodes, defensive backs coach.

Rhodes continued, "But in the process of doing that, [if] you draft this kid, [if] you like this kid, he's going to play. If you're going to bring him in here, he better be a player and he gotta play. And I had no problem with that. He wanted to make sure that if you brought a guy in, [that you would] have a role for him [and] be able to identify exactly what that guy's gonna do for the football team. I think that's the accountability of a coach. You gotta be accountable. If you're going to draft a guy and you feel strongly about the guy you want, he better play. That [lesson] I learned from Bill."[7]

The coaches first evaluated college athletes by position after lengthy discussions about the team's needs. Coaches then were given specific projects. "He put us on the road to look at the fifteen best guys at our position. What he was interested in was a character check more than what they could do physically. We could see all that stuff on film. I want to know what kind of guy he is. So take him out, ask the trainer what he's like. Ask the equipment guy what's he like, because the coach will tell you he's a great kid, but some of those people [trainers, equipment men] will say, 'This guy's an asshole. You don't want to draft him.' He wanted to know those kinds of things," said Fred vonAppen, special teams coach.[8]

"When the season was over, the coaches were actually the scouts. They went on the road and they were gone for months at a time. They did most of the legwork. We had an outstanding scouting department with Tony Razzano, John McVay, and Allan Webb [director of pro personnel]," said George Seifert, defensive coordinator. "But we always incorporated the feelings and the scouting of the coaches as well, so there were two groups of people that would come together. Bill would send us on the road according to position. Like when we drafted Ronnie Lott, Eric Wright, and Carlton Williamson [1981 draft], I went on the road and scouted all those players. When I became coordinator, I had a more varied role and I backed up my position coaches. So we were always on the road for a week or so, and we'd come back for a few days and go on the road again for a week or so to evaluate players. Then all of the information was pooled together. Everybody was involved. It was a team effort."[9]

Throughout the draft process 49ers scouts and coaches were encouraged to ask themselves, "What specifically can this man do that can help the 49ers?" They did not necessarily judge an athlete based on his merits as a standout player but on his ability to fulfill a particular need on the team. Players who might be considered journeymen were viewed as players who could play, in whatever category, giving the team depth.

At this time most scouts would say, "He's just good enough to get you beat" or "He's someone you'll always want to replace." But Walsh wanted his staff to ask, "Is there anything that he can do that will improve the 49ers?" As an example, Dwight Clark or even Joe Montana could flourish in the West Coast system without meeting the requirements elsewhere (size, speed, etc.). At 248 pounds, Dwaine Board wasn't as bulky as other defensive linemen, but he performed extremely well doing what the 49ers asked of him.

For 49ers scouts, the scouting process was year-round, not just around draft time. Led by Tony Razzano, they visited every school in the nation and then met with Bill Walsh to provide their input. In 1984 the 49ers scouting department consisted of two directors:

Tony Razzano—director of college scouting
Allan Webb—director of pro personnel

and seven scouts:

Billy Atkins—South (joined 49ers staff in 1984)

Vic Lindskog—East (49ers scout since 1980)

Michael Lombardi—Midwest/West (joined 49ers staff prior to 1984 draft)

Ernie Plank—Northeast Region (49ers scout since 1978)

Neil Schmidt—Southeast Region (49ers scout since 1975)

Bob Whitman—Southwest Region (49ers scout since 1983)

Billy Wilson—West Region (49ers scout since 1981 who was also a star end who played ten years with the 49ers, was the team's franchise leader with 407 catches, scored forty-nine touchdowns, and was named to six Pro Bowls)

Tony Razzano oversaw the top players nationwide while the other scouts covered specific regions. Sometimes Razzano assigned the scouts different regions so that the team would get two or more opinions about every player heading into the draft. All the scouts came into the draft armed with information about the player's junior and senior years, spring practice, and film documentation of at least four games but more likely six. In addition to the physical statistics (height, weight, forty-yard dash time, etc.), the 49ers compiled a complete personal dossier on each athlete by means of a short "job interview" that included the player's priorities in education, sports, material desires, and personal relationships. This testing was done casually, not in a classroom. Coaches sat down with the player at a meal and asked him questions during the course of a relaxed conversation. By comparing an athlete's answers to those of the players already on the team, the 49ers got a better feel about how a prospective draftee might fit into their organization.

Forty-niner scouts were treated as important members of the organization, not as second-class employees. As a result of their excellent relationship and communication skills, 49er coaches and scouts worked beautifully together for years. "Bill respected everybody's position and Tony Razzano was the same way. But how you graded a player was up to you. . . . When the draft board went up, the players ended up being ranked by consensus, but everybody's individual grade was on that player's card," said Neal Dahlen, director of research and development. "If Bobb McKittrick, the offensive line coach, graded an offensive lineman, and Tony [Razzano] had graded him, and the area scout had graded him, and the regional scout had graded him, and then I had graded him—all those grades went on the card, equally weighted. . . . Bill would say they're all valid, all of the opinions valid. And then it was up to him to decide, 'Would I lean more on Bobb McKittrick's grade on this guy than Neil Schmidt's grade on this guy?'"

Dahlen continued, "As [time] went [on], Tony, John McVay, and Bill also [got] a sense of who their best graders were for different positions. And they would say, for example, 'Neil Schmidt was really good with receivers.' So they'd give that a little more weight but everybody, when they put their grade on the player, knew that it was respected and figured into the process. And it was up to Bill and John to eventually rank the players."[10]

Walsh had created an environment where there was no competition between coaches and scouts. During meetings, both scouts and coaches could express themselves completely. Walsh wanted input. He was only interested in results. On draft day Walsh's tactics varied but the overall goal remained the same: to improve the team. There were three constants in every draft:

1. Philosophy first. Most teams eliminate prospects if an athlete doesn't meet their physical specifications, which might be speed for a defensive back or size for an offensive tackle, whereas the first question the 49ers staff asked themselves when evaluating a player might be, "Could he ultimately start in the NFL?"
2. Extremely thorough preparation.
3. An atmosphere among coaches and scouts conducive to making the best decisions.

THE 1984 DRAFT CLASS

Throughout his years with the 49ers Walsh ran a calm draft room. "The college draft is the very foundation of the National Football League. It is the point from which everything begins. . . . We had talented people who were well organized and who felt a real commitment to their work," remarked Walsh.[11] By finishing with a 10–6 regular-season record in 1983, the 49ers held the twenty-fourth overall pick in the 1984 draft. They would miss out on the top fifteen or so players, so

Walsh would keep to the board and draft the best remaining players available.

Held on May 1–2 in New York City, the 1984 draft lasted twelve long rounds with 336 players chosen. In the end the 49ers selected nine players. Walsh's board was ready, and he was willing to deal to get the guys he liked. In the first round with the twenty-fourth overall pick, the 49ers selected Todd Shell, the six-four, 225-pound linebacker from BYU who Walsh had scouted himself.

"[Todd Shell] was a very versatile athlete; he was a very good, skilled linebacker," said Dahlen.[12] In the second round, fifty-sixth overall, Walsh selected John Frank, a six-three, 225-pound tight end out of Ohio State. The premed student was ideal for the West Coast offense and fit in nicely with the other two tight ends. "John Frank was a young rookie at the time. Great guy. Kind of uncanny about the way he does things. 'Coop, you got to do this; you got to do that,' I'm trying to tell the rook, 'Hey man, I got this.' But he was just so much help coming from Ohio State, that drive that he had to win and just a tenacious player. He made things happen when it looks like it's not gonna happen," said tight end Earl Cooper.[13]

As the third round began, the 49ers looked to move up. They had their eyes on a certain offensive lineman. Walsh traded up seven spots, giving up a fifth-round selection to the St. Louis Cardinals to pick at number seventy-three overall, and selected Georgia tackle Guy McIntyre. The six-three, 270-pound McIntyre had played tackle in college, blocking for Heisman Trophy–winner Herschel Walker, but he knew once he got to the NFL, he would be changing positions to guard. "Knew that was going to be the transition. So I wasn't surprised," said McIntyre.[14] McIntyre was perfect to play guard under Bobb McKittrick, who lobbied for the Georgia athlete. "I found out later that he said, 'If you're giving me my choice of whom I want to pick, this is the guy I want to go with.' So when it was up to him, they moved up and got me. It was destined to be," recalled McIntyre.[15]

Forty-niners teammates quickly recognized the athleticism of their third-round pick, as well as his bright future in the NFL. "The guy could just flat-out play football. I watched him on film and he's somebody who just kept his feet moving all the time and never stopped. You'd just see defensive players come up, and he'd put them on their back just before the whistle blew. This guy . . . can play football. Taking nothing away from the other guys, but there's a guard that is the future here. And he played there for almost ten years," said offensive tackle Allan Kennedy. [16]

After trading away his fourth-round pick to acquire Manu Tuiasosopo, Walsh had two fifth-round picks. In that round he chose two unique players who would contribute in big ways throughout their 49ers careers. Selected 121st overall was Michael Carter, a six-two, 280-pound nose tackle at SMU who didn't appear on most teams' boards because he was trying out for the Olympics as a shot-putter. He was one of America's best. "He had a bad knee at one time during the season [as a senior], and we thought if he did well in the Olympics, he might go on tour in Europe. But he was so good, such an athlete. A couple of the coaches at SMU said, 'Take this guy. He's one of the best guys we ever had.' In fact, the coach used to call him 'pit bull,'" said Bill McPherson, defensive line coach. [17]

"The *Dallas Morning News*, our local paper, had a mock draft that told what teams were looking for and what would be the best fit for each of our [SMU] players. It said San Francisco was interested in me and I thought that would be a pretty good fit because I dreaded going to Pittsburgh or someplace where it was cold. In the fifth round San Francisco chose me. I was happy," said defensive tackle Michael Carter. [18] Carter was happy to be going to San Francisco, but when he made the Olympic team, he told Walsh that he would be three weeks late to camp. For Walsh and the coaches, Carter was worth the wait. They knew they were getting a good player who was participating in a once-in-a-lifetime event.

The other fifth rounder and 139th choice overall was Jeff Fuller, a fast, physical linebacker at Texas A&M whom the 49ers envisioned as a safety. "Jeff Fuller was a big player for his position and he was tremendously gifted physically," said Dahlen. "He was maybe better than [former Broncos safety] Steve Atwater as an athlete." [19] At six-two, 216 pounds Fuller quickly gained the respect of his teammates as a freak athlete who would fit in with the other defensive backs. "You got Jeff Fuller. He was big; he was fast. This guy would run with wide receivers, and I was just so impressed with his athletic ability, being such a big guy. He had great speed, and he was a hitter, too. Strong. So it was another example of having a really strong group in the secondary who took a lot of pride in the way we played the game," said Carlton Williamson, strong safety.[20]

"He was my roommate that year, me and Jeff. Probably the best athlete on the team. Big, strong, fast—he can play every position. He can play all four defensive back positions, and he can play linebacker. He was that gifted," said defensive back Dana McLemore.[21]

Walsh had no picks in the sixth, seventh, and eighth rounds, all of which were offered up in trades to the Falcons, Patriots, and Chargers, respectively. In the latter rounds he sought additional depth at defensive back with ninth-round choice, Lee Miller, and fresh legs to run routes with wide receivers Dave Moritz (tenth round out of Iowa) and Kirk Pendleton (eleventh round out of BYU).

But it was the second ninth-round pick that would defy all odds to make the 49ers. Derrick Harmon of Cornell was the 248th player chosen in the 1984 draft. The five-ten, 200-pound Ivy League running back was excited about joining the 49ers. "I was happy and surprised by going in the ninth round, but I was happy to be drafted. Getting drafted was an honor [as was] coming into the atmosphere of San Francisco," said Harmon.[22]

The scouting and film study paid off. "[Walsh] had a real knack for picking guys. I mean, he would look at some film. There'd be a lot of film or little film. Boom," said Bill McPherson, defensive line coach. "He might be in the draft room the day of the draft, and he'll say, 'I want to get that Carter kid. I want that kid. I saw him a little bit. I want him. I'm going pick him right here.' I mean, he had a knack for talent. He really did."[23]

It was another banner draft for the 49ers, as six of their nine draft picks would make the team: linebacker Todd Shell, tight end John Frank, offensive guard Guy McIntyre, nose tackle Michael Carter, safety Jeff Fuller, and running back Derrick Harmon. While playing for the 49ers, the 1984 draft class would go on to win thirteen Super Bowl rings.

Walsh wasn't done building his roster after the draft. On June 14 Walsh signed a player whose last name was very familiar to 49ers fans. Inside linebacker Jim Fahnhorst, younger brother of tackle Keith Fahnhorst, was signed to a four-year contract. The younger Fahnhorst had just finished playing two years with the Arizona Wranglers of the USFL. In the spring of 1984 he played eighteen games with the Wranglers under George Allen, losing in the USFL Championship Game against the Philadelphia Stars. His contract up, he was very happy to be joining his brother in San Francisco. "Yeah, that was great. He was older than me, more than six years older, so I was never able to play with him. . . . I knew I had a lot to live up to, but it was just a chance of a lifetime to play with him," said linebacker Jim Fahnhorst.[24]

For the elder Fanhhorst, it was also a dream come true. "That could've been a distraction, playing with your brother for the first time, but we didn't let it. It was fun," said Keith Fahnhorst, offensive tackle. As the team was being assembled, the veteran group of returning players got to work to prepare for the 1984 season. It would take hard work to get back to the Super Bowl.[25]

6

LUNCH BOX TEAM

People ask me about that team. I say they were the 'lunch box team.' They were good guys. They were not selfish. I think they all saw a role that they had to play, and they brought their lunch boxes and they did that.
—Jerry Attaway, 49ers physical development coordinator[1]

The 1984 off-season was one of determination and hard work for 49ers players. They would not shy away from the task at hand. "We knew we had the team to win. Dwight Hicks made the speech in the locker room. Basically [after] that speech in the locker room, everybody made a commitment to work hard that off-season," said Wendell Tyler, running back. "We made a commitment as a team to be back in that position next year. That's where it all started, because we should've won that game. We had the talent, but it made us hungry for the next year."[2] The hard work to get back to the Super Bowl started at the team's headquarters.

The 49ers facility in Redwood City, about forty-five miles south of San Francisco, was located at 711 Nevada Street in the middle of a suburban neighborhood. Operated by Redwood City's recreation department, it was a dump by most standards, certainly not as luxurious as one might expect, especially for a franchise that had won a Super Bowl in 1981.[3]

In 1984 the beauty of the building at 711 Nevada Street was its location—just a seven-mile drive down El Camino Real (Route 82) to Stanford Stadium and the campus of Stanford University, where Super

Bowl XIX was to be played. On December 14, 1982, in Dallas, Texas, the NFL owners awarded Stanford Stadium the rights to host the biggest sports event in the world. Beating out five other cities (Detroit, Houston, Jacksonville, New Orleans, and Pasadena), San Francisco would host its first-ever Super Bowl. "It is a great traditional university and stadium, it seats 85,000, and we like to move the game around. We've done it since the start, and San Francisco is a very attractive city," declared NFL commissioner Pete Rozelle at the 1982 owners meeting.[4]

49ERS TEAM FACILITY

The journey to the Super Bowl in 1984 was even more special with the knowledge that the game would be played just down the freeway. To prepare themselves to get back to the big game, most of the 49ers players stayed in Redwood City during the off-season. One of the league's least attractive facilities, 711 Nevada Street didn't even have a full 100-yard field. It made do with two fifty-yard fields—half grass, half turf, surrounded by cyclone fencing—which were used most often for tennis. Walsh called them "semifields." A common scene occurred when the receivers ran deep post routes on the grass and then attempted to stop on the Astroturf field. When it rained hard, the fields flooded so they moved practice to the higher grounds of the youth soccer fields.[5]

The building itself—a gutted tract home onto which a second story and a single-story wing had been added—was painted red and suggested the headquarters of a professional football team during the league's mom-and-pop era with its smaller rosters and staff. But that era had long since passed by the time the 49ers won their first Super Bowl in 1981. At a distance the structure might have been mistaken for a school or a library.[6] "I remember when I first got there, I'm thinking, 'OK, this is the big-time NFL.' It's kind of an older rustic-looking town, then I go to this little facility. A flat, two-story place, and I go, 'OK, it's not bells and whistles. They just do it the old-fashioned way,'" said wide receiver Renaldo Nehemiah. "It was all about the game. Not about anything else. You check the egos at the door and everybody came together. It wasn't about all the great state-of-the-art stuff at the time."[7]

Parking was located right outside, next to the facility that was shared with the community center next door. Walking through the main front door at 711, the reception desk was on the left, with Eddie DeBartolo's plush office to the right. Down the hall on the right were the scouting offices of Tony Razzano and his staff, with the stairs leading to the second floor on the left. There was also an unimpressive-looking weight room, part of which was located under a tent outside, and a media trailer where the 49ers coaches and players held interviews and press conferences.[8]

To the left of the stairs was a narrow hallway with several offices and rooms. On the right was Jerry Walker's public relations department, a rather small meeting room usually used by the defense, a small locker room with showers for the coaches, and another small classroom. On the left was the team's main meeting room, which was the size of a large college classroom. When the team meeting was finished—usually in less than ten minutes—the offensive players and coaches would remain to go over the game plan and watch film.

The first floor's narrow hallway came to a dead end at the player's locker room, which was no bigger than a large studio apartment. To the immediate left was the equipment room, overseen by Chico Norton and Bronko Hinek, to the right, the exit to the practice field. Along the right side of the locker room were the defensive player's lockers: defensive backs, linebackers, then defensive line. On the left side were the lockers of the 49ers offensive players: offensive line, wide receivers/tight ends, and running backs. Next to the trainer's room, a small door in the back led to the parking lot. Run by Lindsy McLean and John Miller, the trainer's facility amounted to several benches and two old whirlpool baths. Quarterback lockers were next to the building's showers.

"The facility was absolutely terrible. It was the worst around," recalled a chuckling Jeff Stover, defensive end. "If you were showering and someone flushed the toilet, it would scald you. It was terrible. There were only six showers for what, fifty guys? It was ridiculous. But you know what? It brought us all that much closer together. To accomplish what we did in a facility like that says a lot about the individuals and the coaching and the system. It's not about where you're at. It's about playing football."[9]

The 49ers weight room, headed by physical development coordinator Jerry Attaway, was nothing to brag about—hundreds of colleges had better ones. Rehab equipment for injured players was stored in the corner near the lockers. "It was a humble facility. With no disrespect, it was no better than my high school facility. These guys today don't appreciate what they have with all these mega complexes," said defensive tackle Manu Tuiasosopo. "It wasn't pretty, but it was functional. It had what we needed, and it had heart. It had togetherness. . . . We walk into this facility here, then we're transformed into this family. Then we're focused."[10]

"Bill Walsh couldn't have designed a better facility. Because every place was intimate. There was no place to hide. There was no place to have a clique. There was no place to be your own guy and do your own thing," said linebacker Ron Ferrari. "It was a very intimate setting. That's what continued to bring us closer, spending this much time together. You shower together. You work together. You eat together. You laugh together. You're disappointed together, and there are really no secrets. You can't fake it for that long. So all your insecurities, everybody knew. It was great. But that locker room, we didn't understand it and we thought it was cheesy at the time. But it was probably 50 percent of our success. That intimacy and that chance to get to know the other players and to respect and to tolerate each other even when you're hot. It was a huge part of it. We actually didn't understand it at the time. It was so much later, you look back and you see what the good Lord had for you, what he was preparing for the guys. It's pretty special."[11]

Upstairs on the second floor, the first door was the office of John McVay. Down the small hallway on the left were the 49ers business offices, headed by Keith Simon, and the rooms for the offensive coaches: Bobb McKittrick, Paul Hackett, Sherman Lewis, and Fred vonAppen. "This is Bill Walsh philosophy. Number one: get one big room. We were all in one room. He wanted the coaches to be totally on the same page. Now what better way to be on the same page [than] if you don't have individual offices? You're all in the same room," said quarterbacks and wide receivers coach Paul Hackett. "When I first got there, I went over and I got by the window, which was a great spot. Bobb McKittrick was to my right and Sherm [Lewis] was behind me. If anything was being discussed, if there was a question, Bobb was always right there, and Bobb could help us out and teach us."[12]

On the right side of the hallway was the marketing office, led by Ken Flower, and one large office for the defensive coaches. Within the defensive room were small desks for each coach: George Seifert, Bill McPherson, Norb Hecker, Ray Rhodes, Tommy Hart, as well as Neal Dahlen, the director of research and development. In the middle of the room was a big conference table, and along the walls were blackboards to design the game plans.

Beyond a small hallway with a bathroom was the two-room corner office of head coach Bill Walsh. The first room was the office of his secretary, Nicole Gisele. Through Gisele's office was Walsh's, which was no bigger than twenty square feet. Covered with wall-to-wall wood paneling, the smallish office was decorated by Gisele, who chose pictures of San Francisco's skyline and a fog-shrouded Golden Gate Bridge to give the office some life. Walsh's desk faced the door, putting his back to the only window in the room, which overlooked the practice field behind the facility.

Every morning a hot cup of coffee sat on Walsh's desk. In front of his desk, slightly to his right, was a small table with a film projector. A small couch, some books, stereo speakers, and chairs completed his no-frills, brown-and-beige office decor. If Bill wanted to contact one of his staff, he need only speak up and he would be heard even at the other end of the building. "He saw the cramped offices as an asset. When somebody was talking on the phone or having a conversation, everybody could hear what was going on. In a strange way, it meant that everybody on the staff was in the loop," recalled John McVay. [13]

Members of the 1984 49ers loved coming to work at 711 Nevada Street. Despite the thirty years that had passed, they all had their own memories of the unique building. "It was really tight. Little small rooms and, trust me, Bubba Paris used to clean out some of those rooms after eating beans. He would cut some real big ones, man, and he would clean us out. But it was kind of cool to be quiet, small, and tight," said a laughing Roger Craig, fullback. "It really brought us together. It wasn't an attractive place for our headquarters, and we took pride in that. We took pride in that community. It's a small city but the community of people was so supportive of us. It did keep our team together. Our locker rooms didn't have that much room, so you had to learn how to live [together]. Basically it was just like being in a house with a family. So you gotta learn how to adapt." [14]

"We were all squished together. It was a tiny place, but it had character," said Riki Ellison, linebacker. "Everybody was together. You couldn't run away from stuff, you couldn't go somewhere and escape. You were there. With good things and bad things. You were right next to each other in the locker room and everybody was part of it. . . . I loved the place. I think it was one of the coolest places. . . . This was definitely the closest team and had the most diverse personalities and guys that really enjoyed the game and enjoyed each other."[15]

"People kept it pretty loose but there weren't any distractions. You didn't have any crazy personalities. If you did, the veterans took it upon themselves to straighten that person out, or if they couldn't, then they were traded. So you saw a core that didn't change much," said Allan Kennedy, offensive tackle.[16]

All of the 49ers players were ready to get to work. "Walter Payton gave me some valuable advice. He was a mentor to me. Walter said, 'Never lose your endurance, never lose your endurance. Take two weeks off, get back into your training. You don't have to do nothing crazy. Just never lose your endurance.' I live by that today. I run marathons today, so it's kind of cool," said Craig.[17]

During the 1984 off-season the 49ers players were guided through workouts by Jerry Attaway, the physical development coordinator. "At that time I think Jerry [Attaway] was ahead of the game. He had very specific things that we would work on. Agility, speed, quickness, stretch, and then just old-fashioned [getting-]in-shape stuff," said Ron Ferrari, linebacker. "We were a pretty loyal group of guys who did them."[18]

"He would dream up these drills that were skill and aerobic. So you might work on the particular skill and combine it with a conditioning drill. You'd have to perform that skill under duress. He would dream it up and he'd do it with everybody," said safety Tom Holmoe. "We might ride a bike to San Francisco one day, get in the pool the next day. Then we'd do stuff on the field and be on the rowing machines the next day. Most of it was specific to our positions. . . . I really credit Jerry for keeping me in condition to do it. I was in tip-top shape."[19]

Forty-niners players knew who was in charge of getting them ready for the upcoming season. Everything was organized and coordinated daily by Attaway. "I always thought that the way we conditioned was a little bit stupid. We'd run 100 [yard sprints]. We'd run 220s. We'd run forty-yard dashes. We'd do all that stuff. But very seldom do we ever play that way. So our stuff was always position oriented. If I wanted you to run a forty-yard dash, you started from a stance or you might back-pedal and break into it. You did something that was related to how you played. And my emphasis to people in the off-season, I said, 'You need to sit down with your position coach. You need to look at films. What we need to do is determine what it is that you're worst at.' Guys who are really good weight lifters will lift weights all day long but don't want to run. Guys who are really good runners but aren't real strong will run all day but don't want to lift weights. So let's identify where your weak-nesses are and make the skills you lack part of your off-season condi-tioning program," said Attaway. "So not only do you get in shape, but maybe you can get better at the skills that it takes to create a starting position for yourself or maybe it makes you better if you are a starter."

Attaway helped build the football dynasty at USC, so he knew what he was doing. One of his former Trojans was a big believer in what he preached. "Probably a guy who was the best at it was Riki Ellison. He would come in—probably within three or four weeks after the end of the season—and say, 'OK, here's what we have to get better at,'" said Attaway. "He would identify it, and then . . . he'd walk out the door and there'd be cones and bags and stuff. Very seldom did we do things that ran in a straight line. So whatever your skills were, when we ran this obstacle course, you would run it as a defensive back, where you might backpedal, shuffle into it. You'd run it as a receiver, make cuts. You would make it as an offensive lineman, where you would start and pull and go through. We always tried to make it position specific, skill specif-ic."

Attaway continued, "Everybody did the same workout. We'd set up bags, we set up cones, and we had drills and went through it. But if you were a running back, you carried a ball when you went through it and you started from a stance. If there was a quarterback there, he would hand you the ball, and as soon as you broke out, we threw you a pass. We used to actually throw passes to the offensive and defensive line-men. They thought that was fun because they got to catch the ball."

Attaway worked with all the 49ers players on their specific skills regardless of what they needed to improve. "Perfect example, Riki Elli-son, who I talked about earlier. He came to me after his first year and said, 'People are cutting me.' He was an inside linebacker, and he was only 225 pounds at the time, and he was not real fast but he was quick and could read. Hacksaw taught him well. He could react really quickly . . . he hit them so fast [that] people would just cut him. So what I said is, 'I'm gonna get on my hands and knees with a [medicine] ball'—I had the biggest medicine ball I could get—'and what I want you to do is get in your stance and then come straight at me. Just pretend it's an isolation play where the center and the guards block down the double teams and nose guard over the center. Fullback's gonna lean on you and you've gotta fill the hole.' I said, 'Just play like that and run right over my right shoulder. Don't run over me. Just run over the shoulder.' Well, when he would get a step away from me, I would take the medicine ball and I would throw it at his legs or I'd throw it at his upper body. If I threw it at his legs he would push it down in the ground, go right over the top of it and keep going. If I threw it at his upper body, he would shed it like it was a block and keep going straight forward. Well, as soon as we got him to where he could do that without me tripping him up, then we said, 'now as soon as you go by me, I want you to break to your right,' or 'as soon as you go by me break to your left.' He'd shuffle down the line and then break past me. So he and I actually did that after every workout. It was just the two of us doing that. Well, the next off-season there was one of the new pictures over the stairwell of him pushing the guard right into the ground, and he was trying to cut him with Eric Dickerson. That's what he had done the whole off-season because that was the problem that he had as far as his skill," continued Attaway.[20]

Another player Attaway focused on during the 1984 off-season was kicker Ray Wersching. "In my earlier career I lifted weights, and that just tightened up my muscles and I pulled a quad. I went up to Jerry and said, 'Can I do something besides lifting weights to improve my strength? Something to improve my longevity because I want to be around awhile. I'm having too much fun.' So he devised my program to work out in the pool," said Wersching. "Boy, it was brutal. You came out of the pool and you could barely walk. Your legs were like noodles. It helped me mentally, doing something that improved myself. Later in the season when the body starts to break down, I think it helped me stay stronger. It helped quite a bit and he developed that plan."

Wersching continued, "You did all sorts of stuff. You would go into the deep end and do jumps. In other words, you would go to the bottom and explode to the top, you would take a breath, go back down, and do that numerous times. You would hang on to the side of the pool, then extend your legs and work your groin—swishing your legs back and forth. Then he would throw you in the deep end—you couldn't swim—you would have to run, you would have to pump your arms, pump your legs, and you had to keep going to keep your head above water. Those were your sprints. He kept you going about 30 to 45 minutes. [Laughing.] Some of the other guys on the team who were hurt and couldn't practice on the field [were given] to Jerry [who] put them in the pool. Those guys got healthy real quick."[21]

During the months before training camp the 49ers players were bonding during the workouts like no other team in the NFL. Jerry Attaway could see that the members of the squad were pushing each other to get better. He also saw that they were having fun with the workouts. "First thing, you don't ever want to hurt somebody in your off-season program. So we'd wait for three weeks to a month to go by because now everybody's getting in pretty good shape. They can sprint. They can stop. They can change direction. Now what happens is we run two at a time. Well, all those guys are genetic freaks and mutants, but they're all competitive. So when you run two at a time, what happens is they really start to bust their asses because they want to beat the other guy. So it wasn't like a game, but it was [close]. . . . I remember one day I looked over and there were like four guys face down in the grass and a bunch of other guys on their knees and they were all laughing. They had fun at it. They really liked it and they busted their asses doing it because they felt they were getting better at it," said Attaway.

The voluntary workouts were a success in getting the 49ers prepared for the upcoming season. Even the best players were there working hard—perhaps even harder than anyone else. "Guys didn't have to be there, so it's not like we had the whole team there. Two different sessions of guys and probably between twenty and thirty people, I'm guessing. The two leaders of the team were Joe Montana and Ronnie Lott. And neither one of those guys was flamboyant. You never heard Joe Montana talking about how many completions he had or Lott talking about interceptions. They just came to work and prepared for the next game. The big thing for them was winning. They didn't care about stats as much as they cared that we had a 'W' at the end of the day. When two guys of that caliber aren't selfish, no one else is," said Attaway.[22]

"I think everyone was especially dedicated. The work ethic that we had on that team was incredible," said Bill Ring, running back. "Most of the guys were there in the off-season working out even though you didn't have to be there. But a lot of people were there. We had groups that we worked out with: the quarterbacks, the running backs, and the receivers. . . . That work ethic really never stopped. It had carried through and I think we had great leadership in people demonstrating how to work hard and how to dedicate yourself."[23]

During the summer of 1984, most of the 49ers stayed in the area to work out. "We did and I stayed there. I'd been going back to Clemson, where I'd gone to college, and decided to stay up there for the off-season," said defensive end Jim Stuckey. "It brought us together. . . . [If] we're gonna get back to the promised land . . . then we would have to be together during the off-season. We would have to do things together. Work out and things like that."[24]

Every 49er who worked out made himself a better player. "I was still a young player, but I was really trying to mature and establish myself . . . and trying to keep up and be an equal part of what I thought was a great group of guys. So I benefited from having Fred Dean and Ronnie Lott, Dwight [Hicks] and Eric [Wright], and all the great players we had on defense, along with Joe [Montana], who really set our standards on that side of the ball and for the whole team," said Keena Turner, linebacker.[25]

Even for the few players who didn't stay in the area to work out, they could see that the team was working hard to get back to the Super Bowl. "I always lifted in Minnesota in the off-season. But when I came back to mini-camp, you could feel it, because a lot of the guys had stayed around. That is where it started," said Keith Fahnhorst, offensive tackle. "[Also], there were guys who had a lot of success but didn't have a ring. That was one of the reasons why we all were focused like that [and why] those guys were especially focused, and they made sure the pieces fit. That was the key."[26]

"Everybody came back in shape; everybody came back committed and focused for one thing and that was to win the Super Bowl that year. I knew in everybody's heart—I knew in my heart—we were going to be in the Super Bowl," said Wendell Tyler, running back.[27]

All of the coaches and even front office personnel at 711 Nevada Street could see the team working hard and bonding toward a common goal in 1984. "Wow, we are working hard. We are zeroed-in. I was at the facility and the guys that were around in the facility were always working, and I just really felt there was a sense of purpose right from the beginning," said Paul Hackett, quarterbacks and wide receivers coach.[28]

"That whole off-season it seemed like players came in more often in the off-season and worked harder [than before]. I remember [seeing Ronnie Lott and Dwight Clark embrace]. I thought, 'Coming from Ohio, you don't see many guys embrace like that. Man, this team's got chemistry. Those guys are glad to see each other.' That whole off-season I just felt like '84 was going to be our year, and I think we all approached it that way," said Jerry Walker, director of public relations.[29]

"I remember we used to go and work out together as a group. I mean, on our own, by our old complex in Redwood City. A group of us, we'd just go over there and just work out together," said defensive end Dwaine Board. "I think that was a big part of it, too, because it was a really close team. It was probably the closest team I have ever been associated with as far as players and the way we would do things together."[30]

"People ask me about that team. I said they were the 'lunch box team.' They were good guys. They were not selfish. I think they all saw a role they had to play, and they brought their lunch boxes and they did that," said Jerry Attaway, physical development coordinator.[31]

Part II

Training Camp

7

ROCKLIN

Practice was like a game to us. We'd treat it just like a game. Every practice was an opportunity to get better, and our players took advantage of that.
—Ray Rhodes, 49ers defensive backs coach[1]

Hot.

When most people think of Rocklin, California, in July, the word most often used to describe the town is hot. "It was brutal. As soon as you walked out in the morning there's nothing up there but that beautiful sun," said Bill McPherson, 49ers defensive line coach.[2] In 1984 the small town more than 100 miles north of San Francisco had a population of just over 8,000 and was perfectly suited for Bill Walsh and his team. The campus of Sierra College, usually deserted by the student body in the summer, and its dormitories offered the squad a quiet atmosphere to learn 49ers football. Since Walsh was a teacher at heart, his camps were all business—and all football—twenty-four hours a day.

Sierra College had been the 49ers training camp site since 1981. Walsh selected the school and the tiny town of Rocklin mainly for its remoteness. He wanted the players away from their friends and families so they could concentrate on football with relatively small crowds to watch their practice mistakes. "The atmosphere that was created there by Walsh was spectacular," recalled Paul Hackett, 49ers quarterbacks and wide receivers coach. "We had total isolation and it was great."[3]

For Bill Walsh and his coaching staff, training camp was a time to teach. With a veteran team returning in 1984, Walsh decided to put his squad through a "mental" summer camp. It wasn't going to be survival of the fittest. His team was already in shape from the off-season workouts directed by Jerry Attaway. It was now time to put his plan into place. In 1979 before his first training camp with the 49ers, Walsh took a "vacation" with his family to Lake Tahoe, though he barely left the condo while there. During the brief vacation Walsh drew up the entire schedule for training camp, something he learned from his college mentor. "So much of our practice was situational. This goes back to my coach at San Jose State, Bob Bronzan. He organized every practice almost to the play. When I became a head coach, I isolated every different situation that might occur in a game," wrote Bill Walsh in his autobiography. "We might have, for instance, six short-yardage plays in a game, eight plays where we'd be backed up against our own end zone, six plays with third down and twenty yards to go. In training camp, we'd regularly practice all these contingencies. Over a period of years, we became very proficient at dealing with each particular situation."[4]

When Walsh returned to San Francisco he presented the whole schedule to his coaching staff. Every practice was detailed, every situation covered. Every hour, every minute. Before camp started Walsh met with his coaches, both collectively and individually, to discuss the four basic categories of team development he wanted to accomplish at training camp.

1. Teaching individual fundamentals (techniques) and skill
2. Choreographing the actions of groups (offensive line, defensive backs, etc.)
3. Developing team execution (offense, defense, special teams)
4. Implementing situational football (related to specific game circumstances)

The drills and sessions needed to accomplish these goals would make for some long days for the 49ers coaching staff. "I remember nothing but football from the time you got up in the morning until late at night. The coaches would be up till 1:00 in the morning before [going] to bed after [putting our] practice schedule together," said 49ers defensive coordinator George Seifert.[5]

"Coach [Walsh] was very tough on us and we'd meet every morning before practice. We met every night. Actually we had organized tomorrow's practice at the night meeting, and in the morning we'd go through it again," recalled Bill McPherson. "Then we'd sometimes meet in the afternoon. We'd practice, then we'd meet after the players meeting at night. Bill would always keep the offensive guys later, poor Bobb McKittrick, bless his soul, he'd always keep him and his guys till about 10 or 10:15."[6]

Additionally, a precise training camp schedule ensured there was no wasted time on the practice field; it accelerated the learning process; and it enabled the staff to approach the game on a broad base rather than piecemeal. In other words, at each training camp, starting with the 1979 camp, the staff taught the system on a long-term basis. The players who were with the team in the early years didn't have to relearn the offense or defense; they already knew parts of the playbook and could continue to master their specific positions.

With the whole schedule mapped out for camp Walsh concentrated on mentally getting the best out of his players. To accomplish this he wanted his coaches to be positive and to teach using phrases like "let's try this," "do more of this," or "think about this" rather than to yell at the players and to point out what they did wrong. "It is important for the players to produce and reach their top physical potential. Do whatever it takes to get a player to that level," commented Walsh once to his staff.[7] He coached the coaches, too.

"During practice Bill always had a habit of carrying these three-by-five cards with him. He would record what he didn't like about practice," said Fred vonAppen, special teams coach. "He was a believer that if something went wrong in practice, that it was the coach's fault, the individual assistant coach's fault. But he told us this up front, so we knew. He said, 'If anybody's gonna get taken to task, it's going to be you. And I'm going to rip your ass in front of the players. So don't swell up and get all upset about it because it's gonna happen, and there's some psychology involved here to get the players to rally on behalf of the coach.' So, he would go through these three-by-five cards. And that was a painful experience because he'd go around the room; he liked to walk around and observe. So there were long days and nights at that place."[8]

The time had come to put the plan into motion. As camp neared Walsh and general manager John McVay weren't dealing with camp schedules; they were dealing with holdouts. The success the 49ers enjoyed during the past couple of seasons had left a few players under-paid. With the reporting date for camp coming up, several stars threat-ened to hold out if not given new contracts. Without new deals, Freddie Solomon, whose contract had expired, Eric Wright, Ronnie Lott, and Fred Dean all promised not to show up for camp. The rest of the 49ers knew it was the business side of the NFL. "Truth of the matter, hold-outs in training camp don't affect the team a whole a lot," said lineback-er Milt McColl. "It's usually players who have been around awhile, so they can get back into it more quickly than if they were injured. But I don't think the holdouts affected us too much."[9]

A few days before camp Bill Walsh headed to Rocklin and the cam-pus of Sierra College. "As soon as I leave my driveway and head to training camp, my whole life changes. I revert to the football part and it consumes me for months—more than it should, more than it should—it consumes me and it takes my life," said Walsh in a 1982 interview.[10] The Genius was now in football mode and the 1984 49ers were the beneficiaries. On his drive to Rocklin, the loss to the Redskins in the 1983 NFC Championship Game and the words of Dwight Hicks prob-ably crossed his mind. The 49ers had to get back to the Super Bowl.

On July 16 Walsh and the other coaches opened camp with the arrival of the rookies and selected veterans. "It was like entering into the unknown. As a rookie, [it was] your first exposure to the professional level and [to] where and how you would fit in. I was very nervous. This was my chance to make my dream come true," said rookie running back Derrick Harmon.[11] For the next thirty-four days Rocklin would be the home of the 1984 49ers and the beginning of their magical journey toward a nearly perfect season.

"Dwight [Hicks] summed it up in the locker room—about how bit-ter that taste was—and reminded us not to forget it. That was some-thing that stayed with us. That whole off-season was uncomfortable. So that meant the last two off-seasons had been uncomfortable. We won it [in 1981], then the next two off-seasons were just uncomfortable, and fortunately, things lined up that we had a pretty darn good team in '84 and a pretty good mind-set," said Keena Turner, linebacker.[12]

Players checked into their dorms with a sense of urgency. The no-frills dormitory rooms had air conditioning and televisions but little else. "Training camp is a necessary evil," said Allan Kennedy, offensive tackle. "They didn't give us a whole lot, put it that way."[13]

At 6:00 p.m. on July 19 the 49ers met as a team for the first time. The collective group of men who met that night had the mind-set of a team with no weaknesses. Everybody checked their egos at the door and put the team first. Every player knew his role. In Walsh's introductory speech to the team, he spoke of one thing that was in the back of everyone's mind. "The Super Bowl. Bill Walsh talked about that," said Bill Ring, running back. "He said 'this is our goal, to be world champions. Here's how we have to do it.'"[14]

Everything that the 49ers did in 1984 had a purpose. "When we came in for training camp—even for physicals—it's like everybody, without even talking about it, could just feel it. I think you could just feel [from] the thickness in the air that these guys are ready to go and to go to camp. We went to Rocklin and worked our butts off. Nobody complained. Everybody stayed healthy. . . . Everybody worked their butts off to push each other to that special place," said tight end Earl Cooper.[15]

"Training camp's never comfortable, but I think because the focus was so driven for that season and the preparation and not wanting to be in that position again [losing the 1983 NFC Championship Game] where it comes down to those kinds of plays, that really was the focus," said Keena Turner, linebacker. "Rocklin was something we were familiar with. We knew what to expect. It was really a process for us to get the work done. So it was intense, but that was expected."[16]

As Walsh spoke of getting to the Super Bowl, he looked around and saw a few missing faces. Absent were Freddie Solomon, Ronnie Lott, and Fred Dean. He signed Eric Wright to a new deal right before camp, but he also made a trade to protect his team in case the Lott holdout went longer than expected.

Walsh and McVay dealt a fourth-round pick to acquire ten-year veteran cornerback Mario Clark from the Buffalo Bills. "I had a relationship with Bill Walsh when he was at Stanford and I was at Oregon, so he knew about my one-on-one skills. When Ronnie was holding out, they got me for insurance at cornerback and [to] be the nickel back," said Clark. He quickly saw the difference between the Bills and the 49ers. "It was pretty rough. In Buffalo . . . you worked yourself in shape while training camp went along, but in San Francisco you had to be in shape the first day. That was the mentality that I noticed. So you had to get in shape pretty fast."[17]

The training camp practice schedule went as well as the weather allowed. "Those camps were very hot. In fact I always remember saying, 'My God, if I ever coach I'd move us out of Rocklin. I want to get out of here. It's too damn hot.' And yet, I realized when I became head coach, there was no better place," said George Seifert. "Bonding. It was a spot where you could all bond and come together in a very tough situation. The heat of some of our practices, I mean, there were times we couldn't even practice. But I think the team came together with that."[18]

Walsh didn't want his players beating up on each other in Rocklin's heat. He scheduled the more strenuous practice in the morning, when the heat wasn't as unbearable, and a shorter afternoon practice, enabling the team to remain fresh throughout camp.

"By that time Bill had adjusted the training camp schedule. So we probably had one of the best training camps and one of the most sensible training camps in the league," said Keith Fahnhorst, offensive tackle. "Bill saw the talent that we had on that team. So he wasn't going to beat the hell out of us in training camp. There wasn't any need to."[19]

"That was part of Bill's thing, you have to learn how to practice. Most of the afternoon practices were not in pads—there may be shoulder pads and helmets—but basically in shorts, shoulder pads, and helmets," said Jerry Attaway, 49ers physical development coordinator. "His big thing was that you have to learn how to practice. We don't want to hit all the time, and, of course, if you tell the guys that, they can buy into it. But once again, they can't buy into it thinking we're going to have an easy practice. So they had to learn to practice hard. Not have collisions and be prepared to do things full speed, learn how to practice because you can't beat each other up all year long. It's too long a season."[20]

The 49ers staff taught the players to go full speed without beating up their bodies, and the players noticed. "The most important thing that we focused on was the mental aspect of the game. So we did a lot of practicing with just helmets and working on our steps, our feet, our alignment. Let's take our first two, three steps. Need to be fast and gamelike so that we can have the timing down. Coach Walsh was big on speed. He felt like there was power in speed," said Manu Tuiasosopo, defensive tackle.[21] The typical two-a-day practice schedule looked like this:

7:15 a.m.   Wake-up call

7:15–8:00 a.m.	Breakfast
7:15–8:45 a.m.	Tape schedule
9:00–11:30 a.m.	Morning practice (full pads)
12:00 p.m.	Lunch break
3:00–3:45 p.m.	Group meetings
4:15–5:15 p.m.	Afternoon practice (sweats or shells)
6:00 p.m.	Dinner
7:00 p.m.	Special teams/meetings
9:30 p.m.	Staff meeting
11:00 p.m.	Curfew[22]

But when the schedule allowed, practices that involved hitting were a sight to behold. Some duels pitted friend against friend. "During the morning when it was cooler, it was a fistfight out there a lot of times. It got hot. We got hot. Player to player. My best friend Bill Ring, I remember getting in fights with him, and Bill would just go crazy, these two guys swinging at each other. Then later on we'd go have lunch together. I can't explain it. It was intense, and we knew the expectations were rising, and we knew something was special here. We just had no idea how special it was," said Ron Ferrari, linebacker.[23]

Usually 49er practices were the most competitive arena in the NFL. "[At camp] we didn't have real hard practices, but if you had one-on-one drills, that was always full speed," said Keith Fahnhorst, offensive tackle. "It was always taken seriously as far as developing technique and so on. So, yeah, 'Pee-wee' Dwaine Board was one of the better pass rushers; he didn't let up during practice at all. That was one way to get prepared."[24]

When the 49ers did hit, the coaches saw how competitive their players were and how they wanted to be the best they could possibly be. "I remember thinking that team was pretty special. We were very talented defensively. I remember sometimes in those practices, I talked about where we'd run blitzes, our offense couldn't even get the ball off. That's how good we were and how good our offense was," said George Seifert, defensive coordinator. "I remember that our practices were always very competitive. We did script some things, but a lot of it was just our defense versus our offense. Our practices were always very competitive. I think that had an awful lot to do with the success that we had, is that players every day practiced against outstanding people."[25]

"Practice was like a game to us. We'd treat it just like a game. Every practice was an opportunity to get better, and our players took advantage of that," said defensive backs coach Ray Rhodes. "Every day you went out and competed at a high level, every day. You wanted to make sure you were on that practice field, that you're not gonna let the offensive guys beat you. You're going to go out there every time the ball's in the air . . . that's what we looked at. We're competing for the ball. We're gonna make a play on it and Bill allowed you to do that."[26]

Even Bill Walsh got in on the act. "Bill was a competitive guy. We'd go out there and stop one of his plays, and he'd draw up a play in the dirt," continued Ray Rhodes. "He would draw one up in the dirt and then break the huddle. They'd come out and run the play against us, and they beat us on the play, and Bill turned around to the defense, 'Alright men, now go in and go to work.' So we'd have to always be ready to adjust to whatever Bill would do in practice. Some nights we'd be there two or three hours trying to figure out what Bill did."[27]

The competition on both sides of the ball never stopped throughout camp. The 49ers offense against the 49ers defense: the NFL's best versus the best. Both units always pushed each other to the limit to get better every practice, every day. "It was always great because we would practice against the best passing game in the world at the time. Most of our opponents were so much less complicated and less difficult to defend against than our own guys," said linebacker Riki Ellison. "Our offense was very quick, so we had to become quick to handle them. I thought it was a great training period, because we really trained against the best offense in football for the whole summer camp. That's what we did. So when you have to play against—for four weeks in camp—the best offense in the NFL, then [playing against other teams] it's not cake, but it's pretty damn easy. The other teams are not as challenging."[28]

Throughout camp the one-on-one battles of All-Pros and Pro Bowlers were a sight to see. Whether it was Ronnie Lott in man-to-man coverage on Dwight Clark, Keith Fahnhorst in pass-blocking drills against Dwaine Board, or Riki Ellison going head-to-head with Roger

Craig, the 49ers players got the best possible competition on a daily basis. "Yes, we got after it. Our run drill, I loved that. We knocked the shit out of the offensive line and the running backs as best we could," said Ellison. "I lived for that every day. I mean, John Ayers was unbelievable; he was an animal. I thought Ayers was one of the best guards I've ever faced. I had to play against him all the time. Randy Cross was great at the other guard position. Randy was super quick around the corner. Keith Fahnhorst was good down blocking. There were guys in that group who liked to hit. I was one of them. I'd do that drill every day for the rest of my life if I could. It was fun stuff."[29]

"We had one-on-one sessions with our wide receivers and our defensive backs—man, it was like game time," said Roger Craig, fullback. "Even with our linebackers, it was vicious. Bill would only allow us to do it for a short period of time because he believed in keeping us fresh and keeping us mentally sharp in our game and not getting us hurt."[30] Walsh and his staff let their guys compete and then called them off enough to save their legs and body. But Walsh was giving his players a platform to perform and, more importantly, to compete.

It was also a time for the players to bond. "How impactful our practices were stemmed all the way back from training camp. They just kept the practices hard, tough. By the time we got to the game, that was the easy part. Because we had practiced all week so hard against each other and, as we say, would talk smack back and forth. We're practicing our skills and we're trying to shut them down and not allow them to catch a ball. The sideline, we would just roar and cheer. The receivers core, they would be quiet. Then when the receivers would make a catch, all of a sudden, the receivers are yelling and screaming. We were basically making each other better. We did that very well for many years," said Carlton Williamson, strong safety.[31]

Even when the one-on-one competition was going on, there was also time for teammates to help each other. "There wasn't a day that went by that John Ayers didn't take me aside and say, 'Hey Stov, I saw you lean in here. I saw you looking in here.' He always helped me and there aren't a lot of players who will do that," said Jeff Stover, defensive end. "With John Ayers it was just very special. He worked with me all the time on things he saw. Then I'd work with him. A lot of times he'd stay after practice and work with me. We went against All-Pros. All that did was make us better."[32]

As training camp progressed, Walsh heard some good news from general manager John McVay: Freddie Solomon, after missing five days, and Ronnie Lott, after missing eleven days, signed new contracts and reported to camp. "It's been difficult not to be at camp. I've wanted to be with my teammates. You want to be loyal to them," said Lott to the media.[33] He was needed more than ever when backup cornerback Tim Collier tore his Achilles tendon and was out for the year.

Upon the advice of his agent, Fred Dean was the only remaining holdout. "I'd been in the league for a few years. I'm getting to the end of the game. I wanted to set myself up after football," said Dean. "Football lasts as long as you're playing it. It made me understand that there's much more to the game than just the game itself. I wanted to help myself and my family."[34] Walsh wasn't confident about signing Dean, his best pass rusher, because the two sides were miles apart. He called the current offer by Dean's agent a "Star Wars–type contract."[35]

On the practice field the team was nearly complete and putting in the hours to get itself ready for the season. There was little time for anything else. Walsh made sure of that. But any football team needs some time to wind down. Although their free time in Rocklin was limited, the 49ers found ways to cast off the daily grind of training camp.

PRACTICAL JOKES

One of the timed-honored traditions at 49ers summer camp in Rocklin was the practical joke, especially those perpetrated by superstar quarterback Joe Montana, nicknamed "bicycle thief." With the dormitories on one side and the locker room and meeting rooms on the other side of campus, most players were given a bicycle to get around. After a long day of practice and meetings, most 49ers wanted to get back to their dorm rooms to sleep. Lo and behold, after a 10:00 p.m. meeting, players would find their bicycles missing or chained up outside the meeting building.[36]

"Some guys would bring bikes and some guys would just bring their Ferrari up there. Number 16 [Montana]. If you didn't lock your bike, guys would steal your bike. It got so ridiculous. I always knew who stole my bike. It's freakin' Montana trying to steal my bike," said a laughing Ron Ferrari, linebacker. "So I remember I put his bike so high in the tree. I almost got hurt climbing the tree to put it up there. It's heckle or be heckled. And there's nothing more irritating to see than somebody riding your bike. You'd have to be a detective, like Columbo, and casually ask, 'Did you see Joe ride here? Did Joe come by here?' Then when he was caught he'd smile and just say, 'Yeah, I got it and there's nothing you can do about it,' and ride off with your damn bike. It was a good time. It was always comic relief. If I was the butt of the jokes, it was great. If we could make fun of Joe, that was good, too."[37]

"Joe always had a great sense of humor, and I mean that was all in fun and games. He was just fantastic. During that time when you're at camp, you need something to . . . break that hard ice. Something different to take your mind off whatever else might be going on," said defensive end Lawrence Pillers.[38]

"People used to steal my bike. Put them in trees, put them on top of roofs of the dorms, we did all those things to keep entertained," said fullback Roger Craig. "I can remember one day somebody put baby powder all over Freddie Solomon's bed. They put spiders and snakes in the rooms. That's what kept us going."[39]

Sometimes the practical jokes occurred on the field. "Did anyone tell you the story about Russ Francis and his friend . . . the P-51 at training camp? . . . He wasn't in the plane. A friend of his was in the plane. They dive-bombed the practice, and we all [nearly] had a heart attack. The guy got suspended for a year, the pilot. He almost hit Robert Yanagi [49ers staff assistant who was in the tower]. . . . I swear this plane was probably thirty feet from the top of the tower. Very scary," said Bill Ring, running back.[40]

Walsh had a great sense of humor, but probably didn't laugh at Francis's prank. Only later would he shake his head about the stunt. While practical jokes were acceptable at 49ers camp, hazing was a different story. Walsh felt hazing was dehumanizing, especially for rookies. He recognized that rookies had a lot of work to do during camp— learning a new system, adapting to a new environment—and that hazing would limit their progress. Hazing did nothing to bond a team, said Paul Brown frequently when discussing the issue. "There should be none of it. We're all professionals."[41]

BUNZ & COMPANY

When the players did get a free evening from camp, usually Wednesday night, some of them went to the White Front Tavern in town or to a new watering hole in Roseville, a ten-minute drive from Sierra College. During the summer, linebacker Dan Bunz, a Roseville native who lived on a ranch just outside Rocklin, opened a new restaurant and bar called Bunz & Company. "There was nothing really big in Roseville, nothing. So I thought [of opening] a sports bar and restaurant. There was a little nursery there that I bought the property. I redesigned the building and that was the spot everybody would go to in Roseville. The people loved it," said Bunz. [42]

During training camp several of Bunz's teammates visited his new restaurant. "We'd go to Bunz & Co. all the time. He had a great bar there. On our day off, all the guys would go over there. A lot of the fans lived in that area. They would come over and knew that we would be there," said Jim Stuckey, defensive end. "It was a chance for us for a couple of hours to go relax and get away from the everyday grind of training camp. But he had a great bar. It was good fun all the time." [43]

Forty-niners players repeatedly stopped in to offer support to one of their teammates, as well as to get some food and drinks that weren't from the team's training table. "Remember going over there, eating some hot wings for a meet and greet," recalled Dana McLemore, defensive back. [44] They also caught some of the Summer Olympics on ABC, cheering "USA! USA!" during the gymnastics competition and rooting for teammate and shot-putter Michael Carter. "We went over to Bunz & Co. and watched him throw in the Olympics," recalled defensive end Dwaine Board. "It was great." [45] Carter would make his country and his teammates proud by winning a silver medal in the shot put. His best toss of 21.09 meters was topped by Italy's Alessandro Andrei's throw of 21.26 meters.

"I always thought sports brought people together. People love sports—it brings people together—so bringing food and good sports—a little bit of music once in a while—brought people together," said Bunz. [46]

POOLSIDE AND FISHING DERBY

One of the favorite spots for players between practice sessions was the outdoor pool on campus. Tight end Russ Francis spent so much time there going off the high dive that he was given the nickname "Flipper." Players relaxed and soothed their bodies in the pool's cool water, especially the defensive line. "Bill kept us fresh. I remember going to the pool after the morning practice and lying in the pool. It was the only time I've come out of training camp with a tan," recalled defensive end Jim Stuckey.[47]

"I always cooled down with a couple of the other linemen," said Manu Tuiasosopo, defensive tackle. "That was just part of my ritual at training camp to go and take a dip in the pool there at Rocklin."[48]

Walsh also lightened the rigors of training camp by bringing his squad together for an annual fishing derby. The players relaxed away from the practice field trying to lasso a fish or two. "Walsh would stock the watering hole there in Rocklin with catfish," said Manu Tuiasosopo. "It was a way to create morale, to help bring guys together. I mean, gosh, that was awesome. It worked."[49] One player—fullback Roger Craig—caught something totally different. "It's called the catfish derby and they named it after me," said Craig. "Freddie Solomon nicknamed me 'catfish' because of the way I ran through the holes and [the way that] my eyes would light up. I was running to see where the hole was to get through, no so much of someone tackling me. So they had this catfish derby where you could win prizes. So that kind of broke up the monotony of training camp."[50]

Solomon also found time to play catch with a coach's son. "I always took my oldest son up there with me and he would be a ball boy," said special teams coach Fred vonAppen. "Freddie Solomon used to stay after practice and throw him some balls and teach him how to catch the ball. Unfortunately, he didn't teach him how to run fast enough, but he taught him how to catch the ball."[51]

It was truly a family forming in Rocklin. The 49ers family. Even while enjoying the fun and sun, football wasn't far from the minds of the 49ers players. "You might find a little time to watch TV, but I don't remember watching a whole lot, because you're always meeting in the evening too, after dinner. You might have an hour or two to your own," recalled Allan Kennedy, offensive tackle. "Either you were studying the playbook or you found some time just to relax. We didn't have computers, laptops, or cell phones. We got a couple of watering holes there, but more often than not it was pretty much focused on just making the team."[52]

At Rocklin the 49ers were bonding. But the lessons that the coaches wanted to impart to the players had to move from the Sierra College classrooms to the professional football field.

8

STUDENTS OF THE GAME

It was heaven. To me training camp was heaven, because I was in great shape all the time. But it was a time of learning because we didn't beat ourselves up in training camp. We did more of the mental side of the game. We studied. We were students of the game.
—Roger Craig, 49ers fullback[1]

Within the classrooms at Sierra College, the 49ers coaching staff installed the team's offensive and defensive systems. "The core of any type of detailed preparation is the need for maximizing 'meaningful' repetition. Accordingly, as the head coach, you have to develop and implement a plan that ensures that every player gets the meaningful repetitions he needs to refine his skills and techniques," Walsh told his coaches.[2]

Sierra College became Football 101, where 49ers players learned from the best staff in football. Both playbooks were incredibly detailed—around 800 pages each—and players had to learn them in roughly thirty-four days. Veterans of the system had a head start on everybody else; the rookies and newcomers had to learn everything, even how to line up. "George Seifert had some sophisticated schemes, and it took me awhile to get used to them. Even the way I lined up, my stance, was different than [when I was in] Buffalo. So I had to learn and he was a great teacher," said cornerback Mario Clark.[3] Learning the playbook started in the classroom and lasted all day.

DEFENSIVE MEETINGS

Getting to the defensive meetings involved a leisurely stroll across campus. "We had to do that trek every damn morning up the hill. The meeting rooms were about a half a mile away from the sleeping arrangements," said Riki Ellison, linebacker. "You were struggling to stay awake in the damn meetings after morning practice. They put the thermostat down to 40 degrees to make sure you can't fall asleep. Then you had those night meetings that would go on and on and on, and you're falling asleep and you only have an hour before bed check. But they were fun times."[4]

"[Our meetings] had to be specific. That was part of our teaching method. Bill was one of the first in the NFL to be specific during that particular era and he probably learned that from Paul Brown, who was very specific for his era and who was an innovator. Bill was an innovator," said George Seifert, defensive coordinator. "So it was kind of our method and our theme to be specific in those meetings."[5]

In 1984 situational substitutions were the hallmark of the 49ers defense. Seifert would use every man on the roster. "George was a perfectionist. He wanted everybody to know his responsibility and to do his job. That was the bottom line. Know your responsibility and do your job," said defensive end Dwaine Board.[6] Walsh would eventually use nine defensive linemen and nine linebackers throughout the 1984 season. The 49ers base defense was a 3–4 front, but they were not likely to use the same eleven players for two consecutive downs unless the other team made a first down.

The starting 3–4 unit in 1984 was usually, from left to right, Lawrence Pillers, Manu Tuiasosopo, and Dwaine Board on the line and Dan Bunz (strong side), Riki Ellison, Jack Reynolds, and Keena Turner (weak side) at linebacker. If they stayed in a 3–4 with second-and-long, Jim Fahnhorst would often replace Reynolds. If they switched to a 4–3 formation, Bunz and Reynolds would come out, and Ron Ferrari and another lineman—either Michael Carter or Jim Stuckey—would go in.

If it was second-and-medium (five or six yards), the 49ers would likely shift to a nickel package, adding a defensive back, usually safety Tom Holmoe. Seifert would replace Pillers with Fred Dean, their best pass rusher; Tuiasosopo with Jeff Stover; and Bunz with either Milt McColl or Todd Shell.

For second-and-short, they used a four-man front of Board, Tuiaso-sopo, Carter, and Kelcher, and either Pillers or Stuckey with Ellison, Turner, and Bunz at linebacker. When it appeared that the other team wanted to throw on third down, the 49ers would make sure their best pass rushers were in. With goal line or short yardage, Louie Kelcher and the best run stoppers would be in. Overall, the down, yards needed for a first down, the score, and the quarter dictated the alignment Seifert would use.

Every defender knew his role and learned his position. "It was inspiring to be around guys who wanted to learn the game and try to keep it simple: 'Do your assignment and everything will just fall in place,'" said Tuiasosopo.[7]

"I don't think our schemes are that much different than what other teams use," commented rookie linebacker Todd Shell to the press. "That we have so many people is what makes us different."[8] Seifert had the depth to use his players strategically, as if playing chess. "Different players have different styles, and they can be fresher when they come into the game. It's like when a team has three good running backs. Here comes the third one to start hammering you," he remarked during the 1984 season.[9]

The secondary—which featured cornerbacks Eric Wright and Ronnie Lott and safeties Dwight Hicks and Carlton Williamson—had been together since 1981. Playing mostly zone with a mix of man-to-man defense, Seifert and defensive backs coach Ray Rhodes counted on this veteran group to set the tone for the rest of the defense. "In practice or in the game, we're pushing each other to get better. We often tried to make it game-situation plays. We had to make those plays in practice because Ray [Rhodes] instilled in us that we're going to practice the way we play," said Carlton Williamson, safety. "If we were making mistakes in practice, we had to iron it out and get it corrected then, because we knew what it was gonna take in the live situation in the game. And Ray was great at that with us. He kept us laughing. He kept it free spirited in the secondary. We were loose because of that. He would keep us laughing and relaxed at all times. We really admired that about Ray."[10]

Professor George and his staff challenged his players to understand what they wanted to do in 1984 with all the variations to the scheme. The combination of the front seven working with the secondary created a learning curve for every player. Seifert's 800-page playbook was both very detailed and very advanced by NFL standards in 1984. "Just unbelievable. George would systematically implement these plays, and there were over 100. Of the 100, there were three to six different audibles, and you had to know them all," said Williamson. "But in the course of the game, if something's not working, George would call a play out of that playbook. We may not have practiced this in three weeks, but he'll reach back in that playbook. So you had to be prepared and know what's going on even though we didn't get a chance to work on it all the time. So it was detailed, but that's what training camp was all about. All of that was drilled into us while we were in training camp."[11]

"Well, we came into camp in shape. So we knew that you'd come to camp in shape, and it was the mental aspect of the game that you had to digest. You had to ingrain it in your mind. He had his time lines down and he expected us to get it. Get it fast, get it done, and get off the field. But it was a fun time. . . . He was a forward-thinking coach," said defensive end Jim Stuckey.[12]

"That thing [playbook] was thick. I couldn't even believe it. I felt like I was in my first year at UCLA in poly science. The reading material was something else," said Blanchard Montgomery, linebacker.[13]

Learning the playbook was equally daunting for both rookies and free agents new to the 49ers. "I remember when I first got there, the playbook was 800 pages. He handed me it and told me to memorize it in two weeks. He said that tongue-in-cheek," said linebacker Jim Fahnhorst. "There were so many calls that you had to make as an inside linebacker. If there is a change depending on our defense, almost all our defenses were where the passing strength was. If you had two wide receivers, that was a passing strength, or if you had a tight end and a wide receiver, that was a passing strength. So if the passing strength changes, you have to call out the line changes to the other side. For instance: east, go to the right; west, to the left. Port to the left, star to the right; you would have to get your nose down there so they could hear the call. 'Port, star, star, rocket, rocket!' So you're making sure you're giving all the calls to the defensive linemen, [while listening to] what Ronnie [Lott in the secondary] was saying, any changes in coverage. So you had to listen and shout, because linemen have their heads in the dirt and they can't hear you unless you're right down there; you had to tell them and get right back to your spot. It was a great scheme. We had some great players; we were always in the top five in defense. I don't think we were ever number one, but we were always in the top five in [fewest] points given up during that time."[14]

Entering his second season as defensive coordinator, George Seifert adopted Walsh's philosophy of a sophiscated scheme. He wanted his players to strive for perfection. That's why Walsh promoted him. "George was a lot like Bill. He was into more complexity, whereas [Chuck] Studley was simple and simplified. George had a complexity to his thought process and how he saw defenses that really mirrored what Bill thought about execution and scheme and strategy, which we then started to develop on the defensive side of the ball," said Keena Turner, linebacker.[15]

The 49ers defensive players came to learn every day during camp. There were no easy days in the classroom. During the month at Sierra College defensive players always helped each other. "It was all football. It was hard. It was in your face. It was certainly at a high level. It really felt like a new team from the year before. They were all enthusiastic to learn about this special system. So there was a lot more tension. There was a lot more mentoring. There was a lot more guys helping guys. And when you have that kind of communication, you're going to have a successful organization. So we talked about it in film. In film and practice is excruciatingly detailed and some of these guys are like, 'Wow, you guys do this all the time?' 'Yep. Get used to it.' Everything was serious. As Bill would say, 'no ass grabbing in practice,'" said Ron Ferrari, linebacker.[16]

OFFENSIVE MEETINGS

On the offensive side of the ball Bill Walsh and his staff were installing the West Coast offense. Mirroring the same work ethic and philosophy Seifert instilled in his defense, Walsh and his offensive staff worked long and hard getting the offense drilled into their players' minds. Absorbing an 800-page playbook was no easy task. "That was another challenge. I didn't know so many plays could exist in a game of football. I never knew linemen could have so many ways of blocking," said Derrick Harmon.[17] The rookie from Cornell had no need for worry because

Walsh drafted and signed intelligent men to learn a complicated system.

"It was heaven. To me training camp was heaven because I was in great shape all the time. But it was a time of learning because we didn't beat ourselves up in training camp. We did more of the mental side of the game. We studied. We were students of the game," said fullback Roger Craig. "It was like going back to college again, because we installed over 100 passes a game. Different routes, different formations. So it's all about timing. Bill Walsh made us really smart football players. . . . Our system was complex. Very complex. You can't fake it and go out and try to run it. The timing was so critical. Everything is all timed out, from Joe's three steps, drop back, to his five steps, to his seven steps. All those steps were timing routes for our receivers to run their routes to the proper depths where you could get the ball to them on time. Bill was big on timing."

Continued Craig, "We would run one play 100 times till we got it right. He was a perfectionist and that's what we needed in our system. We needed that kind of guidance from a guy because we had the talent. But we needed the guidance of the guy who will always step in, pull you aside, and say, 'you're not doing it right.' He did it to Joe [Montana], he did it to all of us. He didn't show any favoritism."[18]

"[Walsh] was a great believer that you practice absolutely full speed because timing is the reason that you have teamwork. It's the reason that you work together, and you can't get that in the off-season. You have to get that in training camp," said Paul Hackett, quarterbacks and wide receivers coach.[19]

Absorbing Walsh's playbook not only took timing but also intelligence. Training camp was set up to give his players the maximum number of opportunities to learn the system. "We had about 165 plays usually, which is pretty daunting, especially when Joe [Montana] could audible to a combination of different plays off that 165," said running back Bill Ring. "You had to have that. If you think in football, you're dead. It's gotta be automatic. So you gotta really do your homework, you had to be a student to master that playbook. To really know all the intricacies of all the different nuances within the playbook. Picking up different reads on the defense. Looking at the defensive fronts and adjusting to that."[20]

For one rookie who was also learning a new position, it was an eye-opening experience. "I was lost. Especially [after] moving positions, and the terminology was vastly different at Georgia. We were basically a running team, and they had all these passes and these different types of passes. It took a while to grasp the concept of what we were doing. Just moving from where I was at Georgia to this big [playbook], it was very intimidating," said Guy McIntyre, offensive guard.[21]

The 49ers became a bunch of football nerds who absorbed everything they were taught— even the stars continually gained useful knowledge from the coaches. Every day at camp Joe Montana put on his thinking cap. "Joe didn't take off any plays in training camp. He didn't take off a play and say, 'Hey, let the third-string guy take it.' Joe got in there just as if he was still learning the craft," said tight end Earl Cooper. "That's the character that he brought to the team and that's what a lot of guys really appreciated about Joe Montana. Being a hard worker. Being himself and not looking down his nose at anybody. He just got right in there and worked just as hard as everybody."[22]

Walsh's playbook included nearly 200 passing and running plays, several of which would be covered every day at camp. His multiple formations, motions, shifting, blocking, and everything else that was in the playbook was covered during the thirty-four days at Rocklin. Because Walsh took a detailed approach to his practice schedule, he was able to take full advantage of the available practice time. This minute-to-minute plan provided his offense with more than 450 offensive snaps—not including live scrimmage plays—in its initial fifteen training camp workouts. An average NFL team runs approximately 1,000 plays during the regular season; the 450-plus offensive snaps represent less than half a season's work in just two weeks' time.

The first two preseason games came and went with a whisper (against the Los Angeles Raiders and at the Denver Broncos). Walsh was happy that his team came out with no serious injuries. He did have a problem with his punting competition. Neither Orsoz nor Skladany was standing out. But he got some good news about one of the two remaining missing players: rookie Michael Carter, his fifth-round pick from SMU, was coming to camp.

After winning a silver medal in Los Angeles at the Summer Olympics on August 14, Carter finally made it to Rocklin. "It was great. I met a lot of people from around the world. It was a great experience. I wouldn't trade it for anything else in the world," said Carter.[23]

"When the Olympics were over and he came to camp, everybody stood up and gave him a standing ovation," recalled offensive tackle Allan Kennedy.[24] His new teammates quickly noticed that Carter was all business as a rookie. "Michael was quiet, didn't smile, and he was always angry. Then after awhile he kind of loosened up, and the guys got used to his demeanor and the things he did," said Dwaine Board. "The guy had the strongest hands I've ever seen on a player."[25]

Carter had a lot of ground to make up. First was tackling the playbook. "When he [Seifert] put that book in my hand, I just looked at it. 'You got to be kidding?' College wasn't that much [work]. So I went to my dorm room, and I just studied it. I highlighted everything that pertained to a nose tackle. I didn't even try to worry about the ends or the linebackers. I said, 'Let me just focus on me for right now.' So I learned it," said Carter.

Carter had only four days at Rocklin and nineteen days till the 49ers first regular-season game. "I knew going in I was going to be two and a half weeks late at training camp. But once I got there, I didn't really know what to expect," said Carter. "I believe I showed up on a Wednesday or Thursday. All I remember is that I had one day of watching them practice. I believe it was a walk-through—they had a game on Friday—and Bill McPherson, he looked at me and said, 'Big fella, you ready to suit up? You ready to go at it?' I looked at him. I said, 'Tomorrow?' He said, 'Yeah.' Oh my Lord. I hadn't practiced or anything. But going into the game, I was telling myself, 'I don't know the plays. Just show them that you can play football. Show them that you have speed. Show them you have quickness and strength.' When the ball was hiked, I was going to hit whatever was in front of me."[26] The rookie from SMU had nothing to worry about. He was a football player. Throughout 1984 he would prove it.

As training camp at Sierra College was coming to a conclusion, the players took time to enjoy their last days by the pool. One day a *San Francisco Chronicle* photographer, Fred Larson, captured some photos of the 49ers relaxing poolside. One of the photos appeared in the sporting green section of the paper. The photo showed Dwight Clark and Joe Montana in their bathing suits soaking up the sun. The paper was flooded with thousands of requests for the photo, mostly from males.[27]

After a 35–15 shellacking by the San Diego Chargers—and another poor performance by his punters—Walsh was ready to break camp. "This is my thirty-fifth [NFL] training camp," said linebackers coach Norb Hecker to Frank Cooney of the *San Francisco Examiner* as he packed up to leave Rocklin. "And I'm already looking forward to my thirty-sixth training camp. So, either I must like it and think it is fun, or I must be nuts."[28] The following day, August 19, the 49ers left the peaceful environment of Sierra College and the 100-degree temperatures of Rocklin to return to the team facility at Redwood City. What a difference 100 miles makes. Temperatures were 95 degrees or higher—including seven days with temperatures greater than 100 degrees—on twenty-one of the thirty-four days spent in Rocklin. The first day back in Redwood City the thermometer read 81 degrees.[29]

Walsh and his staff were now just nine days away from having to set their roster at forty-nine men. The last preseason game was an uneventful 17–7 win over the Seattle Seahawks at Candlestick Park. No major injuries occurred and Walsh made his final assessments for the roster. Tom Orosz beat out Tom Skladany for the punter's job. But the main battle was the last remaining spot at running back, where veteran Jeff Moore lost the final spot to Carl Monroe and rookie Derrick Harmon, the ninth-round pick from Cornell. Walsh's team was so deep that he released veterans Frank LeMaster and James Scott. He would keep seven defensive linemen—eight counting holdout Fred Dean—and nine linebackers.

A week before the season opener the 49ers checked the waiver wire and found a name they liked. Walsh and McVay signed linebacker Mike Walter, who had just been released by the Dallas Cowboys. The Cowboys drafted four linebackers in the 1984 draft, so they cut Walter, whom they drafted in the second round in 1983. "It was tough. It was devastating. Everything in my career before that had been a positive step forward, and all of a sudden it's just done and you don't know whether you're going to be picked up by anyone. They have a twenty-four-hour waiver period once they put you on waivers," said Walter. "But I was all ready. I was packing up my apartment, ready to go back to school at Oregon, and I ended up getting a call from John McVay, their general manager, saying they had claimed me off waivers."[30]

Walsh liked what he saw of Walter on film when he was at the University of Oregon, so he was delighted to pick him up off waivers from the Cowboys. "It was a completely different organization when I got there. It was amazing because I got there on a Wednesday and we left on a Friday to play a game. The first game was in Detroit. So you get there on a Wednesday, midday, and they threw me a locker between Matt Cavanaugh and Joe Montana. I wasn't even with the linebackers," said Walter.[31] It didn't matter that he wasn't with the linebackers. Walter would fit right in with the 49ers family, spending the next ten years playing in San Francisco.

Walsh and his staff had now accomplished what they wanted to do in preparing the squad for the upcoming season. The players knew their time in Rocklin would make a difference. "When the season started we were always fresher than everybody else. We all had fresh legs, no bumps, no bruises," said Dana McLemore, defensive back. "I would talk to my friends around the league, and they said, 'Man, we been hitting, we practice in pads all year long.' And I would tell guys, 'We practiced in shoulder pads, shorts, and helmets.' We tried to get through training camp as healthy as possible."[32]

The Genius had a fresh, veteran team that spent their time at Rocklin learning the system and becoming a very close team, an experience that only training camp can provide. Thirty-four days with just forty-nine players and eleven coaches. This team would fight for each other and were hungry to prove they were the best team in the National Football League.

Part III

The 1984 Regular Season

9

SEPTEMBER

Week 1 at Detroit Lions (September 2)
Week 2 vs. Washington Redskins (Monday, September 10)
Week 3 vs. New Orleans Saints (September 16)
Week 4 at Philadelphia Eagles (September 23)
Week 5 vs. Atlanta Falcons (September 30)

With training camp finished and the season opener against the Detroit Lions just a week away, Bill Walsh and his staff started putting together their initial game plans for week 1. Like every other Monday throughout the season, Walsh got his cup of coffee and holed up in his corner office in Redwood City, organizing the offensive side while George Seifert gathered with his defensive staff down the hall. At his desk Walsh watched film and drew up every single play—running and passing—by hand. Sometimes up to 100 plays a week.

"This was the first time that I saw fifteen to twenty runs in a game and close to seventy-five, eighty passes in a game. There was a little package of plays for every possible situation: on your own one-yard line, on the goal line, or in the last minute of a game. Everything was very situation oriented," said Paul Hackett, quarterbacks and wide receivers coach. "So that meant that there would be a lot of drawings and a lot of passes that would go into the game plan, most of which Bill drew every week. He drew them in longhand by himself. Then he had me go over them to sort of check them over. So it was very extensive."[1]

It was something Walsh did since becoming the 49ers head coach. It was a ritual he loved.

Taking a quick break on this particular Monday, Walsh walked down the hall to chat with Neal Dahlen, head of research and development. He had an idea he wanted to run by him. "He wanted somebody to document each offensive installation and team meeting so that he could refer to them during the week. Just taking notes was basically what it was," said Dahlen. "If he said something on Tuesday, he wanted it documented if he had to refer back to it and so on. I thought, 'Gee whiz, this would drive me nuts.' I didn't like taking notes in college, let alone [here] . . . so I suggested that we tape them instead . . . and, of course, that worked out just fine. Ever since that time, we taped every meeting. I had a recorder at my desk upstairs. There would be times when I'd get called a little bit late or have to run up and turn the tape on. Of course, you'd have to change the tape and you'd miss a couple of minutes or something, but basically 95 to 98 percent of what he had to say in the offensive meeting room was taped."[2]

Throughout the 1984 season Dahlen videotaped every 49ers team meeting and offensive installation meeting. These tapes showed Walsh at his most comfortable and best as a teacher. "He was the most skilled teacher that I've ever encountered. He was able to explain [things] extremely well. When he was in a room with a team and teaching the group, he was just marvelous," said Dahlen.[3]

Walsh's offensive meetings tended to be very long. He went over each play himself, explaining to all eleven men their responsibilities, whether playside or backside. The 49ers players were never restless or dull when Walsh was at the head of the classroom. "The funny thing is, we had long meetings—they would go for hours—but they weren't boring. They were engaging," said fullback Roger Craig. "Every time Bill Walsh would talk, I had goose bumps listening to his motivational talk before practice or before our meetings. He was one of those guys who captured your attention when he talked. He made it feel real, and that's what kept us motivated and so energetic to go out and be willing to sacrifice and do something different. Those are the things we focus on. How we make ourselves better and by having that kind of attitude, you gotta bring greatness out of it. Out of yourself and our system, and you're going to win. That was our mentality."[4]

Walsh spoke to his team about everything. Before the team broke up into offense and defense meetings to plan for the Lions, he lectured his squad on diet (meet with Jerry Attaway), sleeping habits, living arrangements, salaries (save your money, he preached), business deals, drugs, and drinking (don't get into bad habits). He also talked about winning. "Bill was way ahead of his time. He'd talk about what it would take to win a world championship. He talked about the teams, the entire league. He'd always make a point of letting everybody know before the season started. 'So all the teams, this time of year, they all want to win the Super Bowl. Everybody wants to win the Super Bowl, but there are only a few teams that are really competing, and we're one of them. We'll be competing each year for a Super Bowl run.' He would explain it to everybody, and he'd meticulously go through every aspect of the season—every game, what it would take to win each game. I just thought that he was way ahead of the league at that time and its thinking," said Ray Rhodes, defensive backs coach.[5]

The 49ers then turned their attention to the Lions. Each game Walsh and the offensive coaches evaluated the defensive personnel of their opponent. Looking at the Lions defense, Bobb McKittrick talked highly of Pro Bowl defensive tackle Doug English, describing him as "one of the best in the game." The Lions ranked eleventh in total defense in 1983 and gave the 49ers all they could handle in the 1983 NFC divisional playoff game, holding the 49ers offense to just 291 total yards. A missed forty-three-yard field goal attempt by Eddie Murray of the Lions enabled the 49ers to salvage a 24–23 victory. Speaking to his offense, Walsh stressed better red zone execution.

> Blocking has to be crisp, ball carrier running crisp near goal line. We've gotta get into the end zone. You start getting those three pointers—they got Billy Sims on their team—it will hurt you. We'll be down there and get three field goals, and they'll get one touchdown and one field goal and they'll beat us, that simple. Have to get into the end zone.[6]

Scoring touchdowns against the Lions is what Walsh preached all week to his offensive players. If they were going to get back to the Super Bowl, Walsh wanted his offense to focus on scoring touchdowns, not field goals. In 1984 he instilled this into every player, not just his stars like Joe Montana or Dwight Clark. While watching film of the Lions, he noticed one of their outside linebackers struggle in pass coverage to the flat while in the red zone. So Walsh drew up a goal-line play for backup running back Carl Monroe, one of the quickest players on the team. In one of the meetings during the week, he went over the play. "Double Wing Left, Sprint Halfback Option: our halfback, Carl Monroe, will do this, so be ready. Stutter, then break flat—should be a touchdown,"[7] Walsh told the whole offensive team. The 49ers coaches would give every man on the team a role in 1984 and expect him to perform. Instead of talking to the starters only, the coaches—especially Walsh in the offensive meetings—made clear these roles while allowing the rest of the team to see who was included in the game plans.

"Walsh was one of those coaches who was called a genius. But what Walsh did [was], if I could run the quick trap, that's the play he would design for me. Whatever you did well, he designed that play for you. And that fit into the game plan. He fit the players into the game plan. So he got the best of every player, designing a play or plays around that player," said running back Wendell Tyler.[8]

"Every player knew. You knew your role, from Roger Craig to Russ Francis or John Frank, to Dwight Clark to Mike Wilson. He made it so that everybody had a play and they felt really good that they were going to contribute. I think it was a good method and a lot of NFL teams still do it," said wide receiver Mike Wilson.[9]

In 1984 the 49ers coaches would use all forty-nine players in every game, and every Niners player would contribute to the team's winning ways. After a great week of practice, the 49ers flew to Detroit for their first regular-season game. At the hotel on Saturday night Walsh met with his offensive team to perform another 49ers ritual, introducing the squad's first twenty-five plays. A tradition he started as an assistant, Walsh improved upon this technique with the 49ers by introducing the plays the night before the game, which gave his offensive players a night to focus on those specific plays. It was a philosophy unique to Walsh— no other NFL coach was doing it at that time.

"All of this is new [to me]. I'm thinking everybody does this. I don't know what other people are doing. I'm just thinking, 'OK, this is the NFL. This is what everybody does the night before the game. They get up and they put plays on the board.' I didn't know how unique it was because I had never experienced anything else," said rookie guard Guy McIntyre.[10]

Most veteran 49ers offensive players knew to expect the scripted plays, and they loved being included in the game plan. "Those wouldn't be put in until Saturday night before the game. By that time you could concentrate on those plays, and you knew what was going to be called the next game. But also you could tell by those plays what the tone of the offense was going to be that day. So that was real important to us," said Keith Fahnhorst, offensive tackle. "What was amazing was that we actually did follow that script. . . . Bill and the offensive coaches had to anticipate not only what we were gonna see early in the game, but the adjustments that the defense would make. So that's why we were able to stick to the script. It was vital as far as seeing what was going to be important that day and being able to concentrate on what the early calls were going to be."[11]

"That was good for me because Bill Walsh knew his analytics. He detected the other team's patterns, what they do. That's where the analytics come in: understanding what [formation] their defenses are in, when they're going to blitz, how many times they blitz. He looked at film over and over and over. He had it down to a science, and he could put [in] his first twenty-five plays and be confident and not deviate from those twenty-five plays. That's pretty amazing. That's a genius. When you can do things like that, that means you know your analytics and your profession," said fullback Roger Craig.[12]

Knowing the first twenty-five plays relaxed the players by preventing them from overthinking them or putting undue pressure on themselves with less than twenty-four hours before game time. "One, it allowed a player to relax. Instead of going to sleep the night before the game with no idea what the first play is going to be—you're nervous and you can't sleep—it put that to rest. It made you relax and focus on something," said Mike Wilson, wide receiver. "You could go to sleep at night, and Walsh always said, 'Go ahead and close your eyes and think about it and say, "OK, if I get this defense, I'm going to do this."' You know, for me as a receiver, did I get press [man-to-man], is this guy off [zone], is he covering two? You know that there are three adjustments that you can make, and you can think through them, go right down the list, and you're ready. It prepared you. It made you relax. You felt confident that no matter what the defense gave you, you were prepared."[13]

Walsh's scripted plays became a staple during his 49ers coaching days, and scripted plays are used throughout the NFL today. However, on September 2, the first twenty-five plays didn't provide a strong start against the Lions. Roaming the sidelines, wearing a white 49ers golf shirt with gold khakis, Bill Walsh put on his headset so he could talk to assistant Paul Hackett, who was up in the booth. Next to Hackett was Jerry Attaway, charting the defensive fronts for the offensive coaches. Most of the time Hackett spoke to Walsh and Bobb McKittrick down on the sidelines. Also in the booth was defensive coordinator George Seifert sitting with Neal Dahlen, who helped chart down and distance, field position, and the defense Seifert called. "I always felt that you could focus most and not get caught up in the emotion—the immediate emotion—on the sidelines. You could focus most on the tactical part of the game," said Seifert. "I always felt like a fighter pilot getting into his jet plane before taking off for battle when I climbed into that [coach's box] seat." In addition to Walsh and McKittrick, Bill McPherson, Norb Hecker, Ray Rhodes, Fred vonAppen, Tommy Hart, and Sherman Lewis were also on the sidelines during a game. [14]

At 1:02 p.m. Eastern Standard Time inside a hot and humid Pontiac Silverdome, Ray Wersching kicked off the 1984 season. The first three plays the Lions ran must have had Bill Walsh wondering what he did to deserve such an awful start. On the second and third plays from scrimmage, the 49ers starting cornerbacks—Ronnie Lott and Eric Wright—left the game with injuries (ankle and knee, respectively). However, the 49ers were a deep team, and the NFL's old adage, "next man up," was invoked. Mario Clark and Dana McLemore both hustled in to take their places. "It was a challenge for me. When those guys got hurt, I had to meet the challenge and step in," said Clark. [15]

After forcing a punt, the 49ers offense didn't fare any better. On the fourth play of the new season Joe Montana was sacked and fumbled the ball, which was picked up by Lions defensive end William Gay, who rumbled all the way to the Niners three-yard line. Two plays later Billy Sims leaped for a touchdown and a 7–0 lead. After the rough start the offense settled down on the next drive. Montana led a nice eight-play, sixty-two-yard touchdown drive that ended with Double Wing Left, Sprint Halfback Option. From the five-yard line, backup halfback Carl Monroe beat his man in the red zone for his first career NFL touchdown. Walsh's extra film study had paid off.

In the second quarter, the 49ers scored another touchdown on a two-yard run to the pylon by Wendell Tyler. "That was a sweep play, a pitch play. I got hit and I stretched over. We emphasized coming out that year starting fast. So that first game was an important game. Especially to come out and establish the run, and we did," said running back Wendell Tyler.[16]

Despite the early fumble, Walsh's first twenty-five plays—twelve runs and thirteen passes—led to fourteen points. Backup cornerbacks on the field enabled the Lions to kick two field goals to narrow the lead to 14–13 at the half. Early in the third quarter Walsh's attitude soured. His punter, Tom Orosz, put the frown on Walsh's face. After a short thirty-six-yard punt, the Lions put the ball back into the arms of Billy Sims. His three carries for thirty-seven yards led to a Lions touchdown and a 20–14 lead.

Then on back-to-back drives, the 49ers offense clicked, gaining ninety-seven yards on twenty plays. But Walsh's biggest concern was realized: they were settling for field goals. Both drives ended with Ray Wersching's right foot. The second kick—early in the fourth quarter—was from fifty-three yards, a career best for the twelve-year veteran. "Kicking inside Detroit, it was like heaven. I loved it. I don't care where we are on the field, put me in there [Detroit]. You didn't have to worry about footing; you didn't have to worry about wind; you had this confidence that you can kick this ball here," said Wersching.[17]

The extra work during the summer with Jerry Attaway paid dividends. Wersching had his best year as a pro in 1984, leading the NFL in scoring with 131 points, which broke the 49ers single-season team record. The game was now tied 20–20 with 10:23 left. The biggest play of the game was about to happen to a player who almost missed being on the field. "Our trainer, Lindsy McLean, told us to hydrate, and I think I overdid it because I drank too much Gatorade. It was indoors and it was real hot. I was feeling sick the whole game," said Dana McLemore, punt returner. "Finally he [McLean] said, 'Well, if you're not feeling good, go over there and throw up.' So I went over to the trash can. I threw up. Got the next punt and did something with it."[18] Despite his queasy stomach, McLemore did do something: his fifty-five-yard return set up an easy score for Walsh's offense. Behind superb blocks on the right side by tight end Russ Francis and wide receiver Freddie Solomon, Wendell Tyler capped a big day—eighty-seven rushing yards—with his second rushing touchdown from nine yards out. The 49ers regained the lead, 27–20. Unfortunately it didn't last. With several starters out, the 49ers secondary miscommunicated on the Lions next drive. Free safety Dwight Hicks missed a call, allowing Leonard Thompson to get wide open for a forty-nine-yard touchdown, tying the score.

On that drive, the 49ers lost starting defensive end Jeff Stover to a serious knee injury when he was putting pressure on Gary Danielson. "I had a hit on the quarterback and I planted my right leg but didn't see Keena [Turner] get hit by the up back. He got hit and nailed my right knee and blew it out," said Stover. "That's part of football."[19] Stover tore his medial collateral ligament and would miss the next ten games.

The 49ers got the ball back with 5:01 left in the game. On the road against a tough opponent, the 1984 49ers responded like a championship team. Starting at their own twenty-five-yard line, the 49ers offense used several different formations to keep the Lions off balance. Instead of passing, they ran the ball frequently. Every time the Lions thought that Montana would pass, Walsh went with the run. Sandwiched around a twenty-three-yard pass to Russ Francis, three of the first four plays were runs. The clock ticked down to the two-minute warning with the 49ers well within field goal range at the Lions twenty-one-yard line.

Since the Lions still had all three timeouts, Walsh called on his most reliable running back to churn out more yards and eat up some more of the clock. Backup fullback Bill Ring knew this was his role and carried the ball four consecutive times for twelve yards and a big first down. "Walsh, he would take time to tell you what he expected of you and what your role was on the team. So there was no confusion and that's a good thing," said Ring. "I knew my role would be to come in on short downs, either to block or to get a third-and-one or a third-and-two. That was my role."[20]

The Lions were now helpless. The clock showed seven seconds remaining when Wersching trotted out for a game-winning, twenty-one-yard field goal. "It wasn't a long field goal, but you [still] had to focus on it and get it through," said Wersching. "I had to make it. That's the approach I took."[21] With a perfect snap by Randy Cross and a perfect hold by Joe Montana, Wersching kicked his third field goal of the second half.

Walsh took his headset off with relief apparent on his face. It was a tough, hard-fought 30–27 victory. "That was one of the best victories I've ever seen," remarked tackle Keith Fahnhorst to the media gathered in the locker room. "To lose both your cornerbacks on the first couple of plays and to have everybody pull together and win, that shows a hell of a lot of character."[22] The plane ride to San Francisco was sweet. Arriving back in the City by the Bay, Bill Walsh unknowingly started a tradition that continued throughout the 1984 season. "When we won the first game, Bill took all the coaches and their wives to dinner. Wow, that was really fun. The next week, we won the next game. So Bill took all the wives and coaches out to dinner [again]. Every game that we won that year, we went out to dinner—the coaches and the wives after the game—and it became one of the great rituals of that season and a bonding point with regard to our staff," said George Seifert.[23]

Although Seifert celebrated the hard-fought victory, his 49ers defense suffered some significant injuries. Starters Ronnie Lott, Eric Wright, and Jeff Stover would all miss games in the coming weeks. "That was part of the mantra of the club. You were expected, if something happened, to be ready, whether it be to our starting quarterback or starting outside linebacker. You were the next guy; you had to be ready. So I think that enabled us to feel like one big unit. That was the standard of the club and, consequently, when somebody went in, he took great pride in how he performed in those ball games," said Seifert.[24]

Walsh and John McVay had built a deep team, so they expected their backups to think like starters, and they damn well wanted them to play like starters. There would be no drop-off in play when backup players entered the game. In 1984 the 49ers coaches would get the most out of all their players. Speaking to his team in Redwood City following the Lions win, Walsh offered praise to those who filled in.

> Everybody will play at some point; there's no way you can be on the ball club and not play an important role. At the most critical times we always talk about the toughest job is to be a backup to somebody [who] is a real fine player, and [to] be ready to play yourself when you're called upon, and [to] play as well as he does. So you got a hell of a player you're backing up, and the superstar leaves suddenly and you need to do just what he did. That's the toughest job and we had guys [who] went in and did it. . . . All in all, it was a hell of a game, but it reminds you what we're up for every week. Every team in the league is good. There isn't a team that you can soften up on. You gotta play well on every down, against every team.[25]

Walsh would turn his attention to the next opponent. The team the 49ers had been waiting to play for eight months—eight months, two days, and four hours to be exact—the Washington Redskins.

> You have the game of the decade coming up. . . . The thing I don't like about them is [that] they're so damn arrogant in the way they treated us last time they played us. . . . We get another turn at these guys, so everybody needs to concentrate. They are a big, powerful team [but a] slow team: big and powerful as you can get, but as slow as you can get. . . . Just a real contrast in ball clubs: we're a skilled, hard-hitting, quick team; they are a big, powerful, slow team, and I like that combo.
>
> This is like the Super Bowl, as far as football is concerned. I don't think anybody is going to have a bigger game than this one [at] this time of year. The difference in the two clubs is speed. They have strength and size, and they've capitalized on it for years, but we've got to be faster. We know we are all faster, but . . . your thought process all through practice and game preparations [has got to be] that you're quicker than they are and you'll explode into them anytime you have the ball. . . . Speed's the essence. Hit them before they hit you.[26]

On film Walsh noticed the difference in speed and quickness on both teams. The game plans would be devised to exploit that. Walsh also wanted to get off to a fast start, unlike the 1983 NFC Championship Game. Practice was sharp. "I don't think that week in practice we had to run a play over [again] because everybody was so in tune and in sync with what we wanted to do," said tight end Earl Cooper.[27] Although it was only week 2 in the NFL, the Redskins–49ers matchup felt like a Super Bowl. It would be the home opener at Candlestick Park and broadcast on ABC's Monday Night Football with the announcing team of Frank Gifford, Don Meredith, and O. J. Simpson. It was a historic year for ABC, as the network would telecast its first-ever Super Bowl at Stanford Stadium at the end of the season.

The prime-time affair got every 49ers player's blood boiling. Revenge was on the minds of some players. "There definitely was no need for any pep talks that week," said Keena Turner, linebacker.[28] "You can certainly say it was a revenge game. It was an obstacle that we had to overcome to get to the Super Bowl," said Carlton Williamson, strong safety. "I was excited. We were on the big stage, Monday Night Football. So it was set up to be a big matchup. We wanted to perform well and we probably gave a little extra energy there."[29]

As game time approached, the 49ers received some good and bad news. Ronnie Lott would play but Eric Wright would not. It was a clear and cool evening in San Francisco with temperatures in the low 60s at kickoff. The 49ers Faithful were already in a frenzy when rhythm-and-blues star Jeffrey Osborne sang the national anthem. At the opening of the game, ABC showed a close-up shot of a fan's sign, written in capital letters, hanging between sections 17 and 19: REVENGE.[30] "I remember how fired up we were for that game. We did want revenge. This was time to get back at the Washington Redskins. We wanted to make a statement," said fullback Bill Ring.[31] The game was now on.

The Redskins took the kickoff and realized early that this was a different 49ers team. The first offensive play set the tone of the game. A gimpy Ronnie Lott fended off a block by massive Redskins offensive lineman Joe Jacoby and drilled running back John Riggins to the ground for no gain. The crowd erupted. "When the game was just starting out, we knew in the secondary . . . that we would . . . charge the team. We took it upon ourselves to try and make a big play and make it early so that we could set the tone. A big vicious hit, a fumble recovery, an interception, whatever it might take—we felt that the secondary had to do that, and we thrived on that," said Carlton Williamson, strong safety. "We would be in the huddle and we'd go, 'OK, who's gonna set the tone?' We felt that the offense would feed off of us if we were playing solid defense. That was the approach, and Ronnie was instrumental in that. Ronnie and I . . . would challenge each other to do that."[32]

With heightened emotions on their side, the 49ers offense went to work on their first twenty-five plays. They never looked finer. It was pure magic on the grass at Candlestick Park as the first three offensive drives ended in points.

> First drive: seven plays for fifty-seven yards, resulting in a one-yard touchdown run by Wendell Tyler
> Second drive: eight plays for seventy-five yards, resulting in a five-yard touchdown pass from Joe Montana to Wendell Tyler
> Third drive: ten plays for sixty-eight yards, resulting in a nineteen-yard field goal by Ray Wersching

Three drives, twenty-five plays, 200 total yards, and seventeen points. The bad taste left in their mouth from the loss of the 1983 NFC Championship Game was now gone. The second quarter saw the 49ers continue to dominate play. After a second Wersching field goal, Joe Montana led another scoring drive. The Redskins defensive front was manhandled by the 49ers offensive line—Paris, Ayers, Quillan, Cross, and Fahnhorst created huge holes for Tyler and Craig. Montana capped the thirteen-play drive by connecting with Dwight Clark on a fifteen-yard touchdown. The Redskins finally got on the scoreboard, but the 49ers led 27–3 at the half.

The first-half stats were hard to comprehend. Walsh's offense ran forty-nine plays, gaining 322 total yards, 20 first downs, and had possession of the ball for nearly twenty minutes. Montana was at his best, going sixteen of twenty-eight for 211 yards with two touchdowns. The only problem for the 49ers was the emotion and energy spent in the first half. Coming out of the locker room, the Redskins looked like a different team, scoring five minutes into the third quarter. On the ensuing drive, disaster struck the 49ers. Trying to heave a pass downfield to speedy Renaldo Nehemiah, Montana was drilled in the ribs by Daryl Grant. After getting up slowly, Montana left the game. On the very next play Tyler fumbled and the Redskins recovered at midfield. Ten plays later Washington scored to cut the 49ers lead to 27–17.

With sore ribs Montana returned to the game after missing only one play. In obvious pain he helped the 49ers regain their momentum. Driving at midfield, Walsh called a pass play for the tight end to block, then run into the flat with the flanker running a slant route first, clearing the flat area. On this particular play, though, Mike Wilson beat cornerback Darrell Green so badly off the line of scrimmage on the slant that Montana fired a perfect strike to Wilson in stride. "That was a slant. We had more slants than anybody and Montana was the most accurate thrower when it came to the slant," said Wilson. "He didn't throw a very hard ball, but he was extremely accurate and threw a soft ball you could catch."

Walsh's assessment of his team's speed showed on this play as Wilson almost outran the NFL's fastest man the length of the field. "I looked to the left and looked to the right, and Darrell [Green] is fast. All I had to do was weave," said Wilson.[33] Green finally caught Wilson on the Redskins six-yard line.

The forty-four-yard gain set up Montana's own touchdown run and a 34–17 lead. Once again the Redskins responded as Riggins—held to just twelve yards on ten carries—scored on a short touchdown run, cutting the lead to ten points with more than eleven minutes remaining. The clock seemed to be moving at a glacier's pace for Walsh as the offense trotted back onto the field. On the first play from scrimmage Montana noticed the Redskins loading up for a blitz. Anticipating man-to-man coverage on the outside, he called an audible to Dwight Clark, who blew past cornerback Vernon Dean on a simple go route. Montana lofted a perfect pass to Clark, who dragged Dean an extra fifteen yards deep into Redskins territory. The fifty-six-yard reception set up a field goal by Wersching—who was now six for six on field goals—and a 37–24 lead.

The 49ers defense was running out of gas and the pass rush in the fourth quarter was nonexistent after four early sacks, three by Milt McColl. Perhaps Fred Dean was missed. Late in the fourth Walsh's blood pressure went sky high when his punter Tom Orosz shanked a thirty-four-yard punt that set up another Redskins touchdown to cut the lead to 37–31 with 3:44 remaining. All the 49ers had to do was get one first down. On an X-Shallow Cross play, Montana found Dwight Clark, who had lined up as a tight end, to seal the 49ers win. "I can't believe how wide open I was. I turned around and nobody was there," commented Clark after the game.[34]

The 49ers were now 2–0 after defeating the two teams they played the previous postseason. "A great, great football game," remarked Walsh to the press. "We played as good in the first half as we ever have here. I just hope we saved a few more of those halves for other games."[35] Walsh was happy to get the victory, as his offense generated 534 total yards. However, the twenty-eight second-half points allowed by the defense alarmed him, although he knew his team had spent most of its energy getting the big first-half lead. A day later Walsh spoke to his team about not becoming complacent.

> As far as our game the other night, it was a great effort on every-body's part. Hell of a win and for those guys who are new to the league, you have to understand what can happen and what often does happen with the ebb and flow with a football game. . . . Final analysis is that we beat a hell of a good football team. We are all pretty proud of it and you should [be], too. We'll have a good week

because of it, but come Sunday again, we have a division game. You can't afford to lose it. Instead of thinking 'That was it,' you think, 'I can't wait to play.' You get after these guys; you can't wait to play again. Like I said, we'll keep you fresh.[36]

With the short week Walsh would have the team practice without pads to keep the players fresh for their next game against the physical New Orleans Saints. Walsh and his staff deeply respected the Saints and their head coach, Bum Phillips. In the past they would struggle with the tough, physical Saints, but more often than not, they ended up with a win. "Assume they'll blitz on every play. They take pride in their defense. . . . We have our work cut out," said Walsh to his offense. "This defense compared to ours is more active and we have an active defense, and I think we're quicker than anybody in the league. It's going to be a hell of a dogfight with these guys."[37]

Before Wednesday's practice, Walsh and McVay made a roster move. Gone was punter Tom Orosz, who averaged only thirty-nine yards a punt the first two weeks of the season. "Bill was a little hard on specialists. He was like a lot of people: 'That's your job. Go out and do it, and do it well, or you're going hear about it,'" said Fred vonAppen, special teams coach. "Tom shanked one in one of our early ball games and Bill just lambasted him. Confronted him and said some things that were [psychologically] damaging. I went to Orosz and said, 'Shake it off. He's hard on specialists.' He turned to me and said, 'Hey, Woody Hayes use to slug me when I came off the field when I missed it.' We made the change."[38]

McVay brought in veteran punter Max Runager, who played the previous five seasons with the Philadelphia Eagles but was one of the last players cut in camp. "He was an experienced guy. He came in with a reputation of being a guy who was very good from the fifty-yard line and going in. He was quick. He was hard to block. So he really helped us," said vonAppen.[39]

"I was at a teammate's house [in Philadelphia] and my attorney called me and said, 'How quick can you get to San Francisco?' I said, 'How quick do I need to be there?' He said, 'Well, you need to leave today.' So I hopped on a plane and flew out there," said Runager. "Had a good tryout and they ended up signing me that day." Initially Runager wasn't impressed with the 49ers practice facility. "The thing that surprised me the most is that we had fairly nice facilities in Philadelphia, as far as where we practiced and the weight room. When I went there [to San Francisco], it was like we were in a little trailer because we used to practice in Redwood City and had a half grass field, half turf field. So I said, 'My goodness, these guys are winning, and they've got these kind of facilities.' But they didn't care what they looked like as long as they put a good product on the field. That's really what they were looking at and that's exactly what they did," continued Runager.[40]

When the players arrived at the Redwood City facility on Wednesday, they met their new teammate. "Fellas, we have a new player with us—Max Runager, will [you] please stand—he's going to punt for us. Please give him a hand," said Walsh at the front of the classroom.[41] The whole team, as well as Walsh, gave Runager a round of applause. Welcome to the 49ers family.

Looking at film, Walsh saw an aggressive Saints 3–4 defense led by linebacker Rickey Jackson and defensive end Jim Wilks. The Saints were ranked first in defense in the NFC in 1983, and they always gave Walsh's offense fits. Heading into the game the 49ers offense had scored on thirteen of twenty-one offensive possessions, and the first twenty-five plays had been clicking. But knowing that Montana was nursing sore ribs, Walsh didn't want him holding the ball too long. He would protect his star quarterback.

For the second straight week Eric Wright would be absent and Mario Clark would start in his place. The night before the Saints game it looked like the 49ers defense would be missing another starter, as Keena Turner spent the night in the hospital's maternity ward while his wife gave birth to a baby girl—Sheena Turner. "It was the night before, so I was up all night. Things went well, but I was going to play because everybody was [OK]. That was a special day for sure," said Turner.[42]

The Saints came in with a 1–1 record as Bum Phillips roamed the sidelines, wearing his trademark blue cowboy shirt, white Stetson cowboy hat, and ostrich boots. After a 49ers punt the defense threw the first punch as Dwight Hicks picked off Richard Todd to set up the offense. Wearing a flak jacket to protect his ribs, Joe Montana didn't take long to capitalize. On the fifth play from scrimmage he sent Freddie Solomon in motion, running a perfect skinny post down the middle for a thirty-two-yard touchdown. On the next drive Todd threw another interception—right to Ronnie Lott. This time the offense didn't capitalize, as Ray Wersching's field goal attempt was blocked. The Saints Russell

Gary attempted to return the block, forcing Montana to make the tackle and subsequently aggravate his rib injury. He would return on the next drive but appeared to be in a lot of pain. Early in the second quarter Montana led a drive that ended in a field goal.

After an exchange of punts the 49ers defense continued its onslaught on Richard Todd, forcing a third interception. This time outside linebacker Dan Bunz picked off a Todd pass and returned it to the Saints twenty-eight-yard line. It was Bunz's first interception since 1979. Montana connected on two passes—twelve yards apiece to both Tyler and Clark—to set up another score. Behind an unbalanced line on the right and blocks by tight end John Frank and fullback Roger Craig, Tyler scored his fifth touchdown of the season.

With nine minutes remaining in the second quarter, the 49ers led 17–0. On the Saints sidelines CBS cameras caught Bum Phillips shouting at his defensive coordinator—his son, Wade Phillips. Bum also yelled at Richard Todd, benching the veteran for Ken Stabler, an even older veteran. Todd finished the day completing just two passes for fifteen yards and three interceptions. The thirty-eight-year-old Stabler was a former four-time Pro Bowler who led the Raiders to a victory in Super Bowl XI. He ignited a comeback that surprised the 49ers.

On his first drive Stabler led a nice twelve-play, eighty-three-yard touchdown drive, connecting with Eugene Goodlow to cut the lead to 17–7. With less than two minutes till halftime Montana made his first big mistake of the season. Trying to hit Dwight Clark over the middle, he threw his first interception of the season (after 81 passes) to Johnnie Poe. The turnover led to a field goal. The lead was now just seven points. Making matters worse, Ronnie Lott hurt his toe in the first half and would be out for the rest of the game.

The first drive of the second half saw the Saints continue their comeback. Stabler completed three passes that ended with a twenty-six-yard touchdown to tight end Hoby Brenner. The score was tied 17–17. Losing momentum, the 49ers also lost their best player. On the second play after the score was tied, Joe Montana took a seven-step drop to throw. Saints defensive end Jim Wilks beat left tackle Bubba Paris on a speed rush, drilling Montana with a blindside hit. The sack forced Montana from the game. With no evidence of rust, backup quarterback Matt Cavanaugh replaced Montana and connected with tight end Earl Cooper for a fourteen-yard gain. But because of the sack the 49ers were still short of the first down and were forced to punt.

With the tide turning against the 49ers after jumping to a 17–0 lead, Walsh got the bad news he expected. Montana was out for the rest of the game with bruised ribs. The Saints continued to put pressure on the 49ers defense as Stabler led another drive into 49ers territory. On a key third down, defensive end Jim Stuckey came up with a big sack to force a field goal. The forty-one yarder gave the Saints their first lead (20–17) as the game headed to the fourth quarter.

On the 49ers bench, one of the team's defensive leaders spoke up. Dwaine Board rarely gave pep talks but felt the need to voice his opinion. "The Saints had just gone ahead of us and I was tired, like the rest of the guys. But I told them, 'No need putting your heads down. Let them put theirs down and we'll raise ours up.' It was a little stronger than that," Board admitted after the game. "I usually don't get emotional. But I felt things were slipping away."[43] He not only talked the talk, he walked the walk, coming up with a huge sack on the next Saints drive, forcing a punt.

Cavanaugh trotted onto the Candlestick Park turf and into the 49ers huddle as the drive started at the 49ers forty-one-yard line. The drive looked as if Montana was still behind center, as their march consisted of multiple formations. Lining up as a single back Tyler went six yards around the left end. With split backs Cavanaugh rolled right, hitting Russ Francis for fourteen yards. Another single-back formation as Craig went for six yards. Out of an I-formation Tyler went up the middle for six yards. On the fifth play, Tyler ran up the middle on a trap play for four yards. Walsh had called five plays with no restrictions or limitations on his quarterback. The next play showed why Walsh had confidence in all his players, regardless of the situation.

Walsh called it the "U-slide": a formation with two tight ends on the left side, Francis flexed out on the line of scrimmage like a wide receiver, and Earl Cooper lined up tight, one yard off the line of scrimmage, next to the left tackle. Cavanaugh sent Cooper in motion to the right, and at the snap, both guards pulled left as Tyler faked the handoff. It looked like a sweep to the left; instead Cavanaugh booted to the right. As Cavanaugh rolled, Saints linebacker Whitney Paul wasn't fooled and was in his face. Cavanaugh calmly spotted a wide-open Cooper in the flat and tossed a perfect strike. Cooper caught the ball and turned upfield, breaking free safety Frank Wattelet's tackle, and sprinted into the end zone untouched. "That's one thing Bill really liked about me as a tight end. That once I got the ball up the field, I could use my running back style as far as breaking tackles," said Cooper.

In the end zone Cooper leaped high with a thunderous spike as the Candlestick Park crowd chanted, "Coop! Coop! Coop!" "Anytime you got sixty or seventy thousand fans hollering your name, you can't help but get fired up and want to do more," said Cooper.[44] Walsh used his whole playbook with his backup signal caller and Cavanaugh responded as the 49ers took a 24–20 lead. With momentum and the 49ers fans back in the game, Stabler's luck finally ran out as the 49ers 1984 rookie class responded with two memorable plays. In the nickel defense safety Jeff Fuller had his first career interception and returned it thirty yards deep into Saints territory. With Cavanaugh holding, Ray Wersching kicked a field goal to make the score 27–20. Another defensive stop led to another field goal.

Down ten points Stabler threw the Saints fifth interception of the game as rookie linebacker Todd Shell capped off the big divisional win with his first career NFL interception. Walsh smiled on the sidelines as the team celebrated the comeback victory. The Saints did give the 49ers a dogfight. The five turnovers forced by the defense were the team's saving grace, since the offense struggled at times, especially on third downs, converting only one of eleven opportunities. They did score more than thirty points for the third straight week.

Once again the 49ers backup players filled in and contributed to a victory. The headline in the *San Francisco Examiner*'s sports section called the bench players "sitsubs."[45] The nickname didn't catch on. The 49ers were now 3–0. The biggest concern heading into the next game, a road matchup with the Philadelphia Eagles, was the health of Joe Montana (ribs) and Ronnie Lott (toe).

While preparing his team's game plan on Monday, Walsh had to deal with something out of his control. At a football luncheon for the Maxwell Club in Philadelphia, Eagles owner Leonard Tose told the crowd that the Eagles would easily beat the 49ers, going so far as to guarantee it. When Walsh met with his team on Wednesday he addressed the owner's prediction.

We have a tough one this week. You know the owner there in Philadelphia [Leonard Tose] has guaranteed a victory for his team, so it should turn into an interesting contest. This is a tough game, I can tell you that. We have to go to Philadelphia to do it; we have a wild crowd; they are a slow team—they're like Washington, not active. Extremely well-coached—damn well-coached—defense, but they are slow on their feet and really don't know it yet. So it will be our job to be so much quicker than them, so they don't have a chance to meet that guarantee. . . . This is a good test to see if our line is better than theirs, because they don't think that we are. That's what their owner is talking about. They think they are a tougher team than we are. They think they're more physical than we are. That's the whole idea: they said, 'we finally have a team we can intimidate.'[46]

While game planning for the Eagles, Walsh recalled the last time they faced them. In week 1 of 1983, Walsh's offense was held to just 126 rushing yards and had three turnovers against a tough Marion Campbell–coached defense, resulting in a 22–17 loss. This time around he wanted his team mentally prepared to run the ball. Discussing the ground game with Bobb McKittrick, they focused on 69 Toss—an outside run off tackle—as being a staple against the Eagles 4–3 front. Walsh didn't want his team to have a letdown.

"This is a game that a championship team wins. A struggling team loses about now. A struggling team would lose about now; a championship team would just march right through them. We're better than they are, because we're faster than they are," said Walsh to his team early in the week.[47] He then turned his attention to his quarterback position.

With the New England Patriots, Matt Cavanaugh had started fifteen games, throwing nineteen touchdowns. It was this success that prompted Walsh to trade a draft pick to acquire him as his backup quarterback. The only problem was that Cavanaugh had never thrown a pass in a 49ers uniform until the Saints game. As the week went on, it looked more and more likely that Cavanaugh would get the start. "If he [Montana] can't function smoothly, then he can't play," Walsh said to the press. "It will not affect our game plan if he doesn't play. Matt is a very fine quarterback."[48] Both Walsh and Paul Hackett had confidence in the seven-year veteran backup. "In the back of Bill's mind, he felt that at some point Matt would have to play a game. [Matt] was a great preparer. He and Montana got along and learned from each other.

[That game we decided to] run the ball and pick and choose our times to throw, the deep routes. Matt had a strong arm and that's what we emphasized," said quarterbacks and wide receivers coach Paul Hackett. [49]

At the hotel in Philadelphia on Saturday night, Walsh went over the first twenty-five plays with Cavanaugh, who was starting his first NFL game since 1982. "I'll never forget when the first twenty-five plays came out; the first three were passes. There's no way that Joe would've ever had that in his first twenty-five!" said Paul Hackett. [50]

Wearing a red 49ers ball cap throughout the game, Montana would dress and hold for kicks but would not play under center. The sold-out crowd of 62,771 at Veterans Stadium would make Cavanaugh's first start as the 49ers quarterback even tougher. "Matt was a great backup quarterback. We appreciated his talent. He was always prepared when his number was called," said Keith Fahnhorst, offensive tackle. [51]

The 49ers defense set the tone early, hushing the loud crowd quickly. Defensive end Lawrence Pillers—who must have been wearing his Mississippi patrol hat that day—sacked Ron Jaworski. The defense would harass Jaws all day. The 49ers first twenty-five plays didn't change with Matt Cavanaugh in the game. "The first play, Matt comes out and makes a little fake. Goes back and drills it. I think that gave everybody confidence. But, again, this was Bill knowing what Matt can do best. Having a great feel for him, putting him in the position to have that kind of success," said Hackett. [52] On the team's first play, Cavanaugh hit wide receiver Renaldo Nehemiah for a twenty-yard gain as the 49ers marched to the Eagles thirteen-yard line, setting up a short field goal attempt. After connecting on nine field goals in the first three games, Ray Wersching went wide right on a 30 yarder. But this failed scoring opportunity didn't derail the 49ers offense. On their third drive Walsh unleashed 69 Toss as Wendell Tyler ripped off fifteen yards behind blocks by pulling guards Randy Cross and John Ayers. Then Cavanaugh took to the air, connecting with backs Roger Craig and Carl Monroe for twenty-eight total yards to set up the first score of the game.

Walsh called for his fullback to beat one of the Eagles best players— inside linebacker Jerry Robinson (who played with Wendell Tyler at UCLA). Out of a split backfield with a tight end and wide receiver on the left, Craig ran an out-and-up route out of the backfield, catching

Robinson off guard. A wide-open Craig streaked past Robinson, grabbing a perfect pass from Cavanaugh and sprinting into the end zone for a thirty-five-yard touchdown. It was Cavanaugh's first touchdown pass as a 49er. "The touchdown pass was perfect. I think it was the first time we called that in a game," commented Roger Craig after the game.[53] Cavanaugh was off to a great start: three series, six for eight for 101 yards, and one touchdown.

In the second quarter the Eagles offense showed some life as two of their next four drives ended with field goals, cutting the lead to 7–6. With just fifty-five seconds remaining in the first half, the biggest play of the game occurred on special teams. On the ensuing kickoff, rookie halfback Derrick Harmon took the short kick at his own twelve-yard line and started up the field. He quickly cut to the right, sprinting down the sideline behind a key block by fellow rookie Todd Shell, away from Eagles defenders before being dragged out-of-bounds at the Eagles thirty-seven-yard line. The nice fifty-one-yard return by the former Cornell star set up an unexpected scoring opportunity. "I was thankful to be productive for the team, a positive factor for the game," said Harmon.[54]

With three timeouts to work with, Cavanaugh went to the running game. After two runs by Tyler and Craig gained fifteen yards, Walsh used two timeouts. Then Cavanaugh went to the air with a perfect comeback route to Dwight Clark for a gain of twenty to the two-yard line. With nineteen seconds remaining in the half, Walsh called Sprint Right Option—the same play call as "The Catch." Cavanaugh rolled right and fired a strike to Freddie Solomon in the flat for an easy touchdown. Harmon's big return had helped give the 49ers a 14–6 lead at the half.

In the locker room the team rested for a physical second half. Back-up Matt Cavanaugh had played extremely well, going fourteen of twenty-three for 184 yards and two touchdowns. Walsh felt so good about his offense that he called twenty-five passes for Cavanaugh compared to just twelve runs. Beginning the second half with the lead, he wanted to "pound the rock" some more.

After giving up a field goal early in the third quarter the 49ers started to control the clock with the running game. Walsh called 69 Toss and the 49ers offensive line began to push the Eagles around. Walsh called ten runs in the quarter for forty-three yards as his offense held the ball for nearly nine minutes. The only thing that kept the Eagles in the game—much to Walsh's fury along the sidelines—was eleven 49er penalties. Early in the fourth with a five-point lead, Cavanaugh began a drive to put the game away. Tyler sprinted around the right end for sixteen yards, then Cavanaugh completed only his second pass of the half with a bullet to Russ Francis for thirteen yards.

After another first down the 49ers found themselves with a third-and-fifteen from their own forty-nine-yard line. On cue CBS announcer Tom Brookshier commented, "Crucial play coming up."[55] Bill Walsh called a pass play, 76-Okie, a formation with two tight ends and two receivers set in the game. On the left Dwight Clark ran a simple go route down the sidelines against the Eagles Cover 2 defense. Cavanaugh took a five-step drop and threw a perfect pass between corner Herman Edwards and strong safety Ray Ellis. Clark caught the ball in stride and outran Ellis to the end zone. Touchdown!

The seven-play, eighty-seven-yard scoring drive gave the 49ers a comfortable 21–9 lead. On the ensuing drive Ron Jaworski, who struggled all day completing only sixteen of forty passes, tried to loft a ball down the middle of the field. But linebacker Jim Fahnhorst made a leaping interception, his first as an NFL player. "The defense was called Moscow, it was Thunder Mike Cover 4, where the Mike [middle] linebacker Riki Ellison rushes his gap, and I drop and cover his side. That might've thrown Jaworski off," said Jim Fahnhorst. "The sun was right in my eyes, so whenever the ball comes with the sun in your eyes, you catch the sun. So I stuck my hand up there and the ball hit my hand and brought it in."[56]

His defensive teammates mobbed him. Coming off the field with the ball still in his hands, Jim Fahnhorst got a pat on the back from his big brother. "It was nice to see Jimmy have success like that," said Keith Fahnhorst.[57] "He just said 'good play.' I dropped a few in the preseason and one in the Detroit game. My brother kept telling the offensive line, 'He's got good hands' so on the plane back from Philly he told me, 'You had good hands,'" said Jim Fahnhorst.[58]

The game's only turnover sealed the game as the 49ers rushing attack ran off the remaining eight minutes of the fourth quarter. Wendell Tyler finished with 113 rushing yards—ninety yards on fifteen carries in the second half alone—a new career high as a 49er. The 49ers were 4–0 for the first time since 1952. They also had a two-game lead in the NFC

West, as the rest of the division was 2–2. "Everybody came through. Roger [Craig] came through. Matt Cavanaugh came through. We had talent on that team, and if somebody got hit, injured, the next guy stepped up. Everyone was prepared. That's what really established us as a great team," said halfback Wendell Tyler.[59]

Walsh was pleased with the performance of his backup signal caller: Cavanaugh finished with three touchdowns and no interceptions. "Certainly it's a relief to know that when a quarterback as great as Joe [Montana] can't play that you have somebody who can step in and you hardly miss a step," Bill Walsh said to the press in the locker room.[60] "Of course I wasn't razor sharp because the last time I started a game was in 1982 for New England. But I'm happy with this one. We won and I felt like I contributed. But I was really just one guy out there who benefitted from help everywhere," commented Cavanaugh after the game.[61]

Cavanaugh did get help from the likes of Derrick Harmon—who would get a game ball— Jim Fahnhorst, and a defense that didn't give up a touchdown. They also made the Eagles owner eat his words. "It was out on the bulletin board and we read it," said Matt Cavanaugh.[62] "I'd hate to be on the other side of that. Imagine Eddie DeBartolo guaranteeing a win," commented Russ Francis.[63] "I blew it. But, no, I don't regret it. The only regret I have is that we didn't perform," said a disappointed Leonard Tose after the game.[64]

The victory celebration didn't last long as Walsh quickly turned his attention to the 49ers next game—a home contest against the Atlanta Falcons. It would be a matchup of the NFC's top two scoring offenses (Falcons, 122 points; 49ers, 118 points). But it was their previous meeting in Atlanta that Walsh reflected on, when the Falcons upset the 49ers 28–24 on a Hail Mary pass from Steve Bartkowski to Billy "White Shoes" Johnson. In the same game Falcons defensive back Bobby Butler laid out receiver Renaldo Nehemiah with a violent hit. Both plays were obviously on Walsh's mind when he spoke to the team on Monday.

> We might as well face up to this ball game. We can recall the last time we played these guys. I can't say there is a team we'd rather beat than this one after what happened back in Atlanta the last time we played them. This is a game we're going to have to come out and revisit it. That's all there is to it. They got a hit on one of our

players—lucky, the way they stole that thing, the way everybody acted—I think we deserve this next one. It's going to take a hell of an effort—these guys are the best team we're going to play—all you have to do is look at the film. They're good. They have one hell of a running back [Gerald Riggs], best long passer in the game [Steve Bartkowski], fast receiver, defense that's different, the rest of them, no question about it, it's going to be tough to figure out the defense. So again, special teams are going to be a factor. . . . It's offense, defense, special teams, now that's what has to be the difference in the ball club. [65]

Although the 49ers were unbeaten Walsh had the complete attention of the entire team. They knew this would be a tough, hard-fought divisional game. Walsh and his staff respected quarterback Steve Bartkowski. He had thrown for more than 800 yards with nine touchdowns during the first four games of 1984. As impressive as that was, Gerald Riggs, the six-feet-one, 230-pound running back was even better. He had galloped for 483 yards in ninety-six attempts with five touchdowns. The high-flying Falcons were coming to Candlestick averaging thirty and a half points per game and had just defeated the Houston Oilers 42–10 to even their record to 2–2.

As the week moved on, Walsh worked on getting his team mentally prepared.

Don't let anything distract us now. You'll have the newspaper harping at you. You'll get people wanting to interview you. You'll get people saying how outstanding and great we are: Are you going to go undefeated? Who can beat you? [You'll] hear all that talk. It doesn't mean a damn thing. The only thing that matters is that we stay together as a group and how we concentrate, so when we go on to that field today without pads, it's got to be a mental day. Everything has to be just right, get everybody healthy, but we got to be thinking that today. [66]

Walsh always knew when to mentally prepare his team for an opponent and how to deal with distractions, especially from the media. It was the first time there was talk of an undefeated season. He didn't want that to distract his team into thinking they were better than they were.

He was also worried about injuries and his team's depth. Joe Montana was ready to return after a one-week absence. Although Ronnie Lott wouldn't practice much that week, he was scheduled to play. Assistant trainer John Miller devised a special brace to help immobilize Lott's sore toe. Throughout the week Walsh met with John McVay several times about the 49ers roster. They saw a chance to make their team better. On Thursday before the Falcons game, McVay claimed Billy Shields off waivers from the San Diego Chargers. With Bubba Paris fighting a sore knee, Bobb McKittrick had only Allan Kennedy at tackle. McVay made the move to get the ten-year veteran off the street.

The huge, six-eight, 279-pound offensive tackle started 117 games for the Chargers during the past nine years but a contract dispute led to his release. The thirty-one-year-old Shields felt that signing with the 49ers was a blessing. "I was talking to four undefeated teams at the time so it was a toss-up of who was going to be the favorite," said Shields. "It came down to my relationship with Bobb McKittrick, whom I had worked with in San Diego. I knew some of the linemen through different activities, and Bill Walsh had been a coach with the Chargers, so I knew him [too]. Those relationships were the reason I chose the 49ers."[67]

From the moment he arrived, Shields could see that the 49ers had a special offense, especially their running game, which was different than the Chargers "Air Coryell" passing offense. "It was really different than what I had become accustomed to with the Chargers. We might have a 200 [rushing yard] game once a year, but with the 49ers, it was an achievable goal every week," said Shields. "It was really exciting to have that part of the game as something we were really successful at."[68]

But McVay and Walsh weren't done dealing. The next day the two made a call down the coast to the Chargers to inquire about another ten-year veteran who didn't seem to be playing much. Just two days before the Falcons game, Walsh traded a draft pick to the Chargers for former All-Pro defensive tackle Gary "Big Hands" Johnson. A starter for the past nine seasons, Johnson had sixty-seven career sacks (and led the NFL in 1980 with an unofficial seventeen and a half), had played in four Pro Bowls, and had been named to two All-Pro teams (1980 and 1981). He also had played alongside current Niners Fred Dean and Louie Kelcher on the great Chargers teams of the early 1980s.

But by 1984 he had been relegated to backup with only two tackles and no sacks. He was delighted to join the 49ers. "I figured being up here in San Francisco and out of San Diego would give me a chance to prove to myself and others that I was still capable of playing effectively," said Johnson upon arrival in San Francisco.[69] The 49ers got a motivated athlete who had a reputation for being a team player.

"I love Gary Johnson. We came in together in '75 and spent all our time together and roomed together. When I heard that he was coming, my heart just swelled up. It was just a special thing," said Louie Kelcher, defensive tackle.[70] "He was a great pass rusher. I learned a lot from Johnson. Just about getting off the ball. People [say], 'Watch the ball and take off on the ball.' But Johnson taught me, 'Take off on whatever's moving.' I learned a lot from him," said defensive end Dwaine Board.[71]

"Big Hands is one of the quickest guys I've ever played with. He had the quickest first two steps off the line that I've ever seen," said Manu Tuiasosopo, defensive tackle. "It was a delight for me to see that in practice. I know our guys on the offensive line—I remember talking to Randy Cross, Fred Quillan, and John Ayers—and they had to be on their game, even in our pass rushing [drills], Big Hands came off the ball. If you didn't get him the first two steps, he was gone. He just took over his position on that side of the ball with his first two steps."[72]

Instantly Johnson had improved the 49ers. Johnson and Shields both dressed and played on Sunday. A light mist fell early Sunday morning in San Francisco but cleared just before kickoff. A high near 70 quickly warmed up the players as the 49ers defense set the tone of the game by collecting one big play after another.

Bartkowski came out with the first big strike, hitting wide receiver Stacy Bailey on a sixty-one-yard catch-and-run. Bailey would have scored but for nickel safety Tom Holmoe's shoestring tackle. Big play number one by the defense. Two plays later with first-and-goal from the 49ers fourteen-yard line, Falcons running back Lynn Cain ran a sweep play to the right. Inside linebacker Riki Ellison drilled him and punched the ball out with Dwight Hicks recovering. Big play number two with no points on the board.

The Falcons got the ball back and proceeded to drive back down inside the 49ers five-yard line. On second-and-goal the heart and soul of the 49ers defense made an unbelievable play. Gerald Riggs took a handoff and headed off right tackle. In a blur Ronnie Lott—bad toe and all—shot through a block by Falcons tight end Floyd Hodge and leveled the 230-pound Riggs. On the CBS telecast, color analyst Wayne

Walker, who played fifteen years as a linebacker for the Detroit Lions, praised Lott: "I don't believe you'll see another cornerback in the National Football League be able to make that play. . . . You don't put guys like Riggs on their back very often. Lott just did."[73]

Big play number three for the defense. That big hit forced the Falcons to settle for a field goal, the last points the Falcons offense would score that game. Early in the second quarter the 49ers offense got some bad news: starting wide receiver Freddie Solomon left the game with a hamstring injury and would not return. After a slow start Walsh began to run the ball against the Falcons twenty-seventh-ranked rushing defense. He fed the ball to Wendell Tyler, who carried four times for thirty-eight yards to put the ball on the five-yard line. On the tenth play of the drive Joe Montana ran a quarterback waggle, tossing an easy touchdown to tight end Russ Francis. The six-minute drive gave the 49ers a 7–3 lead.

With less than three minutes left in the half, the 49ers got the ball back at their own twenty. The run game then responded with the biggest play of the game. With a split backfield, Walsh called the perfect play. Falcons defensive coordinator John Marshall blitzed middle linebacker Buddy Curry and free safety Tom Pridemore up the middle. Through a massive hole behind blocks by John Ayers and Fred Quillan, Tyler sprinted all alone down the middle of the field. The forty-yard gallop would be Tyler's longest run of the season.

Montana then scrambled out-of-bounds for fifteen yards, setting up another gem of a call by Bill Walsh. With Solomon out, Walsh called Mike Wilson's number. He lined up in the slot inside Dwight Clark on the left side of the formation. Wilson ran a perfect out-and-up while Clark ran a post pattern in the middle of the field, taking the coverage with him. Montana's seven-step drop allowed time for the patterns to develop. He then lofted a pass down the sideline. Wilson slowed down as the defensive back overran the play, allowing Wilson to make a falling catch for the touchdown. "That was called 2-Flatten Up. Dwight [Clark] ran a post. I ran a five-yard out-and-up. The ball was thrown high and kind of died. I just came back for it and the defender didn't turn around," said Wilson after the game.[74]

Wilson's first touchdown of the season gave the 49ers a 14–3 lead going into halftime. Once again the 49ers hadn't lost a beat when a starter left the game. "I knew what my role was. Any[thing] I could [to] help the team win. And I will say this: everybody had that mentality," said Wilson. Not only did the backup come in to play, but he came in and made a big play—a play that was expected of him. No drop-off.[75]

It was also the second consecutive week that the 49ers offense scored with less than a minute remaining before the half. After the intermission, new acquisition Gary Johnson got into the game for a few plays, and the 49ers defense continued its dominant ways. Linebacker Jim Fahnhorst tipped a Bartkowski pass that was intercepted by Ronnie Lott. Big play number four. On the next drive the Falcons tried a fake punt, but Ron Ferrari made a diving tackle one yard short of the first down. Big play number five. "You had to be suspicious of just about anything. I was just trying to keep this guy from getting the first down. Sometimes it's just luck," said Ferrari.[76]

More big plays and turnovers kept coming in the fourth quarter. With an interception near the goal line, Carlton Williamson denied a score. Big play number six. Then on a thirteen-play drive to the 49ers one-yard line, Riki Ellison and rookie Michael Carter smothered Gerald Riggs on a fourth-down play, denying another scoring opportunity. Big play number seven.

For 49ers defensive players, the goal line means it's time to swell up. Against the Falcons, they did it more than in any other game in 1984. "Swell-up time" was the goal-line mantra for the 49ers defense. "When a team gets close to our end zone, we say, 'Swell up.' It means make the big play. It means, 'I hope the play comes my way.' We say it for everybody. You've got to get big. You've got to play bigger than you are. You've got to feel it," remarked Dwight Hicks in the locker room.[77]

With time running out, Max Runager took an intentional safety to close out the 14–5 win. The Falcons ran seventy-seven offensive plays—the 49ers only fifty-seven—but the Falcons didn't score a single touchdown. It was the second consecutive game—and ninth consecutive quarter—that the 49ers defense hadn't allowed a touchdown. The seven big plays showed the rest of the NFL that the 49ers defense could shut anybody down, including the NFC's top scoring offense, which had been averaging more than thirty points a game.

That it was a team victory made Walsh happy, and he gave credit where it was due. "Our entire defense and the defensive coaches will get the game ball. They have been doing a remarkable job with our defensive calls with every player fitting certain roles," said Walsh at his postgame press conference.[78]

Seifert was using his playbook more and more each week. "Going into today's game, I had ninety-two calls. That's ninety-two defensive variations I could call," commented Seifert in the 49ers locker room. "So, all of sudden we go from a base 3–4, to a nickel, to a Buffalo [4–3 front], to a Redskin [a hybrid 3–4 with four quick linemen], to a Fever, to whatever fits the down and distance and field position."[79] Whatever Seifert was calling was getting the job done. The 49ers defense had played the last nine quarters without allowing a touchdown.

As the month of September came to an end, the 49ers were now 5–0. (The NFL standings after week 5 are shown in table 9.1.) Only two other times in their history had the 49ers started the season with five consecutive wins—in 1948 and 1952. This was virtually uncharted territory for the 49ers.

Table 9.1. NFL Standings after Week 5

AFC EAST		NFC EAST	
Miami	5–0	Dallas	4–1
New England	3–2	New York Giants	3–2
New York Jets	3–2	Washington	3–2
Indianapolis	2–3	St. Louis	2–3
Buffalo	0–5	Philadelphia	1–4
AFC CENTRAL		**NFC CENTRAL**	
Pittsburgh	3–2	Chicago	3–2
Cleveland	1–4	Minnesota	2–3
Cincinnati	0–5	Tampa Bay	2–3
Houston	0–5	Detroit	1–4
		Green Bay	1–4
NFC WEST		**NFC WEST**	
Denver	4–1	San Francisco	5–0
Los Angeles Raiders	4–1	Los Angeles Rams	3–2
Seattle	4–1	New Orleans	3–2
Kansas City	3–2	Atlanta	2–3
San Diego	3–2		

10

THE CANDLESTICK PARK EXPERIENCE

After the 49ers defeated the Atlanta Falcons, Candlestick Park got a major makeover. It was the last home game of the season played with the baseball configuration.

The San Francisco Giants baseball season was over following a disappointing 66–96 sixth-place finish in the National League West. A six-man crew began digging up the pitcher's mound and infield minutes after the 49ers–Falcons game ended. New sod would be planted and the grass field would be ready for the next home game slated for October 14 against the Pittsburgh Steelers. Candlestick Park was now one of the city's hallmark structures. The Bay area was defined by the presence of "The Stick."

HISTORY OF CANDLESTICK PARK

The City by the Bay quickly adopted the San Francisco 49ers, founded in 1946, as part of the All-America Football Conference (AAFC), a rival league of the NFL. The AAFC was comprised of nine original teams including the Cleveland Browns and Los Angeles Dons. At first the 49ers played their home games at Kezar Stadium. Built on the southeastern side of Golden Gate Park at a cost of $300,000, Kezar was home to a very successful, competitive team. Led by quarterback Frankie Albert, a former Stanford star, the 49ers compiled an overall record of

38–15–2 in four years (1946–1949) before the AAFC folded. In 1950 the NFL absorbed the Browns, Baltimore Colts, and 49ers.

In the early years the 49ers built an entertaining team with future Hall-of-Fame players such as Bob St. Clair, Leo Nomellini, and the "Million Dollar Backfield," featuring quarterback Y. A. Tittle and running backs Hugh McElhenny, John Henry Johnson, and Joe "The Jet" Perry. With eight winning seasons from 1951 to 1961, the 49ers gave their fan base—nicknamed the "49ers Faithful"—plenty to cheer. The 49ers consistently sold out Kezar Stadium.

What the 49ers couldn't give the city was a world championship: the 49ers always came up short. After mediocre seasons in the 1960s, the 49ers winning ways returned under head coach Dick Nolan (1968–1975). Following the NFL merger with the AFL and subsequent realignment in 1970, the 49ers won the newly named NFC Western Division for the first time. Behind great play of quarterback John Brodie, wide receiver Gene Washington, and future Hall of Famers, linebacker Dave Wilcox and cornerback Jimmy Johnson, the 49ers finished with a 10–3–1 record. After beating the Minnesota Vikings in the divisional round, the 49ers hosted the first-ever NFC Championship Game against the Dallas Cowboys at Kezar Stadium. In a hard-fought game the 49ers came up short—again—losing 17–10.

The following year the 49ers moved into a new home.

Built and opened in 1958 for baseball's San Francisco Giants, Candlestick Park was named in 1959 in a "name the park" fan balloting contest in which more than 15,000 entries were submitted. Located at Candlestick Point on the western shore of San Francisco Bay and just seven miles south of downtown, the stadium sat on fourteen and a half acres and cost $24.6 million.

When the 49ers made their debut on October 10, 1971, versus the Los Angeles Rams, The Stick had a seating capacity of 61,185. It was 120 feet high and made with 1,034 tons of structured steel and 8,000 tons of reinforced steel. Parking lots accommodated 14,000 cars and 175 buses. Inside the stadium there were just fifty-four restrooms and twenty-nine concession stands. In 1979 the artificial turf surface was replaced by natural grass. The field has been resodded annually ever since, using a Bermuda hybrid with a perennial rye overseed, which takes as long as twenty days to complete.[1]

Since Candlestick was next to the bay, the stadium would become known for sloppy field conditions and strong winds that often swirled down into the stadium, creating tough conditions for football, especially the kicking game.

"I always hated it. I don't know why, but the past few years it's been great there. They don't play baseball there anymore. What I remember is every weekend it would always rain, [and] the mud, the sod would tear up. It was brutal. I was probably the only guy [on the team] who enjoyed the road games—especially inside somewhere—I always loved the domes," said a laughing Ray Wersching, kicker. "I remember one time Morten Andersen [kicker for the New Orleans Saints] came up to me at The Stick and asked, 'Ray, how do you do it?' and I said, 'I have to. I don't have a choice.' You just do your best. You try not to think of all the variables. You try not to think of the wind, try not to think of the mud, the grass. Sometimes they put the ball on the grass—the grass could be an inch, inch and a half deep—the ball disappears. It just made it tough. But I wouldn't trade it for anything. Looking back at it, I love it. Because there are guys who played who never got to the playoffs. Here I am, two Super Bowls. I'm a fortunate guy."[2]

THE STADIUM

Inside the stadium, Candlestick was a strange place to play. The always-wet turf and windy conditions on the field combined with the cramped locker rooms and narrow hallways inside quickly gave The Stick a bad reputation. But most players on the 1984 49ers enjoyed the quirkiness of The Stick. "Candlestick Park was a special kind of place, especially when the fog rolled in. There was one time the fog rolled in, and I couldn't see the receiver across from me," said cornerback Mario Clark. "I'll always remember Candlestick Park. The fans were 100 percent with us every step of the way. It was a great experience."[3]

One special place was the home locker room, a two-level sanctuary—with the offense and defense on separate levels—where the team bonded before heading out to play football on the mostly dirt playing field. "The fighting was done in Candlestick in the dirt, in the mud, in the grass, in this old stadium that looked like a Roman Colosseum. . . . You knew the other players were bitching [about] their facilities. That's what we loved. We knew they were bitching that 'this is the crappiest [place] I've ever played in my life' and 'I hate the crappy shower.' I loved it. I loved knowing that," said Ron Ferrari, linebacker.[4]

The cramped locker rooms—like the old facility at Redwood City—brought the 49ers closer as a team. If they could overcome the limited space to focus on the work at hand on the field, they could overcome anything. Leaving the locker room, 49er players couldn't miss a sign Walsh hung: "I will not be out-hit anytime this season." With those final words, players headed down the narrow hallway that allowed only two to stand side by side, out through the home dugout, and onto the wet grass at Candlestick—a Niner tradition for every player who ever played at The Stick.

Whether it was Candlestick dirt, fog from the bay, or cramped locker rooms, for 49er players, it was their home away from home. "I remember stepping [on the field] at Candlestick more than anything. Out of the dugout onto the field. Saw the crowd and sky. It was like, 'Hey, I'm finally playing on Sunday.' For every guy who put on a helmet, that's their desire. Eventually we can play on Sunday, and I had finally made it. It was a great feeling of accomplishment," said Guy McIntyre, rookie offensive guard.[5]

There were many memorable moments at The Stick but none as memorable as "The Catch" on January 10, 1982. That Joe Montana–to–Dwight Clark play gave the city and the 49ers Faithful a memory for the record books. All Forty-niners fans can recall where they were and what they were doing when that play occurred in the north end zone. "The Catch" also enshrined Candlestick Park in sports history, giving it legendary status akin to that of Yankee Stadium, Wrigley Field, and Fenway Park.

After the 49ers won Super Bowl XVI in 1982, 49ers tickets at Candlestick Park became a hot commodity. It was the place to be and to be seen. For 49ers Faithful, the Candlestick Park experience made The Stick one of the best stadiums in the country. Tailgating was elevated to an art form before home games. Wine, food, and music became a staple at the stadium by the bay.

GAME DAY ENTERTAINMENT

Like everything else in his organization, Eddie DeBartolo Jr. wanted the Candlestick Park experience to be first class. He hired young Michael Olmstead to be the team's entertainment director—a role that his family had held since the early 49ers days in the All-America Football Conference. "My dad started producing halftime shows for the 49ers in 1948, so I kind of grew up on the field at Kezar Stadium," said Olmstead. "I produced my first show when I graduated from Princeton and came back in 1971 for the championship and have been doing it ever since."[6]

"He [DeBartolo] gave you a lot of leeway. He trusted you, and he treated you with respect and like family," said Olmstead about working for Eddie DeBartolo Jr. "I had a lot of respect for him." Bringing star power to Candlestick was priority. Local and national music artists performed yearly, mainly during the pregame shows, which were a special treat for 49ers fans. In 1984 alone Olmstead booked popular musical acts such as Joyce Kennedy (preseason game), Jeffrey Osborne (week 2 vs. Redskins), Andrea McArdle (week 3 vs. Saints), local band Tower of Power (week 7 vs. Steelers), Ashford & Simpson (week 15 vs. Vikings), The Tubes (week 15's halftime show), and Huey Lewis and the News (week 18 vs. Giants).[7]

"We were having rock bands from the Bay area, from Huey Lewis, Starship, all those different groups. Everyone wanted to be part of the 49ers. Eddie was young; he was into it. It was a very exciting time. We were doing things that had not been done before," said Olmstead.[8] "It was an event. It was huge. People would go all out; it was an all-day event. They were ready by the time the game started," said Bill Wash's son Craig.[9]

FORTY-NINERS CHEERLEADERS

After Joe Thomas dismissed the 49ers cheerleaders, Michael Olmstead was in charge of resurrecting the squad in 1983. "We never had cheerleaders even when we won the first Super Bowl. We would have high school dance teams or song leaders perform on the field. We talked to Eddie after the Super Bowl in 1981, and we started our first cheerleaders in 1983. The first team had only twelve girls, and we really focused on dance ability. In fact, we had Paula Abdul for the choreography for the first tryouts," said Olmstead. The first year Olmstead hired Lori Ryan to run the team. The 49ers first cheerleading squad included Hedi Hooper, Angela King, and a future star—Teri Hatcher.

"She was beautiful and talented and had a great personality. She was an immediate star because of her appearance, and cameramen and cameras gravitated to Teri," said Olmstead. "She was very talented and a strong dancer and had bigger plans in mind and moved to Hollywood to pursue her career."[10] Hatcher would go on to star in hit TV series *Lois & Clark* and *Desperate Housewives*. But during the 1984 season she cheered on the sidelines for the San Francisco 49ers.

FORTY-NINERS TEAM PHOTOGRAPHER

Heading into the 1984 season, Candlestick Park was a loud, exciting arena for 49ers fans. On the sidelines was Michael Zagaris, the team's photographer, capturing it all. Zagaris was a native of San Francisco who attended 49ers games at Kezar Stadium with his father during the mid-1950s. Zagaris started his career in photography as a teenager watching the Million Dollar Backfield with his football hero Hugh McElhenny carrying the ball.

After attending law school and spending time shooting the local music scene, Zagaris wanted to get back into sports photography. In 1973 he talked his way into shooting football games for the San Francisco 49ers. After Bill Walsh was hired, Zagaris had a productive conversation with the 49ers head coach about preserving the team's history. "I went to him and [said I] wanted to be [around] the team. 'I think it's going to be special and I want to document this from day one. Shoot the team on the bench, in the locker room, halftime, in meetings, and if you think I am going too far and [becoming] a distraction, just look at me and I will back off.' He said, 'OK, we will try that,'" said Zagaris.[11]

Zagaris shot some of the most iconic images of 49ers coaches and players. From close-ups on the bench to intimate moments in the locker room, he has preserved 49ers history for more than four decades. Most of the photos shot were black and white, giving the images a unique look that is purely his. Forty-niners fans undoubtedly have seen his photos in 49ers programs and publications and might even have some on their walls.

In 2013 he celebrated his forty-first season on the 49ers sidelines. In addition to Walsh's support, he also appreciated the support from Eddie DeBartolo Jr. "From day one, he was visible. He had passion and was always around," said Zagaris. "You could tell he loved and cared for the players and he wanted to win."[12]

FORTY-NINERS RADIO

By 1984 seating capacity at Candlestick Park had increased to 61,413. On Sundays nearly every seat was filled. Forty-niners fans at the stadium and at home could listen to the game locally on the 49ers flagship station KCBS. For the fourth consecutive year Don Klein (voice of The Catch) was the 49ers play-by-play man, with former NFL quarterback Don Heinrich as color analyst. Doing pre- and postgame reports was an up-and-coming young radio voice, Ted Robinson, who had joined Klein and Heinrich in the booth in 1983 before switching exclusively to pre- and postgame reports in 1984.

"Don Klein was in my generation. We were trained to [be] consummate professionals. Absolutely precise in his description, precise in his factual presentational, not emotional," said Robinson. "The most emotion I ever heard [from] Don was The Catch."[13] Klein was a well-known Bay-area announcer who began at KCBS in 1956, broadcasting mainly Stanford basketball and football games. In 1981 Bill Walsh recommended him for 49ers games, and in 1981 Klein became the play-by-play voice of the 49ers. Topping that season off was the radio call for The Catch. "I was sports director at KCBS and I had a daily sports show. That call was just luck," said Klein.[14]

His partner was former NFL quarterback Don Heinrich, who played eight years in the NFL with three different teams—including six years with the New York Giants—and who also participated in the 1958 NFL Championship Game referred to in popular culture as "The Greatest Game Ever Played." In 1984 the two Dons made a perfect pair for listeners. "Don [Heinrich] was a quarterback and that worked out well. I would say, 'tell me what [the offense is] looking for,' and the listener got a full picture of what they were trying to do," said Klein.

"Bill [Walsh] was always very good with the press, and he was very good about giving you time," recalled Klein. The veteran broadcaster spoke to Walsh after games for three five-minute radio spots that aired on KCBS throughout the week leading up to the next game. "After the games I would interview Bill for about five minutes, and he would talk about the game plan or what was expected that week," said Klein. [15]

"Players gave good interviews and were mostly upbeat. If they lost, they really didn't want to talk," said Klein. "I spent a lot of time at the practices and got to know them really well. I liked Dwight Clark. He was always one of my favorites to interview. He was a great guy and was always with a big smile and upbeat." [16]

The radio team of Klein and Heinrich enjoyed a wonderful ride during the 1984 season, as well as teaching a young aspiring play-by-play announcer the ropes. "I learned a lot from Don [Klein]. Just saying the right things, call[ing] the right people, the right yard line, the right score. All of that. [He was] a total gentleman, very welcoming to me," said Ted Robinson. [17] In 2009 Robinson would become the 49ers play-by-play man, continuing a fine tradition of 49ers radio voices that over the years has included Bob Fouts, Lon Simmons, Don Klein, and Joe Starkey.

In 2013 the 49ers played their last season at Candlestick Park, winning more than 200 games at The Stick (1971–2013). But in 1984 the stadium was filled with emotions on the field, on the sidelines, in the stands, and from the radio booth. For 49ers fans, radio announcers, coaches, and players, there will never be another Candlestick Park.

11

OCTOBER

Week 6 at New York Giants (Monday, October 8)
Week 7 vs. Pittsburgh Steelers (October 14)
Week 8 at Houston Oilers (October 21)
Week 9 at Los Angeles Rams (October 28)

After a perfect month of September the 49ers prepared themselves to play three road games in the next four weeks. Bill Walsh had a simple philosophy when taking his team on the road. It was a business trip, not a vacation. "Bill would always have this speech, 'It's us against them.' When you went into a stadium you want them to be booing you as loud as they can. Then every time you hear that, you get a little bit more excited about beating these guys, because that's the way they're gonna come at you. He almost kind of put us into that frame of mind. That it would be a very challenging environment," said Bill Ring, running back.[1] "Us against the world. Bill Walsh always said that. These are business trips. We're not allowed to see family and friends. Might come in a little early, but it was strictly business. After that, on the plane, you guys can have fun, but before that it was a business trip," said defensive back Dana McLemore.[2]

In keeping with the organization's overall philosophy, the 49ers traveled first class, sparing no expense courtesy of owner Eddie DeBartolo Jr. They flew in a full-size DC-10, with each player getting his own row in which to stretch out. They ate first-class meals on the plane, and when they checked into the team's hotel, it was the five-star variety. But in the end it wasn't about luxury, it was about results. "Bill used to always say to us, 'It's a business trip.' That in itself said the focus is all on Sunday. We'd travel on Friday evenings. That allowed us to adjust somewhat to the time change. There was no emphasis on dress code. Our accommodations and focus were always [about] being at the very best at one o'clock on Sundays. The other things weren't that important," said Keena Turner, linebacker. "So we'd travel with that kind of mentality. He just minimized all that stuff. And I think a lot of it was still driven by the relationships of the guys on the team. It really was about that group of guys going into an environment together and shutting all of the other things out."[3]

The first trip in October started with an East Coast flight to the Big Apple to face the New York Giants on Monday Night Football. Bill Parcells's team was 3–2 but coming off a bad 33–12 loss to the Los Angeles Rams. At 5–0 the 49ers were the only undefeated team in the NFC, joining the unbeaten Miami Dolphins of the AFC, who were riding the hot hand of Dan Marino. The second-year phenom from the University of Pittsburgh had already thrown for 1,527 yards and fifteen touchdowns in the season's first five games. On the day before the 49ers were to play the Giants, Chicago Bears running back Walter Payton broke Jim Brown's all-time rushing mark of 12,313 yards at Soldier Field against the New Orleans Saints. Down the coast, Eric Dickerson of the Rams was off to a tremendous start with 498 yards rushing. Throughout the 1984 season, the NFL record book was under fire from stars around the league.

Before the season started Bill Walsh circled several games on the calendar to challenge his team. The Redskins in week 2 was one of those games. The trip to New York was another. Speaking to his team on Monday he reiterated the importance of playing well on the national stage in New York.

> Just want to set it straight as far as this week's game is concerned. Little different for those of you who've done it—go to New York City to play a game—in the fight game, you go to Madison Square Garden. Guys would spend their whole career trying to get there one time. In New York City, it's a crazy place, but it's the mecca of the whole country. When you're an athletic team or entertainer, actor, musician, or whatever, you want to perform in New York City. [It] is the ultimate. We're going there as an undefeated football team. This

is where your performance is looked at by everybody. As you guys know, the critics usually start there. Everybody looks at you from there. Pressure is on you there to perform. The pressure is on you. There've been a lot of hyped athletes and musicians who've gone in there and failed and staggered out of town.

We'll go in with a lot of pride and a lot of accomplishment and test [ourselves] in New York City. This is not Duluth or Albuquerque; this is the Big Apple. This is the mecca of the United States or the world. The sport critics there, the sports fans there are the most active, the most vocal, the most critical. [There are] all kinds of ways to be a good football team: one is to be a great performing team that goes into New York City and methodically destroy their finest. Just go in and destroy their finest and leave town, and know you went into New York City to do it. It's that simple.

That's the challenge. The other way to do it is go in there flat, go in their distracted. When a plane flies over, you see these tall buildings. You know there is a little action in town. You go in there and do that. You make a fool of yourself, and you fall on your face. Generally goes either way. It's my job, the coaches' job, leaders of the team [to] make sure to go in there as champions and dismantle the New York Giants football team and leave town knowing we did it in New York City.

A lot of you have been through it going in there, but you know we're going in as maybe a great football team—who knows, maybe great—they're going to recall what they saw of us, in the future and rest of this season. If we're going to be great, this is the place to be great: New York City. So we're going to be ready to play our best game. Our best game against this particular team is to shatter them early, to bust them all over the field. That's the way you play this particular team. You play in New York City, you better rise to the occasion.

It's not going to be easy because they'll be playing in front of their home crowd, which is crazy. They have a Monday night game, which means something to them. They can get their self-respect back as a football team if they can win on Monday night. So you're going into a place where you're really not welcome, and you can go into the big city and see how we can perform: are we really able to be a great football team? That's what our job is. So have your mind on it, don't get distracted by coming into town where everything goes on. When you get there, we'll take the field and see if we can join the other people who've gone to New York City to see if they could do it. It's up to us.[4]

Walsh's seven-minute speech to his team set the tone for the week. They would play their best football in the biggest city on the biggest stage. They quickly got to work preparing for the Giants. Since 1981 their main focus on offense was how to block the great Lawrence Taylor. Through five games the All-Pro linebacker was leading the league in sacks with eight. But since his rookie year Walsh and Bobb McKittrick had devised the perfect game plan to diminish Taylor's pass-rushing prowess.

That year McKittrick developed a plan wherein guard John Ayers would block the great L. T. At first, teams usually tried to block Taylor with a running back, then a tight end, and finally a tackle. Taylor beat them all and made them look silly. So the 49ers chose a completely different strategy, asking Ayers to peel back and pass protect against Taylor. In 1981 it worked. "Whenever you think of New York, there's one player you're looking for: number 56! Lawrence Taylor was a force his entire career. John [Ayers] had a great base. . . . He was an offensive lineman, just a big guy [six feet five, 265], big legs. Then he'd get his hands in there, and the guys couldn't get away from him. Great technique. Great balance. He'd get in there and fight the guy. He just fit right in there and they couldn't go anywhere. It was amazing," said offensive tackle Allan Kennedy.[5]

One of the reasons that McKittrick suggested using Ayers to block Taylor was that Ayers would not back down. "John was a tenacious player. And he was a fighter. Regardless of what the challenge was, he wasn't going to give in, and L. T. was the guy at the time. He was the sackmaster on the block, and John knew it. In order for us to be successful, we had to be able to block him. And Bobb used that to our advantage. He knew John was a tenacious, no-nonsense, dig-in-the-dirt type of guy. He had the ability to do it . . . some people are better at blocking certain people than others. That was going be the matchup that we had to win. We had to win it in order for us to be successful," said Guy McIntyre, offensive guard.[6]

While developing the game plan, Walsh received news that wide receiver Freddie Solomon would not play. Walsh turned disappointment into an opportunity to give another one of his players a chance to make a big impact. He drew up a play to involve his speedy fourth receiver Renaldo Nehemiah, which Nehemiah appreciated. "Even though I may not have been starting, I was going to play, and if somebody got dinged up, I had to be his equal," said wide receiver Renaldo Nehemiah. "He was a good manager of men, and he had great personal skills. That's something that either you have or you don't."[7]

Along with using Nehemiah more, Walsh wanted to get the ball to his backs out of the backfield. Because the Giants tended to blitz leaving their inside backers on backs out of the backfield in man-to-man coverage, he thought it would be tough to cover Craig and Tyler on outside routes. With the game plan installed, Walsh once again spoke to his team about playing on the big stage of New York City.

> We're not going to New York and coming back with our tails between our legs. It's that simple. We're not going back there to be embarrassed. We're going to play our best football game in that city. Everybody [has] got to make up their minds to [do] it. You're personally going into that city to win a football game. It's that simple, and I [will] not let anything get in the way of that.[8]

"Take it as a business approach. Let's go in there, do our business, and Bill was, 'It's us against the world. Everybody's watching: all these New York people, all these New York reporters. The damn world is watching. Let's go show them about the 49ers. Let's kick their ass, get on the plane, and go back home,'" said defensive end Jim Stuckey.[9]

The 49ers arrived in New York as well prepared as any other time during the 1984 season. A sold-out crowd of more than 76,000 fans filled Giants Stadium as TV sets in San Francisco tuned into ABC's Monday Night Football to watch the 49ers play a nearly perfect game.

But during warm-ups the 49ers lost a player in an unusual way. Backup offensive tackle Allan Kennedy passed out in the middle of Giants Stadium. "That game wasn't a real highlight in my career, because that's the one game where I hyperventilated and passed out. Fell on my face before the game even started! A little embarrassing there," said Kennedy. "We came out for pregame and we ran up the fifty [yard line]. We came back to the end zone. I took my helmet off and took a knee. Next thing I knew I woke up and there were three doctors going, 'Al, do you know where you are?' I said, 'Yeah, I'm in New York. What happened?' I get up and I walked back to the locker room. The New

York fans are just needling me left and right. I come back out in my street clothes. So, not a highlight. But I was able to bounce back from that."[10]

The 49ers won the toss and elected to receive. The crowd was going wild, and it was as loud as a stadium could get. The 49ers soon would hear the sweetest sound of all when playing a road game: silence. Putting his headset on, Walsh paced the sidelines wearing his traditional white 49ers V-neck sweater with gold pants. After one first down, Walsh called Fox 2 Winston. Montana was under center with Roger Craig lined up behind him. Nehemiah was in the slot to the right. Lined up outside Nehemiah, Dwight Clark went in motion, leaving the speedy Nehemiah alone on the right, creating a one-on-one matchup with cornerback Mark Haynes. At the snap Montana took a quick five-step drop and fired a ten yard out to Nehemiah, who made the catch and turned up near the sideline. Haynes took a bad angle on the out route and never caught up. It was all she wrote as Nehemiah sprinted fifty-nine yards for a touchdown. With Nehemiah's sprinter's speed, it was no contest.

"It was a basic play. It freed me up one-on-one, and [Walsh] said the guy would be trailing me and if Joe threw the ball on time, there's no way the guy could be step-for-step with me," said Nehemiah. "I remember running down the sidelines. I was saying to myself aloud, 'It worked, it worked.' I remember running down the sidelines, just cracking up, going, 'This guy just drew this play and it worked. This guy is pretty impressive.'"[11]

"Skeets" grew up just twenty miles from Giants Stadium, making his first touchdown of 1984 even sweeter. "My family was there and not too many people can say they scored a touchdown on Monday Night Football in their home state. So that was nice for me," said Nehemiah. After just six plays, the game was 7–0. It was just the beginning of a scoring barrage. After a quick three-and-out by the Giants, Walsh went back to his first twenty-five plays. The 49ers offense started gaining big chucks of yardage: Wendell Tyler ripped off twenty-five yards on a sweep, followed by Montana hitting Craig for twenty-one yards. The script continued with a twelve-yard completion to Mike Wilson and another twenty-one-yard catch-and-run by Craig, putting the ball on the Giants one-yard line.

On the sixth play of the drive Montana executed a perfect play-action fake to Tyler up the middle, then pulled the ball back and lofted a soft pass to a wide-open John Frank in the corner of the end zone. The first career catch for the rookie from Ohio State was a touchdown. When Frank caught the ball he wanted to spike it, but he just handed the ball to the official. With only six and a half minutes gone in the first quarter, Walsh had called twelve plays that led to two touchdowns. The 49ers were making a big statement in New York City.

The Giants offense had another quick three-and-out. It was now time for the 49ers special teams to get involved in the prime-time party. Giants punter Dave Jennings booted a booming punt that had five seconds of hang time. As Dana McLemore settled under it, he never considered making a fair catch, although the Giants were bearing down on him. Terry Kinard, the Giants starting free safety, got close enough that he made contact with McLemore. Not breaking his concentration, the third-year pro from the University of Hawaii fielded the ball cleanly, made the first man miss, broke an arm tackle from rookie linebacker Carl Banks, sprinted upfield, broke another tackle by linebacker Robbie Jones, juked another tackler at the Giants forty-five-yard line, and sprinted past everybody else into the end zone. Holding the ball above his head with his right hand, McLemore jump high in the air, celebrating his big play.

The seventy-nine-yard return was his third career punt return for a touchdown. The first quarter was barely half over and the 49ers led 21–0. Finally the Giants responded by driving for a field goal, but the 49ers defense didn't want to be left out. On the Giants next drive, Dwight Hicks picked off Phil Simms to set up the offense again. Although Walsh had already used his first twenty-five plays, he knew how to attack the Giants defense. This time, he used Roger Craig, who gained twenty-seven yards on three touches. Not to be left out, Wendell Tyler then ripped off thirty-six yards around the right end as the 49ers drove to the Giants eight-yard line. On third down Montana threw a swing pass in the flat to Craig, who found himself one-on-one with linebacker Harry Carson. Making a serious juke to move back inside, Craig made Carson grab nothing but air. Four yards later Craig was in the end zone for the 49ers fourth touchdown of the first half.

The New York crowd was silent. On the ABC broadcast, O. J. Simpson commented that the Giants were "playing one of the finest teams in the game today."[12] Walsh's speech early in the week had been heard. The 49ers were playing like a team on a mission. The second half saw the 49ers defense continue to shut the door. A Jim Fahnhorst interception led to a Ray Wersching field goal. Walsh pulled Joe Montana, who had thrown three touchdowns in the game, early in the fourth quarter. The only thing left for the 49ers was to see if the defense would give up a touchdown. With just over a minute left in the game, the Giants scored on a one-yard touchdown run by Butch Woolfolk. An opposing team had not crossed the 49ers goal line since the third quarter of the Saints game during week 3. The defense had played twelve quarters without surrendering a touchdown.

The 31–10 victory was a dominant performance in every respect. Offense, defense, and special teams contributed to a complete and satisfying victory. It was the first time since 1948—when the 49ers were in the All-America Football Conference—that the team had started the season 6–0.

After this convincing win, the national and local media started talking about a perfect season in earnest. The *Washington Post*'s Christine Brennan wrote her recap of the game under the headline, "49ers Look Perfect for the Season." "We'll play them one at a time," said Walsh after the game.[13] Spoken like a true coach.

Walsh gave a game ball to Roger Craig. The second-year running back from Nebraska had a breakout game on national television totaling 128 yards from scrimmage on sixteen touches and one touchdown. "He may be the most versatile back in football. He has the size and strength and certainly the concentration and intelligence. And he blocks beautifully," commented Walsh at his postgame press conference.[14]

The other game ball went to the unsung offensive line. Along with Craig's big game, Wendell Tyler ran for 101 yards on just fourteen carries behind a very quiet offensive line. John Ayers dominated the great Lawrence Taylor, who finished with just four tackles and no sacks. Walsh spoke to the team:

> As far as game balls for this game [Giants], we looked at the film, the whole offensive line should get one. [Cheers and yelling in the 49ers meeting room] . . . You did a hell of a job the other night. We did what we talked about doing at the start of the week. That's one project completed. The next one of course is the Steelers.[15]

The 6–0 start gave the 49ers a comfortable three-game lead in the NFC West:

NFC West Standings
(as of October 9)
49ers: 6–0
Rams: 3–3
Saints: 3–3
Falcons: 3–3

With the short week the 49ers prepared for a home game against the always-tough Pittsburgh Steelers, coached by Chuck Noll. The future Hall-of-Fame coach was impressed with the play of the 49ers. "I don't think I've seen a better team on film. I haven't seen a team play with the intensity that they've played with. They're relentless," commented Noll.[16]

Looking at the film on the Steelers defense, Walsh was concerned about attacking the Steelers 3–4 front coached by one of his former players. Tony Dungy, the youngest coordinator in the league at twenty-nine, played one year for the 49ers in 1979—Walsh's first year in San Francisco. Now he was calling defensive signals for an aggressive, physical defense that loved to hit. "We have to get ready, offensively and defensively, to play these guys. It's a game we can't skip a beat on," remarked Walsh to his squad.[17]

On game day the 49ers found out that one of their key starters would miss the game. After warm-ups offensive tackle Keith Fahnhorst just couldn't play. On the long flight back from New York his back flared up and never improved throughout the week or during pregame. After ninety-five consecutive starts, the durable right tackle would miss his first game in six years. "That was real frustrating, standing on the sidelines watching," said Fahnhorst.[18]

In his place, McKittrick called on Allan Kennedy. Just a week after his most embarrassing moment—passing out before the Giants game—Kennedy would get his first NFL start. "The coaches had enough confidence in me to say, 'OK, Keith, take the day off, and we'll put Allan in there,'" said Kennedy. "My folks were there. They didn't come to many games. They came to that game. I think my dad was more nervous than I was!"[19]

The 3–3 Steelers came to Candlestick Park as eight-and-a-half-point underdogs to the unbeaten 49ers. Starting for the Steelers at quarterback for the first time that season was Mark Malone, who replaced an injured David Woodley. The glory years had passed by the Steelers, but there were a few remaining stars from the Steel Curtain. "I watched Jack Lambert and Donnie Shell as a kid growing up, and here I am on the field playing against them," said Roger Craig, fullback. "I was a captain that game. I can remember they were captains and I shook their hands. Donnie Shell, he just kind of snarled at me."[20]

On their first drive of the game Malone guided the Steelers deep into 49ers territory. With a balanced offense of seven runs and five passes, Rich Erenberg capped a twelve-play drive with a two-yard touchdown run. The first drive of the game took nearly six minutes off the clock. After a couple of punts by both teams the Steelers made another long scoring drive.

This time the Steelers took eleven plays to march fifty-three yards to set up a field goal by Gary Anderson. With eight minutes left in the second quarter, the 49ers trailed 10–0. On the ensuing drive, the 49ers offense got going. Starting at their own twenty Montana used the whole field and every available receiver. Completing passes to five different receivers, he drove the team to the Steelers seven-yard line. On second down Montana ran a bootleg to his right. With nobody open, he tucked the ball away and sprinted to the corner of the end zone. Touchdown! The nearly seven-minute drive took the 49ers into the locker room trailing only 10–7.

The second half started with the most unusual drive. After the 49ers punted, the Steelers launched an eighteen-play drive that resulted in a strange situation: third-down and forty-one yards to go for a first down. Three straight penalties and a Dwaine Board sack led to the huge negative yardage. The drive took nearly eight minutes off the clock, but the long delay didn't slow down Walsh's offense.

Montana converted two key third-down plays with completions to Dwight Clark to put the 49ers in scoring range. Two plays into the fourth quarter, a thirty-yard field goal by Ray Wersching knotted the game. With a rested defense, George Seifert got a big play that helped change the momentum of the game. Mark Malone faded back to pass, but up the middle came Gary "Big Hands" Johnson, drilling the Steelers quarterback just as he threw the ball. The pigskin flew right into the hands of linebacker Keena Turner. "I think he was trying to throw it over me, but it just came right to me," said Turner after the game.[21]

Turner brought the interception back to the Steelers twenty-yard line. The 49ers Faithful cheered the game's first turnover loudly. Four plays later Wendell Tyler plowed up the middle, running through safety Eric Williams, for his sixth touchdown of the season. With 10:48 left the 49ers took their first lead of the game, 17–10. The 49ers looked like they would pull it off. But something wasn't right. "I'd have to admit that looking back, I think that Pittsburgh did a great job of evaluating what we did defensively and had a specific plan and did a good job of attacking what we did," said defensive coordinator George Seifert.[22]

The Steelers did have the right game plan. After losing the lead Mark Malone engineered a surprising drive deep into 49ers territory that included converting a fourth-and-one with a quarterback sneak. The 49ers defense then "swelled up," forcing a fourth-and-goal from the 49ers six-yard line. The game's biggest play was then put into the hands of the officials. The Steelers lined up with three wide receivers, one tight end, and one back who stayed in to pass block. Two of the Steelers receivers ran crossing routes: one at the back of the end zone and the other, John Stallworth, at the goal line. While crossing at the front of the goal line, cornerback Eric Wright stayed behind Stallworth step for step. After taking a five-step drop, Malone pump faked once. Then with time running out, he forced the ball to Stallworth at the front of the end zone.

Wright made a great jump on the ball, diving in front of Stallworth, knocking the ball down with his right arm. Great play. But hold up! Field judge Don Habel threw his penalty flag. Pass interference on Wright, giving the Steelers a new set of downs. Television replays showed that Wright knocked the ball away with his right hand while diving in front of the receiver. His left hand never touched Stallworth. NBC announcer Bob Trumpy reacted, "I don't know about that call."[23]

Wright came out of the game, tossed his helmet off, and sat on the end of the 49ers bench. "It was an awful call. Doesn't mean we win the game, but we thought it was an awful call," said linebacker Keena Turner.[24] "I felt like those officials had never seen an athlete as good as Eric [Wright] make a play like that. It was a spectacular play that he made," said Seifert.[25]

The Steelers had new life. After a false start penalty Malone made a gutsy call. He drew up a play in the huddle for John Stallworth. On the fifteenth play of the drive, Malone threw a fade pass in the corner of the end zone. Stallworth leaped over Ronnie Lott to make the catch. The extra point tied the game 17–17. It was another long drive, running 7:27 off the clock and leaving just 3:03 remaining in the game.

The 49ers made their worst play of the year on the following drive. On the third play from scrimmage Montana tried to hit Bill Ring out of the backfield near the sidelines. Without enough loft on the throw, linebacker Bryan Hinkle made a leaping one-handed interception near midfield. "Anytime Joe did something like throw an interception, everyone just gasped because he just didn't throw interceptions," said Paul Hackett, quarterbacks and wide receivers coach.[26] Gaining his balance, Hinkle sprinted up the sidelines forty-three yards to the 49ers three-yard line before John Ayers knocked him out-of-bounds, saving a touchdown.

The 49ers defense once again "swelled up" and did not allow a touchdown. Walsh used the two-minute warning and his last two timeouts to stop the clock. The Steelers settled for a short Gary Anderson field goal. The 49ers trailed by three but got the ball back with 1:42 left and no timeouts. Starting at their own twenty-six-yard line, Montana Magic brought the fans to their feet.

Montana to Clark for thirteen yards
Montana to Cooper for four yards
Montana to Cooper for eight yards; Cooper gets out-of-bounds with
    forty-three seconds remaining
Montana to Craig for five yards with twenty seconds remaining
Montana to Cooper for thirteen yards
Montana to Cooper for eleven yards; Cooper dives out-of-bounds
    with ten seconds remaining

Montana had gone six of seven for fifty-four yards, using tight end Earl Cooper to get his team in field goal position to tie the game. "We ran that 70 series and I caught four passes and got out of bounds. We were so conditioned to get what you can and get out of bounds," said Cooper.[27]

Ray Wersching trotted onto the field to attempt a game-tying thirty-seven-yard field goal. He tapped Montana on the shoulder—"line me up, Joe," said Wersching. The snap was perfect. The hold was perfect. Wersching, with his head down, drilled it. The ball veered left from the beginning and never came back. Wide left. No good. Wersching knew it. As soon as he kicked the ball, he immediately jumped in the air and spun in a circle.

"Once you get the ball moving from a right-footed kicker . . . if you get any kind of wind, it brought it over, and it was like, 'Oh, noooo!' I couldn't believe it didn't go through, because I hit it pretty well," said Wersching.[28]

Steelers players started to celebrate. Malone kneeled down and the game was over. The 49ers had suffered their first defeat. There would be no perfect season, although nobody on the 49ers was thinking about that. It was a tough loss for everybody. "I think it was probably a good thing that we did it then, because everyone was very angry and we didn't want to lose again," said Bill Ring, running back. "It was a tough game and it was very close the whole way. But I think in some respects that was a great wake-up call for the whole team."[29]

"That was probably the best thing that could've happened to us, losing that game. That was a reality check," said safety Carlton Williamson. "We were feeling like we cannot be beat because we will find a way to win. But coming out on the other side of that game with a loss, it made us realize that [if] we get into the playoffs, there is no second chance. So we can't lose. That means we have to play our very best every time. And we learned from that. We learned a lot from that game we lost and I really believe that helped us. That's what I took from that game."[30]

It was the first loss since the 1983 NFC Championship Game against the Redskins. That heartbreaking, lousy feeling had reemerged. It would be the last time the 49ers would lose in 1984. "I don't remember us having ideas going into that game that we were going to be undefeated for the season. But . . . the next challenge was one we expected to win. We got to a point where, when we lined up to play, we expected to win. When we didn't, there was disappointment that went with it," said Keena Turner, linebacker.[31]

In the locker room after the game, one player didn't shy away from talking to the press. Ray Wersching stepped up to the mic and answered every question about his miss. "I thought I hit it well. I'm just really depressed and disappointed. . . . I like to contribute to this team. I have the opportunity to tie the game up and something like that happens, I feel hurt. I felt like I let the guys down and I don't want to do that. I want to contribute," said Wersching to KGO-TV after the game.[32] But nobody on the 49ers blamed Wersching—even thirty years later. "You can't put it on the kicker. It didn't come down to that one play," said Earl Cooper. "You never lose confidence. That's one thing I know about that team. You miss a pass. You drop a pass. You miss a block. You miss a field goal. Everybody had each other's back. Hey, we'll get the next one. We'll put you in a better position to make the next one. I think that's all the confidence that every one of those players had in each other."[33]

"That was a credit to the leadership we had on the team. Certainly nobody panicked after we got beat by Pittsburgh. But we certainly knew that we didn't want it to happen again," said Keith Fahnhorst, offensive tackle.[34] In the end the 49ers didn't play their normal sixty-minute football game. George Seifert's defense gave up 175 yards rushing—the Steelers had the ball for thirty-four minutes—and surrendered eight of fifteen third downs. They couldn't get off the field. The following day's local headlines focused on the nearly perfect season and one bad call.

"There Goes the Perfect Season"[35]
"49ers Break Date with Perfection"[36]
"Million Dollar Game, 10-Cent Officiating"[37]

On Monday at 711 Nevada Street in Redwood City, the 49ers got back to work. "It took a lot of pressure off everybody. Everybody just started playing football and we're concentrating on just getting through the season and getting to the Super Bowl," said running back Wendell Tyler.[38] "It really taught us that we cannot play like that and expect to meet our goals. I think it got us to focus on small things," said Carlton Williamson, safety. That morning, Walsh addressed his squad for the first time after the loss.[39]

> We have a great team. We haven't lost a thing from the standpoint of our future. In this competitive league, you have to give credit to the opponent on occasion. But the next time we take the field, men—I don't care which team it is—we've had this taste in our mouth one too many times. I don't have to suffer through this anymore than you do. I don't want that sick feeling of losing a game that you should've won or that you could've won, that sickening, lousy feeling. We know

how it is; it's not fun. So the next time you go out, the Houston Oilers, they are going to have to take the wrath with what we're going to have to give out to them. Whether they like it or not, they're going to have to take it. That's the only way to get it out of your system—to knock the hell out of somebody as soon as you can.[40]

Walsh didn't want any distractions going forward. But there was a small one the week of the Steelers game. On their day off Ronnie Lott and Renaldo Nehemiah invited twelve other 49ers players to a recording studio operated by Narada Michael Walden, a well-known music producer in San Francisco, to record a team song. "He was a friend of mine. One day Ronnie and I had gone to his studio. We were singing background on one of Phyllis Hyman's songs. He came up with the idea, 'Hey, how about we make this song?'" said Nehemiah. "Of course we all got into it."[41]

"Nobody had any idea what the heck we were doing. We just went out to have fun. It was Tuesday night and everybody said, 'Hey, we're going to meet over here and do it,'" said Mike Wilson, wide receiver.[42] "I think somebody said, 'Hey, man, we're going be doing this record. If you want to be a part of it, come on.' [I'm] a rookie; I'm trying to hang out with the guys, so I said, 'OK, I'm there. John Frank's there, too,'" said Guy McIntyre.[43] "Ronnie had the relationship with Narada Michael Walden. He had been producer of the year. He was pretty hot back in those days. So through that relationship he came up with the tune and got a group of us together and the rest is history!" said a smiling Keena Turner.[44]

Calling themselves "The 49er Squadron," the diverse group of teammates consisted of Dwight Clark, Roger Craig, John Frank, Dwight Hicks, Tom Holmoe, Ronnie Lott, Guy McIntyre, Blanchard Montgomery, Renaldo Nehemiah, Bill Ring, Keena Turner, Carlton Williamson, Mike Wilson, and Eric Wright. Titled "We're the 49ers," the song was nearly four and a half minutes long and featured the lyrics: "We're the 49ers! We will rock you till we win the fight, because we're the 49ers! We're dynamite. We're dynamite!"[45]

"They blended it, mixed it, so I can't distinguish my voice from anybody else on there. But Keena probably would say he was the best," said Guy McIntyre, laughing.[46] "Well, I was the best. I still like the song. It's a classic. It's one I think will stand the test of time," said a joking Keena Turner.[47] Some teammates might disagree. "Keena was the worst singer. I was the best. Ronnie couldn't carry a note, either, so I had to carry those guys. I had to sing louder so I could drown them. I think we even turned Keena's mic off. He didn't know that," said an equally amused Carlton Williamson. "None of us was the greatest of talents. It was all Michael Walden. But we teased. We like to tease some of the guys, 'Yeah, man, your mic was turned off.'"[48]

"It was a little theme song you'd hear in the stadium warming up, and [then] . . . you'd hear it on the radio. For the record, none of us made a cent from it, but it was fun. Those are the memories and the camaraderie that you have with your teammates that you can look back [on] and say, 'Wow, it was more than just first-and-ten and catching the ball. It was about friendships,'" said Mike Wilson.[49]

Some teammates caught the fever of the "We're the 49ers" tune. "I thought it was catchy. They did a great job on the song," said Dwaine Board.[50] Produced and written by well-known music producer Narada Michael Walden, the song was distributed by Megaton Records. Playing bass on the song was Randy Jackson, known for his twelve-year run on *American Idol*.

Locally, Bay area fans fell in love with the song. "It was cool. The city embraced it and rallied around it, and all of a sudden you started hearing it all the time," said Wilson.[51] "I was happy that I was asked to be a part of it. I still have the record," said Williamson.[52] Today the song gets overlooked because there wasn't a video shot for it, unlike the more famous "Super Bowl Shuffle" performed by the Chicago Bears in 1985, despite the fact that the 49ers recorded their song a year earlier. "You kind of laugh [at it]. We were just having a good time, and of course, it turned out to be pretty cool after you did it, and it was very popular. Then of course the Chicago Bears did it. Then everybody was doing it," said Wilson.[53]

Walsh wasn't happy that the players were preoccupied off the field, mainly because it occurred the same week as a loss. "[Walsh] never wanted us to do things outside of football because he thought it would be distracting. He wanted you to kind of fly below the radar," said Ring.[54] "OK, we just lost one game. It's not the end of the world. But to Bill, he made it seem like the end of the world!" said McIntyre.[55]

"From Bill's perspective, he never rested. Our days were filled with 'How do I get better?' Bill had an amazing way of keeping our environment on edge. It was a very edgy environment that—at least this is one guy's opinion—was never comfortable. Just wasn't a comfortable environment. You came to work feeling the edge of expectation consistently. And I think that was why it produced. It worked and our season was an example of that," said Turner.[56]

The loss to the Steelers was followed by a matchup with the winless Houston Oilers, who were 0–7 under rookie head coach Hugh Campbell. The former prep star from Los Gatos High School had actually played against Bill Walsh's Washington Union team in the Bay area. The forty-three-year-old Campbell had coached five years with the Edmonton Eskimos of the CFL before getting the Oilers job. He won five Grey Cups with Warren Moon as his quarterback, and when he was hired as the Oilers head coach he quickly signed Moon to be his starting quarterback.

As for Walsh, he wanted to get back to running the ball. Throughout the week he wrote "200 rushing yards" on the blackboard to remind his offense of the goal for the week. He wanted his team to be physical. Because the Oilers did not look good on film, Walsh wanted his team to refocus on the task at hand to get back in the win column. They would face a 3–4 defense led by a familiar coach. Jerry Glanville, who had been with the Atlanta Falcons, was now the Oilers defensive coordinator. Although the Oilers were ranked twenty-eighth in team defense, Walsh knew they would be aggressive and hit.

> It's always a test of a football team to see how you react to a loss. There's only been one team ever who's gone all the way without a loss, so all the great championship teams have basically lost games. It's how you bounce back. . . . What we need is spirit and intensity that we had two weeks ago in New York. If you come in with that, we'll explode on these guys and you're sailing again and we can reflect on the Pittsburgh game that we learned something from it. But that's what it's going to take.[57]

Saturday night in Houston, a few of the 49ers players, mostly defensive starters, ate some hotel food that didn't sit well. "I remember playing and I was sick. I was sick as a dog. Pretty much the whole defensive line was sick. It was from food poisoning. It was the food from the hotel," said Dwaine Board.[58] "For whatever reason I didn't get sick. It didn't bother me. But, yeah, there were some guys with some kind of stomach virus," said Carlton Williamson.[59]

The next day at the Astrodome the 49ers almost got more than they could handle. Keith Fahnhorst was back at right tackle as the 49ers offense got off to a great start. Joe Montana completed four passes on the opening drive, which ended with a touchdown toss to tight end Russ Francis. A second scoring drive concluded with a Ray Wersching field goal. It looked like it would be a rout. Then Montana made an uncharacteristic mistake, throwing only his third interception of the year. The Oilers capitalized on the turnover, cutting the lead to 10–7.

On the Oilers next possession Moon made the same mistake. Backup cornerback Dana McLemore dove in front of an Oiler receiver for his first career NFL interception. Montana made the turnover count with a very long scoring drive. Although Russ Francis and Mike Wilson would leave the game with injuries (neck and knee respectively), Montana capped an eighteen-play drive by throwing a perfect screen pass. "It was just before half. I was going down the left side and they thought I was going to run out-of-bounds. I stayed in bounds and I cut it up toward the end zone. I knew the situation, and they relaxed because they thought I was going out-of-bounds, but I cut it up. It was definitely an intelligent move on my part with the situation," said Wendell Tyler, running back.[60]

Tyler's quick thinking gave the 49ers a ten-point halftime lead. With twenty-nine seconds remaining, Moon scrambled up the middle for a twenty-five-yard gain as the clock ran out at halftime. This twenty-five-yard run was the longest run from scrimmage that the 49ers defense would give up all year. It showed that the 49ers defense had no weaknesses. They might bend at times but George Seifert's game plans in 1984 truly dominated their opponents, especially when the longest run of the year was a meaningless twenty-five-yard scramble to end the half.

As the rain began to fall outside the Astrodome, the 49ers defense quickly returned the ball to the offense. On the second play after halftime Dwaine Board stripped the ball from running back Larry Moriarty, and fellow defensive end Lawrence Pillers fell on it at the Oilers nine-yard line. Walsh wasn't happy when his team was called for holding on a Tyler touchdown run and settled for a field goal. The 49ers were in total command with a 20–7 lead, but the winless Oilers fought back. Moon connected with wide receiver Tim Smith on a forty-five-yard touchdown pass to cut the lead to six points.

As the fourth quarter started the 49ers made another long scoring drive. Using all his weapons, Montana took twelve plays to get his team to the Oilers five-yard line. On the next snap Roger Craig plowed up the middle, broke a tackle, and spun into the end zone. With 7:50 left in the game the 49ers led 27–14, but they couldn't shake the Oilers, as Moon continued to challenge Seifert's defense with passes downfield. This time Moon looked to his tight ends, connecting first with Chris Dressell on a forty-two-yard completion into 49ers territory, then hitting Jamie Williams down the middle of the field for a twenty-nine-yard touchdown. The quick ninety-two-yard drive took only two and a half minutes.

With the lead again cut to six points, Walsh discussed his next call with Paul Hackett. He wanted to throw. He called 78 X Hook: If the Oilers played zone, Dwight Clark would run a twelve-yard hook. If they blitzed and played man, he would run a post. To confirm the coverage in advance, Walsh sent Wendell Tyler in motion toward the left sidelines. When Oilers free safety Carter Hartwig went with the motion, both Montana and Clark knew it was man coverage.

Montana saw the blitz on his seven-step drop. Behind nice pass protection, he saw Clark make the adjustment to the post, and he launched a pass down the middle of the field. As the ball got to Clark, cornerback Willie Tullis tipped the ball into the air. Clark deflected the ball back to himself, making an incredible juggling catch. Tullis got turned around trying to find the ball as Clark streaked into the end zone for an eighty-yard touchdown. "As the ball was coming I actually thought it was overthrown. But as it hit my hands, I think he hit the ball, and it just popped straight up because I felt like it was right between us. It came at the right time for me and the team," commented Dwight Clark after the game.[61]

"Dwight Clark's catch was one of his greatest plays as a football player," said Walsh to the press.[62] The game-clinching score helped the 49ers finish off the Oilers. As the 49ers walked off the Astrodome turf with a 34–21 win, CBS announcer Wayne Walker applauded them. "They're deep and talented, and I think more than anything, the smartest team I've been around. When I go talk to all of them, real sharp guys that know the game."[63] Walsh and his staff knew the type of players they had. Not only were they physically gifted, but they were intelligent. They were definitely students of the game. Starting with training camp, they continued to learn the game of football throughout the 1984 season, this time winning a big road game regardless of the Oilers record.

In the locker room, not everything was so rosy. Owner Eddie DeBartolo thought his squad played down to the level of the winless Oilers. He voiced his opinion. "It sucked, and you can print that. Bill [Walsh] is proud of this team and so am I. But what this team needs is to pull together. I'm not disappointed with the effort, but we're not hitting on all eight cylinders."[64] The young 49ers owner might have let his emotions get the best of him. Talking to the press after the game, he discussed what really put him in a bad mood.

Originally not scheduled to be at the game, he was to attend a Michael Jackson concert with his family the night before, but he made the surprise trip. "Worst plane ride of my life," DeBartolo said of the trip on his private jet. "One time we dropped straight down for ten seconds, and the plane was sideways. I've never been so scared," said DeBartolo. DeBartolo said he took his three daughters to see Jackson in Cleveland as promised. "We spent an hour with Michael Jackson backstage and my daughters thought it was fantastic. Michael told me he liked the 49ers, no kidding," continued DeBartolo. "I said, 'Aw, c'mon, you're not interested in the 49ers really, are you?' He insisted. He said he likes their style."[65]

As emotions calmed the 49ers found themselves 7–1. Although the 49ers allowed 356 passing yards to Warren Moon, it was a bounce-back victory after the tough Steelers loss. It also would be the last time the 49ers defense would surrender more than seventeen points in a game that season. Montana had 353 passing yards and three touchdowns as the offense piled up 517 total yards. They did come up shy of the 200 rushing yards Walsh wanted, gaining only 164. It was good enough for the win.

Next up was the divisional rival Los Angeles Rams. "The games that we played against the Redskins or even some of the other NFL teams were special. But I'm going to tell you something. There is nothing like Ram week. There is nothing like playing the Los Angeles Rams," said Manu Tuiasosopo, defensive tackle. "When you get ready to play the Rams, it's like a whole different level. The intensity. Guys like Hacksaw Reynolds, a former Ram, and the intensity that he brought to the meeting rooms and in practice. It just filtered to the other players. Ram week was a special week."[66]

Heading into Rams week, the 49ers faced tough matchups every-where. Offensive tackle Keith Fahnhorst would be matched up against Rams All-Pro defensive end Jack Youngblood. Before facing the Rams, Fahnhorst would get what his wife called "his Jack face. He breaks out in zits. He can't eat, he gets grumpy," said Susan Fahnhorst to the *San Jose Mercury News* in 1985.[67]

"Yeah, Jack was a bitch. I thought he was one of the best players to ever play the game and obviously other people did, too, because he's in the Hall of Fame. But Sue always knew when I was facing Jack and I think she added to the incentive [to show up Youngblood] because she always talked about how cute he was. So I had that hanging over me, too," said Keith Fahnhorst. "I always had a lot of respect for Jack. Obviously I may have lost more battles than I won against him, but he was always one of the classiest players. I played against Jack Youngblood probably forty, fifty games because we played them in the preseason, too, and Jack never said a word one way or the other whether he beat me or didn't beat me."

Her admiration of Jack Youngblood aside, Susan Fahnhorst was very invested in her husband's career. Often she was his biggest critic. "I knew I wasn't going be able to bullshit her when I got home. Whether we won or lost, I knew that she was watching every play, and I wasn't going to be able to bullshit my way through anything," said her hus-band. "I might argue with her for a bit but she knew her football too well for me to talk my way out of it. She was much worse than Bill or Bobb."[68]

Another tough matchup would pit the 49ers front seven against the Rams huge offensive line who were blocking for the NFL's best run-ning back, Eric Dickerson. The Rams starting five linemen—Jackie Slater, Kent Hill, Doug Smith, Dennis Harrah, and Irv Pankey—aver-aged six feet four and 260 pounds. Through eight weeks, the Rams zone-blocking running game was tearing up the NFL. Dickerson had 925 rushing yards and five touchdowns. The previous two games before facing the 49ers, he had shredded the Saints for 175 yards (an 8.8-yard-per-carry average) and the Falcons for 145 yards (a 6-yard-per-carry average). Walsh's speech to the team on Wednesday described Dicker-son as "maybe the best single player in football today."[69]

Seifert and McPherson got to work. They knew early on that their defensive players were totally focused on the task at hand. "It was kind of a match made in heaven for me. I felt that I was a pretty good hitter and I welcomed the opportunity. So I was excited about our game plan. I was excited going into that game," said strong safety Carlton Williamson. "I just wanted to let Eric know that he was going to be in for a rough day. A very physical day. They had a huge offensive line; we would watch him on film. He was huge [too]. These guys were pulling and blocking in front of Eric. But a lot of it [was] designed for me to lurk in the middle like a kind of extra linebacker. Riki Ellison and Keena Turner, those guys would take out the interference. So it's just Eric and me, and we were toe to toe, eye to eye. I wanted to get the better of that every time and that was my motivating force. We felt that if we're going to win this game, we're going to have to stop him and I'm going have a lot of opportunity to do it. Yeah, I was excited about that. And it was a great game plan."[70]

Seifert would design a game plan to get everybody to the ball. It would be big man on big man, with all twelve men attacking the offensive line to get to the ball carrier. He wanted no running lanes or cutback lanes. One 49ers linebacker welcomed the challenge of facing the Rams running game and his old college coach John Robinson. "That was a physical game for me. The Rams could've drafted me before San Francisco [in the fifth round] but they didn't. So I was fired up and that was the USC offense. I knew that offense better than anybody. It was tailback U. It was simplified. It was big man on big man, and I lived for that. Those games were my favorites," said Riki Ellison, linebacker.[71]

"You had to tackle. You had to gang tackle him. You'd have to get all the hats you could get on him. He was good. Very good," said defensive line coach Bill McPherson.[72] Everybody on the 49ers defense bought into the game plan to stop Dickerson. "We did a good job ganging up on him and stopping the run with him. This is one of those things where George [Seifert] would always come up with what I call hybrid-type defenses. He put Jeff Fuller as the linebacker in one of those games. You got Ronnie Lott and Jeff Fuller, two big-time hitters on the field, and Carlton Williamson. He was able to utilize their strengths in stopping the run. He came up with one of those hybrid-type things by stacking Fuller in the box, Ronnie going in the run game. He's going to find a way to get up there quick and we were able to slow Eric Dickerson down. During that era, Eric Dickerson was one of the best backs I had seen. He could break a play at any time. You could hold him for so many plays; next thing you know, he pops one on you. We were able to neutralize him during the course of those games that year. Eric Dickerson was tough; he was a tough back to deal with," said Ray Rhodes, defensive backs coach.[73]

One 49er defender especially wanted a chance to lay a lick on Dickerson. Rookie nose tackle Michael Carter had played with Dickerson while at SMU but never got the opportunity to tackle him. "We were not allowed to even touch our running backs at SMU," said Carter. "Once I got to the 49ers, I knew I was gonna play Eric. He knew I was coming for him. I said to myself going into that rookie year, 'I never want him to ever run for 100 yards on me.' So I was looking forward to those two games that year."[74]

Tackling Dickerson would not be easy. "To this day when people ask me, Eric Dickerson was the toughest guy to tackle, because you never could get a clean hit on him. His body, he was tall. He was rangy, but he had the ability to relax parts of his body when you would try to tackle him. If you tried to tackle him around the waist, he was like a damn snake or something. Really tough. We had to emphasize a lot of gang tackling with him. The Rams always had great offensive lines. They had big physical [players]—Jackie Slater, Irv Panky, Doug Smith—they had some good guys. But George would always devise his plan, stop the run. Take the run away, and they've got to go to what they do second best or third best. It was literally stop Eric Dickerson. An emphasis on getting everybody to the ball because you never knew when that guy was down," said Jim Stuckey, defensive end.[75]

"For sure the game plan was to get as many bodies on him as possible. That was our approach. We talked about if you had the good guys [running backs], you had to hit them more. Hit them often. Hit them in a group. And that was really our emphasis and again it helped us," said linebacker Keena Turner.[76] Going into the game Seifert used the code name "Wolf" to tell Ronnie Lott to switch to safety and Dwight Hicks to move to cornerback. Just to get one more big body at the line of scrimmage.

For week 9, the 49ers traveled south to Anaheim Stadium. Walsh and his staff had prepared the 49ers well to play against their biggest rival. He knew this would be another statement game in a rivalry series that dated back to 1950. "That was just the tone that Coach Walsh set and expected, and everybody else bought into it. We were going to stay focused, and stay focused for four quarters," said Manu Tuaisosopo, defensive tackle.[77] The Rams were 5–3 coming off two consecutive division wins against the Saints and Falcons.

Once again the 49ers defense set the tone early, forcing a fumble on the Rams first offensive possession. Safety Dwight Hicks recovered the loose pigskin. Montana converted a third-and-sixteen to set up a Ray Wersching field goal. Near the end of the first quarter Eric Dickerson ripped off a nice fifteen-yard gain. It would be his last meaningful carry of the game as George Seifert's game plan would stuff the future Hall of Famer.

Early in the second quarter Wersching kicked his second field goal. After another Rams punt the 49ers offense came up with a big play. On third-and-ten from their own thirty-six-yard line, the 49ers came out in a single-back alignment with two tight ends and two wide receivers. Walsh had called a pass play. Knowing the Rams might blitz, Montana had Roger Craig swing to the right as an outlet receiver. After taking his five-step drop Montana felt instant pressure from the Rams blitz, which came up the middle from both middle linebackers, Carl Ekern and Jim Collins. With this particular blitz, the Rams All-Pro defensive end Jack Youngblood would drop back and cover the single back in the backfield if he came to the left side.

As Montana took his fifth step, he lofted a perfect swing pass to a streaking Roger Craig in the flat. Never breaking stride, Craig rushed past a helpless Youngblood down the right sideline. Downfield, Craig got a nice block by Renaldo Nehemiah on Rams cornerback LeRoy Irvin before dragging safety Eric Harris the last five yards into the end zone to complete a sixty-four-yard touchdown.

"When you blitz, you have to pay. So the Rams blitzed both guys and they're going to use Jack Youngblood to cover me. I had the jets, too, but I can't let Jack Youngblood catch me. No way. Was just perfect. It was an audible. He audibled, so I swung out and he hit me with a perfect pass right over the shoulder. Take it to the house. It was awesome," said Craig.[78] "I have coverage on the back [Craig]. I didn't cover him too well. That's the only formation and the only play that really hurts that defense. They hit the perfect play and executed perfectly on it," remarked Jack Youngblood after the game.[79]

The 49ers missed the extra point—their only mistake of the day—to take a 12–0 lead. The ensuing Rams drive was even worse for the home team. Dwaine Board used a power move, pushing left tackle Irv Pankey away quickly, then forced a fumble with a blindside hit on quarterback Jeff Kemp. Manu Tuaisosopo fell on the ball at the Rams eleven-yard line. On the second play after the turnover, on a nice play-action fake, Montana threw a dart to the back of the end zone to a leaping Freddie Solomon, who made a nice catch while managing to get both of his feet in bounds in front of the goalpost. The score was now 19–0. The rout was on.

Shortly before the half the Rams had their best drive. Kemp completed four passes for sixty-five yards putting the ball inside the 49ers five-yard line. It was time to "swell up." With the running game ineffective, Kemp hit Dickerson with a pass in the flat. It was a sprint to the pylon. With Dickerson's speed, it looked like a certain touchdown, but out of nowhere linebacker Riki Ellison not only knocked Dickerson down short of the goal line, but he jarred the ball loose through the corner of the end zone, making it a touchback for the 49ers.

"That was a big hit on the goal line. You knew he liked to go wide and it was just getting the hat on the ball and getting that ball out. That was a big-ass play," said Ellison. "It was a collective group and our game plan was to take Dickerson, to limit him in his yardage and movement."[80]

At the half Dickerson had just thirty yards on eight carries. It would get much worse for the Rams rushing attack in the second half. "We just own those guys for some reason, especially that year with their zone offense. Coach McPherson, Norb Hecker, we learned the zone offense, whether it's inside zone or outside zone: when your guard started blocking on the end, you went up and hit him in the ear hole, and it clogged everything up. When you nailed him, it just stifled the play. The Rams that year were mainly a zone-blocking team and were good at finding the cutback lanes, but we did a good job of shutting them down," said Jim Fahnhorst, linebacker.[81]

On the 49ers second drive Walsh found his offense backed up at its own five-yard line. Up by three scores Walsh wanted his team to work on passing the ball, mainly because through the previous eight weeks, the 49ers had not scored a touchdown in the third quarter. Montana looked perfect, connecting on big passes down the field, twice to Solomon for thirty-eight and sixteen yards and once to Nehemiah for twenty-six yards. A six-yard Roger Craig run capped off the ninety-five-yard drive. The score was now 26–0.

CBS announcer Tom Brookshier said, "San Francisco is thinking about Palo Alto"—Super Bowl XIX.[82] That was the furthest thing on the minds of Bill Walsh and his team. They thought only of finishing off their divisional rival. Midway through the fourth quarter Montana did just that. On a three-step drop he hit Dwight Clark, who beat Irvin badly off the line of scrimmage on a quick slant. Clark sprinted untouched for forty-four yards and another score. Montana jogged downfield with both arms raised to meet his teammates. Montana finished the game on fire, completing his last thirteen passes to go twenty-one of thirty-one for 365 yards and three touchdowns. The Rams–49ers game ranked fifth in 49ers history for single-game passing yards.

The defense shut the door the rest of the game. Late in the fourth quarter Jim Stuckey recorded the team's fifth sack of the game and Ronnie Lott had the squad's fifth turnover with an interception. Five sacks, five turnovers. A convincing 33–0 victory. It was the 49ers biggest defeat of the Rams since October 8, 1961, when they trounced them 35–0.

Of all the impressive numbers, the most impressive was holding the NFL's leading rusher, Eric Dickerson—who would run for an NFL-record 2,105 yards in 1984—to a season-low thirty-eight yards on thirteen carries. Using the 49ers base defense on more passing downs, as well as calling the "Wolf" formation, virtually stopped the explosive Dickerson. "The guys were fired up. Big Hands Johnson, Louie Kelcher, Dwaine Board were very fired up, and we had a great scheme for stopping Eric Dickerson. George Seifert gets all the credit in the world. He drew up some great stuff to stop a lot of opponents," said cornerback Mario Clark.[83]

"Hopefully we have been through that phase of the season and learned a lesson against Pittsburgh, a team we should have beaten. Then in the Houston game, we had the doldrums and almost paid dearly. We can't expect everybody to be full bore every minute of their lives. But I hope we've matured through that two-game session. I can't conceive of us playing this well every week. But I'm hopeful that our standard of play will carry us through with whomever we play. If we are after the championship, then we have to have the best record in the NFC. That's one of the very, very important factors. The weight of the title could be the home-field advantage, so we have to have the best record, and we can't assume anything," explained Bill Walsh at his postgame press conference.[84]

His players knew home field was important. "That's our goal. We want to have the home-field advantage in the playoffs. That really gave us a big help in 1981," said Randy Cross while sitting at his locker. "Have you ever been to Chicago or Washington in late December or January? Then you know why." At 8–1 the 49ers were not only the best in their division, they were the best in the NFC by two games. Their week 9 performance against the Rams compared to their games against the Redskins and Giants. But this 49ers team was looking for a bigger prize—the Super Bowl. That was always the goal. That was the mind-set.[85]

The first two months went as well as could be expected, maybe even better. (The NFL standings after week 9 are shown in table 11.1.) The 1984 49ers were in the midst of a very special season, one that required continual hard work behind the scenes. That's what great teams do to prepare themselves.

Table 11.1. NFL Standings after Week 9

AFC EAST		NFC EAST	
Miami	9–0	Dallas	6–3
New England	6–3	St. Louis	6–3
New York Jets	6–3	Washington	5–4
Indianapolis	3–6	New York Giants	5–4
Buffalo	0–9	Philadelphia	4–5
AFC CENTRAL		**NFC CENTRAL**	
Pittsburgh	5–4	Chicago	6–3
Cincinnati	3–6	Detroit	3–6
Cleveland	3–6	Tampa Bay	3–6
Houston	0–9	Minnesota	2–7
		Green Bay	2–7
AFC WEST		**NFC WEST**	
Denver	8–1	San Francisco	8–1
Los Angeles Raiders	7–2	Los Angeles Rams	5–4
Seattle	7–2	New Orleans	4–5
Kansas City	5–4	Atlanta	3–6
San Diego	4–5		

12

SIX DAYS TILL SUNDAY

Each week of the 1984 season the 49ers coaches and players prepared for each opponent on a strict schedule laid out by head coach Bill Walsh. Like training camp, the regular season was mapped out week by week, day by day, and hour by hour. Usually it was six days till Sunday, unless there was a Monday night game.

MONDAY

Mondays found Bill Walsh in his corner office watching film of the next opponent and drawing up close to 100 offensive plays by hand—up to thirty running plays and nearly seventy passing plays.

7:00 a.m.–12:00 p.m.	Individual coaches finish viewing and grading film of the just-completed game (usually played on Sunday), then review as a staff (offense and defense) and take notes. Lunch.
1:00 p.m.	49ers staff meeting
2:00 p.m.	Team meeting
2:30 p.m.	Coordinators review fifteen to twenty key plays with entire offense or defense, denoting

	major points of emphasis, then break up by positions to review film.
4:00 p.m., approximately	Walsh leaves office
4:15 p.m.	On-field practice
4:45 p.m.	Practice ends
6:00 p.m.	Dinner
9:00 p.m.	Running back/offensive line coaches meet to outline basic runs and pass protection schemes for morning meeting with coordinator. [1]

"Bill always installed [all] the plays, putting in all of the plays. He did it all himself. He did it for the running game. He did it for the passing game. He didn't allow for anybody going off on a tangent from a coaching standpoint. We were totally on the same page with him. It was just fascinating to me, and it was all planned by him," said Paul Hackett, quarterbacks and wide receivers coach.[2]

On Monday mornings while Walsh was holed up in his office—only leaving to speak to the team at 2:00 p.m.—his coaches would grade the previous day's game. Neal Dahlen, director of research and development, would be breaking down the next week's opponent. "My work-week would start as soon as we got the film of the upcoming opponent. I would take down all of the offensive plays that the opponent ran in at least three games, and the last one, of course, was the one we got the weekend prior. So that was my Monday assignment as soon as the film got there," said Neal Dahlen. "Then after that, I got the secretary to put it in the computer. I would take the computer [printouts], duplicate them for all the defensive coaches, and then I could go home. That might be 7:00 or 8:00 at night."[3]

Continued Dahlen: "I would chart all of the opponent's offense. Everything: result of the play, the formations, the personnel groupings, down and distance. There were different sortings that the computer makes: What they do on first-and-ten? What do they do second-and-long with certain personnel groups? What do they do on third-and-three? Whether it was run/pass percentage or personnel groups, you'd get all [that information] out of the report. That's the thing I liked the best about the way Bill Walsh's system worked: everybody worked on his own. You didn't sit in a group and talk back and forth and look at one film."[4]

Mondays would be the start of a long workweek for the coaches. "Monday was a bitch for the staff, because you had to get through the autopsy of the previous game and then start on your next opponent. So once you got through that, it was midnight to one o'clock," said special teams coach Fred vonAppen. "So it was labor intensive from that standpoint."[5]

After grading the previous game's film, 49ers coaches met with the players to review the game they had just played. In the defensive meeting room George Seifert showed his players how passionate he was about the little things that could result in a win or a loss. He was the master of the clicker. "George might run one play back 100 times and wouldn't say a word! It was like, 'Geez, is he ever gonna move on?' and the worst thing about it was, if you made a mistake, you knew you made a mistake. And George would just run it back. He'd run it back fifty times and then he would just go off on you. It was like, 'Geez, George I know, OK!'" said Dwaine Board, defensive end.[6]

"He might run one play back forty times! You're sitting there, 'Oh my God, we're looking at this play again?' But George was very meticulous about the way he went about his work. He didn't care about how many times he played it back. That didn't bother him at all. He went through every player on every defensive play and ran that clicker back, went through every play. Everybody's technique and what he's supposed to be doing. . . . The thing I really enjoyed about the game during that time [was that] there was nowhere for a player to hide. Either you do your job or George Seifert's gonna be on your ass," said defensive backs coach Ray Rhodes.[7]

It seemed as if every defensive player on the 1984 49ers had a George Seifert clicker story. "He made you want to understand what you were looking at, because sometimes watching a play five times, it sinks in," said Jim Fahnhorst, linebacker. "My degree was in psychology so I was a big believer in visualization, and watching film really helped me. Visualization really helped me in knowing the plays. And in learning George's weekly playbook, which was roughly 100 pages, I would go through every play the other team had and know all my responsibilities, run or pass, so that I felt mentally prepared."[8]

"George would see something and if he wants to put an emphasis on it—that little clicker, man! I was wondering if that thing would ever wear out—he would just click that rewind and you'd be going through two steps. You'll see that for like five minutes. He'd be showing just these two steps that you made. But that was George," said strong safety Carlton Williamson. "He would try to show you the angle that you're taking, a block or tackle that if you just took one more step, you would have a more impactful hit. But he was the coach and he was always coaching. Yeah, he would wear [out] that fast forward and rewind."[9]

The defensive meetings—as in training camp—were long and arduous. But nobody was bored. Seifert and Bill Walsh had the attention of their players. "There weren't a lot of really long meetings in San Diego that I could stay up for, but I could with Coach Seifert. He grabbed your attention and kept it. For me, it was fun. It was a breath of fresh air," said Louie Kelcher, defensive tackle. "We didn't sit around eating ice cream and enjoying the film. When it was time to get your ass chewed out, everybody saw it. So it was business as usual. There wasn't anything sugarcoated. We were all men at that point and they treated us that way."[10]

Whether offense or defense, every Forty-niner player learned from watching his performance on film. "I approached the NFL like each play could be your last play. So you better make the most of it. It was very rewarding to come back in on Monday morning after a victory. . . . That was my motivation to go sit down in the meeting and look at the tape and say, 'Hey, I gave it 100 percent,'" said wide receiver Mike Wilson.[11]

TUESDAY

Tuesday was a day off for the players, though some visited the facility to work out, lift, or visit the trainer. Also, the quarterbacks stopped by 711 Nevada Street to get a head start on the week's game plan. Bill Walsh started the day going over the personnel report of the next opponent. He spent at least a half hour with Allan Webb, director of pro personnel, discussing the roster of their upcoming opponent. The coaches

finalized their game plans on Tuesdays, which were the longest days for
the coaches.

8:00 a.m.	Personnel report on opponent by Allan Webb, director of pro personnel
8:30 a.m.	Offensive staff meets and discusses base runs and pass protection
10:00 a.m.	Defensive coaches and offensive line coach, quarterbacks and wide receivers coach, and running backs coach draw up sheets for runs, pass protection, goal line, short yardage, red zone and base passes, play action, etc.
11:30 a.m.	Lunch, work out, etc.
2:00 p.m.	List nickel passes and nickel runs
4:00 p.m.	Begin scripting sheets
5:00 p.m.	Review blitz situations
6:00 p.m.	Dinner
7:00 p.m.	Finalize: Defensive and offensive script sheets; script and cards; scouting reports and installation slides
9:00 p.m.	Begin short-yardage and goal-line discussions

"Basically [Tuesday] was the coach's day to stay late and get our base
game plan ready," said George Seifert, defensive coordinator. "The
base game plan would [be] basically put in for Wednesday practice,
then you would go to subsequent different aspects of your game plan.
Nickel on Thursday and still work on base. Then you'd get to Friday,
and you'd be involved in your red zone and goal-line play. So your
specifics would come as the week unfolded."[12]

"George Seifert was the Bill Walsh of defensive football in the league. We had the most intricate defensive scheme in the league, bar none at that time. He expected you to grasp it quickly. You had to be smart. You had to be on your toes, because we might put in fifteen or twenty blitzes we hadn't even run. But each week, I remember thinking, 'How the hell can he think up all this stuff on a damn Tuesday when we have a day off?'" said Jim Stuckey, defensive end. "But George was extremely intelligent and he demanded mental capability. He always said 'You can make physical mistakes but don't make mental mistakes.'"[13] All of the 49ers coaches knew that Tuesdays were going to be long days. They thought nothing of it, even if they spent the entire day and night at the practice facility. Usually that was when the 49ers coaches found their edge, devising the game plans that win football games.

The long hours combined with the tight configuration on the second floor at 711 Nevada had the coaches bonding—just as the players were in the locker room downstairs. "The facilities were less than posh. I mean, it was kind of a fun place now that we look back at it. We were two, sometimes three to an office. [Paul] Hackett and I shared the same office with Bobb McKittrick. Bill was at the end of the hall and we had a meeting room that wasn't big enough and we had team meeting rooms that weren't big enough. It was all very intimate," said Fred vonAppen, special teams coach. "One of the things that was very big with Bill was staff harmony. We had a great group of men to work with. Bill McPherson was such a wonderful football coach and a wonderful guy to be around. George [Seifert] was, in his own way, a genius defensively. Ray Rhodes was a character and I loved being around him. Tommy Hart helped us and [Paul] Hackett was an interesting guy. He's very creative offensively. He had the toughest job because he was the one who had to cut and paste all of Bill's plays to be ready for the game plan, and he was pretty creative himself."[14]

Continued vonAppen, "Late in the evening Paul lit up cigars, and he had what he'd call an 'Elvis night' every week where he would exclusively play Elvis, which drove Bobb McKittrick, who was in the next office, bat shit because he couldn't stand Elvis. But we'd be playing Elvis and breaking down film and smoking cigars and stinking the place up. It was a good bunch of guys; they really were. They're your family for six months out of the year."[15]

"There were times that I never went home. I would go into the training room, put on a pair of sweats, and roll up some towels as a pillow and sleep there," said physical development coordinator Jerry Attaway. "Chico [Norton] would get there about 4:30 in the morning to wake me up. Shower, and away we go."[16]

Most of the 49ers players never saw the long hours put in by the coaching staff. "He [Walsh] was pure genius. The reason I say that is that you appreciate it as a player. But then you [become] a coach and you understand exactly what goes into the prep and planning. You don't always see that as a player because all that work is done behind the scenes. Then they come to you and you're only part of a certain element. When you realize the planning of mapping out every minute of every practice, [that] is basically what Bill did. That's helped me in my practice here. It's helped me in life after football. I'm sure he's helped all our players on the 49ers with life after football just in terms of the way that he prepared and was organized," said Bill Ring, fullback.[17]

WEDNESDAY

Wednesday. Hump day. This is when the workweek starts for the players as they return to the practice field.

7:30 a.m.	Staff meeting
8:15 a.m.	Quarterback meeting: basic defensive profile, run checks, protection perimeters, and concerns
8:30 a.m.	Special teams meeting
9:00 a.m.	Team meeting: scouting report; install basic runs, nickel runs, and protection
9:30 a.m.	Offensive line: install base, play-action, action, and nickel passes
10:00 a.m.	Individual meetings
11:15 a.m.	Walk-through
11:45 a.m.	Lunch

12:45 a.m.	Individual meetings: view video of upcoming opponent
1:15 p.m.	Finish watching film
1:30 p.m.	Special teams practice
2:00 p.m.	Practice
4:15 p.m.	Practice ends
5:15 p.m.	Coaches review practice footage; finalize short-yardage and red zone offense and defense; review backup and four-minute offense; review script sheets and prepare cards for Thursday practice

Quarterback Joe Montana always had a head start on the game plan. "That's where the film study [comes in] . . . at home [too]. In those days quarterbacks all had 16mm projectors. I would give them the game film or the cut-up tapes to take home, and we would have a conversation as the week unfolded about specific plays or specific looks," said Paul Hackett, quarterbacks and wide receivers coach.[18]

Montana had played in Bill Walsh's system for six years, so he knew the offensive philosophy and terminology. During the season when he got the week's game plan, Montana watched film and performed a daily ritual to aid in better learning the plays. "I would physically trace over them in my playbook with a red pen. It helped me to visualize what would be happening on the field. When a play was called, the picture would immediately come into my mind. I would trace the plays at least once a night after learning them, and sometimes four or five times during the week," wrote Joe Montana in his book *Joe Montana's Art and Magic of Quarterbacking*. "Then I would go through each play in my head and try to visualize where the players were supposed to be. Then I would visualize the pass patterns—the end of the route, to be exact. I would see the linemen in front of me, then I would concentrate on where the receivers were instructed to end up. You need to visualize what will be happening once the ball is snapped."[19]

For defensive players, the morning walk-through gave them time to learn the game plans. "We'd bring our papers onto the field. You couldn't miss a mental repetition in a walk-through. You were given the plays an hour before, and there was pressure to get it right. It was so intense. It was crazy," said safety Tom Holmoe. "They forced you to learn. But they knew people learned in different ways. So you'd see diagrams. That was for players who could learn through pictures . . . then below, for every position, it would be written in some form exactly what your assignment was, so some people read it. Some people never read the words, they would look at the pictures. So once you'd read it and seen it, you could actually physically put yourself in it. We did a ton of that and walked through it. . . . They were going to give you every resource to do it. I thought that was brilliant. But it also took time."[20]

Time spent preparing for their opponents is what the 49ers did. Besides morning walk-throughs, every player hit the film room. Sherman Lewis literally kept his running backs in the dark. "He taught me the game. Coming into your seventh year, you're a veteran, [but] he taught me to look at more film," said halfback Wendell Tyler. "I started looking at more film when I was with the 49ers. He taught me about the little details. I already knew a lot about training but I did more film study when I was with the 49ers. They were like, 'practice makes perfect.'"[21]

In the defensive meeting rooms several players set the tone for watching film to gain an advantage over the upcoming opponent. "Hacksaw [Reynolds] taught me to look deeper into the game. You sit with Hacksaw after practice and watch film. You look at alignment; you learn things that you're like, 'I never saw that,'" said Ron Ferrari, linebacker. "He would look at finger pressure. He would say, 'When this guard lines up here, he's gonna to do this.' I'm like, 'How'd you know that?' He was like, 'Well, this always happens. If he's cheating over here, he's trying to get over here.' He just showed things . . . and we'd have to look at them again and again, and it was literally going to the complete next level in understanding football."[22]

"Dwaine Board led by example. He was very smart, his film studies. I know he studied a lot. I can remember him taking film home. I can remember him asking questions in our meeting. So he really prepared himself and that just showed up in the game," said defensive tackle Manu Tuiasosopo.[23]

"One of the things that Coach Mac [Bill McPherson] and Dwaine Board were so great at [was that] they spent a lot of time on film work.

We studied. They studied the guy and the group of guys. So if it was Dwaine Board looking at the offensive tackle and the offensive line that we were going against, we really understood what they liked to do, what they didn't like to do. What they liked to do in situations, what their tips were. Just like everybody studied us, but I really think that was part of our culture. Linebackers with Hacksaw Reynolds, and defensive line with McPherson, and in the secondary, Ronnie [Lott] was a student of the game. He really was. That went throughout our whole defense, for sure—that we were prepared mentally—and the game plan," said Keena Turner, linebacker.[24]

Forty-niners players put in the time to get to know their opponents. "I had to get up front. I sat in the front row just to get it. [Meetings] were so long and tedious. A lot of the guys were struggling back there. I know that. They struggled to stay awake if they're not engaged with this stuff. I think the middle linebacker had more responsibilities than anybody," said linebacker Riki Ellison. "So we were putting in a different defense every night as we'd go through it. Then Hacksaw was obviously coaching over the coach, critiquing and bitching, so that kept the linebacker group pretty entertaining. It kept us focused on that aspect of it. George [Seifert] was an intense guy. I don't know if he was much of a joker. He was intense."[25]

Throughout the week the players saw how the game plans came together, especially starting on Wednesdays. "You could just see what they're doing on the blackboard and you're going, 'Yeah, this is all going to work here. There's just no way they can stop us there,'" said Allan Kennedy, offensive tackle. "Seeing how they would put together the game plans there and the plays that were put in, you didn't fall asleep in those meetings, though. You wanted to absorb everything. And you went out there and practiced it."[26]

As the workweek progressed, the practice schedule began to resemble training camp with twice-a-day practices. With Bill Walsh's energy and attention to detail, the practice field became another classroom for the 49ers coaches. "Basically we had two practices a day, all year long. I mean, who were we trying to kid? The players knew it," said Fred vonAppen, special teams coach. "We would meet, put things in, and then go through a walk-through at eleven [a.m.], and the walk-through was really a run-through, so it was a misnomer. We ran through everything, didn't have pads on. Then we'd break for lunch, come back, meet again with the players. More game plan and film and so on, and then we go out and practice. And Bill [Walsh] was a marathon practicer. They were two and a half, three hours, almost without an exception. One more play. One more play. That's the way he was."[27]

"Bill was a perfectionist. Bill was very precise. If he scheduled practice for two hours and fifteen minutes, by God, you better make sure everything is done right; everything is done precisely. Because when he had to stop practice and explain it, that means that's another five minutes of practice. Because he wasn't going to cut practice short just because he had to stop and explain something," said Earl Cooper, tight end.[28]

THURSDAY

7:30 a.m.	Staff meeting
8:15 a.m.	Quarterback meeting: review blitz, outline red zone approach
8:30 a.m.	Special teams meeting
9:00 a.m.	Team meeting
9:30 a.m.	Offense/defense meeting: install short-yardage, goal-line, red zone, and backup plan; defense nickel review
10:30 a.m.	Individual meetings: view video of upcoming opponent
11:15 a.m.	Walk-through
11:45 a.m.	Lunch
12:45 p.m.	Individual meetings: view video of upcoming opponent
1:15 p.m.	Meetings end
1:30 p.m.	Special teams practice
2:00 p.m.	Practice
4:15 p.m.	Practice ends

5:00 p.m.   Coaches review practice video;
                                         discuss openers.

Whether it was in the classrooms or on the practice field, the players on the 1984 roster bought into everything that the coaching staff presented to them. The veteran team with twenty-four players from the 1981 Super Bowl–champion squad had set a standard to learn and practice. It was the "Forty-niners way." New players and rookies quickly picked up what they were supposed to be doing from everyone around them, from the starters to the scouting team. "I remember that there were a few number-one picks on the scouting team. We dropped our egos at the door, and that was the attitude of that whole team. If I'm going to be a scout [practice team] guy, I'll be a scout guy. That was the attitude of that team. It was such a great attitude and that's what got us over [the top]," said Mario Clark, cornerback.[29] "I was always prepared [for games] because practice was exhausting physically and mentally," said linebacker Dan Bunz.[30]

Regardless of status, every player helped each other. "Keena [Turner] was so valuable that he was one of those guys who was going to be on the field pretty much all day long. I found a little niche to help him on all of the nickel adjustments," said Ron Ferrari, linebacker. "We had a little deal that I'd help him on all the nickel adjustments during practice. They would always be in on Thursday. So it was great because he had so much on his plate that I could literally just have focus on him on a few specific nickels."[31]

Even if it meant staying after practice to get more work in, it was done. Even the team's superstars paid the price by staying late. "I had the opportunity to work with Joe [Montana] after practice a lot, which was cool. We worked on play-action fake, and we wanted to perfect it to a science so people thought that I had the ball. If I didn't get hit, I didn't do my job," said Roger Craig, fullback. "We took pride in everything we did. We took ownership of our team. Bill Walsh gave us a platform—that's the key. We bought into Bill Walsh's platform and when we bought into it, we took it to another level. That's what defines a coach. If you get your players to do that, then you got something."[32]

FRIDAY

7:30 a.m.	Staff meeting
8:15 a.m.	Quarterback meeting: discuss openers
8:30 a.m.	Special teams meeting
9:00 a.m.	Team meeting
9:45 a.m.	Offense/defense meetings: review checks and alerts; review game plan by personnel and formation
10:00 a.m.	Individual meetings
11:30 a.m.	Practice
1:00 p.m.	Practice ends: finalize offensive sideline sheet; list openers

On Friday the workload began to slow down. If there was a road game, Friday would sometimes be a travel day. Even then the players couldn't escape the coaches. "We could never say we were not prepared when we went to play," said strong safety Carlton Williamson. "Even on the plane. The linemen are relaxed and asleep. George [Seifert] is going around finding defensive backs and he's giving us pop quizzes. I'm laying down listening to music on my Walkman, and George would come up to me through the aisle and say, 'See, we're in Cover 3. They come out in this formation. What do you do? What call do you make?' He just wanted to cross those T's and dot those I's. So we didn't have a whole lot of relaxation time when we were on the road or the night before the game"[33]

SATURDAY

On the day before the game Bill Walsh even put in some time preparing for the opponent looming the following week. "After Friday he would look at some tape of the next opponent on Saturday. He'd use every moment available to him to prepare so that when the week started on Monday, he was pretty well there," said Neal Dahlen, director of research and development.[34]

9:00 a.m.	Individual meetings: review practice footage; hand out final game plan
10:30 a.m.	Practice
11:15 a.m.	Practice ends
11:15 a.m.–6:00 p.m.	Team break
6:00 p.m.–8:00 p.m.	Check into team's hotel
9:00 p.m.	Special teams meetings
9:30 p.m.	Offense/defense meetings: review openers (first twenty-five plays); use cut-ups to support opening calls; view game video to give players a flavor of the game; plan and review key situations (short yardage, red zone, goal line, blitz, etc.)
10:00 p.m	Team meeting
10:05 p.m.	Snack

After a morning walk-through at the 49ers facility, the team would break for lunch, giving the players and coaches time to take care of their family responsibilities before checking into the team's local hotel for the night. Usually the team had two hours to check in on Saturday night before the special teams meeting at 9:00 p.m. Coach Fred vonAppen never found any trouble getting his players motivated to play on Sunday.

"Fred was a great special teams coach. We were very focused on doing a great job in covering. Everyone took it very seriously, because—especially for a guy like me—I knew that was the job I was getting paid to do. So I had to make sure that I did it well," said Bill Ring, fullback.[35]

However, some of vonAppen's players on the special teams unit had a hard time keeping up with his vocabulary. "Fred should have been a poet or an English major. He would use words that 90 percent of the guys couldn't understand. A couple of times you would hear, 'What did you just say?' So we had to slow it down, but he would use the [words] in such a way to make a point," said a laughing Ron Ferrari. "He was always saying, 'Get your happy ass down the field!' and 'you cannot let this guy come through here.' He had a command of the English vocabulary. It kept it entertaining. He could be serious and he could joke."[36]

"[We] would be amazed by the words that he would use. To this day . . . I use some of the same ones. They crack me up. He'd be explaining some things or showing film and he'd say, 'They're doing a yeoman's job of blocking this guy.' A yeoman? I mean, who the hell knew about a yeoman? Awesome. Even Tom Holmoe was like, 'What's a yeoman?' So we heard some great things," said linebacker Blanchard Montgomery.[37]

The offense and defense would then split up to go over the game plans for Sunday. In the defensive room, George Seifert and his staff reviewed everything they had introduced during the week. "We'd watch film. We'd have a team meeting, then after the team meeting, we'd have our defensive meeting. All the defense would be together. It evolved from looking at tape together as far as your position groups. . . . Sometimes we'd look at tape together, the whole defensive squad. George would say what he had to say going into the game—any alerts, any tips. He'd have all this stuff ready to go to let them know to be alert for this, to be alert for that. Just reminders of things that we'd gone through during the course of the week," said Ray Rhodes, defensive backs coach.[38]

In the offensive room Bill Walsh went over the game plan and presented the team's first twenty-five plays. "His presentations on Saturday night were masterful because that was when he would put in his first twenty-five [plays]. So when the players left the [offensive] meeting, I always had this sense that they felt a calmness about knowing [that] this is the way it's gonna be and we'll play through this and see what happens," said special teams coach Fred vonAppen.[39]

At 10:00 p.m. the entire team met to hear from head coach Bill Walsh. During this period Walsh showed a few highlight plays from the previous week's game. He didn't show a touchdown alone, he went over all the elements of the touchdown, showing how all eleven players contributed to the score. "The night before the game [Walsh would] show a video—a highlight video—and the first time I saw this with him,

I go, 'Wow, that's a nice technique,'" said Manu Tuiasosopo, defensive tackle. "So coach would obviously point out that we got a touchdown or we got a sack. But he focused on the peripheral. He took our attention to the reason why he got a sack because of the coverage: 'Look at the coverage. Look at his technique. Look at his feet.' So he was giving props to the guy who didn't get the stats but played every bit a part of the end result. The guys saw that and a mutual respect formed, and it was cemented throughout that year."[40]

"One thing I think was very good that Walsh did was run film of a previous game, and it would be the highlights of the game you last played. That was really an impact and left a high level of confidence when you left to go to sleep and prepare for the big day. He did a good job of keeping a good balance of perfection, and he kept it light so you didn't feel so much pressure," said offensive tackle Billy Shields.[41]

After the team meeting the whole squad would break up for a snack. Most of the individual units took this time to gather one last time to go over strategy. They also took this time to bond. For the defensive line, it might mean gathering to watch film. "We used to sit around after a Saturday practice—we would always get together as a defensive line in somebody's room—and we would watch film. It was just a bunch of guys hanging out, watching film, and jabbing at each other, which was fun," said Dwaine Board, defensive end.[42]

For the offensive line, it meant sharing stories over a snack and a few beers. "I think that was more of a time to relax a little bit. We didn't always talk about the plays or [what] we watched. A lot of us watched films on Saturday, so it was pretty much in the tank already. It was time to relax a little bit and unwind before the game because we were always ready," said offensive tackle Keith Fahnhorst. [43]

"I remember the nights before games. You have a short meeting and a little something to eat, then afterward we'd camp out there and find a table. Other groups did the same things. We would be there at the hotel on a Saturday night, and Randy Cross and John Ayers always liked to have a couple beers," said Allan Kennedy, offensive tackle. "Then Bobb would just sit down with the whole group and—after our 9:30 meeting—just talk. It was a great relationship. We'd all sit and go over a couple things and make sure we were all on the same page. It was easygoing, loose."[44]

"That was their thing, to sit around and have a couple beers. Bond and just talk, talk about the game, talk about whatever. I participated in that as much as possible," said Guy McIntyre, rookie guard.[45]

After the meetings it was off to bed. "Sleeping was never a problem for me before a game because I felt like I had to get a good night's sleep in order to put in a good day's work," said tight end Earl Cooper.[46] For some it was still a time to prepare. "I always studied the night before a game. I'd trace over the plays so they would be stuck in my mind. I always had to go over the formations, too. With all that preparation and to some extent, apprehension, I'd get four or five hours of sleep, at the most," wrote Joe Montana in his *Joe Montana's Art and Magic of Quarterbacking*.[47]

13

NOVEMBER

Week 10 vs. Cincinnati Bengals (November 4)
Week 11 at Cleveland Browns (November 11)
Week 12 vs. Tampa Bay Buccaneers (November 18)
Week 13 at New Orleans Saints (November 25)

After a masterpiece of a game against the Los Angeles Rams Bill Walsh quickly refocused his team, preparing them for a familiar foe. Walsh's squad got ready to host the Cincinnati Bengals, a team owned by his former mentor Paul Brown and coached by Sam Wyche, his former quarterbacks coach on the 1981 Super Bowl–winning team. After one year as the head coach at the University of Indiana, Wyche was hired as the fifth Bengals head coach in franchise history, replacing Forrest Gregg, who had coached against Walsh in Super Bowl XVI.

"We're going to know the 49ers backwards and forwards by the end of the week. I want to do a good job and see if our team is up to beating the 49ers Sunday. I think we'll give them a good game," said Wyche early in the week. Facing his former pupil worried Walsh, as Wyche knew the ins and outs of the 49ers as well as anybody. Although their records were lopsided—the 49ers at 8–1 and the Bengals at 3–6—the southern Ohio team was coming off back-to-back wins against the Browns (12–9) and the Oilers (31–13). The 49ers were listed as a ten-and-a-half-point home favorite. With the hoopla building, the game became personal to Walsh. Facing his mentor's team always meant something to him. Speaking to his team early in the week, he made his feelings known with both humor and inspiration.[1]

> Men, I have a little at stake in this game. Help me out, will you? [Team laughter.] This is a big one in many ways. It's a big one for us to again establish ourselves as an outstanding, if not great, football team. You can't go like this [Walsh moves his arm in a wave-like motion] to win. Only way is to play explosive defense that rocks the other team. That's the one thing that makes you a champion. Teams can have average offenses; they can have average kicking game, but if they don't have that rocking defense, they don't have a shot at it. We have it. Offensively we gotta battle these guys because they play great defense. . . . We can't take a sloppy, sort of easy-does-it approach, sort of like it happened against Pittsburgh: a game we know we're going to win and it's just a matter of time. Then a flag goes up and a missed field goal and game's over. That's not going to happen this time. . . . Just look at the film and decide for yourself what kind of ball game we're in for. Now they have a lot of talent, and they're playing well right now. This is a chance of a lifetime for them. It's that simple. So have yourself ready for this one.[2]

Walsh wanted no distractions this week, especially from the local press. "I remember him saying we got to do interviews with the media. But you don't need to sit down for an in-depth interview. Once you've talked to them for five or ten minutes, you've said enough. If that interview goes too long, you're going to say more than you should. So keep it short," said Jerry Walker, director of public relations. "The more you elaborate, that's when we're going to get misquoted. His basic thing was not 'don't talk to the media'; it was 'don't talk to the media too long.'"[3] Throughout this week Walsh wanted his team's focus on the Bengals, not on answering questions about Wyche or his mentor Paul Brown.

One big concern for Walsh was the secondary. Jeff Fuller would miss the game due to a personal issue, but it was the health of Ronnie Lott that was discussed the most. Lott would play, but Seifert was concerned that Lott's toe would hamper him from chasing receivers from his cornerback position. The coaches chatted about moving safety Dwight Hicks to corner and Lott to safety.

On game day on November 4, the 49ers Faithful celebrated a beautiful 65-degree day by posting signs around the stadium wishing Lawrence Pillers a happy thirty-second birthday. The sold-out crowd at The Stick was anticipating a Niners victory. On their first offensive drive, Joe Montana's hot hand continued, completing his first five passes of the game—and his eighteenth consecutive completion overall—before making a big mistake. In Bengals territory Montana threw a pass down the middle of the field that sailed over Renaldo Nehemiah's head and into the arms of Bengals safety Bobby Kemp. It would be the start of a very generous day for Montana. After the turnover, Ken Anderson, another Walsh pupil, connected on a deep pass to his favorite receiver. The forty-nine-yard catch by Cris Collinsworth set up a Bengals field goal.

Walsh saw his quarterback respond. After a thirty-three-yard kickoff return by Carl Monroe, the 49ers methodically marched down to the Bengals twelve-yard line. On the eleventh play of the drive, Joe Cool hit a wide-open Earl Cooper, who had beaten linebacker Jeff Schuh, for an easy touchdown. Early in the second quarter the 49ers were up 7–3. For the rest of the half Sam Wyche had his mentor off balance.

An eighty-yard drive ended with a short touchdown run by Larry Kinnebrew, the Bengals 255-pound running back, to give Cincinnati a 10–7 lead. After the score the Bengals defense confused Montana again, as he threw his second interception of the game. Montana tried to hit Freddie Solomon down the middle of the field, but linebacker Reggie Williams stepped in front of him for the pick. Williams was knocked out-of-bounds at the 49ers thirty-two-yard line. Despite a sack by birthday boy Lawrence Pillers, the Bengals increased their lead as Anderson completed a dart to Collinsworth, who was well covered by Eric Wright.

The crowd was getting restless as the visiting Bengals held a 17–7 lead over the local heroes. On the last drive of the half, they became even more restless after Montana threw his third interception. As the 49ers headed to the locker room after their most disappointing half of football to date, Walsh thought about what he wanted to say. Instead, one of the leaders of the team stepped up to express his feelings. "I said a few words at halftime. I wasn't a big talker, either, but I felt that things were a little chaotic in the locker room and I just reminded those guys that we were much better than the team that we're playing and we just needed to go out there and play our game. Bill may have thought that I said the right thing at the right time," said Keith Fahnhorst, offensive tackle.[4] After the game, Fahnhorst would get a game ball from Walsh.

At the half, the Bengals had 263 total yards and the 49ers 173: too many yards given up on defense and too many turnovers on offense. No rah-rah speech was required from Walsh. A different 49ers defense would take the field during the second half.

Because they were trailing, Walsh had to put the ball in the air too much: twenty-four passes compared to just nine runs. They needed a good start in the third quarter, which had not happened most of the year with only one touchdown scored during that period all season. As the 49ers started their first drive, Walsh's offense started to move the ball, leaning on the running game. The first four plays were runs: Tyler for six, Craig for fourteen, Craig for two, and Tyler for four. Then on third-and-nine Montana hit Dwight Clark for thirteen yards and a huge first down. Although the drive stalled deep in Bengals territory, Ray Wersching's field goal cut the lead to 17–10.

On the Bengals next drive it looked like the 49ers had momentum. Ronnie Lott, playing safety, picked off a Ken Anderson pass and returned it to the Bengals twenty-four-yard line. The sudden cheers quickly turned to moans. Montana gave the ball right back with his fourth interception of the game. Coming into the game, Montana had thrown only three interceptions all season. He had more than doubled his total in just three quarters. Despite the turnovers Bill Walsh maintained his sense of humor when Montana returned to the sidelines. "How's it going out there?" remarked Walsh to his struggling quarterback.[5] Montana grinned, chuckled, and visibly relaxed.

By now the 49ers defense had settled down. A big sack by Ron Ferrari forced a Bengals punt. With fourteen minutes remaining in the fourth quarter, Montana put the interceptions behind him. "We believe in all our players. Most of all we believe in Number 16," commented Randy Cross after the game.[6] "If it ever affected his confidence, it never showed in the huddle. You couldn't tell on the following play or the next series if he had thrown a touchdown pass or an interception. He was still the same Joe. We all got a lot of confidence from that," said offensive tackle Keith Fahnhorst.[7]

He went to work on a fourth-quarter comeback by mixing the run with the pass. Montana to Cooper for seventeen yards, a Tyler fifteen-yard run, a fifteen-yard pass to Bill Ring, and a Tyler twelve-yard run put the 49ers in scoring position. The four-minute drive led to a Wersching thirty-five-yard field goal, cutting the lead to 17–13. Forty-niners fans chanted "Defense! Defense! Defense!" The defense did not disappoint, forcing a punt. Now it was time for special teams to contribute. Dana McLemore returned a short punt nineteen yards to the Bengals forty-yard line. Quickly Montana connected with Dwight Clark for seventeen yards, then dumped one off to Craig for eight yards. It looked like they would punch it in the end zone, but the Bengals defense stiffened at the seven-yard line. With 5:44 left in the game Walsh decided to kick the field goal. Wersching's third kick of the game cut the lead to one point.

The crowd was louder than ever, giving the 49ers defense more life. They attacked the Bengals on every down, forcing another quick three-and-out. After a short punt the 49ers took over on their own forty-two-yard line with 3:52 remaining. On the first play of the series, the 49ers made the biggest play of the game. Dwight Clark ran a simple, quick out route against cornerback Ray Griffin, who missed the tackle. All alone, Clark sprinted up the sidelines. After thirty-nine yards he was finally brought down at the Bengals nineteen-yard line. The 49ers Faithful were going nuts. They were not thinking about those turnovers. Already in field goal range Walsh wasn't satisfied. He knew the Bengals had a very good kicker in Jim Breech. He went for the touchdown. On third-and-eleven Montana hit Freddie Solomon down to the five-yard line. After the two-minute warning, Wyche called his first timeout. Walsh called another pass play.

On second-and-goal, the 49ers used a formation with two tight ends, a split backfield (Craig/Tyler), and one wide receiver, Freddie Solomon, who lined up tight on the left side. Solomon then went in motion to the right, just outside John Frank. At the snap, Montana made a play fake to Tyler and booted right. Bengals defensive end Eddie Edwards didn't fall for the fake and was quickly in Montana's face. Off his back foot, Montana threw a pass to Solomon, who was in the back of the end zone and outleaped safety Robert Jackson for a clutch touchdown. "I wanted to throw it harder [to get it over Jackson] but I was feeling the pressure and I couldn't step up," commented Montana after the game. "A great catch."[8]

The 49ers had finally wiped out the Bengals lead. With just a minute and a half left, the 49ers led 23–17. The Bengals needed a touchdown to win. George Seifert called for his nickel defense to slam the door. They came up big again. A sack by Gary Johnson—the sixth of the game—pushed the Bengals backward, and Carlton Williamson sealed the game with an interception.

The 49ers were now 9–1 after their most nerve-wracking victory of the year. Walsh walked to midfield and hugged his friend Sam Wyche. After a short chat Wyche then shook hands with Joe Montana, his former pupil, and Keena Turner. Respect for a man who had helped the 49ers to win Super Bowl XVI was evident. Wyche would help the Bengals turn the corner, as his team would finish the 1984 season with an 8–8 record. Four years later, Walsh would see Wyche again as Montana led a game-winning drive to win Super Bowl XXIII in Walsh's last game as 49ers head coach.

The 49ers overcame a career-high four interceptions by Joe Montana by shutting out the Bengals in the second half. After giving up 263 yards and seventeen points in the first half, George Seifert's boys allowed just eighty-three yards and no points in the second. "We were resourceful. At any point in the second half if Cincinnati drove for another touchdown we would have been finished," sighed Bill Walsh after the game. "But we shut them out. We were great in a time of desperation."[9]

"It's almost as if we could hear people saying, 'Let's see what you're made of,'" remarked Ronnie Lott to the press after the game. "Doing what we did, this is what it takes to be a good team."[10] In beating Walsh's former team, the 49ers showed they had the heart of a champion. For just one evening Walsh enjoyed a sweet win by his 49ers.

The next game featured another NFL team from Ohio. This time the 49ers would travel to the Buckeye State—the home state of owner Eddie DeBartolo—to face the Cleveland Browns. As much as Walsh wanted to beat his former team the week before, DeBartolo wanted to see his team beat his hometown franchise. Speaking to his team, Walsh stressed picking up their level of play.

> You gotta concentrate now. Really concentrate on football for six weeks and find a reason for every game. Now this week, naturally, you're traveling. When we get off that field, we're going to be a machine this week. Let's be a machine when you go on the field and we'll be ready to do that, I'll guarantee you. . . . But the critical thing now, as you guys know, is about a three-week drive here when it

comes to our intensity. At the end of the last three, you'll see the end. But these right here are the toughest, and this is where the top teams show up, and you can almost see it all around the league. Certain teams are poking their heads up now, and they're taking command of what their own destiny is. You see what Chicago's doing. Washington, here they come again. Same thing happening around the league and we're there. Now what we have to do is for the next three weeks you have to maintain your concentration on this thing. . . . We're going to keep it going this week.[11]

The comeback win against the Bengals focused the 49ers. Walsh wanted no more letdowns, especially against weaker teams. Their next three opponents—the Browns, Buccaneers, and Saints—would challenge them. The Browns were struggling mightily. After a 1–7 start they fired head coach Sam Rutigliano and replaced him with defensive coordinator Marty Schottenheimer. Despite the lack of victories, his aggressive 3–4 defense was performing well. Led by linebackers Clay Matthews and Chip Banks and cornerbacks Fred Minnifield and Hanford Dixon, the Browns defense was ranked in the top ten. They were physical and aggressive. During practice throughout the week, Walsh had his squad prepare for the weather. Winter was coming to Ohio in November and the forecast called for rain, wind, and possible snow showers. The 49ers would be ready for the elements.

On the practice field Lott moved to safety to save wear and tear on his toe and Hicks to cornerback. "I thought that Ronnie was beat up. He had a bad toe, a bad shoulder, bad everything. Dwight was a smart enough guy. He knew how to cover and he played smart," said Ray Rhodes, defensive backs coach.[12] "Dwight had played some corner and Ronnie played safety in college, so it was a pretty good move for both guys." Left tackle Bubba Paris's knee was hurting him so much that he would miss the game and be replaced in the starting lineup by Billy Shields. All week the Redwood City facility buzzed with gossip about the possible return of Fred Dean. "You [had] the water cooler talk. Is Fred close to coming? We were playing well, but we missed Fred. Because you miss a Hall of Famer when he's not there," said linebacker Keena Turner.[13] Although the 49ers players wanted Dean back, their main focus turned to the Cleveland Browns.

Arriving in Cleveland on Saturday, John McVay, along with team lawyer Carmen Policy, met with Dean's agent David Perrine at the team's hotel. Because of the lack of progress and communication, the two groups brought in a mediator for this overnight session. "We spent countless hours on the phone trying to work out a deal, so finally we decided we need a neutral guy, an arbitrator to sit there with us," said John McVay, vice president and general manager. "After much discussion we decided on Willie Brown to be our arbitrator."[14] Willie Brown, the speaker of the California State Assembly, was also a longtime 49ers fans as well as a future mayor of San Francisco (1996–2004).

"They have to believe in you and [believe that] you have their best interest," said Willie Brown. "I've always loved football and dreamed of being a football player, and clearly this was as close as I was ever going to get. I was able to talk the language and was also a fan."[15] The highly motivated Brown got the two sides talking. For the first time it looked like a deal would be made.

As the two sides worked through the night, the 49ers woke up to bitter Ohio weather with temperatures in the low 30s, as well as rain, snow showers, and a stiff fifteen-mile-an-hour breeze off Lake Erie. Not quite northern California weather. But it was football weather. During warm-ups 49ers players saw their breath in the air for the first time all season. Walsh walked onto the muddy grass of Cleveland Stadium wearing a long gold snow coat with a 49ers ball cap. Putting on his headset, he didn't bother wearing gloves. A few of his players did. Dwight Clark, Freddie Solomon, and Bill Ring wore black gloves that resembled scuba diving gloves to help keep their hands dry.

From the opening kickoff, it would be the 49ers day. Browns rookie running back Ernest Byner fumbled the opening kick after a big hit by Carl Monroe. Forty-niners running back Derrick Harmon recovered it. The turnover set up a forty-seven-yard field goal by Ray Wersching. On the Browns ensuing possession Byner fumbled a bad handoff from quarterback Paul McDonald (who had been coached by Paul Hackett at USC) to set up another 49ers field goal.

As the rain fell harder the 49ers defense continued to force turnovers. Linebacker Keena Turner picked off a pass and returned it deep into Browns territory. Three plays later Walsh called a draw play against a nickel blitz. It proved to be a perfect call as Roger Craig went up the middle, untouched, between blocks by Randy Cross and Fred Quillan for a twenty-yard touchdown. The 49ers forced a fourth turnover later that didn't lead to a score, but it didn't matter as they headed into halftime with a 13–0 lead.

The second half looked like a replay of the first. It was all 49ers. On the second drive of the half Montana, ignoring the rain and wind, marched his team to another Roger Craig touchdown. On the last play of the third quarter the 49ers finished off the overmatched Browns. Near midfield Montana dropped back, looking left to Dwight Clark's side. Not open. Montana drifted in the pocket, looking to his third read to the right, and threw a dart to a wide-open Freddie Solomon across the field. Browns linebacker Eddie Johnson took a bad angle and missed the open-field tackle, and Solomon raced sixty yards down the sidelines and into the end zone in front of the Dawg Pound.

Two more second-half touchdowns made the final score 41–7. The 49ers ran seventy offensive plays and held the ball for nearly thirty-six minutes. Leaving the field, they were met by owner Eddie DeBartolo, who hugged every coach and player. "I came here in 1978 and I thought I had a hotshot football team with O. J. Simpson. [The Browns beat the 49ers 24–7.] Over the years my father and our company have done a lot of things in Cleveland and I wanted to come back here from '78 and win a game," commented DeBartolo outside the visitor's dugout. "I've never been happier in my life. This is my Super Bowl."[16]

The 49ers were now 10–1. Only the undefeated Dolphins (11–0), behind the hot hand of Dan Marino, had a better record in the NFL. At this point in the season, both teams looked to be headed for a super showdown. Elated from their win, the victorious locker room at Cleveland Stadium rejoiced upon hearing the news that Fred Dean had agreed to a new contract and would end his holdout. "My attorney called me and said, 'I think we have reached a deal.' That was one of the highlights of my life, because I knew that Mr. D. wouldn't let me hang out there too long. It was a little bit longer than I expected, but he opened the door and let me come in," said Dean.[17]

With help from Willie Brown the 49ers had their best pass rusher back in the fold. The overnight session had worked, even if John McVay missed a game for the first time as a 49ers employee. "That is the only game that I missed in twenty-three years with the 49ers," said McVay. "But we were in the hotel negotiating the contract with Fred's agent and Willie keeping us going. We finally got everything done."[18]

DeBartolo and Walsh were delighted that the holdout was over. The only bad news of the day was losing linebacker Ron Ferrari for the season with a serious knee injury. "Game's over. We won. There's a lot to be excited about. I just kind of go out to the player's bus early and out comes Eddie D. and he jumps on the bus. Walks all the way down the aisle and wants to have a conversation with me. 'How you doing, Ronnie?' He came and said, 'Are you OK? You're going be fine. Is there anything I can do?' He didn't have to do that. He brought us together, and when you talked to Eddie, you knew he loved you. It was genuine. It was real. He set the tempo and the tone and you felt like family. I still remember Eddie coming out. He came right out to the bus. We talked for about a minute or so and I could not believe it. Eddie was the kind of guy who, if he was talking to you, you knew you were his favorite player on the team. He made you feel that way," said Ron Ferrari, linebacker.[19]

All of the 49ers players appreciated DeBartolo's concern for them. DeBartolo always thought of himself as one of the guys. "I don't mind being regarded as a player's owner because I really think I am. I really care about my players. It bothers me very deeply when something bad happens to them. Their families mean a lot to me, and I think we'll always have this rapport, this closeness, this bond between us," DeBartolo once said.[20]

Ferrari received a game ball for his effort, as did Freddie Solomon and Dwight Hicks, who played the whole game at cornerback. At 11:00 a.m. the next day Fred Dean arrived at the team's facility in Redwood City. He took his physical and signed his contract. He was ready to play. "When I came back, the fellas welcomed me. The 49ers welcomed me. I know that coach Bill Walsh and Mr. DeBartolo made me feel comfortable," said Dean.[21] He was so excited about returning that he wanted to get after the quarterback—any quarterback. Speaking to the local media he commented on seeing Joe Montana for the first time in months. "Been so long since I touched a quarterback, when I shook Joe's hand I wanted to sack him," said a happy Fred Dean.[22]

"It was great because we knew once we got Fred back that we were going to be better. We were playing good defense, but having Fred back and knowing the type of player he was— an impact player who could change the game—brought more life into us on defense," said defensive end Dwaine Board.[23]

"It was great. Here comes the man. Fred was like what Joe Montana was to the offense and gave us an added spark. Everybody welcomed him back with open arms. We needed him. We needed him to take us down the stretch," said Jim Stuckey, defensive end.[24]

At the team meeting Walsh's sense of humor shone through when he introduced the team's newest addition. "We have a new member of the squad. A young kid coming in. Try to show him the ropes. Fred Dean is with us!" said a smiling Walsh. The whole squad welcomed him with cheers. "Speech, speech, speech," the 49ers players chanted in the jammed meeting room. "Glad to be back, guys," Dean said to a big round of laughter, even from Walsh.[25]

Dean would return to face the Tampa Bay Buccaneers, who had just defeated the 6–4 New York Giants to improve their record to 4–7. This would be John McKay's last season as Bucs head coach—the only coach they had known since their inception in 1976. The 49ers would take on a familiar face in quarterback Steve DeBerg, and power running back James Wilder was having a career year (in 1984 he set a league record for rushing attempts in a season with 407).

Wilder would finish the season with 1,544 rushing yards and thirteen touchdowns. He also added eighty-five receptions for 685 yards, making him one of the league's most versatile backs. Seifert had stopped Riggins, Riggs, and Dickerson; he knew how to slow down Wilder. Walsh was more concerned about putting up points against an aggressive 3–4 defense led by All-Pro defensive end Lee Roy Selmon.

On a cool and sunny day at Candlestick, the sold-out crowd—including Willie Brown, a guest in Eddie DeBartolo's box—saw two 49ers return to action. The defense saw the return of not only Fred Dean but also defensive end Jeff Stover. Under the watchful eye of Jerry Attaway, Stover made his way back to the field after ten weeks of rehab for a torn medial collateral ligament in his right knee. "Jerry was key in my rehab, working with me and pushing me. A lot of pool work and stuff that a lot of people didn't even do at that time," said Stover. "Jerry was one of the first to put guys in the pool and rehab them where you don't have that pounding on the knee. You could do water work, where you have resistance. You're not beating the heck out of it."

Also enabling Stover's quick return was the use of a hinge cast that stimulated the muscles around the knee. "With the hinge cast I was able to get on a Cybex machine and work out and build the muscle back up, so I was way ahead of the game," said Stover. "They could be more aggressive with my rehab from there, and it just kept getting better and better where they finally made a brace for it and I was able to start practicing."[26]

With the return of two 49er players came the loss of another early in the game. On the first play from scrimmage Ronnie Lott—starting at free safety with Dwight Hicks at cornerback—shot between the center and right guard, meeting Wilder in the hole and stopping him for no gain. It was an early message the 49ers defense wanted to send to the powerful Wilder. However, Lott left the field with an injured right shoulder after the big hit. After one play, Seifert had to change his personnel, switching Hicks—who had practiced all week at corner-back—back to free safety and inserting Mario Clark at cornerback.

Neither team was sharp for the remainder of the first quarter. The squads combined for three turnovers, two by the 49ers—both fumbles by Wendell Tyler. TV cameras caught Walsh tearing off his headset after the second one. This was not the start he wanted. Early in the second quarter Fred Dean entered the game and immediately made his presence known. After missing the first eleven games, Dean lined up at defensive end across from Bucs tackle Gene Sanders. Dean used a quick swim move with his left hand over Sanders's shoulder to get to DeBerg midtoss. The ball floated down the field into the hands of a diving Keena Turner.

Near midfield Walsh went right back to Wendell Tyler. Calling 18-BOB—a sweep play—Tyler went around the right side behind blocks by Randy Cross and Keith Fahnhorst for a twenty-six-yard gain. Near the goal line Tyler rewarded his backfield mate, Roger Craig, by pan-caking Bucs cornerback John Holt and leading Craig into the end zone.

DeBerg led his team to a field goal to cut the 49ers lead to 7–3. Walsh opened up his playbook and called Halfback Sail, trying to match speedy Carl Monroe against a linebacker on a corner route. It worked. Monroe beat Scot Brantley off the line as Montana hit him in stride for a forty-seven-yard gain. Inside the red zone Walsh called a wide receiv-er reverse: Montana faked to Craig up the middle while Freddie Solo-mon went around the left end. A great block by John Ayers led to the easy touchdown, giving the 49ers a 14–3 lead.

When it looked like the 49ers were taking control of the game, veteran Steve DeBerg responded with a scoring drive before the half. A forty-three-yard reception by Gerald Carter set up a Buccaneers touchdown. In the locker room, Bill Walsh looked befuddled. The 49ers had dominated most of the first half, gaining 238 yards, converting every third down (eight for eight), while leaving Max Runager on the sidelines. The three fumbles were what kept the Bucs in the game, trailing only 14–10.

After an exchange of punts—Runager's first—the 49ers offense got rolling again. Starting at the 49ers eight-yard line, Walsh leaned on the running game. Time to get physical. Roger Craig carried four times for forty-five yards while Wendell Tyler had four carries for twenty-one yards, finishing the drive with his eighth touchdown of the season. Eight of the ten plays Walsh called were runs.

But the scrappy Buccaneers wouldn't go away. With the help of a twenty-five-yard pass interference penalty, DeBerg found Gerald Carter on a nine-yard touchdown to once again cut the 49ers lead. Clinging to a four-point lead, Walsh went back to the ground game. On the first play Tyler ripped off twenty-five yards behind a big block by massive Bubba Paris, who returned after missing one game. On another carry Tyler pounded up the middle for eleven hard yards, which put him at more than 1,000 yards for the season. Tyler became only the fourth 49ers running back to achieve that historic feat, joining Joe Perry (1953–1954), J. D. Smith (1959), and Delvin Williams (1976).

Tyler's runs led to a Ray Wersching field goal and a 24–17 advantage. Over the last two scoring drives Walsh called twelve straight runs, and Tyler was the benefactor. He had rushed for more than 1,000 yards on 193 carries in twelve games for an average of 5.1 yards per carry. On the bench Tyler saw Candlestick Park's scoreboard flash his accomplishment on the big screen. Several 49ers teammates, including Roger Craig, congratulated him as the 49ers fans gave him a standing ovation. Tyler thanked his offensive line. He knew his achievement was a team effort and his linemen deserved credit.

With 8:39 left in the game, it was time for the 49ers defense to step up. Everybody loves a great comeback story like those in Hollywood movies. As the Bucs marched to the 49ers thirty-eight-yard line, Fred Dean appeared onscreen. From his right defensive end spot he beat rookie left tackle Ron Heller on a speed rush, grabbed DeBerg by his left leg, and took him down for his first sack of the season.

Just before the two-minute warning Max Runager launched a beautiful fifty-six-yard punt to pin the Bucs back. On the next play DeBerg fumbled the snap, which was recovered by Gary Johnson to clinch the eleventh victory of the season for the 49ers. Johnson was mobbed by his teammates—including Fred Dean, who was playing with Johnson for the first time since 1981 in San Diego—as he carried the ball with him to the 49ers sidelines. The hard-fought 24–17 victory was over.

Montana threw just seven passes in the second half as the running game controlled the game and clock. The Roger Craig/Wendell Tyler duo combined for thirty-three carries for 183 yards and two touchdowns. The only bad news resulting from the game was that Ronnie Lott would be out for three weeks with a dislocated right shoulder. With four games remaining the 49ers clinched a playoff berth, but they were looking for a bigger prize.

Fred Dean played thirty-one snaps and loved being back on the field sacking quarterbacks. "I'd say I welcomed myself back into the NFL with that sack. I would have been disappointed if I didn't have one," he remarked after the game.[27] The same could be said for Jeff Stover. "It was one of the most exciting things for me, ever," he recalled nearly thirty years later. "I was a little apprehensive at times. But after a few plays I didn't even notice [the brace] anymore. I just remember being excited to be there."[28]

On Monday Walsh spoke to his team about the challenge ahead.

> This was a good game in a lot of ways. We couldn't have beaten the top teams with this past performance and I don't understand why. A lot of good things defensively, offensively we fumbled the ball at critical points at critical times. Just those particular things could cost us a playoff game. You could go all the way, play a team better than the one you just played, and lose to them because of those kinds of things. So what we have to do is stick tight now. We have to finish the season without our fumbles, without our zone coverage, missed responsibilities. Everything has to be right. It's that simple. We talked about being on a three-week program. Two are done. Now you have another one. This one we have to play our best. We look like the best team in football, but there are little gaps that we need to take care of.[29]

They would prepare for a divisional game on the road against the New Orleans Saints. With a win they would clinch the NFC West.

> We're not going down there fat and happy. I want us to go down there and play the best game of the year. This is the time we play a great game. This is the time to do it. You've got the playoffs coming; we've qualified for them. This is the time to play your best game. This will be the best team you play all the way through now. Biggest test you'll have and we've got to be up for it. Don't go into that stadium thinking it will be a cakewalk with this ball club. . . . Just remind yourself, the noise factor alone in that stadium—it's going to be packed with screaming people—it's going to be the toughest game we've had. Personally I hate thinking we're going to lose this game. [30]

Walsh wanted to keep his team fresh, so once again they would practice with no pads. He knew he would be without Ronnie Lott, and during Friday's practice linebacker Jack Reynolds hurt his back. Jim Fahnhorst would start at inside linebacker. It was Thanksgiving week in the Bay area and for the 49ers this meant it was time for the "free turkey gag," the annual Thanksgiving prank played on unsuspecting rookies who are told that they will get a free turkey at a certain local store. For Riki Ellison that meant setting up rookie linebacker Todd Shell. "I conned him pretty good because I carpool with him and I kept using reverse psychology, saying, 'Aw, c'mon you're not going to stop for a turkey?'" commented Ellison to the *San Francisco Examiner* a few days before the Saints game. "He went into Lucky's and asked the butcher for a free turkey and they told him he was crazy. He took it great, though."[31]

"Turkey day story: every year rookies are told to go to a local store [where they] would be treated like stars and get a free turkey," said Derrick Harmon, one of the six rookies on the team. "You would go down to the store thinking they would give you a free turkey. All fun and games but we got nothing. Good memory."[32]

The next day inside the Superdome, the crowd of more than 65,000 saw the 11–1 49ers face the 6–6 Saints. The Saints were coming off a huge 27–24 Monday night victory over the Pittsburgh Steelers, who had given the 49ers their only loss of the season. It would be another physical game.

On the first play from scrimmage Walsh called a trick play. Wide receiver Freddie Solomon took a reverse around the left end for forty-seven yards. It would be the longest regular-season run from scrimmage for the 49ers all season. The drive stalled, though, as Ray Wersching lined up for a forty-eight-yard field goal. The kick was wide left. Not the start Walsh wanted, but this game would be dominated by George Seifert's defense.

Early in the second quarter Max Runager pinned the Saints back with a perfect coffin-corner kick. Rookie linebacker Todd Shell—getting more playing time due to the absence of Jack Reynolds—helped the cause with a key sack, giving the 49ers good field position. Starting from the Saints thirty-six, Montana completed three passes to get to the Saints one-yard line. Roger Craig leaped over for the easy score. The Saints generated enough offense to get one field goal right before halftime.

The 49ers offense seemed to be sleepwalking. Montana was just six for fifteen for sixty-one yards. The second half saw more life. The opening drive saw a well-executed ten-play scoring drive that resulted in Montana connecting with tight end Earl Cooper on a nineteen-yard touchdown. Shell's second sack of the game returned the ball to a suddenly hot 49ers offense. Wendell Tyler ripped off twenty-five yards on 18-BOB, putting him at more than 100 yards for the game (he finished with 110 yards on thirteen carries). Two plays later Montana called an audible, hitting a wide-open Freddie Solomon on a post route for another touchdown. Quickly the 49ers were up 21–3.

The rest of the second half saw the 49ers defense pound Saints quarterback Richard Todd into the Superdome turf. In back-to-back drives Fred Dean picked up two sacks giving the 49ers defense seven for the game. On the Saints first drive of the fourth quarter, the 49ers defense put the finishing touches on a masterful performance. Playing in the nickel defense, rookie linebacker Todd Shell properly read his keys as Todd tried to force a pass in the flat to running back Tyrone Anthony. Stepping in front of Anthony, Shell intercepted the pass and sprinted fifty-three yards for his first NFL touchdown. The first-round pick from BYU had a breakout game with six tackles, two sacks, and an interception returned for a touchdown.

In all the 49ers had eight sacks and held the Saints to just 201 yards of total offense. A late Bill Ring touchdown made the final score 35–3.

In two games against the 49ers Richard Todd was eleven of twenty-five for just seventy-seven yards and had four interceptions. For the 49ers it was the eighth time in twelve games that they had scored thirty points or more. It was the first time since 1953 the 49ers had done that. More impressively, the 49ers were now perfect on the road, 7–0, with just one more road game the following week against the Atlanta Falcons.

Walsh was pleased with his team's effort despite the sluggish first half. He smiled seeing his team run for 219 yards. The bigger accomplishment was clinching the NFC West title. "When you clinch the division and win like that on the road, it's nice, but we can't get high off the hog," remarked Dwight Hicks in the winning locker room. "This is just one step on the road we set in the beginning of the season to be champions."[33] Every 49er player knew the ultimate objective: to get to the Super Bowl. Leaders like Dwight Hicks reminded the team what they were after. The celebration for a divisional title was almost nonexistent.

The 49ers followed a tradition of giving each member of the franchise a belt buckle when they clinched a division title. In 1984 they wanted a different piece of hardware. "They used to give us these little belt buckles for winning the Western Division. People would say, 'Hey, that wasn't what our goal was. Our goal was always to win the Super Bowl,'" said Jim Stuckey, defensive end. "Bill had us focused on greater things. You win the division. Here's the damn belt buckle. That's not what we're after. He said, 'That's good. But we are going for something much bigger than that.'"[34]

It had been ten months since Dwight Hicks's speech in the 49ers locker room in Washington. All the 49ers remembered that message in New Orleans. Only three more games remained in the regular-season schedule. The 49ers were one step closer to their ultimate goal—to get to Super Bowl XIX. The NFL standings after week 13 are shown in table 13.1.

Table 13.1.   NFL Standings after Week 13

AFC EAST		NFC EAST	
Miami	12–1	Dallas	8–5
New England	8–5	New York Giants	8–5
New York Jets	6–7	Washington	8–5
Indianapolis	4–9	St. Louis	7–6
Buffalo	1–12	Philadelphia	5–7–1
AFC CENTRAL		**NFC CENTRAL**	
Pittsburgh	7–6	Chicago	9–4
Cincinnati	5–8	Green Bay	5–8
Cleveland	4–9	Detroit	4–8–1
Houston	2–11	Tampa Bay	4–9
		Minnesota	3–10
AFC WEST		**NFC WEST**	
Denver	11–2	San Francisco	12–1
Seattle	11–2	Los Angeles Rams	8–5
Los Angeles Raiders	9–4	New Orleans	6–7
San Diego	6–7	Atlanta	3–10
Kansas City	5–8		

14

DECEMBER

Week 14 at Atlanta Falcons (December 2)
Week 15 vs. Minnesota Vikings (Saturday, December 8)
Week 16 vs. Los Angeles Rams (Friday, December 14)

With just three regular-season games remaining, the 49ers accomplished much with their 12–1 record. They clinched the NFC Western Division and had the best record in the conference. With one more win they would clinch home-field advantage throughout the playoffs—including the Super Bowl, right down the road in Palo Alto. But in order to achieve home-field advantage, they would have to do something that the 49ers had never done under the leadership of Bill Walsh: win a road game in Atlanta. In four previous trips to Atlanta, Bill Walsh's 49ers had lost all four times—including the heartbreaking Hail Mary game in 1983. In those four games the defense had given up an average of thirty-two points per game. This trip would have a different outcome.

After a 3–3 start the Falcons had fallen on hard times. They had lost their starting quarterback, Steve Bartkowski, to an injury and then seven consecutive games. The team was reeling and it was reflected in their following: only 29,644 fans showed up at Atlanta Fulton County Stadium—meaning more than 26,000 stayed away on that rainy Sunday in the South. With Ronnie Lott out and Carlton Williamson a late scratch due to a pinched nerve in his neck, George Seifert adjusted his starting secondary. Tom Holmoe would start at strong safety.

On the first play of the game, Falcons backup quarterback Mike Moroski challenged Mario Clark, hitting Alfred Jenkins on a forty-seven-yard reception. The defense held the Falcons to a field goal. The 49ers responded quickly. Walsh called a pass play and Montana connected with Freddie Solomon down the middle of the field for a sixty-four-yard touchdown. It was the sixth straight game Solomon scored a touchdown.

Late in the first quarter the Falcons drove past midfield. Then Moroski went after Mario Clark again. This time the 49ers veteran cornerback came up big, intercepting a deep pass in the end zone. Still working though his first twenty-five plays, Walsh called a masterful drive. After eight plays Montana had the ball on the Falcons six-yard line. This time he looked for his other wide receiver, hitting Dwight Clark for his fifth touchdown catch of the year.

The Falcons fought back with a heavy dose of their best player—Gerald Riggs. On a thirteen-play drive Riggs carried the ball nine times, capping the march with a two-yard touchdown run. Trailing only 14–10 the Falcons got the ball back with two minutes in the half. Playing with confidence the home team looked to score again. But for the 49ers defense, it was time to make a big play. From his own forty-two, Moroski faded back. Trying to pass rush from his right defensive end position, Fred Dean blew past tight end Arthur Cox and blindsided Moroski, jarring the ball loose. The wet football lay on the ground for almost five seconds before Gary "Big Hands" Johnson scooped it up. The ten-year veteran rumbled thirty-four yards to the end zone. It was just the third career touchdown for Johnson. The improbable defensive score put the 49ers up 21–10 at the half.

Their joy quickly faded early in the third quarter. After a Ray Wersching missed field goal, Moroski hit Alfred Jackson—who finished the game with 193 receiving yards—on a forty-eight-yard touchdown. After all the positive plays, Bill Walsh saw his team up only 21–17. His offense was forced to punt, putting George Seifert's defense back on the field. The defense came up with another huge play, taking advantage of young Moroski's biggest mistake of the game. Under pressure from Dwaine Board, he tried to force a ball to wide receiver Floyd Hodge on a curl route, but backup cornerback Dana McLemore had other ideas. "I got a good jump on [the ball]. I think I knocked Keena [Turner] down to get it. But I knew I had it in my sights so I got a real good jump on it. I tried to get it as fast as I could to get out of there," said McLemore.[1] Reading the play from the snap McLemore jumped the route in full stride, going fifty-four yards untouched in the mud. It was his first-ever interception return for a touchdown. It was also the second defensive score for Seifert's squad.

In the fourth quarter the Falcons turned the ball over on two consecutive drives: a fumble recovery by Todd Shell and an interception by Keena Turner. The latter set up a Roger Craig touchdown, preserving a 35–17 victory. The defense forced six turnovers, had three sacks, and scored two touchdowns. They were all over the field because the Falcons ran eighty-two plays to the 49ers fifty-seven plays. In the end the 49ers accomplished something special. They were the first team in NFL history to go undefeated on the road (8–0) in a sixteen-game season (instituted in 1978; prior to that, the regular season was fourteen games). In those eight road games the 49ers outscored their opponents 260–94 (for an average of 32.5–11.75 points per game).

Walsh's offense was held to a season-low 290 total yards but he didn't care. He was happy to get his first-ever win in Atlanta. Plus, his team had clinched home-field advantage throughout the playoffs. The road to the Super Bowl in the NFC would go through San Francisco. The only bad news on the defensive side was the loss of inside linebacker Jim Fahnhorst to a knee injury. "It was a draw play. So you take a half-step back, read it's not a pass, came back up to hit the guard. Then our end came inside with the offensive tackle on top of him while I was bracing with the guard. Both came down on my right leg. So you got about 550 or 600 pounds on my right leg while it was planted. I was lucky it was just my medial collateral that tore," said Fahnhorst.[2]

Three weeks after losing Ron Ferrari, the 49ers lost Jim Fahnhorst for the reminder of the season. "I felt bad for him because I knew that we had a good team and I knew we were going to have some success. For any player to not be able to participate in the good times that [resulted from hard work] is disappointing," said Keith Fahnhorst, Jim's older brother.[3]

For the Fahnhorst siblings, Jim's shortened season was bittersweet. Jim, who had played more than two seasons of football in a calendar year including games in the USFL, was close to breaking down. "My body was tired. I was pretty much a noodle at that time. My body was so worn out. I had played about thirty-eight or thirty-nine games and I was beat up. Mike Walter replaced me and did great," said Fahnhorst.[4] Next man up.

With their last two regular-season games at home, plus home-field advantage in the playoffs and Super Bowl XIX in nearby Palo Alto, the 49ers would not have to leave the Bay area for the next seven weeks. Home sweet home. On the same day of the 49ers victory in Atlanta, the Miami Dolphins suffered their second loss of the season to the Raiders, 45–34. Despite the misstep the Dolphins were still considered the best team in the AFC. Most experts expected a Dolphins–49ers Super Bowl matchup.

The 49ers would have a short week since their next game was on Saturday afternoon against the 3–11 Minnesota Vikings. With the short week Walsh challenged his offense to play better than they did in Atlanta. They would face a Vikings team struggling under first-year head coach Les Steckel, who had replaced the legendary Bud Grant. The three-win Vikings faced the tall task of pulling off the upset against the 13–1 49ers. A crowd of 56,670 fans filled Candlestick to watch a perfect first twenty-five plays by Walsh's offense. After an exchange of punts the 49ers took over near midfield. The first play after the punt, Joe Montana hit Dwight Clark on a beautiful forty-four-yard score. The 49ers defense forced a quick three-and-out to return the ball to Montana. This time Roger Craig and Wendell Tyler touched the ball eight times for forty-three yards to set up a touchdown pass to Freddie Solomon. It was Solomon's ninth touchdown of the season, setting a new career high (he had eight in both 1980 and 1981).

After the Vikings cut the lead to 14–7 early in the second quarter, the 49ers offense rolled over the overmatched team from the NFC Central. Following the Vikings only score of the game, Wendell Tyler stole the show with help from Bill Walsh. After one carry for four yards, Tyler sprinted for a six-yard gain over the right side behind blocks by Randy Cross and Keith Fahnhorst. The modest gain gave Tyler 1,206 yards on the season, breaking the 49ers record set by Delvin Williams (1,203) in 1976. Tyler had broken the record in 238 attempts in fifteen games; Williams achieved it in 248 attempts in fourteen games.

"It hadn't been broken in a long time, but I couldn't have done it without the linemen and Roger [Craig], all the guys. Everybody did his part. So I was able to do my part," said Tyler.[5] Tyler continued to add to the new mark by gaining nineteen more yards on a drive that ended with a five-yard scoring plunge—his ninth touchdown of the year. The next 49ers drive saw another big play. Montana threw a beautiful pass down the middle to speedy Renaldo Nehemiah, who ran a perfect post route behind the defense. The fifty-nine-yard touchdown increased the 49ers lead to 28–7. Walsh's first twenty-five plays—twelve passes and thirteen runs—generated twenty-one points. Right before halftime Ray Wersching added a field goal.

The 49ers had run thirty-eight plays and scored thirty-one points. Montana was almost perfect, completing fifteen of twenty-one passes for 246 yards and three touchdowns. He tied his career high in touchdown passes for a single season with twenty-six (set in 1983). The second half started with Joe Montana on the sidelines wearing a black San Francisco Giants baseball cap. Backup Matt Cavanaugh would play the entire second half. He continued where Montana left off by leading the 49ers offense to two field goals. In the fourth quarter Derrick Harmon scored his first NFL touchdown on a three-yard run. "No, I didn't spike it. I kept it. My dad has it," said running back Derrick Harmon.[6] Bill Ring ended the scoring barrage on a fifteen-yard run.

The 51–7 victory proved to the rest of the NFL that the 49ers were ready for the postseason. With one more regular season game—against the Los Angeles Rams—the 49ers were clicking on all cylinders. Fifty-one points was the most ever scored by a Bill Walsh–led team and the most by a 49ers team since 1965, when they scored fifty-two against the Bears. They had 521 total yards on an incredible seventy-six plays (for an average of 6.9 yards per play).

Records weren't on the minds of the players, but Walsh knew this was a special season. Records and achievement come from success. In addition to the success of individual players, the 49ers team had a chance to make NFL history. If they could beat the Rams, they would be the first NFL team to win fifteen games in a season. Since the NFL went to a sixteen-game season in 1978, no team had gone 15–1.

They would face a tough Rams team with a 10–5 record that was fighting for a playoff berth. With a Rams win, they were in, but with a loss, they would need some help. Plus, Eric Dickerson, who had just broken O. J. Simpson's single-season rushing record of 2,003 yards the previous week, was in the backfield, so the defense had their work cut out for them.

In addition to preparing for the Rams, the 49ers coaches also began prepping for their next potential playoff opponents. They had already played the Redskins, Giants, and Rams, who were likely to make the playoffs, so Walsh put in some time to prepare for the Chicago Bears, the champions of the NFC Central. After the Saturday game the 49ers once again had a short workweek. The NFL scheduled their last game of the regular season on Friday night, December 14.

The week of the Rams game, the NFL announced the squads for the Pro Bowl. Nine players from the 49ers were selected.

49ers Pro Bowl Players

Quarterback: Joe Montana (starter)
Running back: Wendell Tyler
Offensive guard: Randy Cross (starter)
Center: Fred Quillan (starter)
Offensive tackle: Keith Fahnhorst
Linebacker: Keena Turner
Cornerback: Ronnie Lott (despite missing four games)
Strong safety: Carlton Williamson
Free safety: Dwight Hicks (starter)

Six days after the Vikings game Candlestick was ready again. The 9:00 p.m. East Coast kickoff time saw the 49ers make history. ABC cameras caught a clever fan's sign on the Candlestick wall: "Hey Rams, This Is the Closest You'll Ever Get to Stanford." Nearly 60,000 fans saw the 49ers start fast. After the Rams kicked an early field goal, Joe Montana picked up where he left off against the Vikings, hitting Freddie Solomon for a twenty-six-yard gain. He then went back to Solomon, down the middle of the field, for an easy touchdown. The forty-seven-yard score was the eighth straight game that Solomon had found the end zone. On the 49ers next drive Walsh saw another score: this time fifty-eight yards in nine plays capped by Montana's one-yard toss to tight end Earl Cooper.

As the first quarter ended, the 49ers ran fourteen offensive plays and scored two touchdowns.[7]

On the last play of the first quarter Dickerson tried to run around the left end. Instead he was hit by Manu Tuiasosopo, who stripped the ball away, which was then recovered by Dwaine Board. The turnover set up a Ray Wersching field goal. It looked to be another rout of the Rams, but they were fighting for a playoff berth. They responded with a short Dickerson touchdown run followed by another drive to the 49ers twenty-three-yard line. This time the 49ers special teams made a special play as Lawrence Pillers blocked a field goal attempt. But the Rams responded again just before the half with a successful field goal. Behind the running of Eric Dickerson, who had ninety-five yards rushing, the Rams had cut the lead to 17–13.

The second half saw both defenses dominate. After a scoreless third quarter the Rams finally sustained a drive. Mike Lansford's third field goal narrowed the 49ers lead to one point, 17–16. With 3:43 left in the game, the 49ers tried to run out the clock, but near midfield they were forced to punt. Max Runager again proved to be the right man for the punter's job. He dropped a perfect coffin-corner kick that was downed by rookie linebacker Todd Shell on the Rams seven-yard line. Backed-up Rams quarterback Jeff Kemp tried to mount a game-winning drive. The team that had given up the fewest points in the NFL was about to shut the door on the Rams in dramatic fashion. Dropping back to throw, Kemp got immediate pressure up the middle by midseason acquisition Gary "Big Hands" Johnson, who dropped Kemp in the end zone for a safety.

The 49ers defense had given up only 227 points all season (13.1 points per game). George Seifert's unit had been outstanding in the second half. After giving up ninety-five yards rushing to Dickerson in the first half, they held him to just three yards on six carries in the second half. He would finish with an NFL-record 2,105 rushing yards for the season. But in two games against the 49ers he never topped 100 yards, making Michael Carter very happy. The final seconds ran off the clock and began a celebration at Candlestick Park. The crowd knew it was witnessing history. No team had ever gone 15–1, but their 49ers had just done it. After the free kick was recovered by the Niners, Montana took a knee.

Offense, defense, and special teams had once again combined for a complete team effort in the 49ers victory. But for one brief moment— or bad call—in one game (against the Steelers) the 49ers nearly had a perfect regular season. "It's great to be part of history. I've never been on a team where all forty-nine people played a part," commented Gary Johnson after the game.[8] "The forty-nine men on the squad were the difference. Our punter was the difference. Our special teams were the difference. It's really a tribute to the squad to win one like this, because it took the entire squad to do it," remarked Bill Walsh to the press in the locker room.[9]

"Fifteen–1 is something we can cherish but now it's down to business. It's great to be 15–1, but who the heck cares if we lose [in two weeks]? It's only good when you retire," remarked Joe Montana in the locker room.[10]

The 1984 49ers experienced the most successful regular season in NFL history. Their 15–1 record for the season and their 8–0 record for road games were both firsts in NFL history. The Niners broke or tied thirty team and individual records. They scored a franchise-record 475 points. Throughout the regular season the 49ers racked up a team-record 6,366 yards on offense. "We just established the NFL record [15–1] and we're going to stop for a minute and take pride in it. We have future games and we'll be ready for them but we're proud of this. This was football at its finest," said Bill Walsh after the game.[11]

The rest of the NFL was equally ready for the postseason.

NFC Playoffs

1. 49ers (West champs, 15–1)
2. Redskins (East champs, 11–5)
3. Bears (Central champs, 10–6)

Wild Cards

1. Los Angeles Rams (10–6)
2. New York Giants (9–7)

AFC Playoffs

1. Dolphins (East champs, 14–2)
2. Broncos (West champs, 13–3)
3. Steelers (Central champs, 9–7)

Wild Cards

1. Seahawks (12–4)

2. Los Angeles Raiders (9–7)

It was now playoff time. All records, individual achievements, and honors were thrown out the window. It was time to get down to business. The NFL's second season was here. It was what the 49ers were really working toward. A team—following a standard of performance presented to them by their head coach—nearly accomplished a perfect regular season. Since January 1984 in Washington, D.C., 49ers players and coaches had dedicated themselves to this moment—to getting back to the Super Bowl. It was time to finish the journey.

Part IV

The Postseason

15

NFC DIVISIONAL PLAYOFF GAME

New York Giants at San Francisco 49ers
Candlestick Park
December 29, 1984

For the 49ers, the accomplishment of a 15–1 regular season was be-hind them. It was now the NFL's second season: the playoffs. By win-ning fifteen games they had worked hard to gain home-field advantage. "When you got into the playoffs, you knew automatically [the intensity level] was going to pick up. You had everything that you'd worked so hard to get to this point, and you got to make sure to take advantage of it. We really believed that we needed to have home-field advantage. You tried not to let that slip away from you," said Ray Rhodes, defensive backs coach.[1] The playoffs were where they wanted to be. The level of intensity would now increase even higher than in the previous sixteen weeks.

"Once you get to the playoffs everything ratchets up. The intensity is accelerated at an unbelievable rate for all these games. There's usually mayhem during a regular-season game, but when you get to those playoffs and the intensity is really turned up—at least 30 percent—every step you go, the intensity is even greater. And Bill tried to impress upon us not to get too wound up about any particular game. But the hitting was harder, the intensity was much more fierce in situations like that," said running back Bill Ring.[2]

The bye week did slow the 49ers momentum. "I think the worst thing about that first postseason game was that we had a bye the first week. That kind of breaks up your momentum a little bit. You're used to playing every week and all of sudden, you don't. I think that's what our main concern was. I've seen a lot of teams who got beat in that first playoff game when they had a bye the first week," said Keith Fahnhorst, offensive tackle.[3] In the end, the time off brought the team closer together. During the past year the 1984 49ers had bonded more and more, making this as close a team as the NFL had ever seen.

"I remember the camaraderie. I remember the closeness of our team, not only the offense but the defense. I mean, we as a team were close. We made mistakes in 1981; we didn't make many mistakes in 1984. I didn't feel there was anybody who could touch us," said defensive end Jim Stuckey.[4]

As the 49ers prepared for the postseason, they would be able to fully unleash their pass rush, a unit that was now at full strength with the return of Fred Dean and Jeff Stover. Heading into the playoffs, these nine men knew their specific roles in George Seifert's defense. Defensive line coach Bill McPherson would keep them fresh throughout the game with a simple rotation. "Everybody knew his role and played hard. Everybody contributed," said Dwaine Board, defensive end. "The nice thing about it was no one had any animosity toward each other. All we wanted to do was win together."[5]

Off the field the group frequently spent time together. Fred Dean's home was often a hangout, and Dean was more than happy to entertain. "We used to call Fred 'Grandma' because Fred would cook for us. We would all go over to his house. Fred would cook us big meals. Fred could cook anything," said Dwaine Board. "He used to make gumbo, fried chicken, collard greens, and Fred used to make great cornbread. He could cook. Anything you wanted to eat, Fred could cook it up." Continued Board: "Fred could play any instrument, too. He could play the saxophone. He could play the guitar. He could play the piano. And he would always sing. Fred used to think he was Luther Vandross."[6]

"Basically all of them would show up and I'd fix a big spread. A lot of the defensive linemen would come over, and then we had other people, running backs, Ronnie Lott, and other guys. They would show up from time to time. There was Thanksgiving turkey or whatever. We'd eat and enjoy the food," said Fred Dean. "Besides the food we could entertain each other. To hear players talk about the game and things that happened in the game, that made a big difference in what we would try to get done. Because the things that you say in private, they would come out in the open. Some of the things that you do, how you did them, and how you played in certain situations, you would bring about what you needed in order to [be] a player. . . . So what I'm saying is a lot of that was done. I think a lot of that came from conversations that we would have."

Dean loved to host his teammates, and they appreciated his hospitality—and his cooking: eating became a competitive sport at Dean's house. "It was a competition when it comes to Lawrence Pillers. I didn't do too bad myself. I'd eat a lot when I was cooking, too. But the bottom line is, [the get-togethers] were always pretty good. I didn't have too many leftovers after it was all over," said Dean.[7]

"We spent a lot of time together eating meals. Everybody'd take turns. Again, there's Lawrence Pillers. He's another special individual; he's one of the guys. It was like a puzzle and everyone had a place in it. [Pillers] kept everybody laughing [with his] great sense of humor. But, yeah, I ate a lot with Fred," said Louie Kelcher, defensive tackle. "There wasn't a lot that Fred didn't cook. I mean it's the basic ribs and stuff like that. Sausage. He'd cook some different types of food every once in a while. It was a great time, I enjoyed it all."[8]

"We enjoyed each other on the field and enjoyed each other's company off the field," said Jim Stuckey.[9] "I'll tell you, that whole crew—the defensive linemen—we hung together. We were a family. We pounded beers together; we hung out. We were close as a unit, and if one of us was stumbling, we stood up and did what we had to do because we were a family," said Lawrence Pillers, defensive end.[10]

A week before their first playoff game the coaches watched the NFC Wild Card Game. The New York Giants pulled off a 16–13 playoff win on the road against the Los Angeles Rams. Since they had played both wild card teams during the regular season, the coaches had game plans for those teams, as well as for the Redskins. During the bye week Walsh and his staff spent additional time planning for the Chicago Bears—the team they hadn't faced during the regular season. Their preparation ensured they would be ready to play any opponent. "We knew we had home-field advantage throughout the playoffs, so our confidence was high, but we weren't done yet. We had a bye week. We just waited and watched and took it easy that first week," said offensive tackle Allan Kennedy. "Then we saw who we were going to play. The coaches had already planned for either team. We had a lot of film on them. So we knew what worked against them."[11]

Now knowing that their opponent would be the Giants—a rematch of an opponent they dominated 31–10 in their week 6 victory in New York—gave the 49ers confidence. Walsh then put his team on edge, refocusing their energy after a week of not playing. "Great leadership by Bill Walsh and the coaches. He made sure we were on task. Bill actually treated us like we were 9–7 or 8–8 instead of 15–1. He said, '15–1 is good, but we haven't done anything if we don't go ahead and take care of business.' I'm [thinking], 'Is this guy kidding me? We have the best record in the NFL.' But then you go up there on Monday and he would tell you: 'We're going to practice our butts off,'" said Earl Cooper, tight end.[12] In his initial offensive game plan on Monday, Walsh put a trick play at the top of his first twenty-five plays. A hook-and-lateral pass play would start the game.

Walsh left no stones unturned in preparing for the rematch with the Giants despite off-the-field distractions. During the week, two players were handling family issues. Keith Fahnhorst's wife was due to deliver their third daughter on December 26, just two days before the game, and defensive end Jim Stuckey suffered a painful family loss. His grandmother, who raised him, passed away in South Carolina. He flew back to his hometown to take care of his family. "It was really tough. It was my mother's mother. She basically raised me. My parents died when I was six. So it was a very emotional time for me. . . . I wanted to get back to my teammates, to be able to play. . . . I needed them and hopefully they needed me at some point," he said.[13]

Both players would ultimately play and be prepared to contribute. On Thursday the team was loose and ready. In the locker room before practice the 49ers held their annual domino tournament. "That was one of the things that Bill liked to have us do to keep loose in the locker room. Freddie Solomon was the ringleader of dominoes. Fred Dean [too], I was afraid to play him. He was great at dominoes and Freddie was great," said safety Tom Holmoe. "It was just a social thing to bring people together."[14]

In the domino finals it came down to two defensive backs. Tom Holmoe—who had defeated Carl Monroe, Danny Fulton, and John

Ayers—faced off against rookie safety Jeff Fuller—who had defeated Earl Cooper, Joe Montana, Dwight Clark, and Milt McColl. In a very competitive final match, Holmoe came out on top, winning 150–120. "After I won, there were some guys saying I should have had to play four [matches] instead of three. But I've got the crown," commented Holmoe after winning. "I guess it just shows that on any given day, anyone can win," remarked Jeff Fuller.[15]

In the early playoff game on Saturday, the Dolphins, who finished the regular season with a 14–2 record, beat the Seahawks 31–10 behind three touchdown passes by league MVP Dan Marino. The 49ers took notice of the impressive performance by the favored Dolphins. They, too, wanted to have a dominant performance in their first playoff game. The Giants came to Candlestick with momentum after upsetting the Rams. Phil Simms led their passing game, throwing for more than 4,000 yards and twenty-two touchdowns, but he also had eighteen interceptions. The 49ers forced two picks from Simms during their week 6 matchup. George Seifert was confident about stopping the run and putting the ball in Simms's hands. "The emphasis hasn't changed much over the years. You gotta stop people from running the ball and you gotta get pressure. And maybe it's not in that order always, but you gotta discourage the run. You gotta get people in third down. It's that simple," said linebacker Keena Turner.[16] The pass rush was ready.

The 1:00 p.m. local kickoff saw a cool, damp day at The Stick. Only 44 degrees at game time, Candlestick saw the second-largest crowd ever at 60,303. Only the 1981 NFC Championship Game—which had featured The Catch—had a larger crowd. Michael Olmstead, 49ers entertainment director, brought out Huey Lewis and the News to sing the national anthem, putting the 49ers Faithful into a frenzy. The players were ready for the playoffs. "There is not another day. It's now or never. The bar just raised. I mean, you've been studying hard and now you live, breathe, sleep, and you know nothing else matters. You got to be perfect and you can't look back. You can't second-guess yourself. You just got to go and it is the best of the best," said Dan Bunz, linebacker.[17]

"So now we're finally in the postseason. We thought, 'OK, this is it. This is the new season. This is the one that we've been waiting for.' We were ready. We were fired up, and we just knew that our level of play was going to have to go up another notch," said safety Carlton Williamson.[18]

Forty-niners players were nervous and excited with excess energy. Even Ronnie Lott, who was returning to the starting lineup at corner-back, felt the nerves. This was the playoffs. "I really felt like the bigger the game, the better our players played," said defensive backs coach Ray Rhodes.[19] The Candlestick Park crowd was ready. The CBS broadcast with John Madden and Pat Summerall was ready. The 49ers were ready.

The Niners received the opening kickoff. On the first play Walsh called his trick play. Montana completed a quick hitch to Dwight Clark, who lateralled perfectly to Freddie Solomon, who took the ball down the sideline for a thirteen-yard gain and a first down. The Candlestick crowd went nuts. The first drive was a clinic. Behind runs by Tyler and Craig totaling twenty-eight yards and a third-down conversion by Clark, the ball reached the Giants twenty-one-yard line. Walsh called a formation with two wide receivers, two tight ends, and one back. Clark went in motion from left to right and lined up just past tight end John Frank. At the snap Frank ran a corner route and Clark ran a skinny post to the middle. Montana doubled pumped, then threaded a pass to Clark down the middle of the field between Giants linebacker Andy Headen and free safety Terry Kinard. Three minutes into the game, the 49ers had their first touchdown. The crowd went into another frenzy.

The Giants needed to respond quickly, but the 49ers defense would make the situation worse for the road team. Making an early statement this time would be a team effort. On the fifth play from scrimmage, Giants quarterback Simms dropped back to pass. Throwing downfield for wide receiver Lionel Manuel, a blitzing Dan Bunz tipped the ball at the line of scrimmage. The ball carried downfield, glanced off the back of linebacker Riki Ellison, who was in trail mode in pass coverage, and floated in the air as Ronnie Lott dove for the interception. Untouched, Lott got up and ran the ball back to the Giants twelve-yard line before being knocked out-of-bounds by Manuel.

The 49ers Faithful got even louder—the stadium was rocking. "That's a huge turnover. That was the first big momentum change and the crowd went crazy. It was nuts. You could feel the whole crowd and the momentum change right there. I mean, it was already with us but it just picked up volume," said Ellison.[20]

Because of the great field position Walsh adjusted to his red zone plays. With a trips formation Montana dropped back to pass on a five-step drop. He went through his reads: first and second options, both covered. Turning to his third option, he finally lofted a ball over inside linebacker Gary Reasons to tight end Russ Francis. Just seven minutes gone in the first quarter and the 49ers had run ten offensive plays and had a 14–0 lead. Everything was going well.

Late in the first quarter the 49ers offense made a mistake. A Montana toss glanced off the hands of Dwight Clark into the hands of Gary Reasons. Simms took advantage of the turnover, going five for six for forty-three yards, leading to a Giants field goal. In the second quarter the 49ers lost their momentum. After an exchange of punts the 49ers offense found themselves backed up inside their own five-yard line. On second down Montana made an uncharacteristic misread that would cost his team. On a five-step drop into his own end zone, he tried to hit Clark on a deep curl but he didn't see linebacker Harry Carson. The thirty-one-year-old veteran picked off the pass and sprinted fourteen yards for a touchdown. His defensive teammates—including Lawrence Taylor, who tackled Carson in the end zone—celebrated the big play.

The quick start had now stalled. The Giants converted two turnovers into ten points. But Walsh and Montana responded like champions. The following drive started with two Roger Craig carries for a first down. Montana connected with Freddie Solomon for sixteen yards, and he was hit late out-of-bounds, giving the 49ers fifteen extra yards of field position. The next play Montana returned to Solomon. Running a perfect post route Solomon beat cornerback Perry Williams. Montana hit him in stride for his third touchdown pass of the first half. Approaching the 49ers sidelines, Solomon gave a low five to Dwight Clark as The Stick grew loud again.

Covering seventy-three yards in just two and half minutes, the 49ers had regained momentum. They went into the locker room with a 21–10 lead at halftime. The second half would belong to the 49ers defense. While the 49ers were in the Candlestick locker room, the halftime entertainment on the field featured dogs with Frisbees. On the CBS broadcast, host Brent Musburger talked to Terry Bradshaw about the first half and also interviewed Bears head coach Mike Ditka from Arlington, Virginia, where he was preparing for his team's playoff game on Sunday against the Washington Redskins.[21]

The 49ers defense had held the Giants to just 128 total yards—only fifty-six yards on the ground—in the first half and had given up only one completion to a wide receiver (Bobby Johnson for eleven yards). After halftime they continued their stellar work. A Jeff Stover sack ended the Giants first drive, giving the ball back to the 49ers offense. "The coaches were telling us to gear up and go after it. That's pretty much what we did," said Stover.[22]

Surprisingly, Joe Montana then used his legs. Facing a third down Montana scrambled around the left end, aiming to get out-of-bounds, but the Giants defense let up. Sprinting down the sidelines in front of the Giants bench, the 49ers signal caller gained fifty-three yards before being knocked out-of-bounds. Montana's run was the longest by the 49ers all season—eclipsing even Solomon's forty-seven-yard run in week 13 against the Saints. But the long sprint took a lot out of Montana. Two plays later he tried to hit Solomon over the middle but Gary Reasons leaped up for the interception at the Giants five-yard line. It was Montana's third interception of the game. He had only ten throughout the regular season.

But the 49ers defense was not giving up any more points. Dwaine Board sacked Simms to end one drive. Riki Ellison intercepted a pass to end another. In the third quarter alone, the Giants had three drives, ran fourteen plays, allowed two sacks, had one interception, and punted twice. After the Ellison interception the 49ers offense put itself back into scoring position. Ray Wersching trotted out for a thirty-nine-yard field goal attempt. Coming off the edge Elvis Patterson blocked the kick. Trying to make the tackle, Wersching suffered the 49ers biggest loss of the game.

"I didn't wear a mouthpiece and wore a single-bar facemask, and I just got crushed in my mouth. We were coming off the field and I was thinking, 'Damn, what is that?' All of sudden I spit something out like a piece of popcorn and it was my tooth. I went to the dentist [on the sidelines] and said, 'Doc, what do I do?' and he looked at me and said, 'Nothing we can do right now. We'll see you in the chair tomorrow,'" said Wersching.[23]

Wersching's chipped tooth didn't make Walsh laugh along the sidelines. Despite the block the 49ers running game moved the clock forward, frustrating the Giants defense even more. Keeping the ball for another twelve plays made the Giants best player crack. On a short run by Wendell Tyler, Lawrence Taylor began a wrestling match with rookie tight end John Frank, who didn't back down from the NFL's best defensive player. L. T. even punched Frank's face mask. In the CBS booth Madden liked Frank's spunk. "Frank had L. T. pinned . . . one, two, three . . . Frank gets the pin," yelled Madden to the television audience.[24]

"That's just the kind of person John is. 'I'm not gonna back down. I don't care who he is.' That's what he'd be saying after he got finished. That drive he had to win and just be a tenacious player," said Earl Cooper, tight end.[25]

In the end it was the defense that would put the exclamation point on a postseason victory. Fred Dean sacked Simms, forcing a fumble, which was recovered by fellow line mate Dwaine Board. It was the team's sixth sack and third turnover of the game. Of the ten points given up by the 49ers, only three fell on the shoulders of the defense. The 49ers were back in the NFC Championship Game. The 21–10 victory wasn't pretty, but it was a sweet win for the 49ers. "We were a little frustrated offensively in the second half, but our defense played exceptionally well and it was good enough to take us to the next step," commented Bill Walsh at his postgame press conference.[26]

Maybe the 49ers had some rust from the bye week. All along, the 49ers were built as a team, and they would always win as a team. It was the 49ers tenth consecutive victory since the loss to the Steelers. In the locker room the press wanted the 49ers to comment on who they would rather play next, the Chicago Bears or a rematch with the Washington Redskins. "It hurt to lose that game last year. I don't care who we play. Just give me another chance," remarked Russ Francis.[27] "It doesn't matter. We're in the same position we were last year. Whoever shows up, that's who we have to play," commented Eric Wright.[28] "I don't really care who we play. We have to play somebody to get to the Super Bowl," said Dwight Clark.[29]

The celebration lasted through the night. The next day, it would be back to work as usual.

16

NFC CHAMPIONSHIP GAME

Chicago Bears at San Francisco 49ers
Candlestick Park
January 6, 1985

The day after their playoff win against the Giants, the 49ers gathered to review the game film. They quickly put the victory behind them. Their next opponent would be determined more than 2,400 miles away in Washington, D.C. Early Sunday morning (10:00 a.m. PST) the Bears faced off against the defending NFC champion Redskins. The Bears played a very fast, physical game, sacking Redskins quarterback Joe Theismann seven times and forcing three turnovers. Bears quarterback Steve Fuller threw two touchdowns and Walter Payton—who rushed for 104 yards—tossed a halfback pass for another score to lead the Bears to a 23–19 upset victory at RFK Stadium. Moments after the Bears victory, they started boasting about playing in the Super Bowl.

Even the national media favored the Bears in the title game because of their great defense. Peter Richmond of the *Miami Herald* billed the upcoming NFC Championship as "a match between one good offense and one great defense," forgetting that the NFL's number-one scoring defense was the 49ers.[1] In the locker room the 49ers took the news in stride. "By that time we had played a season and we had an incredible amount of confidence," said safety Tom Holmoe. "I think everybody believed that Coach Walsh and his coaches were going to put us in a position to be successful. When I played for the 49ers, I never went into a game where we didn't expect to win."[2]

Sunday night Walsh went to his office to finish the offensive game plan, all the while hearing the Bears brag. His thoughts turned to the last time he faced the Bears, a team coached by Mike Ditka and a defense guided by Buddy Ryan. He flashed back to November 27, 1983, at Soldier Field. Played on a frozen gridiron in Chicago, the game pitted Walsh's West Coast offense against Buddy Ryan's 46 defense. The 46 was an innovative defense with a unique defensive front designed to confuse and put pressure on the opposing offense, especially the quarterback.

Compared to a 4–3 base, the 46 dramatically shifts the defensive line to the weak side—away from the offense's tight end—with both guards and the center "covered" by the left defensive end and both defensive tackles. This alignment forced the offense to immediately account for the defenders in front of them, making it considerably harder to execute blocking assignments such as pulling, trapping, and especially pass protection. Moreover, the weak-side defensive end—usually Richard Dent—aligned one or two yards outside of the left offensive tackle, leaving him on an "island" to pass block. In 1984 Dent led the NFC in sacks with seventeen and a half.

Another key feature of the 46 was that both outside linebackers tended to play the strong side. The linebackers lined up between one and three yards from the line of scrimmage. Their primary tactic was to rush the quarterback. Usually between five and eight players rushed on every play. Buddy Ryan wanted pressure and confusion.

In the 1983 game against the Bears, the 49ers tied the score 3–3 heading into the second quarter. It was all downhill after that. A Jim McMahon–to–Dennis McKinnon touchdown gave the Bears a 10–3 lead. Right before the half the 49ers drove all the way to the Bears one-yard line. On the eleventh play of the lengthy drive Wendell Tyler fumbled at the goal line; the Bears Steve McMichael. In the second half the 49ers defense gave up only a field goal, but Walsh's offense continued to struggle with the Bears defense. Montana threw an interception to end one drive, and Tyler's second fumble ended another. The Bears rushing game behind Walter Payton ran out the clock for a 13–3 victory. It was a disheartening loss under miserable conditions.

While watching the game film from 1983, Walsh sat at his Redwood City desk looking at the dismal numbers. Only 290 total yards, five sacks allowed, and four turnovers. But the only stat that really mattered to Walsh was points scored—three points. It was the lowest scoring output by a Walsh-coached 49ers team. In seventy-two previous games (1979–1983) under Walsh they had not scored so few points. After the game the Bears mocked, "What Genius?" Because of the 1983 loss the Bears Buddy Ryan claimed he had the "book" on Walsh. He said that Walsh's offense was predictable and that the Bears would stay in the Bay area for two weeks after defeating the 49ers. Walsh heard all of this while preparing his game plan.

"Buddy Ryan was talking about how the 49ers offense was predictable, and that's the worst thing you can say about a Bill Walsh offense. So Bill didn't let us forget that he said that. There were a lot of reasons to play well against Chicago," said Keith Fahnhorst, offensive tackle.[3]

Walsh devoted much time to watching that 1983 game. He could see an impressive and very aggressive group that was the NFL's number-one ranked defensive unit. What to do? "Bill took a little extra time on that one. We would not have as extensive a game plan. We would zero-in a little bit more. Fewer protections, fewer pass routes, fewer runs. But all really designed for the 46 defense," said quarterbacks and wide receivers coach Paul Hackett.[4] Walsh knew what he had to do. Throughout that 1983 game he had Montana go back on too many five- and seven-step drops, allowing the blitz to get to the quarterback. This was a mistake most teams in the NFL made playing against the Bears 46 defense. They took deep drops without getting the ball out quickly; in turn they suffered poor pass protection. Walsh put together a package of plays that Montana would run, mostly three-step drops to get the ball out quickly before the pass rush/blitzes could get there. Quick outs, quick hitches. Get first downs, move the chains, make them cover the whole field, keep them off Joe and his timing.

Meeting with his team Walsh set the tone for the week: they wouldn't be intimidated.

> Every detail is important for every man. . . . Another thing, there's no question about it: we know what the Bears think they're going to do. They think in their own stupid way [that] they're going to intimidate us and knock us around the field. That's what they think. It's the only way they can think. They're strutting, because all they have to do is

come in here and kick the shit out of us. This game is going to be a goddamn grudge match from our standpoint.[5]

Looking at the Bears offense on film, defensive coordinator George Seifert and his staff became confident that they could shut them down. First they'd deal with the great Walter Payton, their only big weapon. Stop the run, which they had been doing all year. So he turned his attention to the Bears passing attack. After Jim McMahon had gotten hurt, Mike Ditka turned over the reins to Steve Fuller, the man Walsh worked out at Clemson in 1979, having him throw passes to Dwight Clark, whom Walsh had drafted instead in the tenth round. Seifert's game plan was to stop Payton first, forcing Fuller to beat them through the air. Fuller had started four games in 1984, throwing for 568 yards, two touchdowns, and no interceptions. Ditka told him, "just don't make mistakes." Seifert wanted to unleash his defensive front. Meeting with his team during the week, he preached "not to play careful, just go out and play football, and be aggressive."[6]

"We took that as a personal challenge. That was a team that lived because of their physicality. Because of their bigness, their toughness. They're the Bears. They got the best running back, Walter Payton; they got Matt Suhey. They're gonna run the damn ball down your ass. We wanted to define our defense in that game to the country that we were the best defense in the league, and that was a one-to-one personal thing. Personal with Chicago. So we brought it," said Riki Ellison, linebacker.[7]

The Bears had seventy-two sacks—an NFL record that still stands—but the 49ers had fifty-one sacks of their own. The 49ers defense led the NFL in fewest points allowed, surrendering only 227 all season. They had not given up more than twenty-one points since the Oilers game on October 21 and gave up only three points against the Giants. They knew that they had a great defense and they wanted to show the Bears.

"We knew we had a very talented defensive unit and the Bears were getting a lot of notoriety for their abilities and for not allowing many points. But we knew we were just as good, if not better. We knew we had a much better offense, and we felt all-around that we were the better team. It was that they were in the way. They were one step away from where we're trying to go, and we're going to have to show them what kind of defense we got, that we are just as tenacious. We're just as intimidating as they felt they were. We got brand[ed as] a finesse team and not physical. But we felt that was far from the truth and we were just as physical as any other team out there, and we wanted to show the Bears that we were," said safety Carlton Williamson.[8]

"That week I saw more of the veterans start talking. All the guys that I knew that I played with on the defensive line, they did more talking," said Michael Carter, rookie defensive tackle. "When I say talking, in the position meeting rooms and then in the defensive room, when all the defense is together. They get up and say what they're going to say. There's more talking going on that week than I've ever seen in the whole year that I was there. I said, 'this is serious.' It came to a point where everything was riding on this. You win this one; you're in the big dance. Seifert wanted to make sure everyone was prepared, everyone was focused, and everyone knew why we were there."[9]

On Wednesday in Redwood City Walsh met with his offense to review the game plan. After watching the Bears on film he discussed how they were going to beat them. He went over the pass plays and outlined short drops and quick passes.

> Our three-step drop patterns are the things that will make the difference in this ball game. Now we have to throw the ball on time and we have to catch the ball. Today Joe will [practice] for fifteen to twenty minutes on all the three-step drops. You won't need a defense group out there. Just run them and throw them to get the timing. Because that'll be the difference. . . . The other thing [is] I think we can knock their ass off running the ball. We have the plays to do it. We have some excellent concepts; we'll just take off and knock their cans off the field with them.[10]

"We came up in that game and said, 'OK, what do we do?' We went to our quick passing game. Some teams were just determined to take a five-, seven-step drop and throw it down the field. They were going to get you there; they were always going to bring an extra guy. . . . We knew our opponents well enough that we knew their weaknesses; you stayed away from their strengths. I mean, you don't take a seven-step drop against Chicago because they're going to get you. But we knew we matched well with the receivers, and we could beat their corners one on one, and Joe would get the ball there, so that's what you do," said wide receiver Mike Wilson.[11]

"The reason we took three- and five-step drops was because that kept Mike Singletary, Otis Wilson, and those guys from getting there [to the quarterback]. Whereas with the seven-drop, it would be too long for Joe to hold the ball," said Earl Cooper, tight end. "That kind of focus on what we needed to do as far as getting the ball out, defeating the 46 defense, whether both linebackers are going to be blocked or not, I think that's a tribute to everything that we did as far as putting a cap on that season."[12]

In order to get the short passing game on target they had to protect Joe Montana. To the 49ers, the 46 defense was known as the "20 flop" because the Bears tended to flop two defensive ends and two linebackers on different sides of the ball. Line coach Bobb McKittrick was primarily concerned about the pass rush: the Bears, who set an NFL record with seventy-two sacks, did most of their damage from an unbalanced set featuring all three linebackers on one side and sometimes eight men at the line. In the 1983 game the offensive line didn't adjust to the pressure. The new 20-flop pass protection that McKittrick presented would be so radical that it scared the 49ers offensive linemen. But Coach McKittrick had learned from the 1983 loss. He wanted Montana untouched.

When the 49ers saw the Bears in their favorite pass-rushing formations, McKittrick told guards Randy Cross and John Ayers to drop back a step so that the tackle would block the defensive linemen across from the guard. That enabled the guards to help out with a blitzing linebacker or another blitzing defender.[13] "That was the 46 defense and that caused a lot of problems with pass protections. I remember one of the most important adjustments we made was having the tackle block the defensive tackle who was over the guard. When they first put that in before the playoff game, I thought, 'Oh shit, this isn't going to work.' I was worried about it, but they were right. Our coaches were right. We were able to make that adjustment. But scheme-wise I was really nervous about that because I thought it was kind of an impossible task that they were asking us to do, but it worked," said Keith Fahnhorst, offensive tackle.[14]

Forty-niners players were absorbing everything. Walsh then reviewed the run game: 68 Toss Solid would be a staple. He also went over a few veer plays that grabbed the attention of Wendell Tyler. When he was going over his game plan, Walsh talked to one of his closest coaching friends, Dick Vermeil, a CBS announcer at that time. Vermeil had coached Tyler in college at UCLA, and he suggested a few veer runs that Tyler was successful in running. The veer plays just might work against the Bears 46 defense. "It was Bill being creative," said halfback Wendell Tyler.[15] The room grew excited about the plan.

The next play put the team in a frenzy. Walsh presented a play he had been tinkering with during the past few weeks, something he had thought about when it looked as if they might play the mighty Bears. On the overhead projector was a hand-drawn trap play. It didn't look like anything special. But the formation and personnel made it different. The formation was a basic pro formation with one receiver on each side and a tight end on the right side (strong side). It was a split backfield. Walsh explained that Tyler would line up as the halfback but at fullback would be rookie guard Guy McIntyre.

There was a buzz in the room when Walsh explained the play. It was a simple trap play to the right. Guard Randy Cross would pull and double-team the end with tight end Russ Francis. Tackle Keith Fahnhorst would block the defensive tackle over him; the center Fred Quillan took on the nose tackle, with McIntyre leading through the hole between guard and tackle. Walsh grew excited presenting it to the team.

> We'll . . . run this with fullback, but basically this will be Guy McIntyre. One of the things now, Guy, is we'll do [it] every day so you can get [used to] lining up real smoothly back there and getting a picture of where you belong. Because they see you measuring back there, they measure you, look at you, and follow you right to the hole. So just get into your position without much fanfare. . . . We figure Guy can take his guy on, knock his ass off the goddamn line. He doesn't have much leverage. He's powerful and he's quick. Guy intends to get into him and knock him flat out of there. When we run it Wendell [Tyler] will break outside of Guy's block.[16]

"That was probably the [result] of Buddy Ryan saying that we were predictable," said Keith Fahnhorst, offensive tackle.[17] The athletic McIntyre was surprised and excited about the play. "We knew that it was going to be tough, that defense, the Bears defense. It was a chance opportunity for me to do it," said Guy McIntyre, guard. [18] "That was one of those things where I think the whole team got excited when Bill put that in and we ran that the first time. Guy goes up through there and Wendell comes in right behind him. That was just a great time to watch him," said Earl Cooper, tight end. [19]

The team was fired up about the game plan. Walsh was far from predictable, and the Bears would see it up close. On the practice field, the heavy duty backfield play got rave reviews. "Hats off to Guy for them having the confidence in him and for him being the athlete to execute that. He was a blocking fool," said offensive tackle Allan Kennedy. [20]

A hit on the practice field, the play also got a cool nickname with a great backstory. Thirty years later McIntyre explained the origin of the play's famous nickname. "The genesis of that started [with] a place called Stuart Anderson's Black Angus Restaurant. I would go there because I used to live in San Mateo on Fashion Island. I'm new. I'm just trying to find somewhere to eat and watch football. But on Thursday nights at Black Angus, they would have dancing. So I would hang out there on a regular basis. It was kind of a popular spot. Prior to the playoffs, all the guys went to the Black Angus with their wives and girlfriends. We're out there having a good time. They used to call it my place. What happened was, they were playing 'Shout' from *Animal House*. Back in college at the University of Georgia, I was in a fraternity, and we used to have a toga party, which was kind of the first African American toga party. So we would always play 'Shout,' and we'd get on the floor and do the gator. So when we're at Stuart Anderson's, 'Shout' came on. I was very familiar with the song, and all the guys were familiar with it. So we did the gator. Then [linebacker] Mike Walter, who was there, said, 'Black Angus' when Bill put me in the backfield at practice. And that's how it got coined. And Bill being Bill, it's 'Angus.'" [21]

All week the 49ers felt confident about playing the Bears. They were playing at home at Candlestick, and they had a few chips on their shoulders guiding them all week. But they didn't wage a war of words with the Bears. Late in the week Walsh spoke to his team.

> Do a walk-through. We want to be as fresh as we can for this game coming up. You understand the dialogue going on. The Bears believe

they're going to intimidate us. That's what they believe. They think they are going to shatter us, intimidate, and we're going to fall apart. It's never happened to this team since I've been around. In fact we've done the other. Nothing better than to have someone strut in here and somehow think they're going to intimidate you. They'll come in and we're [going to] knock them on their ass. It's that simple. The key to this thing is to get a jump on everything we do.[22]

It was going to be a challenge, but the Bears were blocking their way to the Super Bowl. It had been twelve months since the speech by Dwight Hicks in the locker room in Washington. "We wanted a Super Bowl and we went into that game, 'let's just kick their ass, and let's go onto the next one,'" said defensive end Jeff Stover. "All the hype and the talk. We just took that and said, 'You know what? Let's shut them up.' That was pretty much our whole [take on it]. Let's just shut them up and go on to the next game."[23]

The night before the game a relaxed Bill Walsh and his wife Geri had a quiet dinner with owner Eddie DeBartolo and his wife Candy. "I think it was good for him because it took his mind off the game. We didn't talk football at all that night," revealed DeBartolo to Glenn Dickey of the *San Francisco Chronicle*.[24]

On the morning of the game Keith Fahnhorst was still awaiting the arrival of his third child. He would make the start at right tackle. As the 49ers warmed up on the field they saw the score of an earlier game. The Miami Dolphins had just defeated the Pittsburgh Steelers 45–28 to advance to Super Bowl XIX at Stanford Stadium. Led by league MVP Dan Marino's four touchdown passes, it was no surprise that the Dolphins would be heading to the Super Bowl.

Looking up into the stadium, the 49ers players saw the largest crowd ever to attend a 49ers game at Candlestick Park. A record 61,040 fans filled The Stick, topping the previous mark set during the 1981 NFC Championship Game that saw The Catch. It was a clear, windy, 52-degree day on the first Sunday of 1985, making The Stick the perfect home-field advantage. The 49ers Faithful were loud early and often. "I'll never forget the crowd and how loud it was. The cheers and the 'Go Niners!' It was an incredible environment," said linebacker Michael Walter. For the second straight week John Madden and Pat Summerall would be in the CBS broadcast booth. The television coverage started with Brent Musberger saying, "you are looking live at Candlestick

Park." A fan's sign reading, "This is Montana Country Not Payton's Place," greeted millions of television viewers.[25]

It was game time, time for the 49ers to show the Bears the best team in the NFL. "They were overconfident. Buddy Ryan and [Mike] Ditka, they had a chip on their shoulder. But I remember Bill used to always tell us, 'Hey, they call us a finesse team but we're not a finesse team. We're going to go out and show them, toe to toe, what kind of team we are.' And that's what we did. We went out and played the Bears toe to toe," said Dwaine Board, defensive end.[26]

The Bears won the toss and elected to receive. The first drive was all Walter Payton. He had seven touches for thirty-one yards as the Bears attempted only two passes to get to the 49ers twenty-three-yard line. Seifert's defense stiffened to hold the Bears to a field goal attempt. The six-minute drive ended with a Bob Thomas missed field goal. Wide right. A bad omen for the Bears. Montana jogged onto the field and into the huddle to call the first play. He drilled a quick hitch to Freddie Solomon for eleven yards. He then called 324 Double Hitch. A three-step drop got the ball out quickly once again, to Dwight Clark. The aggressive Bears made the first mistake. Todd Bell and teammate Dave Duerson collided while trying to make the tackle, leaving Clark sprinting down the sidelines for a thirty-eight-yard gain. Two more quick passes to Renaldo Nehemiah and Solomon had the 49ers on the doorstep of the Bears end zone. But a rushed snap led to Montana covering a fumble and stalling the drive. Reliable Ray Wersching booted a twenty-one-yard field goal to give the 49ers the first score of the game. Despite the bobbled snap Walsh liked what he saw on the ten-play, seventy-three-yard drive. Points wouldn't come easy and the 49ers struck first.

On the ensuing drive the 49ers defense put the Candlestick fans on their feet. Trying to start something on offense, Steve Fuller threw to his speedy receiver, Willie Gault, over the middle, but a diving Dwight Hicks intercepted. Gault would finish the day without a catch. Unfortunately the offense didn't take advantage. Montana underthrew his receiver in the back of the end zone and his pass was picked off by Bears safety Gary Fencik.

On the sidelines Walsh shook his head at the missed opportunity. Early in the second quarter the 49ers defense started flexing its muscles. Fuller was sacked on consecutive plays by rookie Michael Carter and Gary Johnson, giving the ball back to Montana at his own thirty-yard line. Walsh went back to the short passing game against Buddy Ryan's 46 defense: three-step drops combined with a slant to Solomon, then a pivot to Solomon gained twenty-eight-yards. Then Walsh called the Angus play.

"I was very surprised. Bobb [McKittrick] called me up and said, 'Hey we're getting ready to probably put you in,'" said Guy McIntyre, guard. "I'm trying to remember this [play] and run in because if you get any part of the play out of sequence, you can mess up the whole thing and you have to call a timeout. So I'm trying to memorize this play, and I'm running out on the field. Joe sees me coming in, and he steps out of the huddle to meet me. I'm not really aware of that, but I step on his foot. I mean I really stepped right on [it] . . . to the point where he pushes me off and in my mind—in those quick seconds that go by—I'm like, 'I broke his foot.' So, luckily, tough as Joe was, he shook it off and I got him to the play and we ran it."[27]

There was no gain on the first Angus play. The next, Tyler sprinted behind McIntyre for eight yards and a big first down. Montana then continued his hot hand: fourteen yards to Clark on a quick out. Scrambling to his right he connected with Mike Wilson for another fourteen yards. The Bears pressure defense was not getting close to Montana. Walsh went back to the Angus play for just one yard. The 49ers ran the Angus play three times for nine yards in the first half. But the momentum again ground to a halt when Bears defensive tackle Dan Hampton knocked down a third-down pass near the goal line. Wersching trotted back out to kick a twenty-two-yard field goal to give the 49ers a 6–0 lead. The first twenty-five plays generated three red zone trips but only two field goals. It was disappointing for Walsh not to have punched a touchdown over. The Bears next three offensive drives allowed Walsh to calm his nerves.

Calling his defense from the 49ers coaches box, George Seifert had his unit pushing around the Bears offense. They were punching the Bears in the mouth on every play. "We knew upfront that our front seven had to do a job on Walter. That had to happen and then we felt comfortable with the pass rush. So the key was really shutting Walter down and then making them beat us with the pass," said Keena Turner, linebacker.[28]

Over the next three drives, the Bears ran nine plays for a total of four yards and three punts. The great Walter Payton was slowly disappearing from the game. It was going to be a long day for the Bears offense. The first half ended with the 49ers leading 6–0. The 49ers were just thirty minutes away from the Super Bowl. They could taste it now. The 49ers defense was all over the field in the first half, holding the Bears to just seventy-three total yards, an unbelievable zero net passing yards, and four sacks of Steve Fuller. The 49ers offense had 224 total yards on thirty-seven plays. Although they didn't have many points on the scoreboard, they were controlling the game.

On the 49ers bench after halftime, tight end Russ Francis yelled to his teammates, "Thirty minutes left, how bad do you want it?"[29] As the second half was about to start, right tackle Keith Fahnhorst looked up into the crowd for word about his wife. "My sister-in-law was sitting in the stands and I looked up there. She was going to phone periodically during the game. I finally spotted her in the crowd and she yelled, 'No baby yet,'" he commented after the game.[30]

To begin the second half the 49ers drove past midfield but were forced to punt. Max Runager's kicking paid off again, pinning the Bears back at their own eleven-yard line. Fuller ran three plays gaining just one yard. Fred vonAppen's unit contributed once again when punt returner Dana McLemore ran the Bears short punt fifteen yards to the Bears thirty-five-yard line, putting the team in field goal range. This time Walsh intended to punch it in. He recalled the trash talk by the Bears all week. It was time to make a statement. No more field goals.

He used the veer play to Tyler, who gained five and eleven yards on consecutive carries. After a short Roger Craig run Walsh called for Angus. Guy McIntyre trotted back onto the field. On first-and-goal from the nine-yard line the 49ers ran the Angus play to perfection. Randy Cross and Russ Francis took out the end, Keith Fahnhorst blocked the tackle, Fred Quillan got the nose tackle, and rookie McIntyre blocked tackle Dan Hampton, giving Tyler a hole to run through. Tyler did the rest. In the hole he broke arm tackles by safety Gary Fencik and cornerback Mike Richardson, then dragged linebacker Al Harris into the end zone holding the ball above his head over the goal line. Forty-niners touchdown! "I said, 'Just beam in on a color and just hit something.' I kind of knew where I was going, but I just was going to hit anything that got in my way. I hit it and moved the pile pretty good.

Wendell followed me through. We scored a touchdown and at a critical time, too," said McIntyre.[31] The Angus touchdown gave the 49ers Faithful a special playoff moment as the noise from Candlestick could be heard throughout the Bay area. The 1984 NFC Championship Game would always be remembered for the "Angus touchdown."

The lead was now 13–0. For Ditka it must've felt like it was 40–0. The frustration began to show on the Bears sideline. "I remember we had the Angus formation and we were doing well against the Bears and Ditka was not very happy with the 49ers. He was across the sidelines actually flipping us off! Because I think he thought it was so unorthodox. But Bill was all about being unorthodox," said Bill Ring, fullback.[32]

The Bears showed some life when Fuller finally completed a pass to a wide receiver. Dennis McKinnon caught three passes on a drive that had the Bears at the 49ers twenty-one-yard line. Once again the 49ers pass rush came up with some big plays. Dwaine Board beat left tackle Jim Covert to blindside Fuller for a loss of eight yards. The next play Gary Johnson came up the middle, throwing Fuller down by his jersey for an eleven-yard loss. Two sacks pushed the Bears out of field goal range. "You had guys who were playing at their very, very best. Michael Carter was sealing stuff down on the inside. You had Lawrence Pillers, Big Hands Johnson who came in and helped out. Then you had Fred Dean coming off the end. That was just killing them. Everybody played as good as they could play," said linebacker Blanchard Montgomery.[33]

Taking over the ball at their own twelve, Montana started a drive that would get them to the brink of the Super Bowl. As the fourth quarter began Montana hit Mike Wilson for eleven yards. Tyler ripped off a run of sixteen yards. Walsh then called 69 Toss Solid. Roger Craig took the pitch around the left end behind perfect blocks by Bubba Paris, Russ Francis, John Frank, and John Ayers, giving Craig a huge alley where he chewed up thirty-nine yards—the longest offensive play of the game. On third-and-goal Walsh put the ball in Montana's hands. With two tight ends on the right side with Solomon split out wide, the formation looked like a run. It was a one-man route for a quick out. Before the snap Solomon saw that cornerback Mike Richardson had positioned himself to take away the outside route. On the fly, Solomon took his man to the inside first as Montana sprinted to his right. Noticing what Solomon wanted to do, Montana waited for Solomon to make his move.

It worked perfectly. Solomon got Richardson to bite as Montana hit him with a strike in the front corner of the end zone. Another touchdown. Solomon had scored a touchdown in his tenth consecutive game. The Bears defense was tired and defeated. The 49ers had driven eighty-eight yards on eight plays, increasing their lead to 20–0. Even with 11:15 left on the clock, the game was over. The celebration in Candlestick had begun. The Bears had to pass, which was music to the ears of the 49ers pass rush. On the Bears last three drives, the 49ers recorded three more sacks and set up a third field goal by Ray Wersching. "It was fulfilling to contribute to the win. There are guys out there busting their butts the whole game. So I felt fortunate enough to be there and put some points on the board to help us win," said Wersching.[34]

At the two-minute warning Joe Montana went to talk to Bill Walsh on the sidelines. With a long TV timeout the coach and quarterback both kneeled spontaneously. It was a quiet moment in the middle of chaos as the 49ers fans started a chant of "Super Bowl! Super Bowl! Super Bowl!" The pair had a short conversation while both of them picked at the Candlestick grass. Forty-niners team photographer Michael Zagaris snapped a famous photo of the two while they chatted.

"I remember I was on the bench. I don't study a lot of things, I just try to be open and alert and react," said Zagaris. "I started to gravitate toward [Walsh]. Then I got on my hands and knees about five feet away. Bill was aware; I don't think Joe knew. I didn't want anyone to be aware. It's one of the greatest shots I've ever taken. The right place at the right time."[35]

The Super Bowl chants vibrated throughout the stadium. On the sideline 49ers owner Eddie DeBartolo made his way down from the owner's box to celebrate with his players. He cried while embracing each player. Three hours and four minutes after kickoff the 49ers had obliterated the feeling of the loss in Washington one year earlier. In two weeks they would be playing in Super Bowl XIX, just down the road at Stanford Stadium. As the Candlestick clock counted down to zero, a police escort led Walsh across the field to shake hands with Mike Ditka. "We don't have any excuses. We were beaten soundly by a good team," remarked Ditka after the game.[36]

The Candlestick Park scoreboard read "Please Stay Off Field," but it was a useless plea as 49ers fans descended on the field, tearing up the turf for souvenirs. "For us it was about business. We were on a mission, and beating the Bears was an obstacle in front of us. We really weren't even looking at the Bears. They were just in front of us [in the way of] our mission. Then once we beat the Bears, everybody was talking about Dan Marino, [Mark] Duper and [Mark] Clayton," said halfback Wendell Tyler.[37]

The Dolphins would have to wait. For now, the 49ers celebrated. The locker room atmosphere at Candlestick differed markedly from the locker room scene twelve months earlier in Washington. All the hard work had paid off. Plus, they achieved it against the big, bad Bears. "We know we can go out and play good football. Matter of fact, we can go out and play great football. That's what they [the coaches] want us to do, not run our mouths off in the paper, saying [that] we're going to dominate people. My job is to go out and play football. I'm not a public speaker," remarked Gary Johnson.[38]

"I think their biggest mistake was shooting off their mouths after they beat us last year. All they said was that our offense was predictable, but that was saying enough to rile Bill, so he was more intense this last week than I've ever seen him," commented Keith Fahnhorst in the locker room.[39] The 49ers offensive line had protected Montana, and the offense finished with 387 total yards.

The 23–0 victory was sweet in many ways. "Anytime you shut anybody out defensively, you feel like you've accomplished a great feat," said Louie Kelcher, defensive tackle.[40] A shutout proved they were the best defense on the field. They held the Bears to 186 total yards—just 37 net passing yards—and the pass rush generated nine sacks! It was an onslaught of sacks against a team that had set an NFL record for sacks. In two postseason games, the 49ers pass rush had fifteen sacks (six against the Giants). "We took it to their ass. We shut out that team that was known for its running ability. We took great pride in that," said Riki Ellison, linebacker.[41] "We just went out there and beat the living dodo out of them. We beat them physically and we beat them mentally. They couldn't do anything. We shut Walter down. Fuller couldn't get any passes off. We sacked him, I don't know how many times. We were just rolling. It was a statement. I think that not only was our offense good, but our defense was as good as anybody in the league, too," said defensive end Jim Stuckey.[42]

Everything worked for the 49ers: their short passing game, the Angus formation, the veer plays. Every unit contributed: offense, defense, and special teams. Just like the previous seventeen games, it was a team victory. "Mistake-free football. There aren't a lot of mistakes in that game from an offensive standpoint and defensive standpoint. We had some guys who were playing that game who just had some outstanding plays, outstanding gains," said Blanchard Montgomery, linebacker.[43] "I feel this team has something no other team has, and that's forty-nine people who go all out every time they line up," said Dwaine Board to the press in the locker room.[44]

Nothing changed in the way the 49ers had played. The coaches and team showed up again for another win. A happy Eddie DeBartolo continued to thank his coaches and players. "The Bears are a good football team. I think this team today wanted it a little more. I think it's extremely satisfying. The players deserved the recognition. They are deserving, but we have one game to go. The big thing is getting into the Super Bowl, but it's been a team effort from the front office to the water boy," remarked DeBartolo in the 49ers locker room.[45]

For one Forty-niner, the chance to play in the Super Bowl seemed unrealistic at the start of the season. "Just total excitement came over me, because I could not believe it. Here I go from being unemployed for two weeks, to now I'm in the biggest game of my career," recalled punter Max Runager.[46]

The 49ers were established as an early two-and-a-half-point favorite over the Dolphins—mainly due to their proximity to Stanford Stadium.[47] The two teams playing in Super Bowl XIX had the best combined records of any previous Super Bowl. The Dolphins (16–2) and the 49ers (17–1) had a combined record of 33–3. "It will be the two teams with the two best records, and that's how it should be," said Pat Summerall in the CBS booth.[48]

One game to go.

Part V

Super Bowl XIX

Miami Dolphins vs. San Francisco 49ers
Stanford Stadium
Palo Alto, California
January 20, 1985

17

THE GAME PLANS

I knew everybody on that defense was on the same page and we were going after the same goal. All we wanted to do was get on the field and play. The game plans were all dialed in. The coaches had us ready to go and we had ourselves ready. We believed in each other. We just couldn't wait to get out on the field.
—Jeff Stover, defensive end[1]

Despite being a slight favorite the 49ers coaches knew that they had their hands full trying to game plan for the AFC Champion Miami Dolphins. The Dolphins had lost only two games all year—week 12 against the San Diego Chargers (34–28 in overtime) and week 14 against the Los Angeles Raiders (45–34). They scored 513 points in sixteen games (second in NFL history behind the 1983 Redskins), as well as seventy-six points in two playoff wins against the Seahawks and Steelers. They were averaging thirty-two points per game.

Dolphins quarterback and league MVP Dan Marino was the hottest player on the planet. The second-year quarterback passed for 5,084 yards and forty-eight touchdowns during the regular season—both setting NFL records. Then there were his two favorite targets—"the Marks Brothers." Mark Clayton (seventy-three for 1,389 and an NFL-record eighteen touchdown catches) and Mark Duper (seventy-one for 1,306 and eight touchdowns) had combined for more than 2,600 yards and twenty-six touchdowns. Their stats read like video game scores. However, their leading rusher Woody Bennett had just 606 rushing yards on the season. They ranked first in the NFL in passing but only sixteenth in rushing. George Seifert was confident about stopping the run—the defense had done that all season—it was the Dolphins passing game that concerned him.

Including the two playoffs games, Dan Marino had thrown for an amazing fifty-five touchdowns. He had been sacked only fourteen times—a league low—in the regular season and he was untouched in both playoff games. In the eighteen games he had played, Marino had dropped back to pass 630 times. Only fourteen times had he been put on his back—unbelievable numbers for perhaps the greatest single season for any quarterback in NFL history. And he was only twenty-three years old. In 1983 the 49ers got to Marino only once in a 20–17 loss to the Dolphins at Candlestick Park, a game marred by a crucial fumble by rookie Roger Craig with less than two minutes to go while within field goal range of tying the game. "It was really painful, knowing I had let the club down," remarked Craig to the *San Francisco Chronicle* during Super Bowl week. "It gives me extra incentive for this game. I want to make this game the best of my career."[2] Craig would get his chance. Seifert also would get his chance to stop Marino and the Dolphins vaunted passing attack.

The Dolphins defense was a different story. Playing most of their games with a lead, they were ranked nineteenth in the NFL in total defense (twenty-second against the run and fourteenth against the pass). Led by Walsh's old friend, defensive coordinator Chuck Studley—who coached eleven years with Walsh and was the defensive coordinator on the 1981 49ers Super Bowl champs—the Dolphins played sound fundamental defense. They did not take any big chances. "Bill's going to be looking across the line at me wondering, 'What is Chuck thinking?' And I'll be looking across the line at him wondering the same thing about him," remarked Chuck Studley a few days before the Super Bowl.[3] Walsh knew Studley would do what he had done during the season. He knew that he would be conservative.

The 49ers had the NFL's second-ranked offense—behind the Dolphins—and the tenth-ranked defense. The 49ers were also the NFL's best in points allowed, surrendering just 227 points all season—14 points per game—and hadn't allowed more than twenty-one points in a single game since week 2 against the Washington Redskins, when they gave up thirty-one points. The Dolphins scored twenty-one points versus the Bills in week 3—their lowest score of the season—and scored twenty-eight points or more in sixteen of the eighteen games they had played. Seifert would have his hands full.

The day after winning the NFC Championship Game against the Bears, the 49ers coaching staff got to work on their game plans for Super Bowl XIX. "Bill believed for the Super Bowl, you plan early. But this was a unique Super Bowl. We were at home. We didn't have to go anywhere. So this really played into our hands. We were able to do the normal game planning pretty much exactly the way we'd always done it. We were at home. We were in our own facility. It was really business as usual," said quarterbacks and wide receivers coach Paul Hackett.[4]

"Bill kept it like a normal practice schedule. You went home and drove to practice the very next day. Just like we've been doing for what seemed like forever—that was a long season," said Jim Stuckey, defensive end.[5] "Guys could go to their own homes. I think that helped us. Certainly worked to our advantage," said Carlton Williamson, strong safety.[6]

OFFENSIVE GAME PLAN

The workweek started with film study. The staff gave the players the last eight regular season games that the Dolphins played, including their two losses to the Chargers and Raiders, to help them evaluate their opponent. The 49ers offensive coaches focused on watching film of three games—the AFC Championship Game against the Steelers, the AFC Divisional Game against the Seahawks, and the December 17 regular-season game against the Cowboys—to gain a better grasp on the Dolphins 3–4 defense.

Sitting in his corner office Walsh drew the offensive game plan by hand. He included nearly forty runs—twenty-seven basic runs, six run specials, and six draws—as well as twelve goal-line and short-yardage plays. For the passing game he drew nearly 100 passes on the call sheet. In the end Walsh's game plan binder would consist of 134 pages of plays and notes, as well as nearly 150 hand-drawn plays. Early in the week Walsh put his first twenty-five plays together, which ultimately included fifteen passes and ten runs. The opener would be a quick out followed by a run play with an unbalanced line—left tackle Bubba Paris would line up next to right tackle Keith Fahnhorst—just "to demonstrate that was part of our game plan so they might take more time looking at what we were doing than they would if we ran a simple run or two," commented Bill Walsh about his first twenty-five plays.[7] The third play would be a play-action pass—to see how Dolphins linebackers would react—followed by two runs.[8]

Walsh definitely wanted to be balanced. Watching the game film of the Dolphins 3–4 defense, he did not see a fast, athletic unit. Dolphins linebackers were somewhat slow footed, especially when covering backs. He instantly knew that he would use Wendell Tyler, Roger Craig, and Carl Monroe even more in the passing game. "Without a potent pass rush, Miami was forced to cover the receivers tightly. The Miami defense depended on locking their linebackers into man-to-man coverage on running backs. That had worked well for them during the season, but I doubted that they could cover our backs, particularly Roger Craig, coming out of the backfield," wrote Walsh in his 1990 autobiography. "We had one play in particular that was ideally suited to work against the defense. On 20 Bingo Cross both backs would release between guard and tackle just past the line of scrimmage and then cross."[9]

Along with 20 Bingo Cross, Walsh also installed Halfback Sail among the first twenty-five plays to take advantage of the speed and quickness of his running backs. "That was crucial. Again, our coaches deserved a lot of credit because they saw the weakness. It wasn't necessarily the weakness of the players. It was just a weakness in their scheme, and Bill took advantage of it," said offensive tackle Keith Fahnhorst.[10] "Even though they had great linebackers, they didn't have speed. We practiced on crossing routes the whole week. Bingo Cross. Roger would go one way. I would go the other way," said halfback Wendell Tyler.[11] "I think Bill felt all along that their linebackers couldn't cover our running backs. Bill always made the running backs a big part of his teaching. You could tell by the way he talked to them about where [he thought] the ball might go," said Paul Hackett, quarterbacks and wide receivers coach.[12]

While watching the Dolphins linebackers he also noticed that when they turned to run with the running backs out of the backfield, they also turned their heads, putting their backs to the quarterback. Walsh encouraged Joe Montana to tuck and run if he saw a running lane. During the 1984 regular season Montana had only had thirty-nine carries for

118 yards, but in the two playoff games he had eighty-five yards rushing. Walsh would use Montana's legs in this game. "I declined to remark on it until just before the game, because I didn't want to preoccupy Joe with this option and preferred to be as spontaneous and instinctive as possible," wrote Walsh.[13]

Running backs catching the ball, Montana running when given the opportunity, and a balanced offense: Walsh had his plan.

DEFENSIVE GAME PLAN

Down the hall from Bill Walsh in the 49ers facility, George Seifert met with his staff to begin the daunting task of game planning for the high-powered Miami Dolphins. As with any game plan, Seifert and Bill McPherson felt confident about stopping the run. The Dolphins didn't have a Gerald Riggs or Eric Dickerson to hand the ball off to. Although they had a great center—All-Pro Dwight Stephenson—anchoring the offensive line, the power running game was not going to be a factor. The Dolphins were a passing team. Seifert outlined the keys to stopping Dan Marino, the Marks Brothers, and the Dolphins passing attack on the whiteboard:

Defend Dan Marino and the Marks Brothers
Use nickel and dime packages (maybe fifty percent)
Rotate defensive line to keep pass rush fresh
Play tight bump-and-run coverage; don't let them get off the line

Working with the defensive coaches, Neal Dahlen's main task was breaking down four Dolphins games for George Seifert and the defensive coaches. He reviewed the two playoff games (against the Steelers and Seahawks) and two regular season games (against the Cowboys on December 17 and Raiders on December 2). "That was one of those things where you had the utmost respect for them, but you weren't afraid of them," said Neal Dahlen, director of research and development. "George did a great job of preparing the defense, and it was a question of executing the preparation that George and the other coaches had made on defense."[14] "George would say in our meetings: this is another game. That this is what we gotta do," said Bill McPherson, defensive line coach.[15]

Trying to digest the Dolphins offense, George Seifert had a lot on his plate. But after watching the game film he felt confident he had the right game plan. He had the players who could pull it off. He wanted to use everybody. He instructed Bill McPherson to use all nine defensive linemen. If he was going to pressure Marino, he needed a pass rush with fresh legs. "No doubt in our mind—regardless of Marino or whatever—he wasn't going to get the ball deep on us. He wasn't going to be able to throw down the field. Our pass rush wasn't going to allow him to do it. We were going to pressure him. George Seifert put together a plan that we were going to pressure him as much as possible," said defensive backs coach Ray Rhodes.[16] All nine of the 49ers defensive front bought into the game plan, as they had all year. "If the defensive line controls the line of scrimmage the way that I knew we could and put pressure on Marino, he wouldn't be able to just stand back there and pick people apart. That's the key . . . to get right in his face," said defensive end Fred Dean.[17] "Going against a passing team, we were just licking our chops. All we wanted to do was get after them. I couldn't wait till game time," said defensive end Jeff Stover.[18]

An obvious challenge was Dan Marino's quick release. Most teams couldn't get to him in time because of his quick right arm. "I think one of the concerns with Danny was simply that his release was so quick: were we going to be able to get pressure [on him]? How could we really get that pressure?" said Keena Turner, linebacker.[19]

Because the Dolphins loved to throw, Seifert knew he needed to play more nickel coverage. They would start with their base 3–4 defense with run linemen and run linebackers, but the nickel would be their bread and butter. This would give them the best chance of combining a powerful pass rush with tight pass coverage. He thought they would have to play the nickel at least half of the time. "Dan [Marino] probably had the quickest release ever in pro football. Coach Seifert, Coach Mac had devised a really good plan to keep our best pass rushers on the field, put us in the right defense, keep our best cover linebackers out there," said Jim Stuckey, defensive end.[20] The 49ers nickel defense would be a 4–2–5 formation that included five defensive backs. The front four would be a rotation of all the defensive linemen, but the nickel "Elephant" unit would primarily consist of the team's best pass rushers, Fred Dean and Dwaine Board at the ends, and Gary Johnson, Jeff Stover, and Michael Carter inside. Manu Tuiasosopo, Jim Stuckey,

Lawrence Pillers, and Louie Kelcher would share the first-down role when called upon.

Keena Turner would stay in as the only true linebacker. Rookie Jeff Fuller was going to be what Seifert referred to as the "whip" defender, who often plays up close like a linebacker in the nickel. In the secondary would be cornerbacks Eric Wright and Ronnie Lott, safeties Dwight Hicks and Carlton Williamson, and the nickelback Tom Holmoe. George Seifert planned to use the nickel on passing downs around fifty percent of the time. In theory, with Fuller considered a safety, the nickel defense could be a dime, 4–1–6, front. Whatever you labeled it, the pass rush would be the first element of a defensive combination that Seifert wanted to show Dan Marino. The second part would be the secondary.

Ray Rhodes instructed his defensive backs to be aggressive with the Dolphins receivers, especially the Marks Brothers. "George Seifert talked about it earlier during the week with the entire defense. He said, 'Men, we have to keep them in front of us and, we're gonna have to not give them clean releases down the field. Every play I want somebody up in their face jamming them. Throw the timing off.' That's basically what we were trying to get done that day. We were trying to make sure we didn't give them clean releases. Reroute them as much as we could at the line of scrimmage and the D-line [was] going to get after the quarterback. That was the approach," said Ray Rhodes. "We were gonna beat the receivers up. I mean, beat them up. We're going to have to physically beat them. That's the approach that the secondary took."[21]

It was music to the ears of the 49ers defensive backs. "We felt we were a great secondary. This was going to be a matchup between the skill players. We knew it was the world stage. It was our goal—playing in the Super Bowl—and we felt the victory was going to [be] between the wide receivers or their passing game and how well we react and perform against it. So it was set up to be a great matchup," said strong safety Carlton Williamson.[22] "That was a big part of the game plan: make sure we messed up [Marino's] timing. Make sure we could make him release the ball before his receivers could get open," said defensive end Dwaine Board.[23]

Seifert's game plan would be a perfect example of team defense. Everybody knew his role going in and would execute it. The NFL's best-scoring defense didn't care about video game numbers. All they cared about was playing as a unit. They cared about not giving up points. They were going to be on the biggest stage to show the entire world that they were up to the challenge of stopping one of the NFL's all-time great offenses. "We got to that game and I'm like, 'This is the biggest game of the year. You're at the Super Bowl. Forget about being tired. Forget about your injuries and everything else. You have to play hard. You have to play good. You can't have excuses. You're a professional now,'" said Michael Carter, rookie defensive tackle. "Going against Miami and Mr. Marino, . . . we wanted to prove that our defense was as good as anybody else's in the NFL. . . . In order for us to win, we have to get after Marino. You can't have him sit in the pocket and just throw the ball with ease. We had nine defensive linemen and we were shuffling them in and out. If you were fresh and you were in the game, you better be doing something."[24]

Three days after the win against the Bears, the 49ers went back to work for the Super Bowl. Walsh had put together a comprehensive schedule for the first week of game planning. "Bill's pretty good about eating up all your time. You're always thinking about football," said fullback Bill Ring. "You're so focused because it's a once-in-a-lifetime opportunity to go to a Super Bowl."[25] The daily schedule typically looked like this:

8:30 a.m.	Special teams meeting
9:00 a.m.	Team meeting
11:30 a.m.	Walk-through
12:00 p.m.	Lunch
1:00 p.m.	Special teams on field
1:30 p.m.	Practice on field[26]

During the noon lunch break and after practice, individual units accommodated the media for interviews.

January 9—Lunch: defensive line; Postpractice: offensive line
January 10—Lunch: special teams/tight ends; Postpractice: defensive backs
January 11—Lunch: offensive backs/wide receivers; Postpractice: linebackers[27]

Practice was intense for the 49ers throughout the bye week. Both scout teams gave the first teams a realistic imitation of the Dolphins, from Matt Cavanaugh's best Dan Marino impersonation to Mario Clark's Mark Duper route-running style. "I was banged up but still went to the meetings and played scout team, giving the offense a look. That's the role I took on. I was trying to give them the best look, if I had to be Mark Duper, I tried everything I had to do. I was trying to give them the best look," said cornerback Mario Clark. [28]

Throughout the first three days of practice—January 9–11—the 49ers offensive and defensive coaches organized scripted sessions. On Wednesday the two units ran eighty-eight plays that included eleven-on-eleven and seven-on-seven drills and nickel and shotgun packages. Thursday, another eighty-eight plays, working on base offense and defense, nickel, nine-on-seven, seven-on-seven, and offensive screen-and-draws. On Friday the team practiced at Stanford University, running ninety-four scripted plays. Both offense and defense practiced the nickel, seven-on-seven, and goal line and short yardage; the offense also ran eight "special" plays. At the end of the Friday practice most of the game plan was installed. [29]

"Bill asked me once: 'What should we do running wise and stuff at the end?' My thing was run more plays. Run a two-minute offense. They would put together three offenses and three defenses. Everybody would sprint, recover, sprint, recover. We might do that for ten plays, fifteen plays. But you're doing something that pertains to what you do to make a living," said Jerry Attaway, physical development coordinator. "There's an old rule in physiology that says, 'If rest is not equal to or greater than stress, you won't get better at the fastest rate.' So our normal practice schedule gave them a chance, plus we had two weeks. The first week we prepared. The second week was pretty easy. It was just normal practice stuff. The nervousness probably affected sleep or one thing or another, but we didn't really do anything special." [30] On Saturday, January 12, Walsh gave the players the day off.

When the team returned to work on Sunday, one week before Super Bowl XIX, they picked up where they left off with a team meeting at noon followed by an afternoon practice on the field. Walsh and Seifert had scripted ninety plays that primarily reviewed basic offense and defense plans, a seven-on-seven session, and goal-line plays.

Whether it was running after practice or sitting in the film room, the 49ers players put in the hours required to know their opponent. They were worn out by the coaching staff. "I think we've worked harder these last three days than we did three years ago," remarked Keena Turner to the local press after one practice. "Last night, I was so tired I went home and collapsed while the evening news was still on TV."[31] "We put the bulk of our heavy work in the first week game plan and execution and then it was just a matter of being poised and not making the game bigger than it really was," said wide receiver Mike Wilson.[32]

Most of the Forty-niners were now getting antsy about the game. "I knew everybody on that defense was on the same page and we were going after the same goal. All we wanted to do was get on the field and play. So the game plans were all dialed in. The coaches had us ready to go and we had ourselves ready. We believed in each other. We just couldn't wait to get out on the field," said Jeff Stover, defensive end.[33]

One week down. One more to go. The Super Bowl hype machine was about to begin.

18

THE HYPE

You listen to all the hype, all the local media. If you turned on the TV
it was there. It was a lot of fun. I wish everybody could experience
something like that. I tell my kids all the time, "I wish you could
experience what I experienced." It was a once-in-a-lifetime deal, and
when you have a lot of fun doing it—and if you win the game—it's
unbelievable. The adrenaline rush, there's nothing like it.
—Ray Wersching, kicker[1]

The first week after defeating the Chicago Bears, the 49ers had finalized their game plans for offense, defense, and special teams. As Monday, January 14, arrived—Super Bowl week—the hype machine had
begun in full force. "You pretty much went through the same preparation. One of the things about the Super Bowl: normally the week before
the game [is] when you get all your work done. You get all your preparation done before that. Then the week of the Super Bowl you're doing
your media obligations. Just make sure you go through every little detail
and just keep polishing up for the game. That's basically what we tried
to focus on," said Ray Rhodes, defensive backs coach.[2]

Having the Super Bowl in their own backyard was a blessing and a
curse for the 49ers. They didn't have to travel on Sunday or go through
the pain of dealing with the Super Bowl arrival distractions. They were
able to sleep and wake up in their own beds for nearly two weeks. From
rookies to ten-year veterans, having the game at home helped them
focus on the task at hand. "There was no distraction compared to the
other Super Bowls. We were right at home. We were set. We were in a

routine. We were in a rhythm. We were invincible. We didn't need all the hoopla. We enjoyed each other. We enjoyed each other going to practice every day. We had our own locker room. It was comfort. Playing dominoes and doing the same stuff in our locker room on the week of the Super Bowl," said linebacker Riki Ellison.[3] "You get drafted. You have a big starring role in a game that gets you into the Super Bowl. The Super Bowl is played in your town. What more could any football player ask for? It's like a dream come true," said guard Guy McIntyre.[4]

"It was great for me because I'm from the Bay area. To play basically twenty minutes from where I was living at the time was pretty neat. My wife grew up in Palo Alto, so we had a lot of family who went to the games and participated. So it was a big deal and a very special moment playing at home for me personally," said fullback Bill Ring.[5]

The Bay area was now knee-deep in Super Bowl hoopla. "We got everything out of the way in the first week. [But] it was probably more of a hassle being at home because you couldn't get away from it because everybody knew where you lived. Your friends called you. Everybody wanted tickets and all that sort of stuff," said Jerry Attaway, physical development coordinator.[6] "You listen to all the hype, all the local media. If you turned on the TV it was there. It was a lot of fun. I wish everybody could experience something like that. I tell my kids all the time, 'I wish you could experience what I experienced.' It was a once-in-a-lifetime deal, and when you have a lot of fun doing it—and if you win the game—it's unbelievable. The adrenaline rush, there's nothing like it," said Ray Wersching, kicker.[7]

The 49ers staff who experienced the first Super Bowl helped the current team get through the ups and downs of a game of this magnitude. Especially when it came time to finalizing tickets. "It probably helped being in it in 1981, because we had been there before and we knew what other outside distractions there are," said Jerry Walker, director of public relations. "I think that John McVay, Keith Simon, our business manager, Bill, and the whole coaching staff did such a great job of limiting the distractions. Being organized in that get your tickets out of the way. You have your family contact, Keith, in the business office if they need hotel reservations or if they're not going to stay with you. You know everything was taken off the players' shoulders and done by the business office." Continued Walker: "We were told that first week of meeting: get them done now. After a certain date we're not going to help you anymore. So a lot of the players got that done so that when their third-grade child's playground teammate would call and say, 'Remember me,' they would say, 'I'm really sorry. My tickets are already completed.'"[8]

The players were given an allotment of twenty tickets each, which didn't last long. "I had so many people calling me. You know, people whom I hadn't talked to in twenty years, and I was trying to be a ticket manager. You know everybody and their brother is trying to talk to you, and I'm not into all of that hoopla," said linebacker Dan Bunz. "It was madness. It's a good thing we had been to one before. Our staff had been there and Bill had a way to relax and try to get us focused on all of that. [He'd] try to keep us busy but sometimes when you're in your hometown it's pretty hard."[9]

That Monday, January 14, the 49ers participated in their first official Super Bowl press conference sponsored by the NFL, although they called it "an informal news conference." Head coach Bill Walsh and six players drove to the team's official hotel—AMFAC Hotel—in Burlingame to conduct the interviews. Walsh was in one room answering questions while the players were in another. Seated at individual tables with nameplates were Joe Montana, Bubba Paris, Randy Cross, Keena Turner, Dwaine Board, and Dwight Hicks, most of the team's leaders. "I feel like I'm running for president," remarked a smiling Board, sitting behind the microphone at his table. The press fired off questions for nearly an hour.[10]

Nothing controversial was said. The only thing of note was when Montana's fiancée Jennifer Wallace showed up, upstaging her superstar boyfriend.

SHULA VS. WALSH

As with most Super Bowls, many members of the media searched for stories. One of the first ones taking center stage was the matchup of the two head coaches. Don Shula was making his sixth Super Bowl appearance with a 2–3 record. Bill Walsh was making his second, having won his only appearance after the 1981 season. "Bill had a lot of confidence, but Bill felt a challenge, too, because Don Shula obviously had a lot of recognition, a lot of success, and a lot of fame—deservedly so. So I think Bill realized that was a big challenge for him career wise to be able to beat Don Shula," said Keith Fahnhorst, offensive tackle.[11]

The two coaches had only faced each other twice during the regular season—in 1980 and 1983—with Shula winning both matchups by a combined seven points. Walsh burned to prove to himself that he could beat Shula, though he never admitted it. Not even to his staff. "I think there was a clash of egos to some degree with Bill and Don Shula. Don Shula was legendary at that point. Bill was going after his second Super Bowl. You're so busy that you don't get caught up in a lot of that hype," said Fred vonAppen, special teams coach. "It was a remarkable experience because I'd never been in a game that big before."[12]

Walsh didn't allow the press and upcoming media circus to affect his preparation, something he passed down to his players. "He handled the press so well and taught us how to handle the press—nothing against the press—they do a fabulous job. But when you're trying to get focused and concentrate on the game, there are certain things that can distract you. He wasn't gonna let [the media] do it. He handled it very well," said Jeff Stover, defensive end.[13]

MARINO VS. MONTANA

The other early story line that the press and national media focused on was the accomplishments of the high-powered Miami Dolphins offense led by Dan Marino. Despite being a slight favorite, 49ers media coverage more often related to the Super Bowl's location in their backyard than to their play on the field. "Even though we had such a dominating season ourselves and won fifteen games, the press was focusing on Miami for that Super Bowl. They kind of made our players mad," said Neal Dahlen, director of research and development.[14] "It was a home game for us but it wasn't treated like that. Nobody gave us a chance. The 49ers don't have a chance against Marino and against Miami's defense. It kind of rubbed us [the wrong way], that hey, they didn't respect us," said Dwaine Board, defensive end.[15]

The sportswriters of Super Bowl XIX wrote ad nauseam of the impending battle between the two quarterbacks—Dan Marino versus Joe Montana—although they never would be on the field at the same time. They were the two best quarterbacks in the NFL during the 1984 season. They both were also from western Pennsylvania, Montana from Monongahela and Marino from the Oakland district in Pittsburgh. Early on the media's attention was directed toward Dan Marino.

"We knew that we had Montana's back. We knew that we were going to keep him in the light that he belonged in," said Earl Cooper, tight end.[16] "Joe never really wanted to be the center of attention, and you put him in a room and he'd be more on the side and let somebody else do the talking," said Allan Kennedy, offensive tackle. "I don't think he saw anything different as they're trying to slight him, and the press was saying this and that. I'm sure reporters were asking him the same things. Let's play the game. See who wins. And that's what we did."[17]

Most of the 49ers offensive players could see that the attention paid to Dan Marino, who had played only two seasons in the NFL, was firing the ultracompetitive Joe Montana from within. "We talked about it a lot but Joe never mentioned it. But you could see—you could see it in his eyes—that he heard every one of those comparisons to Dan Marino and I think that's why Joe had the game he did, because you don't want to challenge Joe like that," said Keith Fahnhorst, offensive tackle.[18]

"I remember the game so well because all that whole two weeks before, all anyone ever talked about was Dan Marino. And I didn't understand that because we had Joe Montana. I'm going, 'Come on! We have Joe Montana. Why is the press making a big deal about Dan Marino?'" said Bill Ring. "Dan Marino's a great quarterback, but we have Joe Montana."[19] "I do know that Joe would accept each and every challenge that would come his way. He was a very competitive guy. You didn't have to worry about him being up for the game," said John McVay, vice president and general manager.[20]

On the surface, it seemed like a fan's dream to watch two great quarterbacks face off in the Super Bowl. But judging by the media coverage, it was all about just one quarterback—Dan Marino. Even Marino was feeling the stress. On Thursday before the game he suffered dizziness at practice. At a Super Bowl, this made front-page news. Marino just laughed it off. "It's a good example of Super Bowl hype," he commented.[21]

The hype machine was rolling in the Bay area, but not every player or coach was easily recognized. "I remember going down on the elevator with [linebacker] Mike Walter. There were some fans in the elevator. They looked at us, said, 'Are you part of the 49ers?' We said, 'Yeah.'

And this women said, 'Well, who are you?' to Mike Walter and he said 'I'm Mike Walter.' "What number?" she said. 'Ninety-nine.' She said, 'No. I don't know who you are.' It was like she invalidated this guy who played all year and busted his butt and was a good player for us. It put it in perspective and I thought, 'You don't even want to know who I am because you have no idea.' I'm not Joe Montana. It keeps it in perspective for you a little bit. You're not quite as important as you think you are," said Fred vonAppen, special teams coach.[22]

"They're always talking about how it's an offensive game. That's what sells tickets. We had the best on our side with Joe and that crew. You get a guy like Marino. It caused an uproar. It was a lot of good writing that week," said Louie Kelcher, defensive tackle.[23]

SPORTS ILLUSTRATED COVER

A few days before the game *Sports Illustrated*'s Super Bowl preview issue hit newsstands. On the front cover were two photos of the two quarterbacks with arms cocked, eyes downfield, ready to launch a strike to an open receiver under the headline, "Super Shoot-Out." Finally some respect for Montana. But further investigation revealed once again that the media's hype machine was at work. In an article titled "Armed for an Aerial Epic," Paul Zimmerman, the dean of NFL sportswriters at the time, asked the question, "Can Dan Marino be stopped?"[24] In the eight-page article, Zimmerman mentioned Marino by name twenty-seven times. He went on to mention Montana by name *three* times. How could the game be a "shoot-out" or an "aerial epic" when media coverage was so one-sided? Tellingly, no one asked, "Can Joe Montana be stopped?"

FORTY-NINERS JOURNALS/DIARIES

Despite the media hype that the 49ers tried to avoid they did share their thoughts in the local newspapers. The *San Francisco Examiner* had several Forty-niner players write for their weekly series, 49er Journal. Russ Francis (January 11), Ray Wersching (January 14), Dwaine Board (January 15), John Frank (January 16), Joe Montana (January

17), Guy McIntyre (January 18), and Ronnie Lott (January 20) took turns giving their opinions of the big game. Two other players got a full weekly gig. Dwight Hicks wrote a Super Bowl diary all week for the *San Jose Mercury News* while Randy Cross kept one for the *San Francisco Chronicle*.[25] The Super Bowl media machine couldn't be avoided completely by any player or coach.

MEDIA DAY

On Tuesday (January 15) of Super Bowl week, the two teams participated in the NFL's annual Media Day. The ultimate media hype machine event, it would be an hour-long media circus for every player and coach. More than 2,000 members of the media would attend. The 49ers held their Media Day at Candlestick Park. At 9:30 a.m. the 49ers loaded into buses outside their practice facility in Redwood City to head north. Forty-five minutes later the team posed for the Super Bowl team photo then found different spots throughout Candlestick to talk to the media. Most players wore 49ers gold satin jackets to stay warm on a rather cold morning. Bill Walsh camped out in one of the end zones. He only had good things to say about the Dolphins and the upcoming matchup with Don Shula. He knew not to rock the boat, the same message he conveyed to his players. "Bill Walsh, he's a master at dealing with the media. He knew exactly what to tell us: talk less. Talk about how good they are: 'I don't know. We gotta really work hard to beat these guys.' Use reverse psychology on the media and on the Dolphins. Make them think that they're way better than us. We had something up our sleeve," said fullback Roger Craig.[26]

For some 49ers who weren't around for the first trip in 1981, Media Day was an interesting experience. "The Super Bowl is the biggest spectacle and here I am. I go from looking at Joe Montana and Dwight Clark doing "The Catch" to being here. I'm in the press conference and I'm getting interviewed. It was a lot to take in. You're just wide-eyed and trying to absorb it all," said rookie guard Guy McIntyre.[27] "It was strange. They're asking you the same questions over and over, trying to get you to say something so they can print bulletin-board news. I've done a lot of interviews. I didn't want to put my foot in my mouth. I knew to just give generic answers. But that was wild. It's even wilder now," said rookie defensive tackle Michael Carter.[28]

For thousands of sportswriters and media personalities, Media Day was a time to find that fresh scoop, to get a player to say something outrageous or controversial. One reporter asked tight end Earl Cooper to speak Spanish. Linebacker Jack Reynolds passed out papers with an explanation of how he got his nickname "Hacksaw" so he wouldn't have to explain it hundreds of times to all of the reporters. Linebacker Blanchard Montgomery was asked for the umpteenth time for his thoughts on Dan Marino and the Dolphins passing attack. "Can you stop the Marks Brothers and the passing attack? The amount of yards that Marino put up and how he was touted as the best quarterback ever. Those were the questions that I got asked. I think it was the *Los Angeles Times* that asked me, and I said, 'I know the two best quarterbacks ever. I'm playing with one now and I played with other one in high school.' They asked me, 'Who was the other one in high school?' 'John Elway . . . but Joe Montana's the best one ever,'" said linebacker Blanchard Montgomery, who played with Elway at Granada Hills High School in California.[29]

Some 49ers such as Dwight Clark and Ronnie Lott were mobbed by hordes of reporters but other 49ers got a different treatment. "It was good because they were always looking at guys when no one's around. Joe's got 150 guys over here and I'm across the field in the end zone. So there was always a reporter or two coming over. 'Let's find somebody no one's talking to and get his story.' So I always had a couple come over and talk to me and I'd get a quote in the paper," said Allan Kennedy, offensive tackle. "I think every player had their own little area. They put a sign above and we'd just sit there and go, OK, I'm over here. I'm sure guys now are texting and playing games on their phones if no one's talking to them. But back then, somebody would come over eventually."[30]

Located in one part of Candlestick were the defensive linemen, who chose to stay together as a unit. "It was kind of fun where it was all nine defensive linemen. We sat together and answered questions together," said Jeff Stover, defensive end. "That was kind of cool because we had fun together doing it. It was like, 'What are you going to do against Marino?' 'We're just going to get after him.' Media day was fun."[31]

The 49ers Media Day was defined by one player. Joe Montana, who for nearly the entire hour, answered questions about (1) playing close to home and (2) Dan Marino. Sitting in one of the first rows in the north end zone, Joe Cool calmly let the world know that he was proud of what Marino had accomplished and that it should be a great matchup come Sunday. "Everybody has their time. This is his right now. He's had a great year, so, didn't expect anything less from it," commented Montana to the hordes of reporters. "I think it's great what's happened to him."[32]

After the media session ended the 49ers had a short practice, running more than seventy plays. Walsh had every play mapped out. Then at 1:30 p.m., it was back to Redwood City. The 49ers were relaxed. Media Day was over. In the locker room, some of the players got rowdy while eating lunch and playing dominoes. While enjoying each other's company, Fred Dean tried to swipe Dwight Hicks's lunch, something he always tried to get away with. "We have a showdown every day about it. I tell people how I have to talk up to Fred to straighten him out. . . . But that's the one thing about this team. Everyone gets along," wrote Hicks in his Super Bowl Diary.[33]

UNDERDOG/OVERLOOKED

As the week progressed, the media increasingly focused on the Miami Dolphins "unstoppable" offense. An understandable premise with Dan Marino leading an offense that had scored an incredible 589 points in eighteen games for an average of thirty-two points per game. This was fine with the 49ers defensive players. "I remember Ronnie Lott getting up and saying, 'Good, we'll be under the radar, because they aren't even talking about our defense' and we were playing exceptionally well. We just heard all about Dan Marino, and he deserved attention because he was a great quarterback at that time. But it was just the media forgot to talk about the 49ers defense, which pissed everybody off a little bit," said Mario Clark, cornerback.[34]

The 49ers used the lack of respect by the media to their advantage all week when preparing for the game. "We didn't mind being under the radar. We were happy [about it]. I think the coaches too felt like being downplayed [was OK]. That was going to work in our favor because we knew the talent we had," said Carlton Williamson, strong safety.[35] Some players just couldn't settle down. They wanted to play the game immediately. "I was just trying to calm down because I'm an energy guy. I used that with my game. So the energy was so positive and so great that you had so much of it that it was hard to go to sleep. Hard to wait around for practice," said Riki Ellison, linebacker. "So I struggled with the containment of all this energy and being able to try and rest myself before I went into that game."[36]

Overlooked by the media on Wednesday (January 16), the unit received some news about the Pro Bowl. Because of an injury Giants cornerback Mark Haynes pulled out and was replaced by Eric Wright. Now all four members of the 49ers secondary would play in the Pro Bowl. It was the first time in NFL history that all four members of one secondary unit made the Pro Bowl—a historic feat. "Eric wasn't saying too much about it, but you could see in his eyes how happy he was. . . . That means the whole 49ers secondary was going to the Pro Bowl, and Ronnie [Lott] was saying, 'Let's show the people Sunday [during Super Bowl XIX] why we all got picked,'" wrote Dwight Hicks in his Super Bowl Diary.[37]

TICKETS

Bill Walsh made sure 49ers players had their ticket requests completed during the week leading up to Super Bowl week. But for the paying public, Super Bowl tickets were hard to find. With a face value of $60, some tickets to the big game were being scalped for up to $1,000. One Bay area seller wanted $700 for his pair of tickets—plus forty-nine cans of beer. It was a far cry from Super Bowl I, which had an original face value of $12 and didn't even sell out. In the end Super Bowl XIX would see a sell-out crowd of 84,059 at Stanford Stadium. Some newspaper sources reported that parking spots were selling for a hundred dollars.[38]

PARTIES/CITY/HOSPITAL FOOD MENU

The Bay area saw its share of parties and events. On January 12 in the *San Francisco Chronicle*, the newspaper listed twenty-eight different events. Besides the Commissioner's party, the city's biggest event was held the day before the game and billed as "the world's largest tailgate and locker room party." Held at the Moscone Center from 7:00 p.m. till 1:00 a.m., the "official 49er pep rally" featured twenty San Francisco restaurants, photos with NFL players, three stages of live music with the main stage featuring the Pointer Sisters, and a celebrity football game. Tickets were $30 in advance and $35 at the door.[39]

Even local schools, businesses, and hospitals got into the Super Bowl spirit. Throughout Super Bowl week Mount Zion Hospital served 49ers meals to their patients. You could order Randy Criss-Cross Fries, Ronnie Lott's and Bagels, Eggs Bubba-dict, or a cheese sandwich with Monterey Jack "Hacksaw" Cheese.[40]

ABC BROADCAST

As the two teams continued their preparations for the game, so too did ABC. It would be the first time the network—which broadcast Monday Night Football—would televise a Super Bowl. Shortly after the Dolphins and 49ers won their championship games, ABC made a big announcement regarding its broadcast team. All year O. J. Simpson had been the third member of the broadcast team, along with Frank Gifford (play-by-play) and Don Meredith (color). But for Super Bowl XIX, ABC executive producer Roone Arledge decided to replace Simpson with Joe Theismann, who was currently quarterback of the Washington Redskins and who wanted to get into broadcasting once his football career was over. It was an unexpected move. Simpson would still be part of the broadcast, joining Al Michaels and Jim Lampley for the network's two-hour pregame show. (Yes, just two hours—a far cry from today's day-long pregame shows.) He would also join Cowboys head coach Tom Landry for halftime and postgame analysis.

Super Bowl XIX would be carried by ABC on 211 televisions stations and by CBS on more than 300 radio stations (with Jack Buck and Hank Stram announcing). It was also to be televised in Canada and Mexico. American Forces Television Network beamed the ABC feed to military bases in Germany, Iceland, Spain, Diego Garcia, and the Philippines.

ABC positioned twenty-seven cameras—nineteen stationary, five hand held, one blimp, and two super slo-mo—throughout Stanford Stadium. The truck had seventeen videotape machines with slow-motion capability; four color background graphics generators for on-air graphics; one "paint box" to enhance still pictures; one Telestrator for diagramming plays onscreen; two still-storage systems; and two digital video effects generators for special effects that would be used for the pregame, game, and postgame coverage.

Additionally ABC had sixteen miles of camera and microphone cable lined throughout Stanford Stadium, along with 175 television monitors, fifty microphones, and twenty-four vehicles. More than 200 production, technical, administrative, and support personnel would help ABC to broadcast their first-ever Super Bowl.[41]

COMMERCIALS

Super Bowl XIX would be watched by 100 million viewers worldwide. To reach those viewers advertisers paid the highest price in television for commercial time—$1,000,000 per minute. For Super Bowl XIX ABC charged sponsors $1,000,000 for a sixty-second commercial and $525,000 for a thirty-second commercial during the game. Pregame and postgame spots were less expensive. For the previous Super Bowl, CBS charged $425,000 for a thirty-second spot.

During the game broadcast ABC aired twenty-five minutes of commercial time at $525,000 per thirty-second spot. Sponsors that aired commercials included IBM, Anheuser-Busch, Masterlock, McDonald's, Minolta, Nissan, Sharp, Soloflex, U.S. Marine Corps, Northwest Mutual Life, Sony, Ford, Cullinet Computer Software, Computerland, ITT, National Food Processors, and Coca-Cola.[42]

APPLE SEAT CUSHIONS

A few days before Super Sunday, Stanford Stadium got a makeover. The field was freshly painted with team names in the end zones, the NFL shield at midfield, and Super Bowl XIX logos at the forty-yard lines. On Wednesday before the game 250 Stanford University students, who toiled from sunrise to sunset, installed more than 84,000 seat cushions on the wooden seats at Stanford Stadium. Apple Computers, one of America's hottest companies, provided the cushions and donated $5 to the students' campus clubs for each hour worked.

The cushions were two-sided: on one side was Apple's rainbow logo and on the other the Super Bowl XIX logo. In 2013 the seat cushions were listed for as much as $150 on eBay. In January 1985, they were complimentary souvenirs to keep the fans comfortable on the stadium's wooden bleacher row seating.

MEDIA PREDICTIONS

As hype week was coming to a close, one of the Super Bowl's most common traditions swept the country: the media's game-day predictions. Once again the 49ers were overlooked. Most of the national beat writers were picking the Dolphins to win and to put a lot of points on the scoreboard in the process. Only a few picked the 49ers to win.

> Dave Anderson (*New York Times*): Dolphins, 34–20
> Furman Bisher (*Atlanta Journal-Constitution*): Dolphins, 28–24
> Frank Luksa (*Dallas Times-Herald*): Dolphins, 31–17
> Will McDonough (*Boston Globe*): Dolphins, 24–21
> Leigh Montville (*Boston Globe*): Dolphins, 47–45
> Jim Murray (*Los Angeles Times*): Dolphins, 49–47
> Ed Pope (*Miami Herald*): Dolphins, 45–35
> Vito Stellino (*Baltimore Sun*): Dolphins, 35–31
> Dick Young (*New York Post*): Dolphins, 23–13
> Paul Zimmerman (*Sports Illustrated*): 49ers, 37–31
> Thomas Boswell (*Washington Post*): 49ers, 35–31
> Bob Verdi (*Chicago Tribune*): 49ers, 31–28
> Chris Berman (ESPN): 49ers, 30–21[43]

Even some of the sportswriters who picked the 49ers to win weren't giving the 49ers defense any love, predicting they'd give up more than thirty points, something they had done only once all year against the Redskins in week 2. Friday was a mental day for the 49ers; they ran only forty-six plays, including no-huddle plays, two-minute drills, and the last three plays of the game. They were ready. "Most of the work is behind us. You've done the hard work. We're going to study a little more film. But basically the hay is in the barn," commented Walsh to his team after practice.[44] Walsh allowed his team to check into the AMFAC Hotel in Burlingame a day early. "To get into a more controlled atmosphere where my phone isn't ringing all the time," remarked Randy Cross to the local media.[45]

KEITH FAHNHORST'S BABY ARRIVES

For the Fahnhorst family, the two weeks leading up to the Super Bowl was a zoo. On top of the preparation for the big game, Sue Fahnhorst still had not given birth to the family's third daughter. The whole family took the delay in stride, and Keith took his mind off both the game and the baby by spending time with his brother. "I would go over to his house and we would hang out and shoot the breeze. He knew what I was going through, what I was feeling. It was great. We were as close as brothers could be on the team," said Jim Fahnhorst.[46]

At 9:30 a.m. on the Saturday before the big game, the 49ers held a short walk-through practice at Stanford Stadium. The relaxed 49ers ran twenty-four plays as fog covered the football field. The forty-five-minute practice was short and sweet. But for Keith Fahnhorst, the morning before the biggest game of his career was spent elsewhere. "My daughter was born the day before the game. We went to the doctor—I think it was the Tuesday before the Super Bowl—and he said, 'You're not going to deliver for another two, three weeks. Don't worry about that. Beat Miami and enjoy the Pro Bowl,'" said Keith Fahnhorst, offensive tackle. "Sure enough, Saturday morning I get the call from my sister-in-law, Jim's wife, who went over and checked. 'Get your ass to the hospital because she was ready to deliver.'"[47]

While at the hospital Fahnhorst decided to get something to eat, making his wife a very unhappy camper. "The nurses were concerned about making sure I got my breakfast that day," recalled Fahnhorst. "They asked me what I wanted. So between contractions I was eating scrambled eggs, and my wife will never let me forget about that." Courtney Blair Fahnhorst was born roughly twenty-four hours before Super Bowl XIX. "I think it probably relieved some of the anxiety about having to worry about Sue. So little Court, she surprised us," he said.[48] Despite Bill Walsh's extensive planning, he never prepared for something like this the day before the biggest game of the year, but he and the 49ers showed Fahnhorst some compassion—for a brief moment. "They did. But they didn't want it to be a distraction to me or the team. So they congratulated me but then they said, 'We got work to do.'"[49]

NIGHT BEFORE SUPER BOWL XIX

"I saw dad the night before and I have never seen him more confident than I did for this game," said Craig Walsh.[50] While the 49ers were getting settled into their team hotel in Burlingame on the East Coast, viewers of *Saturday Night Live* watched more of the Super Bowl hype. One of the show's six-minute segments featured a skit with Billy Crystal, a 49ers fan, and Christopher Guest, a Dolphins fan, who were preparing to watch Super Bowl XIX. Getting a few laughs, the two football fans eventually make a $5 bet on the game.

While the East Coast watched Crystal and Guest, the 49ers gathered at the AMFAC Hotel meeting room for their last get together before the big game. First was a special teams meeting at 8:00 p.m. Then both offense and defense met for a half hour to go over last-minute details. In the offensive meeting room, Walsh presented his first twenty-five plays. Then at 9:15 p.m. the whole squad reunited for a team "brunch." "The night before was a special night. But we tried to keep it routine. As routine as we could knowing the magnitude of the game," said Manu Tuiasosopo, defensive tackle.[51]

Now the 49ers players listened to Bill Walsh. "Basically he just [said] 'This is it. This is what we worked for.' Everything came back to boxing because he talked about that a lot. 'This is a big championship game, big boxing match between two of the big heavyweights. That is what we're here for. Get out there and perform,'" said rookie defensive tackle Michael Carter.[52] "I remember Walsh saying, 'This is your day, men. Go out and have fun.' That was biggest thing. Just go out and have fun. This is it. This is it. After this, it's all over. It's your last chance. Go out and have fun," said defensive end Jeff Stover.[53]

Walsh had set curfew at 11:15 p.m. He had no problems with any player breaking it. Although nobody was going to stay out late, the team had a hard time going to bed. "Oh, I didn't sleep well. I never slept well before [a game]. I'm tossing and turning all night visualizing what I need to do. I played the game over 1,000 times in my head. I'd visualize positive things, like how I wanted to play, what kind of mentality I'm bringing to the game that day. I want to be aggressive every time I touch the ball. I visualize what I did in practice. You have to visualize. Because you practice the way you play. So if you practice hard, you're going to play that way," said fullback Roger Craig.[54]

"It was hard to sleep at night before the game, let me tell you that," said Carlton Williamson, strong safety.[55] "For me, always, [I] dream about the Super Bowl. You don't sleep that well because you're excited about the game," said halfback Wendell Tyler.[56] "Ray Wersching was my roommate. I didn't sleep very much. I remember getting up at 5:00 in the morning and going out because we were staying at the airport hotel. Looking out over the bay. Today is the day," said defensive end Dwaine Board.[57]

FRED DEAN'S POETRY

"Oh, no, I never slept good before a game. Never did. By the time I laid down, it was time to get up and go have that pregame breakfast and a meeting or something like that, so I never slept good before a game," said defensive end Fred Dean. "I would either read or write some poetry or something, and that would really get me ready for the game that next day."[58] For Super Bowl XIX he wrote a piece titled "My Self."

I want to live with my self and soul,
I want to be able my self to know,
I want to stand in the setting sun, And not hate myself for the things I've done,
I want to be able as days go by, Always to look myself in the eye,
And feel that I never have to lie, To my self.[59]

Every 49er had a different way of handling the stress of playing in a Super Bowl. One thing was certain: this would be the last time the 1984 49ers would take the field. "It was our last time together as a group. The last night of the entire season and what we battled through from Rocklin all the way to that last night as a group that we would come together, eat together, be in the hotel together. The season was coming to an end. We didn't want the season to come to an end. That last week was painful because we were going to lose all these memories and lose that next week. We would've kept on playing. We could've kept on playing," said Riki Ellison, linebacker.[60]

19

PREGAME

January 20, 1985. Super Sunday. The day of Super Bowl XIX.

For the early risers among the 49ers, a continental breakfast was available at 8:00 a.m., but it wasn't until 11:00 a.m. that the team had its official pregame meal. As the team relaxed at breakfast, one player didn't deviate from his normal routine. "Hacksaw gets up at breakfast, early that morning, fully dressed. Whole uniform on. Taped. I mean, the whole nine yards," said Ray Rhodes, defensive backs coach. "This is early in the morning. We don't play until later that afternoon. He is fully dressed with the uniform, taped up, helmet on, sitting at breakfast eating with his helmet on—eating through his helmet. It was unbelievable."[1]

Hacksaw Reynolds was in full uniform and ready for Super Bowl XIX. So were the rest of the 49ers. "You try to keep it together. You don't make it bigger than it is. You try to treat it like a regular game," said fullback Roger Craig. "As a young guy you just kind of follow the veteran guys, [follow] their lead, do what they do. For me, I never ate much. I couldn't eat that much before a game. You just kind of be cool like the veteran guys. You just sit back and watch them. That's what I did."[2]

GETTING TO THE STADIUM

After the pregame meal it was time to leave the team's hotel. "Being a 3:00 game, we spent more time at the hotel the day of. I hate that. I want to just get up, eat, get on the bus, go to the stadium. But waiting for a 3:30 game, there's just too much downtime," said Allan Kennedy, offensive tackle. "There's nothing to watch on TV. There are no other games. You just read the paper. Read a book. Some guys would get to the stadium four hours [early]. John [Ayers] and Randy [Cross] and a couple of the linemen would get there before the game just to get taped early, maybe walk the field to check it out. Everybody else would get there two or three hours before [game time] and other players would get there just when they had to."[3]

Forty-niner coaches and players had two buses waiting to take them to Stanford Stadium. The first left the hotel at 11:30 a.m., while the second one left at noon. The roughly fifteen-mile drive allowed the 49er players to reflect on what they needed to do to play the best game of their lives. "When we got to the stadium, [it] took a real long time, because for some reason they took the back roads. It took a long time, but he [Walsh] said we should get there in plenty of time. 'So you guys can go do your normal routine,'" said defensive back Dana McLemore. "Stanford had built some new locker rooms just for the Super Bowl. So we got in there and relaxed a little bit. That's how Super Bowls are; they take double the time of normal games. A lot of waiting around, sitting around. We were ready to go and play. We had all the pageantries and the six-hour pregame, and it just took a long time."[4]

At Stanford Stadium, the 49ers were greeted with fog and cool temperatures. It felt like a home game. "That was our environment. It was perfect weather. It was our place," said Riki Ellison, linebacker.[5]

THE LOCKER ROOM

Inside the newly built locker rooms the 49ers got comfortable. The stadium gates opened at 12:15 p.m. but kickoff was still a few hours away. Players got taped, listened to music, or went through the game plans. Most players kept to their game-day routine. "You come out as you did for any other game during the season, and you warmed up the same way. Everybody has their rituals and their routines that they do exactly the same. You get out on the field and when the coin's tossed, you're ready to go," said defensive end Jeff Stover. "A lot of guys tape their fingers exactly the same every time. They go to the bathroom—it's a routine that they do all year long—before every game and we did the same thing for the Super Bowl. You don't want to change that routine."[6]

Ronnie Lott wore his lucky pink plaid shorts. Joe Montana sat next to Matt Cavanaugh flipping through his playbook. "I always wore my T-shirt turned inside out and always had to have my hot dog in my locker. Always had to have a hot dog," said Dwaine Board, defensive end.[7]

BILL WALSH'S LOCKER ROOM ANTICS

Minutes before the 49ers were to take the field at 1:50 p.m. for pregame warm-ups, Bill Walsh walked into the locker room. Three years earlier, when Walsh arrived in Pontiac, Michigan, with the 49ers for Super Bowl XVI, he borrowed a bellman's suit and cap and helped his players carry luggage off their bus. The idea was to create a loose atmosphere and make his players feel at home during the intense week before kickoff. In the makeshift locker room at Stanford Stadium, he once again tried to relax his players. "He came in and laid in the middle of the floor. He had his head propped up on something. His legs were up. He was just whistling, listening to the song, and stuff like that. Here I'm nervous, as defensive backs coach, I'm nervous. I'm worried about Marino. We can't let him do this, can't let him do that. The thing that was really impressive about Bill, he was so relaxed," said Ray Rhodes.[8]

Walsh took a seat on the floor in the middle of the locker room. His casual and relaxed demeanor threw off a few of his players. "Before the Super Bowl, I had my tape on, my eye black on. I was walking around in my T-shirt, had my shoulder pads off, maybe an hour before the game. I walk over this body and I look down and it's Bill Walsh. He had his legs crossed and his hands behind his head like he was chilling out. I look down, I think to myself, 'If he's this relaxed and this cool before the Super Bowl, then we're going to win this game.' And everybody had the same feeling. It was a genius move [by] Bill Walsh. Relaxing everybody, it was another game to us," said cornerback Mario Clark.[9]

After a few minutes spent relaxing on the floor, Walsh started to talk, asking the team, "Oh my, how are we ever going to stop Dan Marino and the Dolphins offense?" and "Who's going to stop the Marks Brothers?" The players understood his rhetoric; they heard what he was really saying. "Bill was such a psychologist and he was such a smart man. I think Bill did a lot of that stuff to try to relax us. Kind of relaxing and keeping us on edge at the same time, if that makes sense. Because he didn't want us to feel too confident that the game plan was ready or that we were ready or [so relaxed] that we didn't have anything to worry about," said Earl Cooper, tight end. [10]

"We'd get ready to go out for warm-ups, Bill Walsh is laying on the floor in the middle of the locker room with his head on top of a bag of footballs with his legs crossed. We were a really relaxed team," said Dwaine Board, defensive end. [11] "He knew how to get you going and get your goat and tug at you to get what he needed out of you," said Michael Carter, defensive tackle. [12]

Walsh had his players in the right frame of mind just minutes before taking the field. They had prepared as well as they could for two weeks. Ever since the speech in Washington more than a year ago the 49ers strove to get to this point. It was now time to achieve their goal. Everybody in the 49ers locker room cared about one another. "I looked over, I saw Eric Wright crying in the locker room. [There] was that much emotion all bottled up inside of you. You can't wait to get the game going and let everything settle into the game," said strong safety Carlton Williamson. [13] "Bill had a great way of just getting you mentally prepared and into the game. We were wound up by the time we got into the game," said linebacker Blanchard Montgomery. [14]

PREGAME WARM-UPS

Jogging out onto the field at Stanford Stadium, the 49ers wore their classic red home jerseys with gold pants. They would sit on the west bench, press side. The Dolphins wore their white jerseys with white pants and sat on the east bench. One 49er inked seven letters on the outside of his shoes to show what the players were all about. Fred Dean wrote "warrior" in red marker on the side of his shoes. "The main reason, we were looking at two warriors going into battle that day, and everybody out there was a warrior in some shape, form, or fashion. The general stood on the sideline and directed us and we executed. When you feel something and you write it down like that, you expose something to everything and everybody. And it gives us an opportunity to say that we are 49ers and we're doing a great job," said Fred Dean, defensive end. [15]

"You treat it as just a regular game, because that's what it comes down to. No one's playing any different there. You need to execute, and the best team's going to win," said Allan Kennedy, offensive tackle. "Running out on the field, yeah, that's awesome." [16] Few NFL players get a chance to play in a Super Bowl. Every member of the 1984 49ers absorbed the atmosphere at Stanford Stadium. "It was great. I kept trying to bring myself down. You're sitting there watching the hoopla of the Super Bowl. I just kept telling myself to come down. Get your feet back on the ground. This is a football game. Even though it's a Super Bowl, it's still a football game," said rookie defensive tackle Michael Carter. [17]

"We weren't overwhelmed with the situation we were in. We were a polished team. We weren't overwhelmed by the situation or the task at hand," said defensive end Jim Stuckey. "But it's pretty damn neat being on the field and looking at all the paint and the markings. Super Bowl XIX etched into the grass. Damn, baby, this why we play. This is why you played since you were seven or eight years old. To be right here." [18]

"It was just so exciting. [Although] a player, I was still part spectator when I could: before the game in warm-ups, looking around, big-eyed and smiling, 'Wow, this is the Super Bowl. I can't believe it,'" said Renaldo Nehemiah, wide receiver. [19]

While his team began its pregame warm-ups Bill Walsh took a few minutes to look at the Miami Dolphins up close. "In any Super Bowl, or any big game, there are some lasting memories, and mine that day came in the pregame warm-ups. As I walked through the Dolphins, I could see a distinct difference between the two squads. We were a much more physical, more athletic football team than Miami. Maybe it was just the color or the uniforms, but the Dolphins didn't look physical. We weren't really a big team, but we were athletic. At that moment my confidence soared," wrote Walsh in his autobiography. [20]

While Walsh's confidence soared, his star quarterback was already making plans for training camp in Rocklin. Joe Montana was throwing warm-up passes next to his position coach Paul Hackett. "In pregame warm-up we were in our own end zone, the far end zone at Stanford Stadium. We're throwing seven-on-seven and he throws four or five in a row, and Bill says, 'Hey, Matt, get in there,' and [Joe] comes over to me and quietly says, 'You know, next year in training camp that three-step drop. I need to work a little bit more on that second step.' And I'm blown away. I'm saying to myself, 'This is the biggest game I've ever seen' and he is zeroed-in on his technique because he was a perfectionist. It had to be just right for him. He had learned that from Bill, and his own nature was that way. Maybe he was just trying to calm me down a little. I don't know. I said, 'Yeah, Joe, we'll definitely get on that, but right now you gotta think about that first quick out,'" said Hackett. [21]

As Montana warmed up, Walsh stopped by to give him some last-minute instruction about running with the ball. "Just before the game, I told Joe, 'If you see it, take it.' With the linebackers chasing the backs, there would be nobody to take Joe," Walsh recalled in his autobiography. [22]

As the sold-out crowd was entering the stadium the tension on the field was building. Young players looked to the veterans to lead the way. A few words of encouragement went a long way. "Just before the Super Bowl Hacksaw came up to me and said, 'Roger, you have to play every play like it's going to be your last. You never know if you're gonna ever play another one of these Super Bowls. So give it your best-ever play.' So that advice gave me motivation because I was shaking in my boots. This is my second year in the league, and I'll be playing in the Super Bowl in front of hundreds of millions of people. That is one of the best offenses in the game with Dan Marino, and they're supposed to blow us out. He had a record-breaking season, threw for 5,000 yards and 40-something touchdowns. They have the Marks Brothers, Duper and Clayton. So I was nervous. I was scared. When Hacksaw came up to me and gave me that advice, that gave me wings like I'm ready to go. That pumped me up. I was so motivated that I was gonna do well for the team every time I touched the ball. Every block, whatever. When he told me that it gave me goose bumps," said fullback Roger Craig. Craig would go on to play the game of his life. [23]

The anticipation of Super Bowl XIX was getting everybody more excited by the minute. The big matchup between the Dolphins receivers and the 49ers defensive backs would be one of the main story lines of the game. Forty-niners defensive backs coach Ray Rhodes made sure his secondary was ready. He covered everything. "I wanted to make sure they had the right cleats, [that] they got the cleats they need to go out and perform. I go out and I walk the whole field. I let them know to make sure to get plenty of foot on the ground. It's a little slippery or whatever. But I always would make sure I walked the field and made sure that they had the proper cleats because we can't slip. You get in a bear fight, you can't slip," said Rhodes.

The defensive backs were focused. They were ready to prove that the entire secondary was worthy of being selected to go to the Pro Bowl. From backup players to starters, all the defensive backs showed the same intensity. The pregame became a battle zone. "Our warm-ups, they were intense. Nobody wanted to go in tackling drills against Ronnie [Lott] because Ronnie was geared up. We're getting ready to go through our tackling drill and I'm seeing guys get out of line. Don't want to go with Ronnie because Ronnie gonna try to bust their chest open. I had certain guys go against Ronnie. Sometimes I'd let Carlton [Williamson] and Ronnie go because Carlton understood what he's going to get. He knew he was gonna get the shit knocked out of him. But he could handle it a lot better than some of the other guys," said Rhodes. "That first tackling drill you hear a shotgun. Babow! He just knocked the shit out of the guy. So then I knew Ronnie was ready to play. I know Carlton is ready to go, because that was a hell of a hit [Lott] put on Carlton, all the cobwebs out of Carlton. He's ready to go. The warm-ups were intense. You see the focus in the players," said Rhodes.[24]

GEORGE SEIFERT, WORRYWART

After warm-ups the 49ers headed back inside their locker room. A place where nervous energy could appear. "When you go in the locker room, you're sitting around. Coach Seifert is also a worrywart. Worry all the time. Sometimes I go into the locker room and make sure I don't get too close to George. Because every time you got around George, 'What if? What if?' Before a game, if you're with Coach Seifert, he's gonna 'what if' you to death. 'What do you think about this? Did you cover this? Did you cover that?' 'Yes, George, I covered it.' 'Well go cover it again.' This is before the game," said Rhodes. "You hate to go to your players before the game trying to cover this or cover that. 'George, we covered that.' So you try to avoid him in the locker room. But he covered everything. He was a very detailed guy."[25]

Walsh then gave one last speech to his team. "The speech that Bill gave us before we went out on the field was, 'You've worked hard and don't focus on anything except for the end result that you want. It will happen. But leave it on the field,'" said linebacker Blanchard Montgomery.[26] Kickoff was getting closer. The team exited the locker room at the corner of Stanford Stadium. The 49ers defense would get the honor of being introduced.

FORTY-NINERS DEFENSE INTRODUCED

The eleven starters in the 49ers base defense jogged through two rows of 49ers cheerleaders as the public address announcer called their names: Lawrence Pillers, Manu Tuiasosopo, Dwaine Board, Dan Bunz, Riki Ellison, Jack Reynolds, Keena Turner, Ronnie Lott, Eric Wright, Carlton Williamson, and Dwight Hicks made the memorable trek in front of a sell-out crowd and a worldwide television audience.[27] "I don't think I felt the ground. In fact, my family members made fun of me because when they were introducing the defense, it looked like I was hyperventilating. So I just enjoyed the moment," said Manu Tuiasosopo, defensive tackle.[28]

PRESIDENT REAGAN COIN TOSS/NATIONAL ANTHEM

Jogging out with the rest of the 49ers, Bill Walsh wore a white wool sweater with the 49ers helmet on the left breast over a collared golf shirt, gold khaki pants, and white Adidas cleats. By their bench on the west side of the stadium, the 49ers lined up for the national anthem. Stretching from one twenty-yard line to the other were soldiers in the formation of an American flag. Red, white, and blue was everywhere. Also on the field was the Super Bowl Children's Choir, with more than 100 youngsters singing the national anthem. Walsh stood proudly with a big smile on his face. Next to him was Joe Montana, holding his helmet behind his back. After the anthem was finished, balloons featuring the colors of both teams were released high over the stadium.

Suddenly it was time for the captains to take the field for the coin toss. They would get a surprise they would never forget. Forty-niners team captains Keith Fahnhorst, Dwight Hicks, Keena Turner, and Bill Ring walked to midfield. Greeting them was referee Pat Haggerty and former 49ers star running back Hugh McElhenny, wearing his gold Hall of Fame blazer. "That was especially meaningful for me, because that was the first time that I had to go out on a Super Bowl coin toss. [It] was a special honor for me to represent the team, the special teams, as a captain. That was a lot of fun. Very memorable," said Bill Ring.[29] "It was a great feeling for me to represent the team because of the way we [chose] captains back in those days. Bill chose different captains for every game. Then when we got to the playoffs, we chose the permanent captains. Those guys would represent the team throughout the playoffs. That was what was kind of nice about it," said Keena Turner.[30]

As a special guest, the NFL had President Ronald Reagan, who had been inaugurated for his second term as president that morning, toss the coin live from the White House. Beamed by satellite from Washington, D.C., Reagan appeared on televisions across the country and on the Jumbotron scoreboard at Stanford Stadium. The visiting team made the call: Dolphins center Dwight Stephenson called heads. Hugh McElhenny then said, "Mr. President, will you please toss the coin?" With his right hand, the former college football player from Eureka College tossed the Super Bowl coin high into the air. The coin landed on the White House's blue carpet, where Reagan glanced down and announced: "It is tails!" Referee Haggerty yelled, "San Francisco has won the toss. They want the ball."[31]

McElhenny then said, "Mr. President, thank you for joining us today." Ever the showman, Reagan commented, "Well, thank you. It was a privilege and all I can say is something that was a little prayer of mine while I played football myself. May everyone do their best, may there be no injuries, may the best team win, and no one have regrets." On the ABC broadcast, Frank Gifford spoke up. "Well, you'll have to admit, the toss of the coin was pretty impressive for Super Bowl XIX."[32] For the players on the field, it was an unforgettable moment right before kickoff. "It was special for me. Here you're talking about a small plantation boy who got a scholarship to play football. And then to be on that

[Super Bowl] stage twice? Ronald Reagan is flipping the coin and I'm standing there. The national anthem is playing. I got all the adrenaline going on. The focus was there," said tight end Earl Cooper.[33]

"It almost felt like it wasn't real. I do remember that it felt like forever before they finally kicked off with all the festivities they had [going on]. I was reminded of that when I watched the Super Bowl this year. I thought, 'How do those guys keep the right frame of mind?' It's such a long delay after the warm-ups and before the kickoff. That took a long time, but I do remember how confident Bill was and how confident Joe was. That's what was important," said offensive tackle Keith Fahnhorst.[34] "It's like you get all choked up and you also can't believe it. . . . When you reach one of the goals that you've dreamt about your whole life as a young boy, and you dare to dream it and dare to think that you can do it. Then you've done it. I'm fifty-one years old and it still takes the breath out of me. It leaves you breathless," said linebacker Blanchard Montgomery.[35]

The 49ers were ready to play. "I remember walking up to Russ Francis, and Russ puts his hand on my shoulder and said, 'Hey, we can do this.' And I looked at him and said, 'Russ, we're gonna do it,'" said defensive end Dwaine Board.[36] "This is an opportunity for us to show the world what we got. What this team is really about. I was just excited. I had butterflies," said strong safety Carlton Williamson.[37]

"I just pictured that perfect San Francisco day, the low fog. It was cool. It had everything that you could possibly want. Everything was perfect. There was no weakness in our group. No doubters at all. I think we all felt as we sat there waiting to be introduced: 'This is our place. This is our time.' Nobody was going to take this away and this was going to be a special game," said Riki Ellison, linebacker. "I've played a lot of games in my life but I don't feel like that. That one was that special, and you could feel it before the game kicked off. You could feel it during the anthem. You could feel it on the kickoff. You could feel it on the first series. It was ours."[38]

As the fog cleared, game time temperature reached a cool 53 degrees. As kickoff approached the 49ers were finally ready to play the game. As for the rest of America, they were ready, too. After two weeks and a two-hour pregame show, ABC televised Super Bowl XIX to 85.5 million viewers—the largest Super Bowl audience ever—barely topping the previous high of 85.2 million for the 49ers victory over the Bengals in Super Bowl XVI. The 46.4 Nielsen rating proved Super Bowl XIX was must-see TV.[39]

20

FIRST HALF

Just a few minutes after President Reagan tossed the coin in the White House, Dolphins kicker Uwe von Schamann kicked off Super Bowl XIX with a beautiful boot to the south end of Stanford Stadium. Rookie halfback Derrick Harmon sprinted to his right to field the kick. As he slowed down near the sidelines, he caught the kick, stopped immediately, both feet inches from the sidelines, then stepped out-of-bounds at the 49ers six-yard line. Backed up deep in their own territory was not where Bill Walsh expected the 49ers to start the Super Bowl. "I avoided Walsh. He just called his play," recalled Derrick Harmon, running back.[1] Despite poor field position, Walsh didn't vary his first twenty-five plays. He went with the quick out from his own end zone.

Montana's first pass was incomplete to Freddie Solomon. Then the 49ers started to move the ball. With an unbalanced line—Bubba Paris lined up on the right side next to Keith Fahnhorst—Wendell Tyler gained eight yards. After two first downs the drive stalled near midfield. Max Runager's punt was returned to the Dolphins thirty-six-yard line. George Seifert's base defense (3–4 front) took the field. "I was walking on air. There was no way we were going to lose this game. No way at all. The first time the ball's snapped from a defensive standpoint, it was on. It was on," said linebacker Blanchard Montgomery.[2] But on the first play from scrimmage the Dolphins threw the first punch. Dan Marino tossed a pass to halfback Tony Nathan in the left flat. With too much energy Eric Wright missed the tackle as Nathan sprinted twenty-five yards down the sidelines. In San Francisco territory Marino had three more completions until the 49ers stiffened to force a field goal attempt. Uwe von Schamann had struggled all season from thirty yards or more, going just three for thirteen. But his thirty-seven-yard attempt was good and it put the Dolphins on the scoreboard first, 3–0.

On the 49ers second offensive drive Walsh returned to his play sheet. Montana started with a quick pass to Roger Craig in the flat for four yards. On a draw play Tyler went up the middle for six yards for a first down. Out of an I-formation Montana's play-action fake led to a quick hitch pass to Dwight Clark for nine yards. On second-and-one Walsh deviated from his first twenty-five. Walsh wanted the first down, so instead of a pass play, he called a power run off the left side behind guard John Ayers and tackle Bubba Paris. Tyler pounded for six yards. First down.

After two plays gained just three yards, Walsh and Montana faced an early third-down call. He kept to the list, calling a nickel pass. "This [play] was off our nickel list. It was really the same as the first nickel play we ran, only the opposite way. Joe saw the opportunity and did the right thing by running," commented Walsh after the game.[3] Dolphins right defensive end Kim Bokamper beat tackle Bubba Paris, forcing Montana out of the pocket around the left end. Montana sprinted for fifteen yards and a big first down.

Montana was just getting started with big plays. In the 49ers huddle he had everyone's attention. "Joe brought a charisma to the huddle that [inspired you] to step your game up. You automatically did it because of the aura of him. He's like the Roman gods. You know how they treated the Roman gladiators. Well, Joe was like that. When he's in the huddle, you stepped up your game to another level. We played up to his level. He would bring that out of you. That's pretty special to have that kind of charisma and flair. Kind of like Michael Jordan, Larry Bird, Wayne Gretzky, Magic Johnson—that kind of aura about him," said fullback Roger Craig.[4]

With new life the 49ers now had a first down at the Dolphins thirty-three-yard line. Walsh then called the sixteenth play on his play sheet: Halfback Sail. Roger Craig lined up as the only back to the right of Montana. Carl Monroe lined up in the slot to the right, inside of wide receiver Renaldo Nehemiah. On the left side was Dwight Clark wide, Earl Cooper tight. At the snap Montana rolled right behind pulling guards Randy Cross and John Ayers. Flooding the right side, Craig ran short, Nehemiah ran his pattern deep, clearing for Monroe to run his sail route in the open space. Perfectly timed, Montana threw a dart to Monroe, who had beaten Dolphins free safety Lyle Blackwood to make the catch near the sidelines. With Nehemiah clearing out the defenders, Monroe turned up along the sidelines running into the end zone alone for the first touchdown of Super Bowl XIX.

Excited, Monroe tried to spike the ball, but the pigskin slipped from his grip, falling to the ground. "He didn't know what to do with it. He was just having a good time," said fullback Roger Craig.[5] Little used backup Carl Monroe had made the first big play of the game. "We practiced that all week and they fell for it. Carl was open. He stumbled into the end zone. He lost the ball as he was spiking it. But he was excited and he did it. He stepped up when it was his time," said halfback Wendell Tyler.[6]

The eight-play drive of four runs and four passes covered seventy-eight yards in just four minutes. After a few commercials on the ABC broadcast, Tom Landry went through the touchdown on the Telestrator. It was a beautifully executed play. The Dolphins responded with a surprising twist that the 49ers weren't entirely ready for. Starting on their own thirty Dan Marino went to a no-huddle offense that kept the 49ers from substituting their defensive personnel. Run linebackers Dan Bunz and Jack Reynolds were stuck on the field and Marino took advantage. Marino connected with Mark Clayton for eighteen yards, then completed to his other outside weapon, Mark Duper, over Eric Wright for eleven yards. This would be Duper's only catch of the game.

Marino got hotter as he hit Clayton for thirteen yards and tight end Dan Johnson, who beat run linebacker Dan Bunz for a big twenty-one-yard gain to the 49ers two-yard line. On first-and-goal Marino rushed to the line and rolled to his right, lofting a pass to Johnson over Reynolds for an easy touchdown. After six plays for seventy yards with just 2:27 off the clock, the Dolphins had retaken the lead. It didn't take George Seifert long to adjust to the no-huddle offense by the Dolphins. "As soon as they went hurry-up, George said, 'When we get back on the field, we're putting a nickel on the field right away,'" said Ray Rhodes, defensive backs coach.[7] Seifert told his staff and Bill Walsh agreed: they'd go with a nickel defense the rest of the game.

On the last play of the first quarter Montana ran a play-action draw to Roger Craig, who slipped through the line and cut to his right, beating the linebacker for an eighteen-yard catch, taking advantage of the lack of speed of the Dolphins linebackers. But after two incompletions, the drive stalled near midfield. Out trotted Max Runager. Overshadowed for two weeks by the Dolphins All-Pro punter Reggie Roby, Runager made the first big play on special teams. He calmly booted the ball out-of-bounds inside the Dolphins twenty-yard line, pinning Marino back. "If it bogged down, then I needed to help out and kick that ball inside the ten. Inside the fifteen. Inside the twenty is a plus, but when you start focusing on that ten-yard line and they've got ninety or ninety-five yards to go, then you know you've done a pretty good job with it," said Runager.[8]

Up in the 49ers coaches box at the top of Stanford Stadium, George Seifert was getting help from an unlikely source: Neal Dahlen's teenage son. "He was fourteen years old. He was a little guy. Stanford Stadium was an old-style stadium with steps straight all the way down from the [coaches] booth to the field. So two or three times he had to take the Polaroid pictures from the booth and run them down to the field and then run back up to the booth," said Dahlen.[9]

Seifert made the call to go to nickel on first down. "George's call. George would like to play nickel all day. You know what I'm saying? We knew before it wasn't going to be a base game. It was going to be a nickel and dime game. The fact that they went no-huddle, that was to keep us from getting our guys there. So once we went to that, we played the rest of the day [in nickel formation]," said Bill McPherson, defensive line coach.[10] Marino had gone nine of ten for 103 yards and one touchdown as the two teams combined for seventeen, the most points ever in the first quarter of a Super Bowl.

"In the early stages of the game and halfway through the second quarter they were moving the ball on our base defense. We didn't quite have the movement in our base defense that we had with our nickel defense. It was more prepared to stop the run and pass but not the pass attack," said George Seifert, defensive coordinator. "The thing that helped us [was that] our offense put some points on the board. Then we felt like the thing we had to do was just put pressure on Marino. They weren't going to spend a lot of time doing anything else other than throw the ball down the field. It became a third-down every play."[11]

When Marino trotted back onto the field he saw a different look. The 49ers nickel defense was on the field for the first-down play with

Jeff Fuller and Keena Turner. Fred Dean exploded through the Dolphins line to drop Woody Bennett for a loss of four. "To me it felt like a sack [of running back Woody Bennett] because we were so far in the backfield on them. Even today that would be one of the things I remember [about] that play," said Dean.[12] Then the nickel rush forced two incompletions. "I thought it was a great move. Because we knew we can stop the run with our nickel on the field. We had some great players who played nickel. We had more speed on the field, too. So we knew we could play with it. We could make it hard on them, too, because they expected us to come back to our 3–4 and we didn't," said defensive end Dwaine Board.[13] "Everybody's running around trying to figure out what's going on and what we're doing. George then switched it up and we went nickel. Once you settled down, this is how we're going to play it. Now we're gonna play ball," said defensive tackle Michael Carter.[14]

Backed up, Roby's punt came up short—thirty-seven yards—giving the ball back to the 49ers offense at the Dolphins forty-seven-yard line. It was now going to be the start of the greatest ten minutes and fifty-four seconds of offense in Super Bowl history. Once again Montana used his legs. "Going into the game I told Joe to take the run if it was there, especially if the defenders turned their backs to him in man coverage. Their defensive linemen are not quick. . . . We know if he got untracked he would make good yardage," recalled Walsh after the game.[15]

With nobody open Montana ran through a big lane toward the sidelines picking up nineteen yards. After the big scramble Montana hit Dwight Clark on a dig route for sixteen yards. Tyler ran for four yards setting up Montana again. From the Dolphins eight-yard line, out of a pro-set, strong right, Montana took a five-step drop. Tight end Russ Francis ran his route into the middle of the end zone taking the coverage with him as fullback Roger Craig went through the line behind him at the front of the end zone. Catching the pass at the three-yard line, Craig dove into the end zone for the touchdown.

"This was the first pass on our red zone list. Russ is the primary receiver but he was caught in traffic. In fact he sort of attracted traffic and that left an opening for Roger to make his catch," recalled Walsh.[16] "It was a curl route. I gave him a good fake. He took the fake, I came under and Joe hit me. They couldn't stop it," said Roger Craig, fullback.[17]

On ABC's broadcast, Frank Gifford said, "This is what we anticipated, an offensive show."[18] Viewers would get an offensive show, but only one offense would show up. Montana wanted more input and returned to the bench to talk to Paul Hackett on the phone. "He was never hesitant to say, 'Paul, talk to Bill about this one.' Because he knew that it was all going to flow through Bill, and he knew what things were better suggested to Bill from me. So we had a pretty good working relationship there," said Paul Hackett, quarterbacks and wide receivers coach.[19] Walsh, Hackett, and Montana would all be on the same page for Super Bowl XIX.

Seifert kept his nickel defense on the field and the 49ers defense forced another three-and-out. "The defensive coordinator did a wonderful job of setting Dan up and disguising the coverage. We did a lot of things off of [the nickel] that changed the whole thing for us," said Fred Dean, defensive end.[20] Once again Roby, who averaged nearly forty-five yards a punt in 1984, came up with a short boot. This time, behind blocks by Tom Holmoe and Mike Walter, Dana McLemore returned it for twenty-eight yards to the 49ers forty-five-yard line.

On the last play of Walsh's first twenty-five, Wendell Tyler—behind a nice lead block from Craig—ran around the right end for nine yards. With every play call, the confidence of the 49ers offense was growing. On back-to-back plays, Montana connected with tight end Russ Francis for twenty-nine total yards. "When we needed a play, Joe made it. When we needed a pass thrown and a play made, Joe threw it," said tight end Earl Cooper.[21] Craig went around the right side gaining five yards and putting the ball at the Dolphins six-yard line. On second down Montana took a quick three-step drop, pumped the ball to his left, saw a big opening, took off up the middle, and dove headfirst into the end zone. Another 49ers touchdown!

"They got frustrated they couldn't get to him, so they started dropping on him. I think every once in a while they overreacted within the zone and there was a big gash and he took it. A number of those times, his primary and secondary receivers were covered. So I think that was him sort of going through the progression, as Bill would say, 'I've got ten yards. I'm taking it,'" said Paul Hackett, quarterbacks and wide receivers coach.[22] Montana had rushed three times for forty yards and one score giving the 49ers a 21–10 lead.

It was now Marino's turn to respond. The 49ers nickel defense had other ideas. Gary Johnson rushed up the middle to hit Marino in the chest, forcing an incompletion. It was the first time viewers saw grass stains on Marino's uniform. On second down Johnson dropped Tony Nathan for a three-yard loss. On third down out of the shotgun Marino tried to force a ball to Mark Duper but Eric Wright broke up the pass. After their touchdown in the first quarter, the Dolphins had gone three straight drives without getting a first down. Nine plays for a total of one yard. Seifert changed the momentum of the game by making the decision to go strictly to the nickel.

For the third time in the first half Reggie Roby got off a bad punt—this one went just thirty-nine yards. The 49ers took over near midfield. Even after a sack by Doug Betters on Montana, the 49ers offense was still clicking. Picking himself up Montana went back to work. Craig beat rookie linebacker Jay Brophy out of the backfield for twenty yards. Rolling out right Montana kept the ball for seven yards; Tyler went around the left end for nine yards; a pass to Francis over the middle netted nine more yards. Walsh then called a halfback pass with rookie Derrick Harmon. Sweeping right Harmon pumped to throw, but didn't have an open receiver. Instead of forcing the pass Harmon tucked the ball and ran for seven yards.

A short run by Tyler put the ball at the Dolphins two-yard line. Behind lead blocks on the left side by Bubba Paris, John Ayers, and Russ Francis, fullback Roger Craig followed Wendell Tyler through a nice hole to score the 49ers fourth touchdown of the first half: nine plays and fifty-two yards in 3:39. It was the first time in Super Bowl history that a team had scored three touchdowns in one quarter. With 2:05 left till halftime the 49ers had a commanding 28–10 lead. Montana was showing viewers who the best quarterback in the NFL was. "You could see it early. Joe played extremely well. I think he took it personally because of all the attention that a young guy who had never had a lot of success in the postseason was getting, while Joe obviously had won a Super Bowl. So I think he took that personally and he always seemed to do that his whole career," said offensive tackle Keith Fahnhorst.[23]

It was an amazing stretch of offense. In ten minutes and fifty-four seconds Bill Walsh's offense ran nineteen plays for 154 total yards and scored three touchdowns. After the offensive domination the 49ers defense relaxed. Marino found a groove against the 49ers nickel, completing six passes for seventy-two yards as the Dolphins settled for a field goal. The big play was a thirty-yard catch by tight end Joe Rose. The field goal left just twelve seconds remaining in the half. Next came a play that one 49er would rather forget. On the ensuing kickoff Uwe von Schamann kicked a low squib that dribbled down the middle of the field to the upbacks. Rookie guard Guy McIntyre scooped the ball up and went to his knees. He heard voices telling him to get up, so he stood and was hit squarely in the chest by Dolphins backup running back Joe Carter. McIntyre fumbled the ball. Jim Jensen recovered at the 49ers twelve-yard line. With four seconds remaining, von Schamann booted a thirty-yard field goal, giving the Dolphins six points in the final twelve seconds and cutting the 49ers lead to 28–16.

McIntyre remembers the fumble happening so fast. "Things are going, but it seems like things just stopped. It's surreal. You see it. You hear the crowd. And you know that these guys are coming down the field, and I picked it up because it's live [ball]. I think the whole stadium was telling me to get up and go. The ball's right there in front of me, and the running backs are behind me. Somebody's gotta get the ball. So I get it and by the time I get up, he hit me. They were down and he hit me right there. I'm not used to carrying the ball and he knocked it out. I tackle him and they got a field goal."[24]

Walking off the field, the Dolphins felt good. McIntyre did not. One of the team's veteran players made a point to offer encouragement to the distraught rookie. "I'm running off the field because right then it was halftime and what's running through my mind is, 'If we lose this game by three points, I'm running out of this stadium,'" recalled McIntyre. "I can remember Hacksaw Reynolds, we were running off the field, and he was like, 'Oh, don't worry about it. You've done good for this team.' He tried to encourage me. Picked me up."[25] McIntyre needn't have worried: the 49ers were a team on a mission. They played as a team. Twelve months of hard work wouldn't be defined by one play.

Al Michaels and Jim Lampley hosted ABC's halftime coverage that featured Cowboys head coach Tom Landry highlighting the touchdowns and key plays. The halftime entertainment was produced by the U.S. Air Force, which performed a magical fantasyland musical titled "The World of Children's Dreams." The show featured the Air Force's

1,000-member musical group, Tops in Blue, comprised of Air Force personnel from Mather Air Force Base in Sacramento, California.

Tops in Blue performed several contemporary songs with brisk choreography atop the largest piano ever constructed. The performance also included a salute to all the athletes who performed in the Summer Olympics in Los Angeles. As the show ended, the fog started to roll in off the bay. With the sun setting, the atmosphere in Stanford Stadium grew eerie as temperatures dropped below the kickoff temperature of 53 degrees. During the second half, players would be able to see their breath. Perfect 49ers weather.

21

SECOND HALF

While the halftime show played on, the 49ers coaches and players were going over their second-half adjustments. As Bill Walsh talked to the team, he felt his legs almost give out. "Halftime is long and I wasn't familiar with that locker room. The whole team is there and coach was at the blackboard. I was shooting low and I was laying down and he stepped back and almost tripped over me. He said 'Mike, it's the Super Bowl,'" said Michael Zagaris, 49ers team photographer.[1] Despite nearly falling over the team's photographer, Walsh would have his team ready for the second half.

The 49ers led 28–16, but the advantage felt larger. In the second quarter they dominated the Dolphins. George Seifert's nickel adjustment after the Dolphins scored ten early points made the difference. "Our nickel defense was really the key. It proved to be a diamond in the rough. Pretty much played the whole second half in our nickel defense, and they overwhelmed them," said George Seifert, defensive coordinator.[2] They exposed the Dolphins as a one-dimensional team. Dan Marino threw twenty-seven passes (seventeen completions for 179 yards) in the first half compared to just five runs (for a measly nine yards).

"They couldn't run against the nickel. You would just see those guys—Fred Dean and Pee-wee [Dwaine Board] and those guys—laying their ears back and pawing the ground. That was when—Marino's not a real quick guy to begin with—his feet got nervous, and right then you said, 'Fuck, this is over. If we don't let up on him it's done.' You go in at halftime. You basically said, 'If we don't fuck this up, we've got it,'" said

Jerry Attaway, physical development coordinator.[3] "Dwaine Board, Big Hands, Fred Dean, we came in at halftime. They said, 'Didn't get any sacks in the first half? We gotta turn up the pressure on this guy. We can't let him get back into the game.' So those guys put it on him," said Dana McLemore, defensive back.[4]

As for the offense, Bill Walsh was extremely pleased. The game plan was working perfectly with eighteen first downs, 288 total yards, and four touchdowns. Montana had gone thirteen of eighteen for 168 yards, and his forty-seven yards rushing contributed to 125 rushing yards in the first half. The third quarter would be more of the same.

With the fog rolling in, the Dolphins received the second-half kick-off. Time to unleash the elephant pass rush led by silent star Dwaine Board. On first down he pursued backside, running down Tony Nathan for a one-yard loss. Then on third down he beat right tackle Cleveland Green to sack Dan Marino—who was dropped only fourteen times all season. After several hits the 49ers defense had their first sack. "When I sacked him I looked at Marino and I said, 'Hey, we'll be right back,'" said Dwaine Board, defensive end.[5] "We were jetting all the time. We call it jetting. Just keying the ball and you're gone. You key the ball, play the run on the run. Shoot, it got where you knew the only thing they were going to do was pass," said Bill McPherson, defensive line coach.[6]

On the 49ers first drive of the second half they took over near mid-field without missing a beat. Montana connected with Wendell Tyler out of the backfield for fifteen yards. After Tyler ripped off seven yards, Montana used his legs again for a twelve-yard gain. His fifty-nine yards rushing set a new Super Bowl record by a quarterback, breaking the old mark of thirty-seven yards by Roger Staubach in Super Bowl XIII. For the first time in the red zone, the Dolphins defense—led by Chuck Studley—forced a field goal attempt. Ray Wersching trotted out to boot a twenty-seven-yard field goal to increase the 49ers lead to 31–16.

Behind by two touchdowns, it was now time for Dan Marino to show why he was the league's MVP. Instead he ran into the best pass rush in the NFL. After an eight-yard completion, George Seifert and Bill McPherson saw their front four attack the pocket. Up the middle, Manu Tuiasosopo brought Marino down for a sack. On the next play, left end Dwaine Board beat Cleveland Green again to drop Marino for another sack. The Dolphins had run six plays in the third quarter for minus ten yards and gave up three sacks. For an offensive line that had given up only fourteen all season, they were getting schooled by the 49ers pass rush.

"Excellent execution. Beautiful. I loved it. Anytime you get a sack, you get pumped up," said Bill McPherson, defensive line coach.[7] "I remember looking down [from booth] and Fred Dean and Big Hands were arguing about who was gonna be setup to get the next sack. They had such control over that situation," said George Seifert, defensive coordinator.[8]

The 49ers defensive line was taking over Super Bowl XIX. For two weeks they heard everybody talk about how to stop Dan Marino. They were showing the country how. They were also enjoying the moment. "The coaches just told us, 'Gear up and go, man. You get in that race stance and go.' We were yelling on the sideline. We couldn't wait to get back in, we couldn't wait till Marino got back out there so we could possibly get another sack," said defensive end Jeff Stover.[9] "I can hear Big Hands and Fred Dean. They were going at it. Big Hands telling Fred Dean, 'Hey Fred, you gotta do this because I think I'm gonna get my guy. I'm setting him up. I'm setting him up.' Then Fred Dean would say, 'Why is it always about you? You're always talking about you.' So it was kind of fun that they would interact that way. But it was all part of how they would challenge each other and then go out and do it. Then it was Pee-wee [Dwaine Board] and then Michael [Carter] and then Jeff Stover. Seeing how the guys were setting up their guys and just executing the different defenses and the interaction that was building in that second half," said Manu Tuiasosopo, defensive tackle.[10]

For 49ers fans in Stanford Stadium the cheering was getting louder. Joe Montana was outplaying his western Pennsylvania counterpart. The 49ers offense began their next drive at their own thirty-yard line. Walsh wanted to attack the Dolphins linebackers. Out of an I-formation Montana faked a handoff to Wendell Tyler, who went through the line at right guard, then beat inside linebacker Jay Brophy in man-to-man coverage by cutting to his left. Montana hit Tyler in stride, and he sprinted away from Brophy for a huge forty-yard gain. "They couldn't keep up with us. Wendell Tyler and I ate them alive. They couldn't keep up with us. We kept them off-balance," said fullback Roger Craig.[11] "It was a pass play and I came through the fake. There was a linebacker on me, I just made myself available. We were just better than their linebackers," said halfback Wendell Tyler.[12]

Montana then went back to Russ Francis for fourteen yards. Then another pass to Tyler for five yards, putting the ball at the Dolphins sixteen-yard line. Walsh quickly looked at his play sheet and called "20 Bingo Cross." At the snap Montana took a seven-step drop to let the patterns develop. Tyler lined up on the left of the backfield, he crossed first as Craig went second, crossing from right to left. Montana dumped an easy pass to a wide-open Craig, who then turned up the field at the ten-yard line and high-stepped untouched for an easy touchdown. The signature shot of Super Bowl XIX would be Roger Craig's high-stepping knees pumping untouched into the end zone as he held the ball high in the air. "Just tears and happiness and joy. I remember looking at Roger going into the end zone high stepping. I was like, 'Man, this is it. We got it now,'" said linebacker Blanchard Montgomery.[13]

Joe Montana heard the talk about Dan Marino all week. On the big stage he was proving to the world who the best quarterback in the NFL was. He pointed to the 49ers sidelines and yelled. He high-fived Randy Cross and Keith Fahnhorst. Roger Craig had just set a new Super Bowl record by scoring his third touchdown of the game. "It was like Roger's coming-out party," said Tyler.[14] The five-play, seventy-yard drive took just two minutes and twenty seconds. The 49ers led the most anticipated Super Bowl ever 38–16. Although there was 6:18 left in the third quarter, Super Bowl XIX was essentially over. The big score made one 49er extremely happy. "I'm feeling better. I'm feeling a lot better," said guard Guy McIntyre.[15]

Dan Marino was going to go down slinging it. After three straight completions for thirty-eight yards, it looked like he was going to get the Dolphins back on the scoreboard. Then from the 49ers twenty-seven-yard line, he went for the touchdown. Out of the shotgun Marino found Mark Clayton with man-to-man coverage. He was going to throw deep. Leaping high at the goal line, Eric Wright, running step-for-step with Clayton, outjumped him for a big interception at the one-yard line. Wright received hugs by his fellow secondary mates Ronnie Lott and Dwight Hicks. "Eric plays big and he plays long. When you throw fade balls and deep balls, I know Eric Wright is going to be able to out-athlete the receiver when the ball's in the air," said Ray Rhodes, defensive backs coach.[16]

Backed-up, Montana guided his team to three first downs, gaining in the field position battle. As the drive stalled early in the fourth quarter Max Runager pinned the Dolphins back at their own twenty-one.

Gary "Big Hands" Johnson then bull-rushed up the middle to drop Marino on his backside. It was the 49ers fourth sack of the second half. "Once they started getting in his face, obviously the complexity of the game changed," said Louis Kelcher, defensive tackle. "I was so proud of Gary [Johnson] and the guys. There were a lot of big plays in there. It was great watching it play itself out."[17] George Seifert was in the zone. He just kept calling his nickel defense. He would give up the short yardage but nothing deep. Marino tried his best to go deep to Clayton again, but Ronnie Lott was all over the pass. Another Dolphins punt. On the kick the 49ers had their second special teams gaff. Returner Dana McLemore muffed the punt, which was recovered by the Dolphins at the 49ers twenty-one-yard line.

On the first play after the fumble the 49ers defense put an exclamation point on their work. Rolling out to his right, Marino forced a pass to the back of the end zone to tight end Joe Rose. Out of nowhere, strong safety Carlton Williamson dove in front of Rose for the interception. Williamson had played with Marino at Pitt for two years, but this time he denied him a score. "He just kind of unloaded the ball. He kind of threw a floater out there where the receiver broke one way and the ball went another way. I read the ball the whole time and was able to go get it," said Williamson.[18]

With 10:45 left in the quarter the 49ers began an eight-minute march to run out the clock. Turning the ball over on downs, the 49ers left the Dolphins at their own three-yard line. "That crescendo at the end of the last five minutes of the fourth quarter kept building. It was magical," said linebacker Riki Ellison.[19] After a few meaningless plays Marino fumbled a shotgun snap, recovering it himself as the clock ran out on Super Bowl XIX. "When that clock ticked down, that's just a moment in time that I'm going to have the rest of my life and I'll never forget it," said defensive end Jeff Stover. "The clock ticks off. You sit there. It's almost like you're stunned. 'Did this really happen? Am I really in a Super Bowl? Did I really win?' And all of sudden, yeah, you did and everybody goes bananas."[20]

The celebration had begun at Stanford Stadium. "I'm just ecstatic. I'm looking up. I'm pointing to my mom somewhere up in the 80,000 people. I know she's up there, and I'm pointing up to her," said guard Guy McIntyre. "I'm just pointing; hopefully she sees me. It was a dream come true. What more can you ask for your rookie year?"[21] "I remember Ray and Max came over and we hugged one another. I put my arm around them said, 'Good job.' Then the crowd hits you," said Fred vonAppen, special teams coach.[22]

"I was able to look up and see my parents and a lot of my family up there because they weren't too far behind us on our bench. My father coached me. We worked together when I got started. A lot of his hard work and efforts paid off. I couldn't wipe the smile off his face. To share that with them, as well, was a dream. An absolutely dream," said punter Max Runager.[23] "It was one of the greatest feelings to experience with regard to my football career. I hugged everybody there that I could," said defensive tackle Manu Tuiasosopo. "It was just surreal and it was great. I'd look up in the stands and try to find my family and my wife. It was just awesome to say, 'Wow, here we are.'"[24]

Super Bowl XIX ended at 6:31 p.m. local time (9:31 EST). The 49ers players gathered around their coach. Two players lifted him up on their shoulders. "I was in a state of shock that we had won. I was in a daze, you know, coming from Buffalo and not really winning. I was just walking and Bill Walsh was right there, and I don't know, it was just instinctual, I just grabbed him . . . and for me I was just so proud of Bill and what he had done. It was a respect thing, really, and I grabbed him and I think Guy McIntyre was the other guy who grabbed him on the other side. It was just a wonderful victory, I can't believe it," said Mario Clark.[25] For nearly twenty seconds a smiling Bill Walsh sat on the shoulders of Mario Clark and Guy McIntyre, once raising both arms above his head in triumph.

Emotions for all the 49ers started to spill out. "It's something I'll never forget. It's electrifying, walking off the field. I feel the goose bumps thinking about it. It's just a special time for anybody who plays sports to say we're the best right now," said Louie Kelcher, defensive tackle.[26] "It was the game of my life. I didn't want it to end. It was that kind of experience for me. I wanted to find a way to get back out on the field and play and run around. It could've gone on forever," said linebacker Michael Walter.[27]

"Seeing those last seconds tick off and having to believe that it was actually true: reality is on your side. Speechless. Then we're running off the field; you always see those NFL Films cameras in one player's face and he holds up the number one [finger]. That is what made me know that it was real and I was not dreaming. I was running off the field; I'm moving there, then I turned around, there is the NFL camera staring me in the face. I held up the number one and I was not that flaunty; I would never do that. It's real; we did it! Here's the camera. I tell you what, that was better than sliced bread," said linebacker Blanchard Montgomery.[28]

Walking off the field, safety Carlton Williamson stopped to chat with his former college teammate Dan Marino, who completed twenty-nine of fifty passes and had two interceptions. "It was very brief. I asked him, 'How are you, man? You alright? I know we got to you a few times.' He said, 'No, I'm good, C. W., I'm fine.' I said, 'Well, you guys will be back next year,' which I really thought they would be. I said, 'You guys will be back. You're a fighter.' But it was just a brief 'hi,' a handshake. I just wanted to make sure he was OK," said Williamson.[29] Dan Marino would go on to play seventeen years in the NFL. This would be his only Super Bowl appearance.

Bill Walsh had led the 49ers to their second Super Bowl win in four years. He helped guide a 49ers offense that generated a Super Bowl–record 537 total yards. He also had the best quarterback. Joe Montana had outdueled Dan Marino and was named the game's MVP for the second time. He completed twenty-four of thirty-five passes for 331 yards and three touchdowns. He also ran for fifty-nine yards and another touchdown. He accounted for 390 total yards and four touchdowns. Walsh and Montana received a lot of the publicity but Super Bowl XIX was definitely a team victory. "Everybody just did what they were supposed to do and no one messed up," said Allan Kennedy, offensive tackle.[30]

On the defensive side George Seifert's near-flawless game plan proved to a lot of critics that Dan Marino and the Dolphins passing attack could be stopped. No other Super Bowl had seen a combination of pass rush and coverage like the 1984 49ers had just demonstrated. "Those guys up front—Fred Dean, Dwaine Board, Michael Carter— those guys played one heck of a game that day. I think that made the difference for us in the secondary. I'd never seen Marino hit as much as he was hit that game. They were rushing him. They put a lot of pressure on him. That made our job a lot more easy and fun," said Williamson.[31]

As the 49ers dodged fans, security, photographers, and cameramen to make their way across the field at Stanford Stadium to the locker room, many thoughts filled their heads. "Can we duplicate this? Can we really do this again? Is this really us getting this job done, to annihilate a team that good and finish it off with such preciseness, with such control? It's almost like you don't want it to end because you don't know if you can ever jumpstart it again," said tight end Earl Cooper. "We're turning and looking up in the stands at our loved ones and our friends and all the people we have shared close moments with at that time to say, 'Hey, we did it. We did it again.' It was expected in '84 but to come back and do it [again]? When it's expected of you, and you put all that together with that kind of preciseness, with that kind of emotion, with that kind of sensitivity, it just makes it so special."[32]

Once inside the locker room one 49ers coach found a little peace within the celebration. "There was always a great sense of frivolity, glee, and hugging. Then there was that moment when you walked away from all that and you were able to sit down at your locker and really savor the moment. There was an inner peace, you might say," said George Seifert, defensive coordinator.[33]

22

AFTERMATH

That's the strength of the ball club. We were motivated basically for every game. We played with the same intensity, play after play, throughout the season and this was typical of it. This is the best game I believe we played. We were ready for it, and I can't say enough of the resourcefulness of all 49er players because all of them contributed.

—Bill Walsh to ABC-TV in the 49ers locker room[1]

Entering the locker room, each 49er was greeted by one happy owner. "Eddie DeBartolo met us at the front of the locker room and gave everybody a big hug and thanked us. We didn't have any champagne, though, no champagne," said Mario Clark, cornerback.[2] The lack of champagne—an NFL rule prohibited it—didn't slow the biggest celebration that the Bay area ever saw. DeBartolo and his father greeted every coach and player coming through the door. Eddie D. hugged almost every person who came through. "We did it, Mr. D.!" yelled Eric Wright while bear-hugging DeBartolo.[3] A few moments later Wright, Dwight Hicks, and Keena Turner gathered in a circle hugging the team's owner.

Turner then hugged Joe Montana, who had just put on a 49ers baseball cap and opened a can of Pepsi. Ronnie Lott entered, hooting and hollering. "Just elation. I remember hugging guys. Eric Wright. We did it. We embraced. Just loved it, because you just knew what that [win] represented," said linebacker Keena Turner. "Mr. D. was just unbelievable. He set a standard. Bill created the environment for that standard to be met. It was a combination of those folks. Without any of those pieces, I don't know that it happens, because I think the pieces are that important."[4] When Bill Walsh walked in, he shook Eddie Sr.'s hand and hugged Eddie Jr.

Veterans and rookies celebrated together. Some players yelled and carried on while others just observed. "I was taking everything in. Everything I saw before was on TV. To be able to be there in person was surreal. I'm sitting there and watching how excited a lot of the players are, even older veterans, ones who were there in '81. Then all of a sudden you have people like Joe Montana and Roger Craig and Ronnie Lott—they're running around like little schoolgirls, jumping and hollering and dancing. Wow, this is something. So as a rookie I sat back and watched it," said defensive tackle Michael Carter, who in one calendar year graduated from college, got drafted into the NFL, won an Olympic silver medal, got married, and won a Super Bowl ring.[5]

It was bedlam in the 49ers locker room. Coaches, players, staff members, and ownership were together as one. The entire organization mingled and enjoyed the moment without the media, without the outside world. "Total elation. What an accomplishment to go 18–1. Nobody had done it. It was really elation and thankfulness to do it for the guys and the coaching staff. We did this together," said defensive end Jim Stuckey.[6] "I was happy to see joy in other people's faces. It was a joy for me to see joy in Roger's face. It was a joy for me to see joy in Ronnie Lott's face. Because as little kids, that was what they dreamed about. That's what I dreamed about. To see that come to reality is a memory that I won't forget. In your life you can get trophies, but the trophies rust. But those little snapshots of the locker room, they're in my heart," said halfback Wendell Tyler.[7]

The team that played all season as one big family was now cherishing the moment as world champions. Every person in the 49ers organization savored the moment even when it brought them to tears. "It was a whole family atmosphere—these were your brothers [with whom] you went through good times and bad times [and] the fulfillment of a great journey. I remember Bill [Walsh] saying at the time that [we were] the best team he has seen. It was huge. We felt that we accomplished a goal that we set out to do," said kicker Ray Wersching.[8] "I'm one of the ones who's not ashamed [of] emotion. Your tears are coming down. You're crying because you're so excited for the organization, for the players, and for the city of San Francisco and the Bay area. It's something you just can't fathom. I'm serious. You're emotional. The tears are flowing. I'm not going to lie to you. Tears are flowing. That's a hell of accomplishment," said Ray Rhodes, defensive backs coach.[9]

GAME BALL

As the emotions continued to build in the 49ers locker room, the players slowly gathered around their head coach "I had the opportunity to watch the whole team interact with Bill Walsh and the coaching staff right after the game. You start to see the emotions, the inner emotions of the team. People were crying. People were laughing. I saw George [Seifert] smiling for the first time," said Carter. "I was just sitting back taking it in. I'm not a very emotional person. I'm just sitting there watching. I'm like, 'there's something special here.'"[10]

Bill Walsh was smiling from ear to ear as he raised his arms to get the attention of his players. "Let's get it together, men," shouted Walsh.[11] All of the players and coaches gathered in a circle around Walsh and DeBartolo and took a knee. The whole squad then recited the Lord's Prayer. Standing up, the players cheered as Walsh gave DeBartolo another hug. Stepping forward to stand in front of Walsh, Dwight Hicks raised his right arm to get his teammates' attention. "Take a knee, everybody, one more time," yelled Hicks. All of the players kneeled as well as Coach Walsh. Hicks spoke up, "First of all, nobody knew what kind of offense we had. It was their offense. Our offense showed them." Continued Hicks, "And then! How in the hell are we going to stop Duper, Clayton, and Marino? Nobody knew but us."[12]

Players started to clap and cheer. Facing his teammates, Hicks raised a football over his head. The locker room was now silent. "Game ball," said Hicks before pausing and turning to face a kneeling Walsh, "to Coach Bill Walsh."[13] Instantly the locker room exploded, growing even louder as players and coaches cheered as Hicks handed the game ball to a smiling Bill Walsh. "Really, how deserving. How [appropriate] that Dwight Hicks stepped up and gave Bill Walsh the game ball. Tears came to some people's eyes, and we just cheered [in appreciation of the] game plan he put together for us and helped us to execute. It's just like writing a perfect story," said Earl Cooper, tight end. [14]

Walsh raised the ball high in the air with both hands. It was a moment Walsh would always cherish when he reflected on winning his second Super Bowl. "One other event made the game very special for me. The players awarded me the game ball with Dwight Hicks making the presentation. I didn't think much of it at the time, being overwhelmed by all the excitement, as I did later, when I realized how much it meant to be awarded the game ball for the world championship. It was the nicest acknowledgement the players could give me," wrote Walsh in his autobiography. [15]

"It was almost a surprise to give the game ball to Bill Walsh. It just gave me goose bumps because Bill deserved the ball," said Jerry Walker, director of public relations. [16] "He was extremely confident [going into that game]. He had worked hard to get this. He always wanted the perfect game, and this game was, in his eyes, the closest to a perfect game in his career," said Craig Walsh, son of Bill Walsh. [17]

PRESENTATION OF THE SUPER BOWL TROPHY

Moments after Walsh received the game ball, ABC-TV was allowed in the locker room. It was now time for the commissioner to present the Lombardi Trophy to the 49ers. On a makeshift stage NFL commissioner Pete Rozelle handed the Super Bowl trophy to Bill Walsh and Eddie DeBartolo, calling the victory a "great performance." Jim Lampley of ABC then asked DeBartolo how it felt to win his second Super Bowl in four years. "Guys, I love you. Coach Walsh, his staff, we're the best. We are the best! We're going to continue to be the best. I'm just very proud of everybody we put together through Coach Walsh and his organization. Commissioner, thank you. This trophy belongs to Bill Walsh and his assistant coaches, our organization, and these great players, my pals!" yelled DeBartolo as the players cheered in the background.

Lampley then told the 49ers coach and owner that there was a phone call from the East Coast from a very special guest. President Ronald Reagan was on the line: "Coach Walsh, there ought to be a better word than 'congratulations' for all that we saw tonight and what you and your team have accomplished. But I just want to say congratulations to you and, of course, congratulations to Joe Montana for his being picked and for the performance of all of that team. . . . Now that the season's over and you fellows don't have anything to do for a while, I have to go up on the Hill and deal with Congress in a few days. How would you like to come back? . . . I could use a front-line four." Walsh responded by saying, "I think we'll stick to football."

"I guess as a coach, you couldn't have asked for anything greater than they gave you tonight. God Bless you all, and it was great," finished Reagan. After the president hung up DeBartolo handed the trophy to Walsh as Lampley turned his attention to the 49ers head coach. Lampley asked him if he was ever concerned about winning the game. Walsh said he knew it was going to be tough and sometimes "I wonder[ed] if we could even score." But he congratulated the players who played outstanding football and told Lampley, "I think this is one of the best teams of all time."

Lampley then asked if lack of motivation had ever been an issue for the team as they made the season look easy with an 18–1 record. "That's the strength of the ball club. We were motivated basically for every game. We played with the same intensity, play after play, throughout the season and this was typical of it. This is the best game I believe we played. We were ready for it, and I can't say enough of the resourcefulness of all 49er players because all of them contributed."[18]

NATIONAL MEDIA

All forty-nine players contributed to every win during the 1984 season. (Including those with injuries, a total of fifty-two players won Super Bowl rings.) They set a goal to be world champion and they accomplished it. As the Super Bowl trophy was passed around, several players were escorted away from their teammates to talk to the national media. "The locker room was makeshift. They were made for the Super Bowl. So the postgame press conferences were outside the equipment room door. So the media is right there. It's cramped. You got very little space. It seemed like it took a long time. You wouldn't think that it would take as long because everyone was on a deadline and stuff, but it seemed like the postgame took forever. It seemed like we were there for hours rather than just an hour after the game," said Jerry Walker, director of public relations.[19]

The 49ers coaches and players spoke of nearly perfect game plans. "We did something everybody said couldn't be done. We put pressure on Marino. We sacked him and we blitzed less than usual," remarked Keena Turner after the game.[20] Thirty years later, some 49ers defensive players recognized an unsung hero of Super Bowl XIX. "Nobody gives that credit to George [Seifert] and how he choreographed that team. You probably can ask him. That was probably one of the greatest game plans he's ever done and executed that night. It came together. The pass rush and the coverage came together in a perfect world. I don't think we made any mistakes," said Riki Ellison, linebacker.[21]

SUPER BOWL TROPHY LEFT IN LOCKER ROOM

As the 49ers coaches and players left the locker room one priceless item was almost left behind. "After we won the game, everybody was excited and they brought the Super Bowl trophy into the locker room. They took pictures of Eddie and Bill with the trophy and Montana and so on," said John McVay, 49ers vice president and general manager. "I was one of the last guys left in the locker room just after everybody had left. And [it's] funny, the janitor came up to me and he had the Super Bowl trophy. He says, 'What do you want to do with this trophy?' I said, 'I'll take it.' I mean, everybody just walked off and left. Nobody thought to bring the trophy home."[22]

A SUBDUED CELEBRATION

Since the Super Bowl was at home, most of the 49ers went straight home to celebrate with their families. "It was kind of a good thing and bad thing in a way. There was nothing planned. There were no big parties. It was really weird. I took the bus back to Redwood City, got back in my car, went back to my apartment, and met with my family there because there was nothing organized. It was kind of strange," said linebacker Michael Walter. No Super Bowl celebration was one drawback of having the big game just minutes from home.[23]

One 49er spent the Super Bowl in a Bay area hospital. Jim Fahnhorst watched the 49ers victory while keeping his sister-in-law company. "I watched the Super Bowl with her in the hospital room. I was hoping to be on the sidelines. They said if I was off the crutches that I could. But the NFL said I couldn't. There was no way I could be up in the stands because of the brace. So I sat in her hospital room with my wife and Sue in the hospital," said Jim Fahnhorst. "It was awesome [watching them win], it was great."

After the game Keith Fahnhorst just wanted to get home to his wife and new baby, who were released from the hospital moments after the Super Bowl. But Fahnhorst had a hard time getting home because he missed the team bus back to the 49ers facility. "John Ayers and I ended up hitchhiking to Redwood City after the game. We got picked up by a couple of cops and they gave us a ride home. I went to my townhouse up in San Carlos and spent the evening there with my wife and the new baby," said offensive tackle Keith Fahnhorst.[24]

SUPER BOWL PARADE

The day after winning Super Bowl XIX, 49ers went in two different directions. One group—ten players—went to Hawaii for the Pro Bowl while the other group attended the Super Bowl victory parade on Monday. "That was amazing. That was just beautiful to see the city come together. Mayor [Dianne] Feinstein was there. It was fun. It was really cool to see everyone come out and celebrate," said fullback Roger Craig.[25]

For the members of the 49ers who participated in the parade, it was a memory they have never forgotten as nearly half a million fans came out to celebrate the team's Super Bowl win. Coach Walsh, Eddie De-Bartolo, and Mayor Dianne Feinstein rode together in one vehicle and the rest of the team followed in trolleys. Thirty years later they remember it as one of the highlights of their playing careers. "Oh, that was fantastic. I had never been involved with anything that big and that exciting as far as the whole city turning out. You're seeing people hanging on buildings, ticker tape, and all that stuff. People yelling, screaming. Everybody yelling 'Niners!' It was great. It was fantastic," said guard Guy McIntyre.[26]

"There is nothing like [it] with the fans and the fulfillment of [seeing] how excited and enthused they are. They are fanatic fans. I don't know how many were there; hundreds of thousands of people lined the streets. This is all for us? You gotta be kidding. It just felt great. You felt appreciated. You can't believe this left an impact like this for the general public and the fans. This is a big thing. Again you feel really appreciated that they loved the game so much," said kicker Ray Wersching.[27]

The victory parade was a chance for the 49ers to give thanks to all the fans and to a city that had supported them for nearly forty years. "Oh, it was great. People were everywhere. People were in trees. It was a great feeling! And the fans—San Francisco's got great fans. They love their teams and it was great. Just unbelievable," said defensive end Dwaine Board.[28] "That was wonderful. My mouth got tired of smiling and grinning," said defensive tackle Michael Carter. "But it was great to see the city excited and all the people excited about the 49ers winning the Super Bowl."[29]

"That was fun. Just taking pride that you could bring so much joy and so much happiness to the people there. That was powerful," said linebacker Riki Ellison. "To go down Market Street in the parade and have people yell and scream [with] happiness and joy. That felt very, very good."[30] "The people in San Francisco and the surrounding area, they love the 49ers. It was a great time to be part of it and they showed their love by turning out that day," said defensive tackle Louie Kelcher. "It really does make you appreciate who you are and what you do. It kind of makes you appreciate what you're doing it for. It's the people who are buying the tickets and showing up every Sunday. That was exciting."[31]

Less than fifteen hours after winning Super Bowl XIX ten 49ers boarded a plane to Hawaii. "It was a big sigh of relief, at least for my part. I felt like it's finally over; we did it. We proved that we could do it again. We deserved to be in this arena and we've shown the world we were an even better team than we were in 1981. So it was just a lot of excitement, a lot of relaxing or exhaling," said strong safety Carlton Williamson. "There was no big celebration that I knew of because a lot of us were getting a 9:00 a.m. flight out of San Francisco to Hawaii the next morning."[32]

PRO BOWL

When the Pro Bowl was the week after the Super Bowl, one of the big perks for players attending was to play in the game as a newly crowned Super Bowl champion. Ten 49ers—Randy Cross, Keith Fahnhorst, Dwight Hicks, Ronnie Lott, Joe Montana, Fred Quillan, Keena Turner, Wendell Tyler, Carlton Williamson, and Eric Wright—got that chance in the 1985 Pro Bowl. "It was a great celebration being there. We felt like we didn't do very much after the Super Bowl [due to the subdued celebration] but going to Hawaii, ten of us were there. So it was great to have that representation in the locker room. Then when we would go to dinner and have dinner together, that was wonderful. It was just a great experience out there. Knowing that we were Super Bowl champs, it gave us great pride, it really did," said Carlton Williamson.[33]

During the game a rival coach allowed members of the 49ers secondary a moment that they would cherish for a lifetime. Because they lost the NFC Conference Championship Game, the staff of the Chicago Bears coached the NFC squad. Three weeks earlier Bears defensive coordinator Buddy Ryan tried to beat the 49ers. But in the Pro Bowl, he played all four 49ers defensive backs on the field at the same time, something that had never happened before in a Pro Bowl.

"You know, we commend Buddy Ryan. Because we didn't know at any time if he was going to allow all of us to be on the field at one time. And he did. I get goose bumps even thinking about it. It was such a great feeling being in a huddle in the Pro Bowl and there are four 49er helmets in the secondary all at once. I was really pleased that he did that," said Williamson. "He allowed us to have that moment and it was just great. It was a great way to end a super season."[34]

A SPORTS ILLUSTRATED COVER

A few days after the game was over, another big milestone was bestowed on one 49er. Second-year fullback Roger Craig was featured on the January 28, 1985, cover of *Sports Illustrated*.[35] In an action shot by *SI* photographer Heinz Kluetmeier, Craig was shown scoring his third touchdown of the game under the headline: "The Niners Nail 'Em." The cover boy was shocked when he found out he was on the cover. "I was going back home to the Midwest and someone said, 'Did you see *Sports Illustrated*? You're on *Sports Illustrated*.' I'm like 'What?' We're in the airport. I'm like, 'Oh, my gosh. I'm on the cover of *Sports Illustrated*!' That was amazing," said fullback Roger Craig.[36]

SUPER BOWL TROPHY AT THE 49ERS FACILITY

"The one moment I do remember following that game wasn't necessarily the parade. Bill called the staff [together] at our facility in Redwood City—all of the people in the facility, whether you were a secretary or involved in the business aspects or scouts. We were all right next to one another. Bill called the staff into our meeting room, which was the size of a large closet. [He was] sitting there holding that second Super Bowl trophy. He had the other one, as well—the first one. And holding that and the look of pride on his face and the emotion that he had, you could tell that inner sense and feeling that you accomplished something. That came out in him at that particular moment. That was a pretty neat thing. It's embedded in my mind," said George Seifert, defensive coordinator.[37]

23

LEGACY OF THE 1984
SAN FRANCISCO 49ERS

Three months after winning Super Bowl XIX Bill Walsh was not resting on his laurels. In the 1985 NFL draft he traded up to select Mississippi Valley State wide receiver Jerry Rice in the first round. Selecting Rice showed that Walsh was ahead of everybody else. Three years after drafting Rice, the greatest receiver of all time, the 49ers won Super Bowl XXIII against the Cincinnati Bengals. Walsh cried in the locker room next to his son Craig, knowing that was his last game as 49ers head coach. A few days later George Seifert replaced his mentor and friend as the head man. Seifert would go on to win two more Super Bowls in 1989 and 1994.

From 1981 to 1998 the 49ers had seventeen winning seasons in eighteen years, winning at least ten or more games in each of those seventeen seasons. In that span the 49ers won a total of 230 games (including postseason), thirteen division championships, and five Super Bowls. Over that time period Eddie DeBartolo's leadership and Bill Walsh's standard of performance (as well as his West Coast offense) became the model for how NFL organizations were operated. They were not only the team of the 1980s, they were the future of the NFL.

As for the 1984 49ers, they are immortalized as one of the greatest teams to ever play in the NFL. They set more than thirty team and individual records during the 1984 season; they became the first team to sweep their conference and divisional games in a sixteen-game regular season; they had ten Pro Bowlers, four future Hall of Famers

(Walsh, Dean, Lott, and Montana), and had set or tied twelve different Super Bowl records. They were the first team in NFL history to go 15–1 and win eighteen games in one season. They were one play away from a perfect season.

During the postseason they defeated three teams that would make their own marks in NFL history. In the divisional round they defeated the New York Giants (21–10), who two years later would win the Super Bowl. In the NFC Championship game they shut out the Chicago Bears (23–0), who in 1986 won the Super Bowl. Then in the Super Bowl they destroyed the Miami Dolphins (38–16), who had lost only two games and had one of the greatest offensive seasons in NFL history. They outscored their opponents 82–26 and gave up only one offensive touchdown in those three playoff games. Not only did they lose just one game during the regular season, they arguably endured one of the toughest postseason stretches in NFL history. They earned it the hard way.

But the 1984 49ers were never about statistics, records, or individual accomplishments. The whole team's personality and soul was about being a team—one heartbeat. They were driven by a single defeat against the Washington Redskins in the 1983 NFC Championship. While in that locker room at RFK Stadium, a whole organization vowed to never feel defeated again. So for the next year they woke up every day trying to achieve that single goal. They strove for perfection. Over the course of nineteen games they nearly achieved it, ultimately proving to themselves and to the rest of the sports world that nobody is perfect. But one can try.

No other team in NFL history had as much focus, dedication, and relentless work ethic as the 1984 49ers. They had one singular motive all year—to win the Super Bowl. For one owner, eleven coaches, fifty-two players, and an entire support staff, the 1984 season was unforgettable even thirty years later. You could feel how much that season meant to them. Every interview I asked the question, "After thirty years, what is your lasting memory of the 1984 season? What was it like, not just winning the Super Bowl, but going through the journey to get there?" Many used some of the same words to describe the process required to be a champion. But one of the themes they all used was that they truly "loved and cared" about each other while trying to achieve the goal of becoming a Super Bowl champion.

The legacy of the 1984 49ers isn't necessarily that they set records, won games, and were Super Bowl champions. It's a given that they were one of the greatest teams to ever play in NFL history, but their legacy is the friendships and memories they created for each other knowing they had earned everything they achieved throughout that 1984 season. These are their own words about what the 1984 season meant to them.

1984 SAN FRANCISCO 49ERS MEMORIES[1]

Jerry Attaway, physical development coordinator: "They just played hard all the time. The coaching staff and the team, it was fun. It was successful. It was a lot of work, but when I think back about the best teams that I was around that's the best one."

Dwaine Board, defensive end: "As a team, we did it together. I think one thing that I'm grateful for is to play with the guys that I did. Because it was a great group of guys. I mean, totally great group of players and people."

Dan Bunz, linebacker: "I'm just happy to be a part of that group of guys. I'm happy to be even mentioned in the same breath because I have great respect for all of those guys. You know, Keena Turner, Eric Wright, Dwight Hicks, Ronnie Lott, Fred Dean—come on now—they're all characters, and to actually be able to direct them on defense and then move outside and work more with the defensive backs again, I don't even know how to say it. It's just sometimes you don't realize what you've done until you do sit back and reflect."

Michael Carter, defensive tackle: "I told my wife what we were all involved in during that year span, from the draft all the way through the Super Bowl, that was a lot [including the Olympics]. We went through each and every piece of it and everything just fell in line. By the grace of God, everything was a blessing. I can sit down and catch my breath. But I don't think that will ever happen to anyone else ever again. . . . That team was the best team of all the teams. There were a lot of accolades to go around with other teams but that one was special because of what we all put together going from losing just one game during the regular season and rolling through the playoffs. That was special. Because when you look at the faces—Ronnie Lott and the defensive backs—they were relatively young. Then you look at Joe Montana, Dwight Clark, Roger Craig, and Wendell Tyler. There were a lot of names and a lot of veterans who came from other teams to join that. You had a great mixture of folks and players on that team who came together and put together a championship team. And they all got along and performed as one team."

Mario Clark, cornerback: "It was a wonderful experience. It was something that will stay with you till the end of your days. The camaraderie, the togetherness—we all really loved one another. . . . We were a team and whatever each individual had to do to accomplish whatever, everybody was down with that. Everybody was on the same page and it was a beautiful thing."

Earl Cooper, tight end: "It's meant an awful lot. Like I say, there are friends I can call on. There are friends I can visit. There are people I can go to. The ones who have passed on, I truly miss. I think about Bill [Walsh] and John Ayers a lot, John being a Texas boy himself. R. C. Owens, Freddie Solomon, Billy Wilson, Bobb McKittrick. And when you lose people like that, it really makes you rewind and remember all the great moments and the great times that you had. . . . When you're living in the moment, you don't really appreciate a history that you're making and what you're a part of. You know you're a part of something special, but at twenty-six, twenty-seven years old, it doesn't really hit you like it does when you retire and you start reflecting back on what you've accomplished in life. Not as a person but as a team, because for people to come from all over the United States and to come together as one and be that machine and do the things that we did in 1984—be led by a great group of guys and be part of a great organization—you just can't duplicate that."

Roger Craig, fullback: "We felt that we could conquer any team that came our way. There was no selfishness. We were one heartbeat. We believed in one another. There was no animosity in the locker room, who was getting paid more or who was getting the ball more. It was like we shared the ball with everyone. It was a great environment, work environment to be in."

Fred Dean, defensive end: "That was a great team and a lot of it was the team. You could accredit it to a lot of different things: the coaching staff, the people, the fans. I'm saying they all were a big part of it. . . . I can remember it as all loving memories."

Riki Ellison, linebacker: "I think the greatness of that team was the diversity of that team. We came from different walks of the United States, came from different backgrounds, and loved each other for that entire season. That chemistry was so powerful on that one team. I would include the coaches in that. I remember that team being invincible. No matter who the opponent was, no matter what the weather, no matter what the calls were, we were invincible. We could beat anybody, at anytime, anywhere. We had that feeling for the entire season. Even that Pittsburgh loss we had that feeling. You gotta give Bill [Walsh] credit for that entire orchestration. That was the perfect season for me. That was more perfect than any other Super Bowl. You can ask the other guys. I played in three of them. This was the most perfect one I felt that I've played in."

Jim Fahnhorst, linebacker: "Going back on that year, it was my first year in the NFL and it was a dream season for me although I did get hurt. It was an amazing year. I remember walking into a rental car place and they recognized me and then driving down 101 and the fans honking at me and saying 'Go Niners!' It was just awesome. The fans are just great. The team was great; everybody got along. This was the most selfless team that I ever been part of."

Keith Fahnhorst, offensive tackle: "I always thought that that was one of the best teams that ever played the game, and I still believe that to this day. So there was a lot of pride in that. We had a reunion of all five Super Bowl teams in Vegas a few years ago. It was just a bunch of old guys hugging each other, telling them how much they loved each other, and it was true. We did love each other and it was a special thing."

Ron Ferrari, linebacker: "I remember thinking 'I'm gonna get a ring!' It's unbelievable. 'I'm going to get a ring!' It was fun then to think about the prize. . . . . You think about it, but you don't even really care about the prize, honestly. I care about the process. I care about the coaches. I care about the owner. I care about the players. . . . The secret sauce was the people. I know Bill [Walsh] thought he had something special. What Bill didn't know [was] if we were going to get along with each other. We not only got along, we absolutely loved each other. Of course, that was always modeled by our owner. Bill loved us. He tried to stay away and act like a coach, but we knew he cared. It was a season we actually never wanted to stop. I mean we could've played ten, fifteen more games. It was that much fun."

Paul Hackett, quarterback and wide receiver coach: "We set out on a mission in Rocklin. This was the culmination. The swelling of people feeling good about themselves, accomplishing their goals, and being on top of the world . . . that's really what we had done."

Derrick Harmon, running back: "It feels magical. [I was] lucky to be part of it and happy to be a part of it. Little kid's dreams came true. I made wonderful friends. It is a great organization; [it] had a great coach. Job well done in a 1,000 different ways. I wouldn't have had it any other way. Fun times and great memories."

Tom Holmoe, safety: "You just see everybody on the sidelines and that's what you play for. You play for the win, but to see everybody else on the sideline in jubilee, it was awesome. I get goose bumps just thinking about it right now. Looking back, it's probably more meaningful now. When you think about how hard it was, but we got through it and we have stayed friends for so long—including Mr. DeBartolo and Bill [Walsh], all the coaches, all the players, our equipment managers, everyone in the organization—that was why we won. Because we had great personnel, great coaches, but we loved each other. There's no other word. We loved each other and we still do."

Louie Kelcher, defensive tackle: "How they made you feel welcome. The sense of family I got that we're all here to take care of each other. I think a lot of love was involved. I think there was a special relationship between Mr. DeBartolo and the team and players. He showed it a lot. Then relationships: the guys you went to work with every day. The friendships that we made out of it that lasted, can last a lifetime."

Allan Kennedy, offensive tackle: "I know that year we had a number of Pro Bowlers but everybody did what they were asked to do and not more. A very unselfish team. It starts with the owner there who gave us everything we could possibly want. For us to return that favor was to give him the trophy."

Guy McIntyre, guard: "It's like you're living a fantasy and you didn't want to wake up. It's just powerful. It just doesn't seem like it was that long [ago]. But it was great. To now look back on it and see that was just another piece of a magnificent puzzle that I was able to experience. It was just a magical year. It was. I'm just thankful to be a part of it."

Dana McLemore, cornerback: "Great bunch of guys. Everybody got along real well. Everyone had each other's back. Never had any issues with the players. Never had anything of that on Niner teams."

Bill McPherson, defensive line coach: "It was one of the all-time greatest seasons to win that many games and to have the group that I had to work with. They made me look like I knew what I was doing. . . . It was really a great effort."

John McVay, vice president and general manager: "As I look back on it, that was probably, if not the most talented team . . . not to take away from any of the other teams that we had that were equally talented—but it just seemed that, that team was exceptionally talented."

Blanchard Montgomery, linebacker: "I think everything lined up from the top to the bottom starting with Eddie D. down to the equipment man. Everybody was 100 percent focused on winning and accomplishing it."

Renaldo Nehemiah, wide receiver: Well, for me, to have carved a path from the great Joe Montana and to play with Ronnie Lott and Russ Francis and Hacksaw Reynolds. . . . We had a star-studded team. So I always pinch myself because I'd go, 'Wow, that was an amazing team that I played for.'"

Lawrence Pillers, defensive end: "They [coaches and teammates] brought out the best in me. They motivated me maybe when I was down. They lifted me up. We became not only a football player or a football team, we became a family. We became close. We did something that a lot of other individuals wanted to do and we did it at home. We won the Super Bowl at our house."

Ray Rhodes, defensive back coach: "As far as my career's concerned, I really felt like that year in particular was probably the biggest year for me in football. Because I had a chance to be part of a group on the back end where they all went to the Pro Bowl. We go 18–1. We won a Super Bowl at home in San Francisco. I don't think you could ask for anything better. You couldn't."

Bill Ring, fullback: "Some of the best players in football history were on that field. We didn't know it at the time, but guys like Ronnie Lott. Who's a better defensive back to ever play the game than Ronnie Lott? Carlton Williamson, Eric Wright, and all those guys. They were just amazing talents back there. But the most important thing is that we were selfless. We always pulled for each other. Bill [Walsh] had an amazing way to ensure that people knew their role and played their role."

Max Runager, punter: "Well, number one, I'm honored to be a part of it and number two, to be able to have the kind of year that I had. I felt like I made a contribution to that. But that was the thing that really stands out: I felt like I made a contribution to that championship team. It was very special. It was a phenomenal year and for me personally too, like I said earlier, to go from two weeks of unemployment to a Super Bowl champion was just something I'll remember the rest of my life."

George Seifert, defensive coordinator: "We were very talented. . . . A lot of people said that was one of the best teams in 49ers history. I always thought that the 1984 team was the best that we had."

Billy Shields, offensive tackle: "Having come to the 49er just that year, I feel like it was a real gift being the next-to-last year of my career. It seems like a gift. The joy of being able to say I was on a winning team."

Jeff Stover, defensive end: "That was just absolutely incredible and to do it with the group of individuals that we did it with was pretty darn special. Just a fantastic year!"

Jim Stuckey, defensive end: "It's something that never leaves you. It's been thirty years now. I remember the camaraderie. I remember the closeness of our team."

Manu Tuiasosopo, defensive tackle: "That was probably the most awesome experience for me as a player to get to that Super Bowl game and to win it. But for me it was about the relationship with the defensive line group. Coach Mac, getting reunited with him. Then learning from Coach Walsh the principles that, to this day, I apply in my coaching experience even though I was at the high school level. So for me that's what I take away from it: the relationships that I built."

Keena Turner, linebacker: "That was a pretty good team. Pound for pound, I would match those guys up against anybody. That 1984 team was the best team I played on."

Wendell Tyler, halfback: "I think it was God's divine perfect plan for all of us. Because we all came together for one season to accomplish one common goal, and that's to win the Super Bowl. That was Joe Montana's dream. That was Dwight Clark's dream. That was Roger's dream. But for one given day, we all worked together to get that dream accomplished and nobody can take that from me."

Fred vonAppen, special teams coach: "That 15–1 had nothing to do with me. It had to do with that group and the pride that they had in the organization and a standard to which they adhered. They were the greatest group of guys about policing themselves. It was a classy bunch of guys and it's not surprising that they were able to play to that level and get that seminal accomplishment in their lives. I'm just proud to have been some small part of it."

Jerry Walker, director of public relations: "My first reflection is, I can't believe it's been thirty years, it seems like three or four. . . . It's just amazing. It was a team effort."

Michael Walter, linebacker: "As more time goes by you realize how fortunate you were to be that one little cog in that whole piece of machinery that worked so well together. . . . That was the greatest year that I played as far as just having fun. How close we were to having that perfect season that would never ever be surpassed."

Ray Wersching, kicker: "I think just the unselfishness of the players. Everybody did what they had to do, each player did their job, their responsibilities that year, and there was nobody out there saying 'I'm better than you.' Everybody was equal and we're all in this together. There were no prima donnas; it was just a group of good guys who were very talented and we all played together and . . . that's what made us successful."

Carlton Williamson, strong safety: "When I put it all in perspective, it was just a super year. One that we basically dedicated to excellence. It stemmed all the way back to the loss of the NFC Championship the year before. It was a coming together of our spirits and our desire to be great because we felt slighted. We went on a mission to make it happen [and] we felt nobody's going to take it away from us. It was just wonderful that we were able to achieve it. It's one thing to say that you're going to do it, but it's another thing to go out there and do it and prove it. That's what we did. . . . I felt very fortunate and blessed to have been with the 49ers organization at the right time."

Mike Wilson, wide receiver: "I could always go back and reflect on the friendships I had and how we worked hard and we accomplished something as a group. That's not an individual accomplishment, I mean Joe got the MVP and he deserved it, but we always knew as a team that it was teamwork that won championships. We were a dominant team. There were no weak links in that chain, and we came to play."

APPENDIX

1984 San Francisco 49ers Results
(15–1 regular season/18–1 postseason)

W 30–27 at Detroit Lions (58,782)/Sept. 2, 1984

W 37–31 vs. Washington Redskins (59,707)/Monday, Sept. 10, 1984

W 30–20 vs. New Orleans Saints (57,611)/Sept. 16, 1984

W 21–9 at Philadelphia Eagles (62,771)/Sept. 23, 1984

W 14–5 vs. Atlanta Falcons (57,990)/Sept. 30, 1984

W 31–10 at New York Giants (76,112)/Monday, Oct. 8, 1984

L 17–20 vs. Pittsburgh Steelers (59,110)/Oct. 14, 1984

W 32–21 at Houston Oilers (39,900)/Oct. 21, 1984

W 33–0 at Los Angeles Rams (65,481)/Oct. 28, 1984

W 23–17 vs. Cincinnati Bengals (58,234)/Nov. 4, 1984

W 41–7 at Cleveland Browns (60,092)/Nov. 11, 1984

W 24–17 vs. Tampa Bay Buccaneers (57,704)/Nov. 18, 1984

W 35–3 at New Orleans Saints (65,177)/Nov. 25, 1984

W 35–17 at Atlanta Falcons (29,644)/Dec. 2, 1984

W 51–7 vs. Minnesota Vikings (56,670)/Saturday, Dec. 8, 1984

W 19–16 vs. Los Angeles Rams (59,743)/Friday, Dec. 14, 1984

W 21–10 vs. New York Giants (60,303)/Saturday, Dec. 29, 1984
(NFC Divisional Game)

W 23–0 Chicago Bears (61,040)/Jan. 6, 1985 (NFC Championship
Game)

W 38–16 vs. Miami Dolphins (84,059)/Jan. 20, 1985 (Super Bowl
  XIX at Stanford Stadium)

NOTES

Most of this book was written from original interviews done in person or by phone with the coaches, players, and front-office personnel of the 1984 49ers. I also used Bill Walsh's 49ers meeting tapes, courtesy of his son Craig, who also allowed me to use his father's game plan binder from Super Bowl XIX. The meeting tapes are labeled by week and opponent (for example, 1984 Bill Walsh Meeting Tapes, Week 1 vs. Detroit Lions). Another key source was the network broadcasts (CBS, ABC, NBC) of all of the 49ers 1984 games, including Super Bowl XIX.

Secondary sources include 49ers media guides and yearbooks, 49ers programs, books, magazines, and newspapers–especially the *San Francisco Chronicle* and *San Francisco Examiner*. I leaned heavily on several books by or about Bill Walsh: Walsh's autobiography, *Building a Champion* (1990), written by Walsh with Glenn Dickey; *Finding the Winning Edge* (1998) by Bill Walsh with Brian Billick and James Peterson; *The Score Takes Care of Itself: My Philosophy of Leadership* (2010) by Bill Walsh (posthumously) with Craig Walsh and Steve Jamison; and *The Genius: How Bill Walsh Reinvented Football and Created an NFL Dynasty* (2008) by David Harris.

INTRODUCTION

1. Forty-niners at Redskins, January 8, 1984, CBS broadcast.
2. Dwight Hicks, archival interview (NFL Films, 2005).
3. Dan Bunz, interview by Chris Willis, December 15, 2012.

4. Jim Stuckey, interview by Chris Willis, December 19, 2012.

5. Roger Craig, interview by Chris Willis, April 18, 2013.

6. *Portrait of Victory: 49ers, the Season* (Salt Lake City, UT: Treacor Publications, 1985), 2.

7. Hicks, archival interview.

8. Ray Rhodes, interview by Chris Willis, February 15, 2013.

9. Jerry Walker, interview by Chris Willis, December 5, 2012.

10. Paul Hackett, interview by Chris Willis, August 8, 2012.

11. Earl Cooper, interview by Chris Willis, January 9, 2013.

I. EDDIE D.

1. Murray Olderman, *49er Pro-Files: The Cartoon Book of the Super Bowl Champions* (San Francisco: Sales Corporation of America, 1982), 6.

2. George Seifert, interview by Chris Willis, February 13, 2013.

3. *New York Times*, December 20, 1994.

4. Jeff Schultz with Michael Tuckerman, *The San Francisco 49ers: Team of the Decade* (Rocklin, CA: Prima Publishing, 1990), 195.

5. *1984 San Francisco 49ers Media Guide*, 8.

6. Eddie DeBartolo, archival interview (NFL Films, 2012).

7. Lou Sahadi, *The 49ers: Super Champs of Pro Football* (New York: Quill, 1982), 18.

8. Schultz, *The San Francisco 49ers*, 197–98.

9. Sahadi, *The 49ers*, 11; Glenn Dickey, *Glenn Dickey's 49ers: The Rise, Fall, and Rebirth of the NFL's Greatest Dynasty* (Roseville, CA: Prima Publishing, 2000), 10.

10. Sahadi, *The 49ers*, 13.

11. Olderman, *49er Pro-Files*, 6.

12. Ken Flower, interview by Chris Willis, June 28, 2013.

13. Schultz, *The San Francisco 49ers*, 200.

2. THE GENIUS

1. David Harris, *The Genius: How Bill Walsh Reinvented Football and Created an NFL Dynasty* (New York: Random House, 2008), 161.

2. Murray Olderman, *49er Pro-Files*, 6.

3. Harris, *The Genius*, 32.

4. Ben Kinnley, "San Francisco's Gridiron Guru," *Saturday Evening Post*, October 1985, 80.

5. Craig Walsh, interview by Chris Willis, April 17, 2013.

6. San Francisco Chronicle, *Super Season: 1984 San Francisco 49ers* (San Francisco: San Francisco Chronicle, 1984), 23.

7. Susan Moyer, *Bill Walsh: Remembering the Genius, 1931–2007* (Champaign, IL: Sports Publishing, 2007), 25–29.

8. *1980 San Francisco 49ers Media Guide*, 7.

9. Schultz, *The San Francisco 49ers*, 201, 204.

10. Bill Walsh with Steve Jamison and Craig Walsh, *The Score Takes Care of Itself: My Philosophy of Leadership* (New York: Portfolio Trade, 2010), 15.

11. Craig Walsh interview.

12. Harris, *The Genius*, 64.

13. Bill Walsh with Glenn Dickey, *Building a Champion* (New York: St. Martin's Press, 1990), 99.

14. John McVay, interview by Chris Willis, April 6, 2012.

15. McVay interview.

16. Dickey, *Glenn Dickey's 49ers*, 24–25.

17. Sahadi, *The 49ers*, 29.

18. McVay interview.

19. Walker interview.

20. Neal Dahlen, interview by Chris Willis, July 15, 2013.

21. Dahlen interview.

22. Dahlen interview.

23. Craig Walsh interview.

24. *1983 San Francisco 49ers Media Guide*, 6–7.

3. THE COACHING STAFF

1. Fred vonAppen, interview by Chris Willis, January 22, 2013.

2. Bill Walsh, *Building a Champion*, 101–2.

3. Bill Walsh with Brian Billick and James Peterson, *Finding the Winning Edge* (Champaign, IL: Sports Publishing, 1998), 76–108.

4. *1983 San Francisco 49ers Media Guide*, 6.

5. Walsh, *Building a Champion*, 106–7.

6. Walsh, *Building a Champion*, 106–7.

7. Seifert interview.

8. Ray Rhodes, interview by Chris Willis, February 15, 2013.

9. Rhodes interview.

10. Bill McPherson, interview by Chris Willis, December 4, 2012.

11. McPherson interview.

12. Seifert interview.

13. Jim Stuckey, interview by Chris Willis, December 19, 2012.

14. McPherson interview.

15. Bobb McKittrick's obituary, *New York Times*, March 16, 2000.

16. Ladd McKittrick, interview by Chris Willis, July 8, 2013.

17. VonAppen interview.

18. Paul Hackett, interview by Chris Willis, August 8, 2012.

19. VonAppen interview.

20. VonAppen interview.

21. VonAppen interview.

22. Jerry Attaway, interview by Chris Willis, December 19, 2012.

23. Attaway interview.

24. Attaway interview.

25. Attaway interview.

26. Attaway interview.

27. VonAppen interview.

4. BUILDING A CHAMPION

1. *1984 San Francisco 49ers Yearbook*, 65.

2. *Portrait of Victory: 49ers, the Season* (Salt Lake City, UT: Treacor Publications, 1985), 98.

3. *1984 San Francisco 49ers Yearbook*, 65.

4. Keith Fahnhorst, interview by Chris Willis, February 14, 2013.

5. Bill Ring, interview by Chris Willis, December 5, 2012.

6. Wendell Tyler, interview by Chris Willis, February 16, 2013.

7. Hackett interview.

8. Tyler interview.

9. Tyler interview.

10. Ring interview.

11. Earl Cooper, interview by Chris Willis, January 9, 2013.

12. Tyler interview.

13. Ring interview.

14. Tyler interview.

15. Roger Craig, interview by Chris Willis, April 18, 2013.

16. Allan Kennedy, interview by Chris Willis, December 4, 2012.

17. Tyler interview.

18. Mike Wilson, interview by Chris Willis, November 13, 2012.

19. Craig interview.

20. Renaldo Nehemiah, interview by Chris Willis, June 26, 2013.
21. Hackett interview.
22. *1984 49ers Media Guide*, 43
23. Cooper interview.
24. Kennedy interview.
25. Keith Fahnhorst interview.
26. Keith Fahnhorst interview.
27. Keith Fahnhorst interview.
28. Kennedy interview.
29. Kennedy interview.
30. Kennedy interview.
31. Fred Dean, interview by Chris Willis, January 23, 2013.
32. Stuckey interview.
33. Ring interview.
34. Stuckey interview.
35. *1984 San Francisco 49ers Media Guide*, 37.
36. McPherson interview.
37. Dwaine Board, interview by Chris Willis, February 13, 2013.
38. Lawrence Pillers, interview by Chris Willis, February 26, 2013.
39. McPherson interview.
40. Stuckey interview.
41. Board interview.
42. Pillers interview.
43. McPherson interview.
44. Dan Bunz, interview by Chris Willis, December 15, 2012.
45. Keena Turner, interview by Chris Willis, December 6, 2012.
46. Riki Ellison, interview by Chris Willis, April 10, 2013.
47. Blanchard Montgomery, interview by Chris Willis, December 27, 2012.
48. Turner interview.
49. Milt McColl, interview by Chris Willis, December 7, 2012.
50. Ellison interview.
51. Ring interview.
52. Rhodes interview.
53. Jim Fahnhorst, interview by Chris Willis, January 28, 2013.
54. Ron Ferrari, interview by Chris Willis, March 21, 2013.
55. Ellison interview.
56. Ferrari interview.
57. Turner interview.
58. Dana McLemore, interview by Chris Willis, December 4, 2012.
59. Carlton Williamson, interview by Chris Willis, January 30, 2013.
60. Rhodes interview.

61. Williamson interview.
62. McLemore interview.
63. Rhodes interview.
64. Williamson interview.
65. Rhodes interview.
66. McLemore interview.
67. Williamson interview.
68. Tom Holmoe, interview by Chris Willis, January 9, 2013.
69. Rhodes interview.
70. Williamson interview.
71. Ferrari interview.
72. VonAppen interview.
73. Ray Wersching, interview by Chris Willis, January 15, 2013.
74. Wersching interview.
75. Wersching interview.
76. Wersching interview.
77. VonAppen interview.
78. Wersching interview.
79. VonAppen interview.
80. Wersching interview.
81. Ellison interview.
82. VonAppen interview.

5. DRAFT

1. McPherson interview.
2. Louie Kelcher, interview by Chris Willis, February 7, 2013.
3. Stuckey interview.
4. Manu Tuiasosopo, interview by Chris Willis, March 19, 2013.
5. Tuiasosopo interview.
6. McVay interview.
7. Rhodes interview.
8. VonAppen interview.
9. Seifert interview.
10. Dahlen interview.
11. Walsh draft quote.
12. Dahlen interview.
13. Cooper interview.
14. Guy McIntyre, interview by Chris Willis, December 6, 2012.
15. McIntyre interview.

16. Kennedy interview.

17. McPherson interview.

18. Michael Carter, interview by Chris Willis, February 8, 2013.

19. Dahlen interview.

20. Williamson interview.

21. McLemore interview.

22. Derrick Harmon, interview by Chris Willis, August 26, 2013.

23. McPherson interview.

24. Jim Fahnhorst interview.

25. Keith Fahnhorst interview.

6. LUNCH BOX TEAM

1. Attaway interview.

2. Tyler interview.

3. Harris, *The Genius*, 61.

4. *Santa Fe New Mexican*, December 15, 1982.

5. Walsh, *The Score Takes Care of Itself*, 14.

6. Harris, *The Genius*, 61–62.

7. Nehemiah interview.

8. The description of the 49ers facility at 711 Nevada Street was based on two visits I made to the building in Redwood City. The first visit was April 18, 2013, and the second was November 7, 2013, with Jerry Walker, the 49ers director of public relations in 1984, who spent an hour showing me around the old facility.

9. Jeff Stover, interview by Chris Willis, June 13, 2013.

10. Tuiasosopo interview.

11. Ferrari interview.

12. Hackett interview.

13. Walsh, *The Score Takes Care of Itself*, 34; Harris, *The Genius*, 61–62. The description of Bill Walsh's office is based on my visit to 711 Nevada Street; Nicole Gisele, interview by Chris Willis, September 2, 2013; and Tony Kornheiser, "The Revenge of Bill Walsh," *Inside Sports*, September 1982, 91.

14. Craig interview.

15. Ellison interview.

16. Kennedy interview.

17. Craig interview.

18. Ferrari interview.

19. Holmoe interview.

20. Attaway interview.

21. Wersching interview.
22. Attaway interview.
23. Ring interview.
24. Stuckey interview.
25. Turner interview.
26. Keith Fahnhorst interview.
27. Tyler interview.
28. Hackett interview.
29. Walker interview.
30. Board interview.
31. Attaway interview.

7. ROCKLIN

1. Rhodes interview.
2. McPherson interview.
3. Hackett interview.
4. Walsh, *Building a Champion*, 39.
5. Seifert interview.
6. McPherson interview.
7. Walsh, *Building a Champion*, 39.
8. VonAppen interview.
9. McColl interview.
10. Kornheisher, "The Revenge of Bill Walsh," 91.
11. Harmon interview.
12. Turner interview.
13. Kennedy interview.
14. Ring interview.
15. Cooper interview.
16. Turner interview.
17. Mario Clark, interview by Chris Willis, April 10, 2013.
18. Seifert interview.
19. Keith Fahnhorst interview.
20. Attaway interview.
21. Tuiasosopo interview.
22. Walsh, *Finding the Winning Edge*, 235.
23. Ferrari interview.
24. Keith Fahnhorst interview.
25. Seifert interview.
26. Rhodes interview.

27. Rhodes interview.

28. Ellison interview.

29. Ellison interview.

30. Craig interview.

31. Williamson interview.

32. Stover interview.

33. Associated Press, July 30, 1984.

34. Fred Dean, interview by Chris Willis, January 23, 2013.

35. Associated Press, August 8, 1984.

36. Roger Craig with Matt Maiocco, *Roger Craig's Tales from the 49ers Sidelines* (Champaign, IL: Sports Publishing, 2004), 55.

37. Ferrari interview.

38. Pillers interview.

39. Craig interview.

40. Ring interview.

41. Walsh, *Finding the Winning Edge*, 263.

42. Bunz interview.

43. Stuckey interview.

44. McLemore interview.

45. Board interview.

46. Bunz interview.

47. Stuckey interview.

48. Tuiasosopo interview.

49. Tuiasosopo interview.

50. Craig interview.

51. VonAppen interview.

52. Kennedy interview.

8. STUDENTS OF THE GAME

1. Craig interview.

2. Walsh, *Finding the Winning Edge*, 232.

3. Clark interview.

4. Ellison interview.

5. Seifert interview.

6. Board interview.

7. Tuiasosopo interview.

8. *New York Times*, January 14, 1985.

9. *New York Times*, January 14, 1985.

10. Williamson interview.

11. Williamson interview.
12. Stuckey interview.
13. Montgomery interview.
14. Jim Fahnhorst interview.
15. Turner interview.
16. Ferrari interview.
17. Harmon interview.
18. Craig interview.
19. Hackett interview.
20. Ring interview.
21. McIntyre interview.
22. Cooper interview.
23. Carter interview.
24. Kennedy interview.
25. Board interview.
26. Carter interview.
27. *San Francisco Chronicle*, August 14, 1984.
28. *San Francisco Examiner*, August 19, 1984.
29. Rocklin and Redwood City temperatures are from the *Farmer's Almanac* website.
30. Michael Walter, interview by Chris Willis, March 7, 2013.
31. Walter interview.
32. McLemore interview.

9. SEPTEMBER

1. Hackett interview.
2. Hackett interview.
3. Dahlen interview.
4. Craig interview.
5. Rhodes interview.
6. 1984 Bill Walsh Meeting Tapes, Week 1 vs. Detroit Lions.
7. 1984 Bill Walsh Meeting Tapes, Week 1 vs. Detroit Lions.
8. Tyler interview.
9. Wilson interview.
10. McIntyre interview.
11. Keith Fahnhorst interview.
12. Craig interview.
13. Wilson interview.
14. Seifert interview.

15. Clark interview.
16. Tyler interview.
17. Wersching interview.
18. McLemore interview.
19. Stover interview.
20. Ring interview.
21. Wersching interview.
22. *San Francisco Chronicle*, September 3, 1984.
23. Seifert interview.
24. Seifert interview.
25. 1984 Bill Walsh Meeting Tapes, Week 2 vs. Washington Redskins.
26. 1984 Bill Walsh Meeting Tapes, Week 2 vs. Washington Redskins.
27. Cooper interview.
28. Turner interview.
29. Williamson interview.
30. Redskins at 49ers, Monday Night Football, ABC broadcast.
31. Ring interview.
32. Williamson interview.
33. Wilson interview.
34. *San Francisco Examiner*, September 11, 1984.
35. *San Francisco Examiner*, September 11, 1984.
36. 1984 Bill Walsh Meeting Tapes, Week 3 vs. New Orleans Saints.
37. 1984 Bill Walsh Meeting Tapes, Week 3 vs. New Orleans Saints.
38. VonAppen interview.
39. VonAppen interview.
40. Max Runager, interview by Chris Willis, February 22, 2013.
41. 1984 Bill Walsh Meeting Tapes, Week 3 vs. New Orleans Saints.
42. Turner interview.
43. *San Jose Mercury News*, September 17, 1984.
44. Cooper interview.
45. *San Francisco Examiner*, September 17, 1984.
46. 1984 Bill Walsh Meeting Tapes, Week 4 vs. Philadelphia Eagles.
47. 1984 Bill Walsh Meeting Tapes, Week 4 vs. Philadelphia Eagles.
48. *Ukiah (CA) Daily Journal*, September 23, 1984.
49. Hackett interview.
50. Hackett interview.
51. Keith Fahnhorst interview.
52. Hackett interview.
53. *San Francisco Chronicle*, September 24, 1984.
54. Forty-niners at Eagles, CBS broadcast.
55. Forty-niners at Eagles, CBS broadcast.

56. Jim Fahnhorst interview.
57. Keith Fahnhorst interview.
58. Jim Fahnhorst interview.
59. Tyler interview.
60. *San Francisco Examiner*, September 24, 1984.
61. *San Francisco Chronicle*, September 24, 1984.
62. *San Francisco Examiner*, September 24, 1984.
63. *San Francisco Examiner*, September 24, 1984.
64. *San Francisco Chronicle*, September 24, 1984.
65. 1984 Bill Walsh Meeting Tapes, Week 5 vs. Atlanta Falcons.
66. 1984 Bill Walsh Meeting Tapes, Week 5 vs. Atlanta Falcons.
67. Billy Shields, interview by Chris Willis, January 25, 2013.
68. Shields interview.
69. *1985 San Francisco 49ers Media Guide*, 65.
70. Kelcher interview.
71. Board interview.
72. Tuiasosopo interview.
73. Falcons at 49ers, CBS broadcast.
74. *San Francisco Chronicle*, October 1, 1984.
75. Wilson interview.
76. Ferrari interview.
77. *San Francisco Chronicle*, October 1, 1984.
78. *San Francisco Chronicle*, October 1, 1984.
79. *San Francisco Chronicle*, October 1, 1984.

10. THE CANDLESTICK PARK EXPERIENCE

1. *1984 San Francisco 49ers Media Guide*, 6.
2. Wersching interview.
3. Clark interview.
4. Ferrari interview.
5. McIntyre interview.
6. Michael Olmstead, interview by Chris Willis, January 16, 2013.
7. Olmstead interview.
8. Olmstead interview.
9. Craig Walsh interview.
10. Olmstead interview.
11. Michael Zagaris, interview by Chris Willis, April 19, 2013.
12. Zagaris interview.
13. Ted Robinson, interview by Chris Willis, December 9, 2012.

14. Don Klein, interview by Chris Willis, July 9, 2013.
15. Klein interview.
16. Klein interview.
17. Klein interview.

11. OCTOBER

1. Ring interview.
2. McLemore interview.
3. Turner interview.
4. 1984 Bill Walsh Meeting Tapes, Week 6 vs. New York Giants.
5. Kennedy interview.
6. McIntyre interview.
7. Nehemiah interview.
8. 1984 Bill Walsh Meeting Tapes, Week 6 vs. New York Giants.
9. Stuckey interview.
10. Kennedy interview.
11. Nehemiah interview.
12. Forty-niners at Giants, Monday Night Football, ABC broadcast.
13. *Washington Post*, October 9, 1984.
14. *San Jose Mercury News*, October 11, 1984.
15. 1984 Bill Walsh Meeting Tapes, Week 7 vs. Pittsburgh Steelers.
16. *Del Rio (TX) News Herald*, October 12, 1984.
17. 1984 Bill Walsh Meeting Tapes, Week 7 vs. Pittsburgh Steelers.
18. Keith Fahnhorst interview.
19. Kennedy interview.
20. Craig interview.
21. *San Francisco Chronicle*, October 15, 1984.
22. Seifert interview.
23. Steelers at 49ers, NBC broadcast.
24. Turner interview.
25. Seifert interview.
26. Hackett interview.
27. Cooper interview.
28. Wersching interview.
29. Ring interview.
30. Williamson interview.
31. Turner interview.
32. KGO-TV (San Francisco).
33. Cooper interview.

34. Fahnhorst interview.
35. *San Francisco Examiner*, October 15, 1984.
36. *San Jose Mercury News*, October 15, 1984.
37. *San Francisco Chronicle*, October 15, 1984.
38. Tyler interview.
39. Williamson interview.
40. 1984 Bill Walsh Meeting Tapes, Week 8 vs. Houston Oilers.
41. Nehemiah interview.
42. Wilson interview.
43. McIntyre interview.
44. Turner interview.
45. Lyrics from *The San Francisco 49ers Sing We're the 49ers*, 1984, Megatone Records.
46. McIntyre interview.
47. Turner interview.
48. Williamson interview.
49. Wilson interview.
50. Board interview.
51. Wilson interview.
52. Williamson interview.
53. Wilson interview.
54. Ring interview.
55. McIntyre interview.
56. Turner interview.
57. 1984 Bill Walsh Meeting Tapes, Week 8 vs. Houston Oilers.
58. Board interview.
59. Williamson interview.
60. Tyler interview.
61. *San Francisco Chronicle*, October 22, 1984.
62. *San Francisco Chronicle*, October 22, 1984.
63. Forty-niners at Oilers, CBS broadcast.
64. *San Francisco Examiner*, October 22, 1984.
65. *San Francisco Examiner*, October 22, 1984.
66. Tuiasosopo interview.
67. *San Jose Mercury News*, January 13, 1985.
68. Keith Fahnhorst interview.
69. 1984 Bill Walsh Meeting Tapes, Week 9 vs. Los Angeles Rams.
70. Williamson interview.
71. Ellison interview.
72. McPherson interview.
73. Rhodes interview.

74. Carter interview.
75. Stuckey interview.
76. Turner interview.
77. Tuiasosopo interview.
78. *San Francisco Examiner*, October 29, 1984.
79. *San Francisco Examiner*, October 29, 1984.
80. Ellison interview.
81. Jim Fahnhorst interview.
82. Forty-niners at Rams, CBS broadcast.
83. Clark interview.
84. *San Francisco Chronicle*, October 29, 1984.
85. *San Jose Mercury News*, October 29, 1984.

12. SIX DAYS TILL SUNDAY

1. Walsh, *Finding the Winning Edge*, 257–59.
2. Hackett interview.
3. Dahlen interview.
4. Dahlen interview.
5. VonAppen interview.
6. Board interview.
7. Rhodes interview.
8. Jim Fahnhorst interview.
9. Williamson interview.
10. Kelcher interview.
11. Wilson interview.
12. Seifert interview.
13. Stuckey interview.
14. VonAppen interview.
15. VonAppen interview.
16. Attaway interview.
17. Ring interview.
18. Hackett interview.
19. Joe Montana with Richard Weiner, *Joe Montana's Art and Magic of Quarterbacking* (New York: Henry Holt, 1997), 133.
20. Holmoe interview.
21. Tyler interview.
22. Ferrari interview.
23. Tuiasosopo interview.
24. Turner interview.

25. Ellison interview.
26. Kennedy interview.
27. VonAppen interview.
28. Cooper interview.
29. Clark interview.
30. Bunz interview.
31. Ferrari interview.
32. Craig interview.
33. Williamson interview.
34. Dahlen interview.
35. Ring interview.
36. Ferrari interview.
37. Montgomery interview.
38. Rhodes interview.
39. VonAppen interview.
40. Tuiasosopo interview.
41. Shields interview.
42. Board interview.
43. Keith Fahnhorst interview.
44. Kennedy interview.
45. McIntyre interview.
46. Cooper interview.
47. Montana, *Joe Montana's Art and Magic of Quarterbacking*, 185.

13. NOVEMBER

1. *Ukiah (CA) Daily Journal*, November 4, 1984.
2. 1984 Bill Walsh Meeting Tapes, Week 10 vs. Cincinnati Bengals.
3. Walker interview.
4. Keith Fahnhorst interview.
5. Walsh, *Building a Champion*, 18.
6. *San Francisco Chronicle*, November 5, 1984.
7. Keith Fahnhorst interview.
8. *San Francisco Chronicle*, November 5, 1984.
9. *San Francisco Chronicle*, November 5, 1984.
10. *San Francisco Chronicle*, November 5, 1984.
11. 1984 Bill Walsh Meeting Tapes, Week 11 vs. Cleveland Browns.
12. Rhodes interview.
13. Turner interview.
14. McVay interview.

15. Willie Brown, interview by Chris Willis, July 1, 2013.
16. *San Francisco Chronicle*, November 12, 1984.
17. Dean interview.
18. McVay interview.
19. Ferrari interview.
20. Schultz, *The San Francisco 49ers*, 190.
21. Dean interview.
22. KGO-TV (San Francisco).
23. Board interview.
24. Stuckey interview.
25. 1984 Bill Walsh Meeting Tapes, Week 12 vs. Tampa Bay Buccaneers.
26. Stover interview.
27. *San Francisco Chronicle*, November 19, 1984.
28. Stover interview.
29. 1984 Bill Walsh Meeting Tapes, Week 13 vs. New Orleans Saints.
30. 1984 Bill Walsh Meeting Tapes, Week 13 vs. New Orleans Saints.
31. *San Francisco Examiner*, November 26, 1984.
32. Harmon interview.
33. *San Francisco Chronicle*, November 26, 1984.
34. Stuckey interview.

14. DECEMBER

1. McLemore interview.
2. Jim Fahnhorst interview.
3. Keith Fahnhorst interview.
4. Jim Fahnhorst interview.
5. Tyler interview.
6. Harmon interview.
7. Rams at 49ers, CBS broadcast.
8. *San Francisco Examiner*, December 15, 1984.
9. *San Francisco Examiner*, December 15, 1984.
10. *San Francisco Examiner*, December 15, 1984.
11. *San Francisco Examiner*, December 15, 1984.

15. NFC DIVISIONAL PLAYOFF GAME

1. Rhodes interview.

2. Ring interview.
3. Keith Fahnhorst interview.
4. Stuckey interview.
5. Board interview.
6. Board interview.
7. Dean interview.
8. Kelcher interview.
9. Stuckey interview.
10. Pillers interview.
11. Kennedy interview.
12. Cooper interview.
13. Stuckey interview.
14. Holmoe interview.
15. *San Jose Mercury News*, December 28, 1984.
16. Turner interview.
17. Bunz interview.
18. Williamson interview.
19. Rhodes interview.
20. Ellison interview.
21. Giants at 49ers, CBS broadcast.
22. Stover interview.
23. Wersching interview.
24. Giants at 49ers, CBS broadcast.
25. Cooper interview.
26. *San Francisco Examiner*, December 30, 1984.
27. *San Francisco Examiner*, December 30, 1984.
28. *San Francisco Chronicle*, December 30, 1984.
29. *San Francisco Examiner*, December 30, 1984.

16. NFC CHAMPIONSHIP GAME

1. *Miami Herald*, January 6, 1985.
2. Holmoe interview.
3. Keith Fahnhorst interview.
4. Hackett interview.
5. 1984 Bill Walsh Meeting Tapes, Week 19 vs. Chicago Bears.
6. *San Francisco Examiner*, January 7, 1985.
7. Ellison interview.
8. Williamson interview.
9. Carter interview.

10. 1984 Bill Walsh Meeting Tapes, Week 19 vs. Chicago Bears.
11. Wilson interview.
12. Cooper interview.
13. *New York Times*, January 7, 1985.
14. Keith Fahnhorst interview.
15. Tyler interview.
16. 1984 Bill Walsh Meeting Tapes, Week 19 vs. Chicago Bears.
17. Keith Fahnhorst interview.
18. McIntyre interview.
19. Cooper interview.
20. Kennedy interview.
21. McIntyre interview.
22. 1984 Bill Walsh Meeting Tapes, Week 19 vs. Chicago Bears.
23. Stover interview.
24. *San Francisco Chronicle*, January 16, 1985.
25. Bears at 49ers, CBS broadcast.
26. Board interview.
27. McIntyre interview.
28. Turner interview.
29. NFL Films sound camera.
30. *San Francisco Examiner*, January 7, 1985.
31. McIntyre interview.
32. Ring interview.
33. Montgomery interview.
34. Wersching interview.
35. Zagaris interview.
36. *San Francisco Chronicle*, January 7, 1985.
37. Tyler interview.
38. *San Francisco Examiner*, January 7, 1985.
39. *San Francisco Examiner*, January 7, 1985.
40. Kelcher interview.
41. Ellison interview.
42. Stuckey interview.
43. Montgomery interview.
44. *San Francisco Examiner*, January 7, 1985.
45. NFL Films sound camera.
46. Runager interview.
47. *San Francisco Chronicle*, January 7, 1985.
48. Bears at 49ers, CBS broadcast.

17. THE GAME PLANS

1. Stover interview.
2. *San Francisco Chronicle*, January 19, 1985.
3. *Associated Press*, January 17, 1985.
4. Hackett interview.
5. Stuckey interview.
6. Williamson interview.
7. Frank Cooney, "Football's Master Strategist: Bill Walsh," *1985 Sporting News Pro Football Annual*, 18–19.
8. Bill Walsh Super Bowl XIX Game Plan Binder.
9. Walsh, *Building a Champion*, 209.
10. Keith Fahnhorst interview.
11. Tyler interview.
12. Hackett interview.
13. Walsh, *Building a Champion*, 209.
14. Dahlen interview.
15. McPherson interview.
16. Rhodes interview.
17. Dean interview.
18. Stover interview.
19. Turner interview.
20. Stuckey interview.
21. Rhodes interview.
22. Williamson interview.
23. Board interview.
24. Carter interview.
25. Ring interview.
26. Bill Walsh Super Bowl XIX Game Plan Binder.
27. Bill Walsh Super Bowl XIX Game Plan Binder.
28. Clark interview.
29. Bill Walsh Super Bowl XIX Game Plan Binder.
30. Attaway interview.
31. *San Jose Mercury News*, January 12, 1985.
32. Wilson interview.
33. Stover interview.

18. THE HYPE

1. Wersching interview.
2. Rhodes interview.
3. Ellison interview.
4. McIntyre interview.
5. Ring interview.
6. Attaway interview.
7. Wersching interview.
8. Walker interview.
9. Bunz interview.
10. *San Jose Mercury News*, January 15, 1985.
11. Keith Fahnhorst interview.
12. VonAppen interview.
13. Stover interview.
14. Dahlen interview.
15. Board interview.
16. Cooper interview.
17. Kennedy interview.
18. Keith Fahnhorst interview.
19. Ring interview.
20. McVay interview.
21. *San Francisco Chronicle*, January 17, 1985.
22. VonAppen interview.
23. Kelcher interview.
24. Paul Zimmerman, "Armed for an Aerial Epic," *Sports Illustrated*, January 21, 1985, 48–55.
25. *San Jose Mercury News*, January 14–20, 1985; *San Francisco Chronicle*, January 14–21, 1985.
26. Bill Walsh Super Bowl XIX Game Plan Binder; Craig interview.
27. McIntyre interview.
28. Carter interview.
29. Montgomery interview.
30. Kennedy interview.
31. Stover interview.
32. KGO-TV (San Francisco).
33. *San Jose Mercury News*, January 15, 1985.
34. Clark interview.
35. Williamson interview.
36. Ellison interview.
37. *San Jose Mercury News*, January 17, 1985.

38. *Chicago Tribune*, January 20, 1985.

39. *San Francisco Chronicle*, January 12–13, 1985.

40. *San Francisco Chronicle*, January 13, 1985.

41. *Super Bowl XIX Media Guide*, back cover.

42. *Fort Lauderdale News & Sun-Sentinel*, January 18, 1985.

43. *San Francisco Chronicle*, January 19, 1985.

44. *San Jose Mercury News*, January 19, 1985.

45. *San Jose Mercury News*, January 19, 1985.

46. Jim Fahnhorst interview.

47. Keith Fahnhorst interview.

48. Keith Fahnhorst interview.

49. Keith Fahnhorst interview.

50. Craig Walsh interview.

51. Tuiasosopo interview.

52. Carter interview.

53. Stover interview.

54. Craig interview.

55. Williamson interview.

56. Tyler interview.

57. Board interview.

58. Dean interview.

59. Poem recited by Fred Dean during interview with Chris Willis; *San Diego Union-Tribune*, January 16, 1985.

60. Ellison interview.

19. PREGAME

1. Rhodes interview.

2. Craig interview.

3. Kennedy interview.

4. McLemore interview.

5. Ellison interview.

6. Stover interview.

7. Board interview.

8. Rhodes interview.

9. Clark interview.

10. Cooper interview.

11. Board interview.

12. Carter interview.

13. Williamson interview.

14. Montgomery interview.
15. Dean interview.
16. Kennedy interview.
17. Carter interview.
18. Stuckey interview.
19. Nehemiah interview.
20. Walsh, *Building a Champion*, 208.
21. Hackett interview.
22. Walsh, *Building a Champion*, 209.
23. Craig interview.
24. Rhodes interview.
25. Rhodes interview.
26. Montgomery interview.
27. Super Bowl XIX, Dolphins vs. 49ers, ABC broadcast.
28. Tuiasosopo interview.
29. Ring interview.
30. Turner interview.
31. Super Bowl XIX, Dolphins vs. 49ers, ABC broadcast.
32. Super Bowl XIX, Dolphins vs. 49ers, ABC broadcast.
33. Cooper interview.
34. Keith Fahnhorst interview.
35. Montgomery interview.
36. Board interview.
37. Williamson interview.
38. Ellison interview.
39. The Nielsen Company.

20. FIRST HALF

1. Harmon interview.
2. Montgomery interview.
3. Frank Cooney, "Football's Master Strategist: Bill Walsh," *1985 Sporting News Pro Football Yearbook*, 18.
4. Craig interview.
5. Craig interview.
6. Tyler interview.
7. Rhodes interview.
8. Runager interview.
9. Dahlen interview.
10. McPherson interview.

11. Seifert interview.
12. Dean interview.
13. Board interview.
14. Carter interview.
15. Cooney, "Football's Master Strategist," 19.
16. Cooney, "Football's Master Strategist," 19.
17. Craig interview.
18. Super Bowl XIX, Dolphins vs. 49ers, ABC broadcast.
19. Hackett interview.
20. Dean interview.
21. Cooper interview.
22. Hackett interview.
23. Fahnhorst interview.
24. McIntyre interview.
25. McIntyre interview.

21. SECOND HALF

1. Zagaris interview.
2. Seifert interview.
3. Attaway interview.
4. McLemore interview.
5. Board interview.
6. McPherson interview.
7. McPherson interview.
8. Seifert interview.
9. Stover interview.
10. Tuiasosopo interview.
11. Craig interview.
12. Tyler interview.
13. Montgomery interview.
14. Tyler interview.
15. McIntyre interview.
16. Rhodes interview.
17. Kelcher interview.
18. Williamson interview.
19. Ellison interview.
20. Stover interview.
21. McIntyre interview.
22. VonAppen interview.

23. Runager interview.
24. Tuiasosopo interview.
25. Clark interview.
26. Kelcher interview.
27. Walter interview.
28. Montgomery interview.
29. Williamson interview.
30. Kennedy interview.
31. Williamson interview.
32. Cooper interview.
33. Seifert interview.

22. AFTERMATH

1. Super Bowl XIX, Dolphins vs. 49ers, ABC broadcast.
2. Clark interview.
3. NFL Films sound camera.
4. Turner interview.
5. Carter interview.
6. Stuckey interview.
7. Tyler interview.
8. Wersching interview.
9. Rhodes interview.
10. Carter interview.
11. NFL Films sound camera.
12. NFL Films sound camera.
13. NFL Films sound camera.
14. Cooper interview.
15. Walsh, *Building a Champion*, 210.
16. Walker interview.
17. Craig Walsh interview.
18. Super Bowl XIX, Dolphins vs. 49ers, ABC broadcast.
19. Walker interview.
20. *San Francisco Examiner*, January 21, 1985.
21. Ellison interview.
22. McVay interview.
23. Walter interview.
24. Keith Fahnhorst interview.
25. Craig interview.
26. McIntyre interview.

27. Wersching interview.
28. Board interview.
29. Carter interview.
30. Ellison interview.
31. Kelcher interview.
32. Williamson interview.
33. Williamson interview.
34. Williamson interview.
35. *Sports Illustrated*, January 28, 1985.
36. Craig interview.
37. Seifert interview.

23. LEGACY OF THE 1984
SAN FRANCISCO 49ERS

1. All of the quotes used for the 1984 49ers memories were from interviews conducted by Chris Willis between April 6, 2012, and August 26, 2013.

BIBLIOGRAPHY

PRIMARY SOURCES

Author Interviews

Jerry Attaway. December 19, 2012. Telephone interview by Chris Willis.
Dwaine Board. February 13, 2013. Telephone interview by Chris Willis.
Willie Brown. July 1, 2013. Telephone interview by Chris Willis.
Dan Bunz. December 15, 2012. Telephone interview by Chris Willis.
Michael Carter. February 8, 2013. Telephone interview by Chris Willis.
Mario Clark. April 10, 2013. Telephone interview by Chris Willis.
Earl Cooper. January 9, 2013. Telephone interview by Chris Willis.
Roger Craig. April 18, 2013. Interview by Chris Willis.
Neal Dahlen. July 15, 2013. Telephone interview by Chris Willis.
Fred Dean. January 23, 2013. Telephone interview by Chris Willis.
Riki Ellison. April 10, 2013. Telephone interview by Chris Willis.
Jim Fahnhorst. January 28, 2013. Telephone interview by Chris Willis.
Keith Fahnhorst. February 14, 2013. Telephone interview by Chris Willis.
Ron Ferrari. March 21, 2013. Telephone interview by Chris Willis.
Ken Flower. June 28, 2013. Telephone interview by Chris Willis.
Nicole Gisele, September 2, 2013. Telephone interview by Chris Willis.
Paul Hackett. August 8, 2012. Telephone interview by Chris Willis.
Derrick Harmon. August 26, 2013. Telephone interview by Chris Willis.
Tom Holmoe. January 9, 2013. Telephone interview by Chris Willis.
Louie Kelcher. February 7, 2013. Telephone interview by Chris Willis.
Allan Kennedy. December 4, 2012. Interview by Chris Willis.
Don Klein. July 9, 2013. Telephone interview by Chris Willis.
Milt McColl. December 7, 2012. Interview by Chris Willis.
Guy McIntyre. December 6, 2012. Interview by Chris Willis.
Ladd McKittrick, July 8, 2013. Telephone interview by Chris Willis.
Dana McLemore. December 4, 2012. Interview by Chris Willis.
Bill McPherson. December 4, 2012. Interview by Chris Willis.
John McVay. April 6, 2012. Interview by Chris Willis.
Blanchard Montgomery. December 27, 2012. Telephone interview by Chris Willis.
Renaldo Nehemiah. June 26, 2013. Telephone interview by Chris Willis.

Michael Olmstead. January 16, 2013. Telephone interview by Chris Willis.
Lawrence Pillers. February 26, 2013. Telephone interview by Chris Willis.
Mark Purdy. December 7, 2012. Interview by Chris Willis.
Ray Rhodes. February 15, 2013. Telephone interview by Chris Willis.
Bill Ring. December 5, 2012. Interview by Chris Willis.
Ted Robinson. December 9, 2012. Interview by Chris Willis.
Max Runager. February 22, 2013. Telephone interview by Chris Willis.
George Seifert. February 13, 2013. Telephone interview by Chris Willis.
Billy Shields. January 25, 2013. Telephone interview by Chris Willis.
Jeff Stover. June 13, 2013. Telephone interview by Chris Willis.
Jim Stuckey. December 19, 2012. Telephone interview by Chris Willis.
Manu Tuiasosopo. March 19, 2013. Telephone interview by Chris Willis.
Keena Turner. December 6, 2012. Interview by Chris Willis.
Wendell Tyler. February 16, 2013. Telephone interview by Chris Willis.
Fred vonAppen. January 22, 2013. Telephone interview by Chris Willis.
Jerry Walker. December 5, 2012. Interview by Chris Willis.
Craig Walsh. April 17, 2013. Interview by Chris Willis.
Michael Walter. March 7, 2013. Telephone interview by Chris Willis.
Ray Wersching. January 15, 2013. Telephone interview by Chris Willis.
Carlton Williamson. January 30, 2013. Telephone interview by Chris Willis.
Mike Wilson. November 13, 2012. Telephone interview by Chris Willis.
Michael Zagaris. April 19, 2013. Interview by Chris Willis.

Archival Interviews

Eddie DeBartolo. 2012. NFL Films.
Dwight Hicks. 2005. NFL Films.

49ers Playbooks

Bill Walsh. 1985 49ers Offensive Playbook (800 pages).
Bill Walsh. Super Bowl XIX Game Plan Binder.
Bill Walsh. First Twenty-Five Play Sheet.

Bill Walsh. 1984 49ers Meeting Tapes.

Week 1—49ers at Detroit Lions.
Week 2—Washington Redskins at 49ers.
Week 3—New Orleans Saints at 49ers.
Week 4—49ers at Philadelphia Eagles.
Week 5—Atlanta Falcons at 49ers.
Week 6—49ers at New York Giants.
Week 7—Pittsburgh Steelers at 49ers.
Week 8—49ers at Houston Oilers.
Week 9—49ers at Los Angeles Rams.
Week 10—Cincinnati Bengals at 49ers.
Week 11—49ers at Cleveland Browns.
Week 12—Tampa Bay Buccaneers at 49ers.
Week 13—49ers at New Orleans Saints.
Week 14—49ers at Atlanta Falcons.
Week 15—Minnesota Vikings at 49ers.

Week 16—Los Angeles Rams at 49ers.
Week 18—New York Giants at 49ers.
Week 19—Chicago Bears at 49ers.

Network Games

January 8, 1984. 49ers at Washington Redskins. CBS broadcast.
September 2, 1984. 49ers at Detroit Lions. CBS broadcast.
September 10, 1984. Washington Redskins at 49ers. ABC broadcast.
September 16, 1984. New Orleans Saints at 49ers. CBS broadcast.
September 23, 1984. 49ers at Philadelphia Eagles. CBS broadcast.
September 30, 1984. Atlanta Falcons at 49ers. CBS broadcast.
October 8, 1984. 49ers at New York Giants. ABC broadcast.
October 14, 1984. Pittsburgh Steelers at 49ers. NBC broadcast.
October 21, 1984. 49ers at Houston Oilers. CBS broadcast.
October 28, 1984. 49ers at Los Angeles Rams. CBS broadcast.
November 4, 1984. Cincinnati Bengals at 49ers. NBC broadcast.
November 11, 1984. 49ers at Cleveland Browns. CBS broadcast.
November 18, 1984. Tampa Bay Buccaneers at 49ers. CBS broadcast.
November 25, 1984. 49ers at New Orleans Saints. CBS broadcast.
December 2, 1984. 49ers at Atlanta Falcons. CBS broadcast.
December 8, 1984. Minnesota Vikings at 49ers. CBS broadcast.
December 14, 1984. Los Angeles Rams at 49ers. ABC broadcast.
December 29, 1984. New York Giants at 49ers. CBS broadcast.
January 6, 1985. Chicago Bears at 49ers. CBS broadcast.
January 20, 1985. Miami Dolphins at 49ers. ABC broadcast.

Newspapers

Associated Press
Chicago Tribune
Contra Costa Times
Del Rio (TX) News-Herald
Fort Lauderdale News & Sun-Sentinel
Los Angeles Times
Miami Herald
New York Times
San Diego Union-Tribune
San Francisco Chronicle
San Francisco Examiner
San Jose Mercury News
Santa Fe New Mexican
Ukiah (CA) Daily Journal
USA Today
Washington Post

SECONDARY SOURCES

Books

Barber, Phil. *We Were Champions: The 49ers' Dynasty in Their Own Words*. Champaign, IL: Triumph Books, 2002.

Craig, Roger, with Matt Maiocco. *Roger Craig's Tales from the 49ers Sidelines*. Champaign, IL: Sports Publishing, 2004.

Craig, Roger, with Garry Niver. *Strictly Business: On Football and My Life with the 49ers*. New York: St. Martin's Press, 1992.

Dickey, Glenn. *America Has a Better Team*. San Francisco: Harbor Publishing, 1982.

———. *Glenn Dickey's 49ers: The Rise, Fall, and Rebirth of the NFL's Greatest Dynasty*. Roseville, CA: Prima Publishing, 2000.

———. *San Francisco 49ers: The Super Years*. San Francisco: Chronicle Books, 1989.

Harris, David. *The Genius: How Bill Walsh Reinvented Football and Created an NFL Dynasty*. New York: Random House, 2008.

Koppett, Leonard. *Forty-niner Fever!* Los Altos, CA: Publishing Services Center, 1982.

Lott, Ronnie, with Jill Lieber. *Total Impact*. New York: Doubleday, 1991.

Maiocco, Matt. *San Francisco 49ers: Where Have You Gone?* Champaign, IL: Sports Publishing, 2005.

Montana, Joe, with Bob Raissman. *Audibles: My Life in Football*. New York: William Morrow, 1986.

Montana, Joe, with Richard Weiner. *Joe Montana's Art and Magic of Quarterbacking*. New York: Henry Holt, 1997.

Moyer, Susan. *Bill Walsh: Remembering the Genius, 1931–2007*. Champaign, IL: Sports Publishing Inc., 2007.

Myers, Gary. *The Catch*. New York: Crown Publishers, 2009.

Olderman, Murray. *49er Pro-Files: The Cartoon Book of the Super Bowl Champions*. San Francisco: Sales Corporation of America, 1982.

Portrait of Victory: 49ers, the Season. Salt Lake City, UT: Treacor Publications, 1985.

Razzano, Tony, with Richard Weiner. *Razzano: Secrets of an NFL Scout*. Chicago: Bonus Books, 1993.

Sahadi, Lou. *The 49ers: Super Champs of Pro Football*. New York: Quill, 1982.

San Francisco Chronicle. *Super Season: 1984 San Francisco 49ers*. San Francisco: San Francisco Chronicle, 1984.

San Francisco 49ers Media Guides. 1979, 1980, 1981, 1982, 1983, 1984, and 1985.

San Francisco 49ers Team Yearbooks. 1983, 1984, and 1985.

Schultz, Jeff, with Michael Tuckman. *The San Francisco 49ers: Team of the Decade*. Rocklin, CA: Prima Publishing and Communications, 1990.

Super Bowl XIX Media Guide

Super Bowl XIX Program

Walsh, Bill, with Brian Billick and James Peterson. *Finding the Winning Edge*. Champaign, IL: Sports Publishing, 1998.

Walsh, Bill, with Glenn Dickey. *Building a Champion*. New York: St. Martin's Press, 1990.

Walsh, Bill, with Craig Walsh and Steve Jamison. *The Score Takes Care of Itself: My Philosophy of Leadership*. New York: Portfolio Trade, 2010.

Articles

Cooney, Frank. "Football's Master Strategist: Bill Walsh." *1985 Sporting News Pro Football Yearbook*, 13–19.

Dickey, Glenn. "Montana's Cool Days and Hot Nights." *Inside Sports*, January 1985, 24–33.

Kinnley, Ben. "San Francisco's Gridiron Guru." *Saturday Evening Post*, October 1985, 44–45, 80.

Kirkpatrick, Curry. "You've Got It Made, Joe Montana!" *Sports Illustrated* (College and Pro Football special edition), September 4, 1985, 196–202.

Kornheiser, Tony. "The Revenge of Bill Walsh." *Inside Sports*, September 1982, 88–95.

McGrane, Bill. "On Top of Their Game." *Pro! The Magazine of the National Football League*, March/April 1985, 15–30.

Rapaport, Richard. "The Walsh Factor." *San Francisco: The City's Monthly*, January 1985, 66–69, 122–25.

Reilly, Rick. "The Hand That Feeds Them." *Sports Illustrated*, September 10, 1990, 122–38.

Zimmerman, Paul. "Armed for an Aerial Epic." *Sports Illustrated*, January 21, 1985, 48–55.

———. "A New Plot, but the Usual Ending." *Sports Illustrated*, January 14, 1985, 22–29.

———. "The Niners Were Never Finer." *Sports Illustrated*, January 28, 1985, 16–32.

INDEX

ABOUT THE AUTHOR

Chris Willis has worked at NFL Films since 1996 as head of the research library. He has written four books on early pro football, all published by Scarecrow Press. His first book, *Old Leather: An Oral History of Early Pro Football in Ohio, 1920–1935*, was published in 2005 and received the 2005 Nelson Ross Award by the Professional Football Researchers Association for recent achievement in football research and historiography. His second book, *The Columbus Panhandles: A Complete History of Pro Football's Toughest Team, 1900–1922*, was published in 2007. His third book, *The Man Who Built the National Football League: Joe F. Carr*, came out in 2010. Willis's fourth book, *Dutch Clark: The Life of an NFL Legend and the Birth of the Detroit Lions*, was released in 2012.

As the resident historian at NFL Films, Willis helps oversee all aspects of research for the company and their producers. In 2002 he was nominated for an Emmy for his work on the HBO documentary *The Game of Their Lives: Pro Football in the 1950s*. He is also a member of the College Football Historical Society (CFHS) and the Professional Football Researchers Association (PFRA). Several of his articles, including "The Pro Football Hall of Fame—The Beginning," "The Bodyguard and Johnny U," "Ralph Hay: Forgotten Pioneer," and "Joe Carr's Vision," have been published in the PFRA publication *The Coffin Corner*. Willis was awarded the PFRA's 2012 Ralph Hay Award for lifetime achievement in pro football research and historiography.

In 1997 and 1998, Willis presented at the Pro Football and American Life symposiums held at the Pro Football Hall of Fame. Before starting at NFL Films, he graduated with a B.S. in physical education from Urbana University in Ohio—while playing four years on the Urbana football team—and attended one year of graduate school at Ohio State University, in sports history. He is a native of Columbus, Ohio, and currently resides in Audubon, New Jersey.